The Wisdom to Doubt

Also by J. L. Schellenberg

Divine Hiddenness and Human Reason

Prolegomena to a Philosophy of Religion

The Wisdom to Doubt

A Justification of Religious Skepticism

J. L. SCHELLENBERG

Cornell University Press

ITHACA AND LONDON

First published 2007 by Cornell University Press

Printed in the United States of America

Library of Congress Cataloging-in-Publication Data

Schellenberg, J. L., 1959–
  The wisdom to doubt : a justification of religious skepticism / J.L. Schellenberg.
      p. cm.
  Includes bibliographical references and index.
  ISBN 978-0-8014-4554-5 (cloth : alk. paper)
  1. Religion—Philosophy.   2. Belief and doubt.
3. Skepticism.   I. Title.
  BL51.S427   2007
  211'.7—dc22

                                    2006036023

Cornell University Press strives to use environmentally responsible suppliers and materials to the fullest extent possible in the publishing of its books. Such materials include vegetable-based, low-VOC inks and acid-free papers that are recycled, totally chlorine-free, or partly composed of nonwood fibers. For further information, visit our website at www.cornellpress.cornell.edu.

Cloth printing   10 9 8 7 6 5 4 3 2 1

To Matthew and Justin
and all the conversations still to come

Contents

Preface: An Uncertain Heritage

Philosophical skeptics of every description are linked by history to the Pyrrhonian *skeptikoi* of ancient Greece. But while in its original meaning the label applied to these famous doubters advertises an inquisitive and inquiring turn of mind (something made use of by Sextus Empiricus when he says that skeptics, unlike dogmatists, "persist in their investigations"),[1] the Pyrrhonians were actually inclined to turn away from inquiry. As is well known, in anyone who reached maturity as a Pyrrhonian the desire to seek truth had long since been exchanged for an attachment to the quietude of uncertainty (*ataraxia*) and simple conformity to convention. Sextus himself seems content to detail quite weak arguments along with the strong, apparently giving as his excuse that the point is to use whatever might succeed in producing suspense of judgment, and thereby bring one to the desired tranquil state.[2]

Though there is much to be learned from the Pyrrhonians, modern skeptics should not, I think, follow them in these tendencies. Another impulse animates my efforts here. The religious skepticism championed in this book lives, moves, and has its being within a commitment to be conformed to the demands of truth-seeking, however discomfiting, with an eye always to the future, when perhaps only after long sojourns without the luxury of either religious or irreligious belief, human vision may be clearer and our grasp of how things fundamentally are more secure. That may be a distant future, and it may not come at all. But it will not come without much more of the same inquiry that leads us to skepticism about

---

[1] Sextus Empiricus, *Outlines of Scepticism*, ed. Julia Annas and Jonathan Barnes (Cambridge: Cambridge University Press, 2000), I, 1.

[2] Ibid., III, 280.

religion now. Because I advocate such persistent inquiry, my work here is best described as seeking sustenance not from ancient skepticism but from the ancient roots of "skepticism."

The Pyrrhonians, famously, had various collections of *modes* of reasoning to a suspense of judgment—sets of Ten, Eight, Five, and Two. In my defense of skepticism also, as a salute to Pyrrhonian resourcefulness and to acknowledge the tie to tradition, tenuous though it may be, certain alternative forms of reasoning are labeled "modes." But a difference is that *my* modes seek to provide rational justification for skepticism that will stand up to the most severe scrutiny, and of course their scope is narrower than that of their notoriously thoroughgoing elder siblings, restricted as it is to the domain of religion. Let me be perfectly clear: in my view beliefs are often rationally justified and arguments successful, and we can show through investigation that justified beliefs about other things, for example, about the limited achievements of the past and the unrealized intellectual and spiritual possibilities of the future, support skepticism in respect of religion. Furthermore, though most of my arguments are for skeptical conclusions, no one should ever think that they represent some cynical atttempt to knock down every intellectual dwelling place and punch a hole in every intellectual dream. Quite the contrary. I myself am much concerned with making intellectual progress on religious matters, and within the context of my general skeptical arguments I will even be offering proposals for how definite results with respect to certain more limited religious claims—such as the claim of traditional theism—might be reached. If we broaden our perspective in the way in which I shall often be urging us to do, it may *look* like we are falling back, losing ground, but if the skepticism involved in such a move is restricted to the most general questions about religion—whether there is a religious reality at all, and what its nature might be—and if such a move is itself essential to ensuring genuine *progress* with those very questions, then appearances will be deceiving.

But it may still be wondered how a religious skeptic like me can get away without being skeptical about *other* matters as well. This perplexity can take two forms, one narrower and one more general. First, and more narrowly, it may be wondered whether the skeptical considerations I draw on in developing my arguments will not also apply *to those very arguments*. This issue about self-refutation is dealt with more fully in Chapter 1 and in Chapter 14, but for now let me say that one who is willing to accept simple inductive arguments and apparent self-evidence as capable of justifying belief will find no problem here. However, a second, more general, form of perplexity is also suggested: how, if we have once begun to listen to the siren song of skepticism, can we avoid being drawn all the way in to the more radical doubt of the Pyrrhonians, which questions even simple inductive arguments and apparent self-evidence? Various arguments against radical skepticism might be elaborated in answer to this question. But perhaps the most honest and straightforward answer (more fully developed in Chapter 8) is that to be inquirers at all—and the Pyrrhonian *skeptikoi*, given the meaning of that label, really ought to pay more attention to this—we must suppose that there is a real world to be examined and worth examining, and also that what seems best and strongest in experience and reason is telling us something about it, and may, over time, tell us a good deal more. If we did not do so, we would be prohibited from arriving at any fuller understanding of the truth that may be possible for us, truth of the sort that inquirers seek.

And what if someone asks about the rational basis for *being* inquirers—for seeking such an understanding? Here one can only report one's belief that something of great worth would be forever lost to us should we relinquish our ambition to know and understand—in particular, that a certain relation to truth, if it can be achieved, is of great intrinsic value, and human dignity, if it obtains at all, such as to warrant our pursuing an ever deeper understanding of how best to support it. Such beliefs we—we humanly sensitive inquirers, at any rate—are not about to lose, for the propositions they involve will seem to us self-evident and necessarily true. But not just that: we would give them up, should we be capable of doing so, only at the expense of our souls. Ultimately, I think, there is something deeper at work here than a sense of self-evidence or even the action or practice in which Wittgenstein said everything intellectual is grounded. It is rather a moral passion embracing both of these and more, the passion of the truly wise and of those who would be wise.

It will be certain and plain, therefore, that this skeptical inquiry is indeed an inquiry, carried out within a scaffolding of assumptions that permit and endorse inquiry, held in common with other investigators, rendered eligible and intellegible by whatever arguments may support them but even more fundamentally by the desire and aim to achieve whatever understanding our frail nature and the nature of the world may permit. Perhaps there will be little of that in the end, at least on the deepest matters, but it is a waste of time to worry about this possibility or take it seriously when our aim is to do whatever is required to achieve such understanding, *if it may be achieved.* Here I part ways with the Pyrrhonians. But this does not mean that we can acquiesce in just any wild notions or let intellectual optimism run free. The key is to strike a balance—which balance, I shall claim, requires us to be skeptics, at least for now, on the most general matters in which religion deals, exercising the wisdom to doubt instead of the will to believe.

Some material from articles of mine previously published has found its way into the present work, often in revised form. The articles were "The

Hiddenness Argument Revisited I," *Religious Studies* 41 (2005), 201–215; "The Hiddenness Argument Revisited II," *Religious Studies* 41 (2005), 287–303; "'Breaking Down the Walls That Divide': Virtue and Warrant, Belief and Nonbelief," *Faith and Philosophy* 21 (2004), 195–213; "The Atheist's Free Will Offense," *International Journal for Philosophy of Religion* 56 (2004), 1–15; "Does Divine Hiddenness Justify Atheism?" in *Contemporary Debates in the Philosophy of Religion,* ed. Michael Peterson (Oxford: Blackwell, 2003); and "Stalemate and Strategy: Rethinking the Evidential Argument from Evil," *American Philosophical Quarterly* 37 (2000), 405–419. Material from "The Atheist's Free Will Offense" is reused with the kind permission of Springer Science and Business Media.

For their help with this book, I am grateful to John Ackerman, William Alston, Michael Bergmann, Paul Draper, Daniel Howard-Snyder, Stephen Maitzen, Paul Moser, Terence Penelhum, William Rowe, Richard Swinburne, Chris Tucker, and William Wainwright, as well as the students of upper-level courses on philosophy of religion at Mount Saint Vincent University and members of audiences at the University of Colorado (Boulder), Purdue University, and Wheaton College and at meetings of the Society for Philosophy of Religion. I am also indebted to the Social Sciences and Humanities Research Council of Canada and to Mount Saint Vincent University for financial support and occasional release from teaching duties. Last and first, as always, come the members of my immediate family: Matthew, Justin, and Regina. This book is dedicated to my sons, Matthew and Justin, who—come to think of it, much like my audiences everywhere—remain cheerfully skeptical about a lot of what I have to say. I cannot imagine life without them and without our wide-ranging conversations in the car. My wife, Regina, was able to provide new insight and stimulation in both the fourth and the four hundredth discussion of matters contained herein. Her unceasing enthusiasm for new discoveries is inspiring, and her love is boundless and boundlessly reciprocated.

J. L. S.

Chester Basin, Nova Scotia

The Wisdom to Doubt

Introduction

Reason requires us to be religious skeptics. This, as suggested in the Preface, is because of all that the past has prevented us from seeing and all we must suppose the future may hold in store, in light of what we know about common human intellectual failings and the special ambitions and failings bound up with religious and irreligious belief. The skeptical potential of such considerations has not heretofore been exploited. Much more will be said about them in Part 1, where they will be fashioned into distinct modes of reasoning to religious skepticism.[1]

In Part 2 of the book, I make a specific application of points from Part 1 to what are the central sources, at once, of nonskeptical attitudes toward religion and of a too common neglect of skeptical reasoning, namely, certain arguments associated with naturalism and religious experience. And the new results arrived at here will, in turn, fortify each of the modes developed in Part 1—any one of which may of course be questioned from either of the aforementioned perspectives.

Finally, in Part 3, I present certain new arguments against a particular type of belief on matters of religion, namely, traditional theistic belief, in illustration of earlier claims about gaps in our information being revealed and filled and unexpected perspectives always emerging (or further illustration, since, as suggested above, our modes have the peculiar feature of illustrating their own contention). By this illustrative means, and of course by means of the arguments themselves, which block support for a theistic

---

[1] There will be some overlapping of material in the arguments—the modes are distinct not because they share no content, but because they reason to the skeptical conclusion in different ways, and because no one of them presupposes the success of any of the others.

2   *Introduction*

refutation of religious skepticism, the modes are vindicated specifically with respect to theism—which is appropriate given the strong focus on support of the latter in contemporary philosophy of religion.

In all these arguments the nature of belief is obviously of great importance. And with this point, to be elaborated in a moment, I come to some more particular assumptions than those mentioned in the Preface, which are taken over from a predecessor to this book, my *Prolegomena to a Philosophy of Religion.*[2] Although the present work's central contentions and the main support it provides for them should be readily comprehended even by someone unfamiliar with the earlier one, they are developed within the distinctive framework it devised. (That work was intended not only to make proposals for how to make progress in the neglected area of philosophy of religion "fundamentals" its title can be seen as naming, but also to lay a foundation for what I will do here and plan to continue elsewhere.) Hence for a full comprehension of my arguments, it will be important to see how the results of *Prolegomena* bear on them.

Let me begin, as I suggested a moment ago I would, by clarifying how I will understand that all-important notion of believing. As defined in *Prolegomena* (p. 50), a belief is an involuntary disposition to apprehend the state of affairs reported by a certain proposition, when that state of affairs comes to mind, under the concept *reality*. More briefly and impressionistically: a believing disposition is activated whenever one *thinks of the world*—as it might be put, the distinctive fact about the thoughts that activate beliefs is that they are "world-thoughts." When the religious believer experiences, say, belief that there is a God, or the irreligious believer experiences the belief that there is no religious reality at all, it is not too much to say that, subjectively, *that is how the world is for her.* Though the propositions philosophers are accustomed to talking about in this context may express the content of our beliefs, and though they may come into play when we are describing or reporting our beliefs, in the throes of the believing experience itself we are thinking not of a proposition but of how things are. And though to experience confidence is to experience a feeling state that may fluctuate and be more or less intense or strong, the experience of belief is, as mentioned above, a matter of involuntarily *thinking* in a certain way, and so not in itself a matter of degree.[3]

---

[2] Ithaca: Cornell, 2005.

[3] It is interesting to note that the Pyrrhonian skeptics may not have rejected or sought to prevent belief *thus* understood, for it corresponds closely to what they appear to have labeled "appearances" and declared intellectually innocuous—or at least it does so on the (apparently correct) assumption that appearances are for them always appearances *of reality.* Sextus himself seems sometimes to miss the latter point: he seems to suppose that the experience of an appearance need not be connected, in the experience, to the concept

Turning now to religious and irreligious belief, what we find are states whose content is expressible by *religious* propositions or else by a denial that any religious proposition is true. But to know more about these states, we need to fix the range of the religious. My proposal in *Prolegomena* (pp. 23, 81), in part a technical definition answering to the purposes of philosophy, was that religious propositions or claims should be viewed as ones entailing that there is a reality metaphysically and axiologically ultimate (representing the deepest fact about the nature of things and also unsurpassably great), in relation to which an ultimate good can be attained. Otherwise put, religious claims are claims entailing that there is an ultimate and salvific reality. These expressions too are taken over from the earlier work, along with the label for this basic religious claim: generic ultimism, or, more loosely, ultimism. Ultimism, it should carefully be noted, is not at all equivalent to theism, though the latter claim (an elaborated form of ultimism) entails the former. Given this terminology, we may say, very roughly, that religious belief is belief that in some way affirms ultimism and that religious disbelief (or irreligious belief) is belief that in some way denies it. According to a religious disbeliever, *no* religious claim, that is, no claim entailing that there is an ultimate salvific reality, is true. That is how a religious disbeliever sees the world.

Now the defense of religious skepticism in this book says that *neither* religious belief nor religious disbelief, thus understood, is justified. What we have here, in other words, is a defense of skepticism with respect to ultimism. Immediately we can see that its claim is a highly general one: we will not be following the usual pattern of focusing, rather narrowly, on traditional theism and atheism and paying little attention to other religious possibilities. Our skeptic is not just an agnostic. (Indeed, his stance is compatible with atheism, since—as Buddhist religion reveals—atheism does not entail the denial of ultimism.) Using a term from *Prolegomena* (p. 98), it is a *categorical* religious skepticism that I will be arguing is justified: skepticism as to whether *any* religious claim is true. Alternatively, we might say that I am supporting doubt with respect to the disjunction of religious claims—which is the proposition saying that one or other of the various claims entailing ultimism is true. Only

---

of reality, apparently because we can, when *speaking* of that experience, dissociate its deliverance from what is real. (See his *Outlines of Skepticism,* ed. Julia Annas and Jonathan Barnes [Cambridge: Cambridge University Press, 2000].) This, however, confuses the experience with subsequent reflection on it. Perhaps if the Pyrrhonians had recognized this, they would have found problematic not only what they called belief—which seems to involve not just a disposition to have such experiences as I have described but also a disposition to confidently assert that they reflect the way things really are—but also belief as understood here.

after defending this completely general stance do I come to the specific question of theism. (By then one way in which at least skepticism about theism can be supported will already have been suggested, but others, distinct from the first, will be added in Part 3.) To my knowledge, a thorough defense of so general a skepticism about religion has not been undertaken before.

Strictly speaking, religious skepticism comes in a variety of forms. One form that should be mentioned, other than the categorical one already noted, is what in *Prolegomena* (p. 100) I call *capacity skepticism*. Capacity skepticism is skepticism concerning humans having the cognitive and other properties required to be able to access truths about whether there is or is not something ultimate, or about the details of the nature any such reality must possess (more briefly: basic truths about religion). Capacity skepticism itself comes in two forms, qualified and unqualified: the former is skepticism regarding the claim that we *presently* are capable of discerning the truths in question; the latter is skepticism with regard to the claim that humans will *ever* possess this capacity. These points are of particular importance here since the modes of reasoning developed in Part 1 of this book sometimes defend categorical religious skepticism by way of a defense of capacity skepticism (thus seeking to lead the inquirer to what in *Prolegomena* I call *complete* skepticism). This is potentially an effective strategy. For to hold or to endorse any belief of the relevant sort about an ultimate salvific reality, we would need to take ourselves to have the capacity in question, to be *exercising* it in our positive assessment of the relevant evidence; and thus doubt with respect to the capacity claim must rationally lead to an absence of any such tendencies in favor of belief and to an endorsement of categorical skepticism instead.

It is important to note that any of these forms of skepticism—indeed, any form of skepticism at all—can be *passive,* by which I mean a state involving involuntary doubt or uncertainty about the truth of a proposition, or *active,* by which I mean a stance or cultivated disposition of skepticism, a kind of "coming out on the side of skepticism," together with reinforcing behavioral dispositions. (I associate the common idea of withholding judgment with the latter notion.) This difference will help the reader make sense of the distinction, sometimes utilized in this book, between seeking to engender and recommending skepticism (only active skepticism is properly recommended since only here is borne out the connotation, naturally conveyed by a recommendation, of something being such as can voluntarily be done).

Back to belief now: another distinction from the earlier work that will be illuminating here, inasmuch as it is critical to an understanding of my precise intent in this book when I say that both religious belief and irreligious belief are unjustified, is a distinction between different senses of "belief that *p*." Sometimes it is a certain *way* of believing, *the* belief that *p*, that we have in mind when we use that expression, and to use it correctly we need not presuppose that the belief is realized in anyone (even if its appropriateness to this or that mental or social context is discussed); but in another sense what we may have in mind is *his* or *her* belief that *p*, and in evaluating the belief thus understood we evaluate the person who holds it by way of assessing his or her relevant dispositions (the dispositions involved in the person's coming to, or not ceasing to, hold the belief in question). In the former abstract case what we have is a belief *type;* in the latter concrete case it is a belief *token.* In considering the justification of a belief type what we are looking for is a kind of worthiness that abstract discussion of what is preferable in the way of belief and should be embraced, or else inferior and should be avoided, can help us discern; whereas in the evaluation of belief tokens the relevant desideratum is what we may call responsibility: the proper fulfillment of all relevant duties and the exercise of virtue in the formation and maintenance of the belief by the believer. Clearly the categories distinguished here are different in important ways—and now the critical point: what I am most directly concerned with in this book are belief types, not belief tokens; and in claiming that religious and irreligious beliefs are alike unjustified I am claiming that those belief types are unworthy of being instantiated. It is compatible with my conclusion that some or many individual religious and irreligious believers are quite responsible in respect of their beliefs. To put it another way, many individuals may be justified in holding religious or irreligious beliefs even if religious and irreligious beliefs (the belief *types* now) are not justified for them or for anyone else.

This way of approaching my defense of religious skepticism—which state, the reader will now be able to see, I am also construing as a type—is influenced by my understanding of (one of) the tasks of philosophers of religion, set out in *Prolegomena.* As I say there (p. 179), "philosophers, in developing their abstract evaluations of possible responses to religious claims and debating their merits, are pioneers and scouts looking for a terrain in which to live; they are seeking to provide an aid and a guide for the concrete choices and pursuits of individuals. To alter the metaphor, they are in the business of assessing and ranking candidates so that we can make a more informed vote." In line with this statement, my claim in this book may be taken as the claim that we should not settle in the land of belief: neither the response of religious belief nor the response of irreligious belief *should* be made. *We can do better.* A suitably informed vote will be in favor of religious skepticism. (This may require active skepticism in some cases, if, because of the psychological power of belief, passive skepticism is not immediately engendered by what are observed to be powerful coun-terarguments.)

Now some may not agree that the "information" I put forward in justifi-cation of religious skepticism is properly assessed. But my task, as I see it, is to express as clearly and powerfully as I can the arguments that seem to me to point in one direction as opposed to another, as part of a community at-tempt to reach wide consensus on where the truth about the worthiness of various responses to religious claims lies. (Such a consensus might still not hit on the truth, but at least if reached as a result of the most careful inves-tigation, it would represent the best indication of the truth we could have, and it is accordingly worth striving for in philosophy, just as in science.) That is what I do in this book. I take my arguments to be sound—I hope responsibly—but their main purpose is not to vindicate any belief of mine with respect to the truth of their conclusions but rather to advance discus-sion. Readers may of course wish to use what I say, together with what oth-ers say on this subject, to seek to determine what intellectual course they can responsibly pursue. In the midst of the less than ideal circumstances in which we actually find ourselves, where a consensus on most important questions has not yet been reached, all of us have to make do with the best we can find. But it may be that over time more and more options will be decisively excluded by work of the sort I am undertaking here, directed to response types, in a manner that is widely recognized as forceful; and this would no doubt significantly contract the range of responses that are responsibly chosen or pursued by individuals. However, as indicated, the latter topic of discussion will not be directly entered into here.

So the aim of this book is to show that the responses (i.e., response types) to ultimism of belief and disbelief should be avoided by thinking persons aware of the relevant facts—that there is a better response to religious claims than either of these, at least at the stage of human development in which we find ourselves: we should, that is, be skeptical as to whether any religious claim is true. But a little more filling out of this conclusion and the framework within which it will be reached may be useful. Already in the previous paragraph and here again I have linked talk of belief and dis-belief and skepticism to the notion of *responses* to religious claims. Two im-portant points from *Prolegomena* concerning this may now be introduced. First (p. 189), philosophers of religion, in assessing responses to religious claims (providing an aid and a guide for the concrete choices and pursuits of individuals), are, among other things, pursuing the higher-level goal of determining whether religious *practice* is justified. And in doing this, it is useful for them to consider responses to religious claims in a full-blooded way—as involving not just this or that propositional or cognitive attitude but also a disposition to *act* on it. Perhaps typically the rational status of the latter component will depend on that of the former, with that of the former in turn depending on the import of truth-oriented considerations, so that we could get away with focusing simply on the propositional or cognitive dimension. But we should be at least open to the idea that the pragmatic benefits of the relevant action dispositions also have a role to play (perhaps, for example, the value that results from acting on religious belief or disbelief can contribute something to the justification of a believing or disbelieving response to religious claims, and so needs to be taken into account when determining which response is best), and in the case of some responses a distinction between cognitive and conative may be harder to realize, at least in practice, and truth-oriented considerations may be largely irrelevant.

This brings me to the second point about responses, which is that religious belief plus a disposition to act on it is not alone where positive responses to religious claims, sufficient to generate religious practice, are concerned: there is also the response of *faith*, which as I understand it is quite distinct from that of belief. The person of faith also makes a positive and religion-generating response to religious claims, and her reasons for doing so may be expected to be quite different from those appropriate to belief, perhaps, for example, involving more of an emphasis on the goodness of what certain claims refer to than on their truth. This is because faith that a proposition is true—and here we have one of the central claims of *Prolegomena* (p. 139)—involves a purely voluntary attitude of mental assent toward that proposition, undertaken in circumstances where one views the state of affairs to which it refers as good and desirable but in which one lacks evidence causally sufficient for belief of the proposition. (There will be no public *verbal* assent—i.e., no verbal affirmation of the relevant proposition as true—by one who recognizes that the presence of belief would contextually be implied by such affirmation.) In mentally assenting to a proposition, one deliberately adopts and subsequently adheres to a certain policy: a policy of mentally going along with the content of that proposition in relevant contexts (as opposed to questioning or criticizing or ignoring it, or simply keeping it at arm's length)—of imagining the world to oneself as including the truth of that proposition and mentally selecting this picture to guide one. Such an attitude is different from belief, which, as indicated above, is more a matter of involuntarily being represented *to* than of actively representing (and which typically issues in unqualified verbal affirmation of the relevant proposition as true). Now all we have mentioned so far is *propositional* faith. There is also what I call *operational* faith, which is realized when someone acts on propositional faith in pursuit of a religious way, or else on propositional religious belief. But the important point here is that when we have the response to religious claims that combines the two forms of faith, propositional and operational, we see a quite distinct full-blooded response to religious claims, the faith response, which must be considered alongside believing, disbelieving, and skeptical responses. A faith response, interestingly, involves passive skepticism (for belief is incompatible with it), so not just any skepticism will represent a distinguishable response to religious claims. The skepticism that does represent such a distinguishable response I call *pure* skepticism. A purely skeptical response to religious claims is a nonreligious response involving categorical religious skepticism but without the admixture of faith.

All these responses—believing, disbelieving, purely skeptical, and faith-full—need to be considered by a philosopher seeking to determine whether religious practice is justified. In considering any such response, the philosopher is of course seeking to determine whether it is justified or unjustified, a task that we have already seen is linked to its worthiness or lack thereof, which I have suggested is a matter of relative preferability. Principles for judging between such alternative responses are spelled out in *Prolegomena,* Chapter 8, and for the reader's convenience they are reproduced in Appendix B at the back of this book. But the basic idea on which they turn is that a response to religious claims may be the best that can be made, or at least as good as any other, or less good than some other. In the first case I say it is *positively* justified, such as rationally ought to be made; in the second case it is only *negatively* justified, not such as rationally ought not to be made; and in the third case it is unjustified. *Epistemic* considerations contributing to or detracting from the justification of a response are ones having to do with the likelihood of truth in religious claims; *non-epistemic* considerations are ones having to do with the extent to which this or that response to religious claims furthers our non-truth-oriented goals. (In accordance with my principles, I shall for most of Part 1 proceed as though only the former sort of consideration is relevant; whether any of the conclusions thus arrived at should be qualified by the latter sort is discussed in its final chapter.)

Now in *Prolegomena* (p. 193) it was determined that, for various reasons, a priority could reasonably be placed on investigating whether religious responses are in every case rationally outclassed by nonreligious ones. What this says, when filled out, is that philosophers should investigate whether, given available information, either a disbelieving or a purely skeptical response is rationally preferable to both believing and faith responses, and thus positively justified in every case—that is, for every religious claim. And we noted that to carry out such an investigation most effectively and with anything approaching alacrity, philosophers are well advised to move to a very general level indeed, where the religious proposition involved is ultimism, the generic religious proposition that, as we have seen, is entailed by every more particular one. If disbelief or pure skepticism turns out to be positively justified at that level, then of course it is positively justified everywhere, and no religious response to any religious claim—and so no form of religious practice—is either negatively or positively justified.

Which brings us directly to this book, where I am starting to take my own advice. We have already noted several times that ultimism will be our focus here. Now we can see why: it is a matter of carrying out the agenda set by *Prolegomena*. Our present inquiry will show that, according to initial indications, the nonreligious side of things does indeed have the upper hand, for there is sufficient and overall good evidence of truth for neither ultimism nor its denial, and non-epistemic factors do nothing to alter the situation in favor of the justification of believing one of these propositions. (Certainly this situation may change—my judgment here could conceivably be overturned by some obvious breakthrough in favor of ultimism or its denial either in the near or in the more distant future—and nothing in my arguments suggests otherwise, but it represents how things are at present and how they must remain without such a change.)[4] Accordingly, some form of categorical religious skepticism is justified, and indeed, positively justified. But I emphasize: *some form.* Our conclusion will in fact deliver only a limited result emphasizing the need to instantiate or pursue passive categorical religious skepticism, not pure skepticism. It follows that such a conclusion cannot yet show whether a nonreligious response to religious claims must be preferable to religious ones. What would be called for to work out the remaining matters is an additional step: a separate inquiry to determine whether pure skepticism or skeptical *faith* is justified, and, if the latter turns out to be justified, to discern what its proper object(s) and associated practice might be, and whether the faith response, whatever form it may take, is positively or only negatively justified. These, however, are matters for another book. Here we will content ourselves with the more modest skeptical conclusion.

The framework for our discussion, inherited from the earlier work, is now fully in place. It is from within this framework, utilizing the concepts and principles here outlined, that I will defend religious skepticism (the set of formal definitions arrived at in *Prolegomena,* some members of which are not mentioned here but will play a role in the book, is reproduced in

---

[4] In my view we do not know enough to know that we will never know more, and so such changes as are here mentioned cannot be ruled out. And they are not ruled out even by such of my arguments as refer to ignorance that lasts far into the future and is relieved only after many generations of further investigation or not at all (see Chapter 4), for my claim is never that things *will* be so but rather that they very well *may* be so—a claim obviously compatible with such turning out not to be the case and thus with the justification *presently* provided by such scenarios being later removed.

Appendix A, for the further benefit of the reader). But as suggested earlier, my arguments should be quite accessible even to one who has little familiarity with this framework. Chapter and part titles are intended as markers to rich veins of reasoning which but a little effort will expose, and which, indeed, I hope readers will be provoked to mine using techniques and principles I have not considered and may not have noticed. But it is to my own exploration of these natural—but long overlooked—skeptical resources that I now turn.

PART I

FINITUDE AND THE FUTURE
Seven Modes of Religious Skepticism

THE HUMAN TENDENCY to form beliefs, it may be, is best understood in evolutionary terms, as bound up with the conditions of our survival in earlier times, and as unavoidable even today in many of the particular contexts of our lives. Whatever the case, for big-brained humans this believing tendency is all too easily, and often illicitly, transferred to what we may broadly term the theoretical or intellectual domain, where ratiocination that we hope will take us to knowledge of matters *transcending* the particulars of our lives is exercised. Now such knowledge, were it achieved, would by its very nature make belief at the intellectual level appropriate (knowledge entails belief), but it could also be that in certain areas—like religion—we need to curb our tendency to form beliefs in order eventually to arrive at such knowledge.

Philosophers may think that the cautionary note I have sounded is accommodated by their omnipresent emphasis on carefully investigated and undogmatic and justified belief, but there is often reason, at the intellectual level, to doubt that belief *can* be justified (at least as things stand), both because of the good chance that we have missed something and are mistaken and because believing by its very nature tends to set up chains of events that will prevent us from seeing this, if it is so. (Because of this last point, assurances of alertness and openness to being wrong do not amount to much here.) And *religious and irreligious* forms of belief are most acutely subject to such difficulties. We all know, for example, how over and over in the history of the West truly terrible things have been done in response to what was taken as a word from the Lord. Over and over grievous errors have been perpetrated in the name of Divine Truth. Today it continues. So why doesn't anyone infer that we have a tendency to think knowledge of ultimate things is present when it is not, and that the next time it seems we have it, we may well be wrong? Why doesn't anyone recognize that we may well have a lot of growing up to do, that we are quite possibly not yet in a position—intellectually, morally, socially—to claim access to the Divine of the sort that is claimed when one expresses belief about such things?

What I want to do, by asking questions like this, is to motivate a transformation in our basic view of the human intellectual situation. We tend to think of ourselves as incredibly advanced, and relatively speaking this may be true, but not absolutely. It is easy to think we are at the end of a long process of development, that all the basic options—and certainly all the religious options—are already "out there." In fact, we may be just beginning: our ideas about how things ultimately are may be primitive precursors of much more complex and intricate and adequate things to come, and we may just have touched the tip of an iceberg where thinking about the Divine is concerned. Of course, it is also possible that our situation in respect of religion will soon be altered by important and obvious new discoveries as to the nature or existence of the Ultimate that quickly win wide support, but in the absence of such a happy state of affairs, radical modesty and even pessimism about the intellectual merits of what has been arrived at thus far, and about our present capacity as individuals or in concert to establish or disestablish claims concerning the existence or nature of an ultimate and salvific reality, is called for. The religious skepticism I support lives on the impression that detailed understandings of the Divine so far developed may be, to borrow from Hume, "but the first rude essays of an infant species." If we take this line, we will see the formation of religious or irreligious belief in the present as wrongheaded, and when it is belief of some specific and detailed religious proposition from extant traditions or of some antireligious naturalism, we will see it as intellectually and morally dangerous—threatening, as it does, to cut off deep and wide religious investigation before it has a chance to properly get started.

In Part 1 of this book I have divided the neglected arguments for religious skepticism bristling here into four main categories, represented by the opening four chapters. First we have what I call the *Subject* Mode, so called because it addresses matters of intellectual oversight and other limitations endemic to human life, affecting the finite subject of any belief at all. These facts of finitude can make the justification of belief difficult. For some beliefs, however, the difficulties prove to be insurmountable, and religious and irreligious beliefs, so I shall argue, are conspicuous among them. The *Object* Mode of Chapter 2 presses discussion in another direction, drawing attention to certain problems deriving from the unique nature of the focus of religious (and, by extension, irreligious) belief, namely, ultimism. In Chapter 3 we consider all the ways in which investigation of matters religious has been stunted by patterns of the past. The new mode of religious skepticism here encountered is the *Retrospective* Mode. And the *Prospective* Mode of Chapter 4 examines various investigative issues that arise when we take seriously our open future.

But these are just four modes of religious skepticism, and the table of contents speaks of seven. So where are the other three? Well, the other three are formed by combining elements from the first four in various ways. Thus we first have four modes, then two, which result from combining material from the four, and arguably are each more powerful than any of the four, and finally we arrive at one, by making the same sort of move again, resulting in the most powerful mode of all. How these new modes of reasoning may be developed is discussed in Chapter 5. Chapter 6 concludes the discussion of this part by examining the bearing of pragmatic considerations on all the foregoing arguments. The conclusion reached is that such considerations not only do not count against my case for religious skepticism but, when properly construed, can be seen to come out strongly in its favor.

The Subject Mode

To say that human attempts to gain reliable information about the world are challenged by our finitude is not to court controversy. This is undoubtedly one of the most obvious facts about us. One would hardly know it, though, given the regularity with which it is overlooked or neglected by intellectually greedy humans in the various areas of human inquiry. My work here on the many sources of human error is designed to make such an error harder to achieve, and to show how the corresponding awareness undergirds categorical religious skepticism.

I begin by introducing and clarifying some central concepts and claims. Let us say that *evidence* is anything providing support for the truth or falsity of a proposition or blocking such support. By saying that something blocks support for the truth or falsity of a proposition, I mean that it is such as must—unless its own force is blocked—prevent that support from being effective, where effectiveness is understood in terms of an epistemic contribution that would remain, even were all relevant information taken into account.[1] Of course support for the truth or falsity of a proposition, whether in this sense effective or not, may be stronger or weaker. Let us say that any support that would be strong enough, were nothing else needing to be considered, to make a proposition certainly or probably true provides *good evidence* that it is true; and that any support that would be strong enough, were nothing else needing to be

---

[1] What I call blocking evidence is in the literature often called an undercutting defeater (as distinguished from a rebutting defeater). But given the needs of this part of the book, I want to develop the notion of a "defeater" in a nonstandard way, and so I will not be speaking of undercutting or rebutting defeaters here.

considered, to make the relevant proposition certainly or probably false provides *good evidence* that it is false.[2]

Here is an example to illustrate what we have so far: You notice that GB faces a dilemma that typically moves a politician to lie, and that GB is a politician. What you notice provides good evidence that GB will lie. But you may also notice that GB almost never lies or that a solution to the dilemma that does not involve lying has just been presented to GB by another politician. In the former case what you notice provides good evidence that GB will not lie, and what you notice in the latter case blocks the support for the truth of the proposition that he will lie with which you began. Since all the things noticed here have a role to play in your attempt to determine whether GB will lie, the term "evidence" may plausibly be applied to them all.

Evidence bears on the justification of a belief at some stage of inquiry if it provides some degree of support for the truth or falsity of the proposition expressing that belief, or if it blocks such support. If it provides support for the truth of the proposition or blocks support for its falsity, it *bears positively* on the justification of the belief in question (such evidence I shall also call positive evidence); if instead it supports the falsity of the proposition or blocks support for its truth, it *bears negatively* on the justification of that belief (evidence of these latter sorts I shall also call negative evidence). If the positive bearing of some piece or collection of positive evidence in relation to other evidence taken into account at a certain stage of inquiry is such that, if the former were added to the latter, and even if good evidence had previously been absent or blocked, the inquirer would be left, on balance, with good evidence that the proposition in question is true, then I shall say its bearing on the justification of the corresponding belief is *strongly* positive. And if the negative bearing of some piece or collection

---

[2] I do not intend to commit myself to any very precise and detailed conception or analysis of probability in this book. Given the current state of our knowledge concerning this vexed subject, and because the various defeaters I present from Chapter 1 on are, if effective at all, effective given various construals of the nature of the probability commonly claimed for religious or irreligious beliefs, to do so would only invite unnecessary disagreement. Having said that, I can confirm a more general point that should be clear from the various expressions I use when discussing probability—that by probability I have in mind a measure of the extent to which the available relevant evidence (or, sometimes, the total relevant evidence) makes a proposition or belief likely to be true, that is, probability of the sort I refer to is always probability *with respect to evidence*. And it is also important to note that, in apparent agreement with what all of us assume when we reason, I take the probability of a proposition or belief on evidence to be an objective matter: our judgments as to probability—for example, the judgment that available evidence makes theism more probable than not, or that it does not do so—are judgments about what we suppose to be the *real* or *objective* extent to which evidence supports the truth of a proposition or belief (which we realize we could be getting wrong).

of negative evidence in relation to other evidence taken into account at a certain stage of inquiry is such that, if the former were added to the latter, and even if good evidence had previously been present and unblocked, the inquirer would be left, on balance, *without* good evidence that the proposition in question is true, then I shall say its bearing on the justification of the corresponding belief is *strongly* negative (notice that a strongly negative bearing does not require that the inquirer be left with good evidence that the proposition involved in the belief is false).[3] A piece or collection of evidence with a strongly positive bearing on the· justification of a belief at some stage of inquiry I shall call a *vindicator* of that belief; and a piece or collection of evidence that instead has a strongly negative bearing I shall call a *defeater* of that belief.

Using these notions we may express a central thesis of this chapter as follows: there are, at any point in any human intellectual inquiry, and in relation to any belief it may be thought to yield, various ways in which positive and negative evidence and also vindicators and defeaters can go *unrecognized* by us. Now such evidence can go unrecognized because it is overlooked; because it is neglected; because it is inaccessible; because it is undiscovered; or because it is undiscoverable (and perhaps there are other varieties of unrecognized evidence I have failed to recognize). For any evidence we fail to recognize, either we are capable of noticing it or we are not; and this provides a way of categorizing unrecognized sorts of evidence, as can be seen in Figure 1. (Here by "capable of recognizing" I mean simply that we presently possess the concepts and breadth of understanding required to observe some evidence's bearing when it comes before us.) As I interpret them, the labels I have used here represent distinct, non-overlapping classes, so when speaking of these different ways in which evidence can be unrecognized, we may correspondingly speak, as I have done, of different sorts of unrecognized evidence.

Let us now identify the defining features of each of these classes a little more carefully, taking them in the order most suited to exposition. (1) *Overlooked* evidence, I suggest, is missed even though it is accessible or, as might be said, part of "one's own" evidence (such as one could take account of without taking account of any fact—apart from the fact of oversight itself—not previously encountered) and despite a capacity to see it and dispositions not unfavorable to seeing it, because of unavoidable features of human intellectual life that contingently prevent one from directing the requisite attentiveness to the matter(s) involved. (2) *Neglected* evi-

---

[3] My phrasing in the previous two sentences is meant to accommodate both situations in which information is in fact taken into account by an inquirer and ones in which it is not.

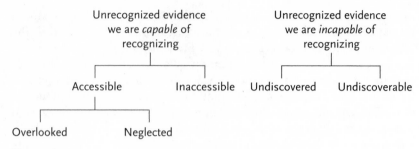

Figure 1

dence is also accessible, and also goes unrecognized despite a capacity to see it, not on account of unavoidable features of human intellectual life contingently interfering with attentiveness or any other unavoidable factors, but because of factors producing desires or other dispositions *unfa-*vorable to seeing it. The failure to recognize evidence is here avoidable because of the avoidable influence of the human will on those dispositions. (3) *Inaccessible* evidence, as I shall use that term, is likewise evidence one is capable of seeing, but it goes unrecognized because it is *not* part of one's own evidence: here unavoidable features of human intellectual life contingently prevent one from undertaking the investigation that *would* have led to an encounter with the evidence in question had one undertaken it. (4) *Undiscovered* evidence is evidence we fail to see because we are not capable of seeing it in our time, in a manner deriving from limited development within what is possible in evolutionary terms (unevolved concepts or dispositions, primitive intellectual environment or resources, etc.). (5) *Undiscoverable* evidence too goes unrecognized because we are incapable of recognizing it, but this time in a manner deriving from limited evolutionary possibilities, in other words, because it is *in principle* impossible for beings like us ever—in any time—to assimilate this information.

In what follows I briefly examine each of these classes of unrecognized evidence in turn and then develop a framework for determining when evidence of these sorts may be realized in a manner militating against the justification of beliefs under investigation in this or that inquiry. In the concluding section of the chapter, I argue that religious and irreligious beliefs are most severely indicted when this framework is applied.

1. *Overlooked Evidence*

There are many ways in which we can unavoidably be prevented from giving attention to items accessible to us—that is, overlook things. Let's start with non-intellectual situations. Suppose I fail to see the woman, bruised and bleeding, who is lying immediately beside the path I take when running in the park every morning. I may do so because, while seeking to be attentive to my environment, I am unavoidably distracted at the relevant time by some external event (just when she is about to come into my visual field, a plane roars overhead and steals my attention until her body is behind me); or I experience a fit of abstraction, with similar effects; or I suffer some distortion in my vision and/or thinking; or, due to one of a multitude of possible causes outside my control, I experience a momentary lapse in alertness, and so on. A completely different way of being prevented from giving attention to items accessible to us involves being non-neglectfully unaware that any special care or attentiveness is even required and, as a result, acted on by causes ruling out such attentiveness (the park in which I run is considered very safe by persons I know to be reliable, I have heard nothing about a missing person in the area or anything similar in its demands on my attention, and so I acquiesce in a seemingly innocent desire to daydream). In all such cases we want to say that we have an instance of oversight as opposed to neglect or inaccessibility or deeper problems like physical blindness or some other relevant incapacity.

Something similar holds for situations in which I overlook evidence bearing on the justification of a belief that is somewhere on my intellectual radar. I may miss a defeater or vindicator that is, as we say, "right there" because of factors (whether weariness or emotional or physical distress or external interruptions or whatever) unavoidably bringing it about that the relevant tract of my mental life is distracted, abstracted, distorted, dull, unclear, etc., even when I am seeking to be attentive. And, just as in the non-intellectual situations, there can also be factors making it the case that I am non-neglectfully unaware that any special care or attentiveness to what I have previously accessed in the way of evidence is required: maybe because of the word of an expert, or because for some other reason I (mistakenly) judge that the evidence overwhelmingly points one way, I am certain the belief is true and so not looking out for evidence either positive or negative.

The possibilities here are endless, and it is easy to see that we often miss evidence bearing on the justification of beliefs, sometimes beliefs we share (i.e., tokens of which appear in our own mental life), in one or other of these ways. We can do so even when we are strongly motivated not to do so, completely responsible in all aspects of our intellectual lives, and possessed of the highest intellectual ability. Perhaps most disturbing, intellectual oversights may occur that are never corrected, by the inquirer or anyone else. Obviously I have no examples of this, but everyone can come up with examples of intellectual oversights that have been corrected even though they might not have been. Famous ones would presumably include the notorious case of Einstein dividing by zero (defeaters for the relevant beliefs formed in the process of that calculation would, we might expect, have occurred to him under optimal conditions, ones empty of all such factors as I have listed above). At this point I do not want to speculate on *how* commonly such things occur or on the likelihood that they frequently occur in a manner that is relevant to the justification of religious or irreligious beliefs (I will develop a framework for dealing with such questions in section 6). Instead I move on to the next class of unrecognized evidence.

2. *Neglected Evidence*

At least as common as oversight is neglect. (We tend to think of this as culpable, and for my purposes it will be all right to go along with this tendency.) Here again we have a situation in which I have failed to give attention to something accessible to me, but in describing it I imply that I *should* have done so. I assume that I have the relevant capacity and upbraid myself for not exercising it. Thus I may with appropriate self-recrimination admit that I did not see the injured woman beside the path. The idea is presumably that I could have been more attentive (by which is meant not only that I was capable in the above sense but that nothing unavoidably prevented me); that such attentiveness would have revealed her presence to me; that I was aware—or culpably unaware—that such attentiveness was appropriate; and so I am culpable for at the time behaving in a manner inconsistent with it and thus also for failing to recognize the fact in question.

In just the same way, I may legitimately say that I should at some time have seen evidence bearing on the justification of a belief which I did not then see. Perhaps, for example, I give up my pet theory of the universe after a defeater that decisively shows it to be false is pressed on me from several quarters, and subsequently discover the clear makings of that very defeater in various articles and books I had been reading a short time before. I may then say that I should have seen the defeater earlier. What I am thinking is that without the desire to save my theory and resistance to counterevidence (something I at some level recognized as inappropriate), I would probably have seen it. Or perhaps I am thinking, more generally, that a level of concern for the truth which I recognized as appropriate and could have instantiated would have revealed it to me. Here I am culpable. And of course I may be culpable for my neglect whether its effects are ever fully noticed by me—as my example assumes—or not. Indeed, the culpable behavior that is causally involved in producing the failure of recognition in the first place may very well continue, and thus ensure that the epistemic effects of my neglect are *never* properly recognized.

Neglect of evidence can occur in many ways, but prominent among them are laziness and self-deception. It may be because of dispositions bound up with an avoidable laziness, dispositions I recognize as unworthy of me, that I fail to investigate thoroughly and so come to miss positive or negative evidence accessible to me when I need to see it. Or it may be because (as the example above suggests) I fool myself into thinking that my evidence has been thoroughly examined or that certain considerations are not as powerful as they seem that the accessible evidence with a bearing on my inquiry goes unrecognized. And of course these two may also work in tandem: a cultivated laziness can make the omissions involved in self-deception easier; and I may deceive myself into thinking that I am not giving in to laziness after all, in order to continue in it and avoid being perturbed about it. Neglect of these sorts is obviously all too common in the intellectual life.

3. *Inaccessible Evidence*

The main difference between inaccessible evidence and the forms of un-recognized evidence already considered is that, as its name implies, it is *not* there for the seeing, part of one's existing or present evidence. What we have here, however, is not something deeply hidden in information I am incapable of assimilating. I am capable of recognizing this sort of evidence, but I don't, because it happens to fall outside my purview (and perhaps it always will).

Now it may occur to readers that something very like the neglect just discussed might contribute not only to missing evidence that is accessible to me but also to making it the case that certain evidence is always inaccessible: laziness and self-deception can prevent us from expanding our evidence base as well as from seeing something that falls within it as things stand. That is true. But having already discussed central cases of neglect, I want here to focus on something else, something at least as important, namely, the way in which even when we are doing our best, much relevant information we are capable of assimilating nevertheless may remain ungrasped.

Indeed, this class of unrecognized evidence may well be the largest of those we are surveying. For, being finite, and given the huge reserves of new evidence we are constantly tapping into insofar as our inquiries are diligent, and the frequent changes in belief consequent on this, it is certainly plausible, at any point in time, to suppose that many more such changes would be recognized as called for if, at that time, we could see more of that evidence. It is necessary for finite beings to be selective in their thinking, and so there are at any given point in time innumerable forays into new evidence we might have taken that would have made possible various insights inaccessible to us now. (Perhaps I hit on a certain argument, and it structures much of my subsequent thinking to the exclusion of points I would otherwise have encountered. Or perhaps because of an illness I start thinking about how to develop a certain chapter in my book on Friday instead of Tuesday, and given the weather, undirected reading, chance thoughts, or even serotonin levels peculiar to Friday, the ideas that occur to me on Friday set in motion a certain chain of intellectual events that are quite different from what would have occurred had I started thinking about this on Tuesday.)[4] And might not some of those insights have involved the recognition of evidence with a bearing on beliefs of interest to us? Is it not ludicrously optimistic to suppose that we should be so fortunate as to live in a world in which the only considerations bearing on beliefs of interest to us lie along the lines of thought and discussion we actually pursue?[5]

The possibility of such missed information is distressing but glaringly obvious, and though, again, it is in the nature of the case impossible to give examples of evidence that is never uncovered by anyone, it is possible to give innumerable examples of relevant considerations that would not have been found had someone's evidence base not been suitably expanded, in a manner that clearly might not have occurred. A famous example can this time be gleaned from the life of Wittgenstein, who labored long and hard over his *Tractatus* and then, a few years later, decided that much in it was mistaken. With regard to his earlier view of logical inference he wrote: "At

---

[4] There seems to be deep contingency here; one often has the sense that a chapter might easily have looked quite different and affected the development of the book and all one's subsequent thinking in ways not actually realized had *that* organizing idea or argument occurred to one instead of *this* one. On a larger scale, we might think about how two persons with very similar temperaments, upbringing, and interests nonetheless may take very different directions through life, with one happening on a book by Russell and being led into analytical philosophy and the other reading Kant's first *Critique* and developing a more historicist, constructivist approach. These two might have much to learn from each other, and each might change his mind on many things if for a few moments he could see with the other's eyes.

[5] Of course, not only such "congenital" factors may prevent evidence from (perhaps ever) becoming accessible to us; we must also take note of all the ways in which we can be stymied by simple bad luck: perhaps my evidence never comes to include some vindicator of a belief of interest to me because a book doesn't arrive when it's supposed to, or a meeting falls through, or my computer breaks down and I miss an important e-mail, and so on.

that time I thought that all inference was based on tautological form. At that time I had not seen that an inference can also have the form: This man is 2m tall, therefore he is not 3m tall."[6] Perhaps no one has mulled over his ideas more thoroughly than Wittgenstein, with a stronger desire to determine what is true, and yet this defeater never came within range at the (most) appropriate time. And had his inquiries taken a different direction (had he, for example, gone back to aeronautical engineering after writing the *Tractatus*), perhaps neither this defeater nor any defeater at all of his former beliefs would ever have become known to him.

It is important, therefore, to give careful attention to the strong possibility of failing to recognize evidence bearing on the justification of beliefs that are of interest to us because it is inaccessible to us, at the time, and perhaps for all time, even though it is possible for beings such as we are to uncover it, and even though we would be able to recognize it *as* evidence were it to come before our minds. Maybe it was in part his recognition of our vulnerability in this respect that led Wittgenstein to suggest that one should always be willing to "see things afresh, as though he had come across the problems for the first time."[7] But, as we have seen, even such an admirable resolution might, on account of the unavoidable limits imposed by our nature and circumstances, fail to prevent us from falling far short of critical insights in many areas of human inquiry.

4. *Undiscovered Evidence*

The Wittgensteinian remark just mentioned may also allude to the need to be always pushing our *understanding* in new directions, opening up unexplored territories in which new and more adequate concepts and other intellectual resources may evolve. Here we turn from surveying possible unrecognized evidence we are capable of recognizing (for the recognition of which no more than our present concepts and breadth of understanding are required) to evidence we are *in*capable of recognizing because the evolution just referred to—or enough of it—has not taken place. Factors analogous to the "congenital" ones discussed in the previous section are at work here. For (slightly revising what I said there), being finite, and given the huge reserves of new ideas we are slowly tapping into insofar as our

[6] Quoted in Ray Monk, *Ludwig Wittgenstein: The Duty of Genius* (New York: Macmillan, 1990), p. 284.

[7] Monk, *Wittgenstein*, p. 276. We might also note the connection between these limitations and the desirability of seeking consensus with other inquirers traveling different pathways, which desirability I have emphasized in the Introduction and elsewhere in this book.

inquiries are diligent, and the conceptual and other large-scale intellectual changes consequent on this, it is certainly plausible to suppose that many more such changes would be recognized as called for by all of us if human intellectual horizons could be pushed forward even a little further. This oversimplifies the situation, however. For we need to see how the very direction of inquiry taken by a finite mind (or community of minds) at any given time will limit what it can see at that time, and might limit it even if we could extend our understanding in that direction indefinitely! It is, again, necessary for finite beings to be selective in their thinking, and a severely limited number of foci or directions of thought can be realized in a finite mind (or community of minds) in any given period of time; so there are in any such time innumerable directions of thought humans *might* have taken that would have made possible various insights unavailable to us now—insights that might have led our understanding to evidence with a bearing on beliefs of interest to us that could not otherwise have been apprehended.

It is instructive in this connection to rehearse to ourselves the many conceptual changes that have occurred in the past, as one mode of thought has been replaced by or incorporated within another. The history of science provides examples, as is shown in Thomas Kuhn's famous book *The Structure of Scientific Revolutions* (even when one makes allowances for occasional exaggeration in his work).[8] And certainly we may expect such changes to continue as our own still primitive understanding of the nature of things is further enhanced. Nicholas Rescher puts it nicely when he writes: "There is nothing epistemically privileged about the present—ANY present, our own prominently included."[9] But this means that we should expect yet more new intellectual resources and conceptual structures to emerge, which may permit humans to grasp and articulate evidence that we cannot now see. As we might put it, paraphrasing what was said at an earlier stage in the evolution of this chapter: it is ludicrously optimistic to suppose that we should be so fortunate as to live in a world in which the only considerations bearing on beliefs of interest to us lie along the lines of thought we can actually pursue at this point in the history of human intellectual development.

5. *Undiscoverable Evidence*

With this final category we come to the most deeply hidden unrecognized evidence of all. Here we have to imagine that all the intellectual

[8] See Thomas Kuhn, *The Structure of Scientific Revolutions* (Chicago: Chicago University Press, 1962).

[9] Nicholas Rescher, *Scepticism: A Critical Reappraisal* (Totowa, N.J.: Rowman & Littlefield, 1980), p. 240.

evolution we are capable of has taken place, and think about what might still lie outside our grasp when that has occurred. Would there be anything at all? The truth of an affirmative answer can surely not be ruled out. It is hard to believe that humans, being finite, will ever be capable of knowing *everything* there is to be known; no matter how far they develop, there must always remain the disturbing possibility of "that which cannot be understood." Accordingly, we must also take note of how there may be undiscover*able* evidence with a bearing on beliefs of interest to us.

Some writers think that, in certain areas of inquiry, we are much closer to reaching this limit than most of us would be prepared to acknowledge. Colin McGinn, for example, has argued in an interesting book that the deepest metaphysical problems—such as the mind-body problem and the problem of free will—have solutions that lie outside the bounds of human cognition and will never be penetrated by the human mind. Our brains are just not cut out for work on problems like these.[10] If McGinn is right, then the pool of the unknown and unknowable is of course a veritable ocean, and we should expect many beliefs, in particular beliefs about abstruse matters of metaphysics, to have undiscoverable defeaters deriving from the facts about these matters, which we have inevitably and irremediably misconstrued. Of course McGinn himself focuses on other, cognitively available defeaters of extant beliefs about mind and will (and so on), and having to his own satisfaction shown by means of them that such beliefs are unjustified, puts forward his "mysterian" hypothesis as a way of accounting for our lamentable failures in this area, which contrast so strikingly, in his view, with our cognitive successes in other areas, notably science. But the point is that if he is right, then there are also *undiscoverable* defeaters (deriving from the facts about metaphysical matters) for all such beliefs, and indeed for all the beliefs about such matters that we may ever entertain.

Is he right? It will be useful to pursue this question a little way, given its bearing on the larger concerns of this book. Interestingly, McGinn's own view, a strong metaphysical view about why certain epistemic states of affairs obtain, is just one more theory alongside others, subject to the same worries about unrecognized evidence that should haunt all the others. (So we can see right away that the points emphasized in this chapter are of broader relevance than McGinn's, and capable of subsuming his.) Some of those possibilities may be realized in considerations of the following sorts, which seem at least jointly to provide a defeater for McGinn's view. First, McGinn's work betrays a rather clear naturalistic bias: he thinks there must be a *naturalistic* solution to the mind-body problem

---

[10] See his *Problems in Philosophy: The Limits of Inquiry* (Oxford: Blackwell, 1993).

undiscoverable by us, and dismisses out of hand certain non-naturalistic alternatives to it, in particular religious ones. Indeed, some religious views do not come in for enough of a hearing to qualify even for dismissal. (In almost every chapter McGinn criticizes an "eliminativist" option that tries to resolve the metaphysical problem under discussion by ignoring it, but he would apparently be in the eliminativist camp himself were the problem under discussion that of whether there is an ultimate salvific reality, and without much more of a leg to stand on, given some of the most general points of the book about our ignorance, than the views he criticizes.) Thus his discussion is at best incomplete. Second, and relatedly, McGinn over-estimates the success (in the sense of approximation to truth) of natural science, thus setting up a less than secure contrast between the results of science and those of philosophy. As suggested in the previous section (and there will be more on this), many scientific theories are in much the same boat as philosophical ones in respect of being subject to future adjustment or rejection. Since his theory depends on the aforementioned contrast, it is weakened by our awareness of its precariousness. Third, it seems that McGinn neglects the fact that, especially when we move into philosophical regions of the theoretical domain, which are unrivaled in generality and depth, there may be just so many possible solutions to problems, and so many components thereof needing to be put together, that because of the demands of sorting through all this or purely through bad luck we could literally go on for many millennia without hitting on the right solutions, even if our present abilities or ones we may develop would suffice to show us that they *were* the right ones should we hit on them. McGinn makes rather a lot of a lack of success spanning only a few thousand years, but the slowness of reason, taken together with the fact just mentioned, might very well suffice to generate our present ignorance on metaphysical matters even if our future success is assured. Thus a favorable light is cast on explanatory hypotheses incompatible with McGinn's—a light that he has yet to disperse, and that it is hard to imagine he might disperse before at least a few more millennia of inquiry have passed.

Whatever may be the merits of McGinn's account (and for the reasons given I do not believe it provides an adequate basis for refraining from metaphysical inquiry), it is clear that he is right to draw to our attention the idea of undiscoverable solutions to certain human problems. This brings with it the idea of undiscoverable negative evidence with a bearing on certain human beliefs, and also—we should now add—the idea of undiscoverable *positive* evidence (unless we unquestioningly go along with McGinn's criticisms of present views on metaphysical questions like the mind-body problem and with his naturalism, we should countenance the notion that there may be undiscoverable *support* for some of those views). Even if he has not managed to prevent his theory on mind and will and the like from being swept into the fray, as one among many to be considered, itself subject to potential defeat (perhaps by negative evidence of the sorts we have discussed),[11] he has at least shown that it is epistemically possible that there is, in relation to many of the beliefs of interest to us, unrecognized evidence including considerations we not only will not but cannot ever know.[12]

6. *Unrecognized Defeat: A Strategy of Assessment*

Suppose now that some human subject *S* is in a specific context of intellectual inquiry, considering whether the belief that *p* is justified.[13] And suppose that after what she regards as extended and careful examination of all the relevant evidence she can lay her hands on, *S* correctly concludes that, in the evidence carefully examined, the positive evidence in relation to *p* is dominant, leaving her, on balance, with good evidence that *p* is true (evidence, let us say, making *p* quite probable). We might be inclined to say that the proper verdict for *S* to deliver to the community at large is that belief that *p* is *justified*, and that our proper response would be to *accept* this verdict.

---

[11] Of course, such defeaters of McGinn's view as there may be cannot, at least if that view is false, all be *undiscoverable* themselves, for if it is false then there are discoverable solutions to the problems he discusses, and these would generate defeaters of his views. But for all that, some defeaters of his view could be undiscoverable, and any of the other varieties of unrecognized defeaters might be instantiated here too. (These need not concern us, however, if, as I have suggested, a clearly recognizable defeater of his view is also available.)

[12] The judgment that a proposition *p* is epistemically possible, which will be making an appearance fairly frequently from here on, is intended as a very general judgment, applicable to all who inquire into the matters it concerns. The intuitive idea is that, given our information and experience, *p* at any rate *may* be true—that it is a live contender, true "for all anyone knows," or—a bit more precisely—that no available information or experience rules out its being true. I suggest that the following analysis will be suitable for my purposes: *p* is epistemically possible just in case currently available information and experience does not justify the belief that *p* is false (sometimes I will apply the central idea here by saying that we should be *in doubt* about whether some proposition is false). Notice that this view does not imply that, if *p* is epistemically possible, the evidence for and against *p* that is available to us does not make the falsity of *p* probable (if the evidence available is not *enough* evidence—if a judgment based on that evidence would be premature, say, because more investigation is obviously needed—then it may make the falsity of *p* probable without justifying the belief that *p* is false), or that the force of available evidence for and against *p* is readily discernible (if we were justified in believing that an assessment of such evidence was beyond our capabilities, then *that* information would make it the case that the belief that *p* is false was unjustified, and thus make it the case that *p* was epistemically possible).

[13] Everything that follows could of course be restated to apply not just to an individual *S* but to *S* construed as an investigative team.

One way of expressing the significance of our results in previous sections of this chapter is to say that, given those results, this might *not* be the proper response. Why? Because, given those results, there may often be justification for doubt about whether the examined evidence is *representative* of *all* the evidence that bears on the justification of the belief in question.[14] Let us say that *S*'s examined body of evidence *E* is representative of the total body of relevant evidence *E** just in case *E** underwrites the same assessment of *p* as *E*. And so if *S* thinks that *E* makes *p* probable and also claims that *E* is representative of *E**, what she claims is that *E** makes *p* probable. But if she takes account of our results and applies them to her case, *S* may see that she has to withdraw this claim. For what she may see is that (i) there is good reason to think there is other evidence (of some kind) she has failed to recognize that bears on the truth of *p*, and that (ii) there is good reason to be in doubt about whether the conjunction of this other evidence with *E* would result in a body of evidence that still makes the belief that *p* probable—that is, good reason to be in doubt about whether, despite her positive evidence, she has avoided a situation in which the *unrecognized* evidence has a strongly *negative* bearing on that belief, constituting a *defeater* for it.

Now in *Prolegomena* (p. 219) I point out that there are several evidential situations incompatible with justification for belief, and these include there not being enough evidence available and the good evidence that is available being blocked. It is clear that *both* these possibilities are instantiated when *S* is in the situation described above. For, first, if she has to be in doubt about the representativeness of her evidence, she has to be unsure as to whether the available evidence provides her with an adequate sample of all the relevant evidence, and thus must wait for more and more illuminating evidence before rendering a judgment as to the truth of *p* (of course she may remain in this situation indefinitely, regardless of the new evidence she unearths, if [i] and [ii] above continue to apply to her). And, second, if she sees that (i) and (ii) apply to her, that itself means that not only may there be a defeater for the belief that *p* in the unrecognized evidence, but there *is* a defeater in information *available* to her, the defeater that emerges from *recognizing* the fact about the epistemic possibility of a defeater lurking in the unrecognized evidence. In other words, (i) and (ii) provide us with new information to offer *S* that may block the support provided for the truth of *p* by *S*'s evidence.

---

[14] The notion of "carefully examined" evidence is not coextensive with that of (what at the beginning of this chapter I called) accessible evidence or one's own evidence. The latter category includes the former, but it is large enough also to include overlooked or neglected evidence—which forms of evidence (by definition) do not belong to the carefully examined evidence.

But why, someone may ask, should we worry about what might happen in the future? Why should unknown possibilities ever be thought to block *S*'s admittedly supportive examined evidence? Well, as for the first question: it can be misleading to speak of the future here, for the total evidence we are talking about, including both recognized and unrecognized evidence, *obtains now;* and there are certain things that can be known right now about the unrecognized evidence, as we saw earlier. As for the second question, and this is important: when we express and endorse a *belief,* we are saying not just that the corresponding proposition is supported by evidence we know about, with the verdict of evidence we don't know about—and so, in effect, of the world—left open, but rather that it is really true. And such a response to a proposition is not one that should be made unless there is justification for believing that the *total* body of relevant evidence supports it; for that the total body of relevant evidence supports the proposition is entailed by its being really true.[15]

It follows that if on careful examination *S* finds justification instead for doubt about whether the evidence she has examined is representative, she is in no position to recommend the belief that *p*. Indeed, if she has done her best to understand the force of all available evidence and this is the result, she must declare such belief unjustified. For now she has become exposed to the following argument: (1) If *p* is true, then the total evidence supports it. But (2) there is good reason to be in doubt about whether the total evidence supports *p*. So (3) there is good reason to be in doubt about whether *p* is true. It is clear that this conclusion, (3), blocks the support for *p* provided by *E*: *S*'s reason for doubt about the representativeness of her evidence has in effect brought it about that her existing evidence base has been enriched through the addition of the proposition "There is justification for doubt about whether *p* is true," which proposition in conjunction with *E* does not provide good evidence supporting the truth of *p*, even if *E* alone does. Any justification for doubt concerning the representativeness of evidence is therefore

---

[15] Notice that—as implied in the Introduction, where the distinction between belief and confidence was made—one is not inevitably *certain* of what one believes: involuntarily seeing the world as such-and-so in a non-degreed fashion is compatible with a variety of different degrees of intellectual confidence. Nor does justification for the view that the total relevant evidence supports a proposition have to justify *certainty* as to the obtaining of that state of affairs. This may seem to leave an escape route for the believer: can she not say that despite holding beliefs on the relevant matters, she is less than certain about them, and that her lack of complete certainty is enough of a concession to the point I am developing? She may say this, but it will not be adequate since it follows from my defense of doubt that *no* degree of confidence is justified here, and no degree of confidence clearly falls too far short of certainty to be compatible with belief.

itself capable of functioning as strongly negative evidence, of blocking the force of otherwise good evidence. It is itself capable of producing a defeater for beliefs of interest to us, an "unrecognized defeater" defeater that once unearthed prevents even the recognized and available evidence—in which it is now included—from providing a sufficiently strong indication of the truth of the propositions concerned.

Of course I have said only that *if* an inquirer is in the position described above, represented by (i) and (ii), such disturbing consequences ensue, and the reader will rightly ask how one is to be assured of the applicability of this conditional's antecedent in this or that context of inquiry. So let us consider how we might go about determining this. Subcondition (i) is surely uncontroversially and quite generally realized—that is, we can see that it is realized in just any significant context of intellectual inquiry. Here the distinctions made in previous sections between the different ways in which evidence may go unrecognized are helpful. For once we have run through all those possibilities, considering how variously, given our finitude, humans can fail to notice evidence having a bearing on beliefs (even if only evidence further supportive of conclusions already arrived at), the idea that we should, at any point of inquiry, have failed to notice *nothing* of importance must surely appear incredible to us. Even if we have looked for and examined much relevant evidence quite scrupulously, the possibilities of oversight and neglect nag, and the extremely high likelihood of relevant evidence of some sort in the huge tracts of information we have not got to because we have been focused on other things, or in what has not yet been discovered or is undiscoverable, seems obvious. Here it should also be noticed that it is not only *S*'s own oversights, neglect, selectivity, or incapacity that may produce unrecognized evidence relevant to her inquiry, but the oversights, neglect, and so on of all those investigators who have come before her, on whose efforts she depends when gathering evidence. It seems clear, then, that (i) should be taken as satisfied: there will in all likelihood be *some* evidence relevant to *p* that has gone unrecognized by *S*.

What about subcondition (ii), with its reference to justified doubt about the representativeness of *E*? How might we come to be in the position *it* represents? This condition may seem quite difficult to satisfy—more difficult, certainly, than has been acknowledged so far. Indeed, by premise (1) of the very argument I use above, if *p* is true then it is supported by the total evidence, and *E* says that probably *p is* true. So—the critic may suggest—given *E* and premise (1) of the above argument, we already have support for supposing that probably *E* is representative. And if we have such support, then to fall into doubt about

E's representativeness we will surely need *counterbalancing* support for supposing that *E* is *un*representative—that there is in fact unrecognized evidence and that it has a strongly negative bearing on belief that *p*. But how could we ever have access to such a thing as that?

This reasoning is mistaken, however. Given *E* and premise (1) of the above argument *and given that* E'*s support for* p *is unblocked,* we acquire the need for counterbalancing support referred to, but not otherwise. And the doubt about representativeness that the skeptic seeks to inspire by reference to unrecognized evidence, if it can be justified, serves precisely to block *E*'s support for *p*. Thus if our reasons for doubt here are any good, then there will be no unblocked support for representativeness that needs to be counterbalanced. (The critic supposes that the force of any reason for doubt that might be produced will be independent of that belonging to the reason for not doubting to which he refers, leaving the latter's force in place; but this is not so.) Another way to see the problem here is to notice that if we successfully block *E*'s support for *p*, then we also block all inferences that we might wish to make from *p* given *E*, such as the inference that the total evidence supports *p*. And just that inference is needed to generate the threatening support for representativeness to which the critic's reasoning refers. Thus we do not need a good reason to suppose that the total evidence in fact includes strongly negative unrecognized evidence and that *E* (therefore) is in fact unrepresentative in order to satisfy the condition specified by (ii). (Indeed, if we could show that much, then we might, all things considered, have justification for declaring that *E* is in fact unrepresentative, and not just for being in doubt about its representativeness.) If we can show as much as that there is good reason to expect much unrecognized evidence whose import *could as easily turn out to be strongly negative as positive*, we will at once block *E*'s support for *p* (thus also blocking the support for believing in representativeness it indirectly provides) and satisfy (ii). For then we will be in a position to restate our argument from above as follows: (1) If *p* is true, then the total evidence supports it. But (2) there is a 50/50 chance that the total evidence does *not* support *p* (or else the likelihood that it supports *p* is indeterminate). So (3) there is a 50/50 chance that *p* is untrue (or else the likelihood of its being true is indeterminate). And this restatement clearly has the same doubt-related force as the original.

Now having said all that, it is still true that, depending on the content of *p*, we may sometimes be faced with evidence for *p* so strong that it *cannot* be blocked, that there is no room for doubt as to its truth—so strong that nothing can prevent us from inferring (should we need to do so) that the evidence in question is representative. (If there *were* room for doubt, the last paragraph's point about blocking would indeed apply, and so we are not questioning what was said there, but in these cases there is no such room. Here we again—though with a different result—see how reasons for doubting and for not doubting in this connection are not independent.)

Simple beliefs of reason such as the belief that if A is taller than B, then B is shorter than A or that 2 + 2 = 4 come to mind as examples. These beliefs are apparently secure in every possible world: one cannot imagine the luminosity of self-evidence coming off them, and it is surely appropriate for the inquiring philosopher to endorse them. Certain general moral beliefs such as the belief that universal justice is good or that respect for others is good apparently fall into the same class. Moving beyond self-evidence, perhaps we can say that if the belief in question is the belief that there is no hippopotamus in a certain room in Winkler, Manitoba (a small room!), even philosophers should be convinced that the evidence of perception will not be cast into question by new evidence if the former has been carefully examined. Certainly, we should now admit that there is a possible world in which we are shown to be mistaken, but we would not rightly admit this to be *epistemically* possible. Or suppose that the belief in question is the belief that my mother, for whose general virtue and particular devotion there are innumerable interwoven strands of evidence, is not out to fool anyone when she says she loves me: we may not be able to imagine a relevant change in our evidence being produced by overlooked or neglected or other unrecognized evidence coming to light. Of course we will still see that there is a possible world in which we learn shocking things that undermine this belief, but we will be sure—and, it seems, legitimately sure—that that world is not the actual one. And maybe such very general beliefs as the belief that the earth is not flat or that *some* sort of biological evolution has occurred are also beliefs that we have obvious reason to think will not be defeated by new evidence because of the sheer quantity and diversity and quality of evidence presently supporting them, perhaps evidence accumulated over a very long period of scrupulous investigation. In such cases the evident truth of the belief itself is our warrant for denying that the evidence our inquiry has generated is unrepresentative.[16]

But notice how narrow a class of cases has been carved out here. However long the list of its members may be (we do not need to fine-tune the

[16] The possibility linked in this paragraph with "possible worlds" and contrasted with epistemic possibility I shall call *logical* possibility (this is of course what some others call "broadly logical" or "metaphysical" possibility).

list here),[17] it is surely going to be an item *on* the list that many, many cases fall *outside* it. Evidently we are often just not in situations like this. In everyday life and also—and this is our focus—in the specific contexts of intellectual inquiry, we often find ourselves in much messier situations, forced to admit that there may well be unrecognized evidence that would, were it taken into account, completely change the complexion of the picture suggested by the evidence we have examined. Indeed, in application to the clear cases that have been mentioned, the term "inquiry" is either not really appropriate (because we are dealing with necessary truths that form part of the *framework or background* of inquiry instead of its subject matter) or else must be thought of in the past tense (since there is no longer any serious questioning or discussion as to whether the proposition in question is really true). So although there are these cases where any argument citing (i) and (ii) would be immediately answerable despite what I have said about unrecognized evidence, this fact has seriously limited applicability.

Suppose, then, that we are in the much more common context where it is *not* evident to just any serious investigator that p is true and (thus) supported by representative evidence. What, if anything, could provide a bulwark against doubt about representativeness in such cases? It is hard to see what this might be apart from some convincing approximation to what we have in the clear cases—some reason, perhaps, to suppose that the thorough and careful investigation undertaken with respect to p has unearthed all the evidence it is important to consider. That we think this *is* needed is suggested by how most of us operate in the theoretical domain: we carry out the most careful investigation we can and believe what that investigation supports, on the assumption that all the important evidence has been examined. But what if that assumption is cast into question? What if we have reason to think that much relevant evidence—perhaps including much important evidence—remains unexamined, despite our (and others') care and attempts at thoroughness? Surely we would then have no basis at all to infer the representativeness of our evidence from the carefulness and apparent thoroughness of our investigation. Surely then we would lack any suitable approximation to the clear cases.

Consider an analogy. If Jane has *just begun* an investigation into, say, the truth of some theory of quantum physics and finds that the evidence encountered thus far is, on balance, strongly in its support, we would not

---

[17] More general considerations about what might guide us in judging certain beliefs to be justified, whether thus clearly and evidently or otherwise, in opposition to a completely *global* skepticism, are introduced and discussed in Chapter 8.

consider it legitimate for her to draw any conclusions about the truth of the theory or the representativeness of her evidence. Jane's sample is much too small, and there is good reason to think that important new evidence (perhaps evidence defeating what her evidence so far supports) may be uncovered by subsequent inquiry. Our situation in nonclear cases can be similar. If there must, on account of human finite limits, remain a great deal of unrecognized and unconsidered evidence *even after* we carry out as thorough an investigation as we can with respect to a (nonclear) issue of interest to us, then we are in an important respect in the same boat as Jane is in. Then the fact of our careful and lengthy investigation, though it is admirable, and though in other respects it certainly puts us ahead of Jane, leaves us in the same position she is in with respect to the matter of representativeness. For we can see that there may be as much unexamined evidence outside the range of our investigation as outside Jane's, if not more. And so we certainly are in no better a position than she to infer from the quality of the relevant investigation that the examined evidence is probably representative.

But should we really fall into doubt on that matter instead? I want now to develop certain points previously adumbrated into a *sufficient condition* for the justification of doubt with respect to the representativeness of evidence in certain nonclear cases, and thus into a sufficient condition for the satisfaction of the condition specified by (ii) above for those cases.

Notice first that the more and the more diverse unrecognized evidence we should expect there to be, the worse any argument against (ii)'s applicability must appear. Here our five types are once again extremely pertinent, for awareness of them gives us a strong initial indication that such an argument's conclusion will be false in many cases. But which cases? Can we narrow things down a bit? I think a reference to the presence of significant (i.e., not obviously false) *alternatives* to *p*—propositions recording the various ways in which *p* can be false—is apropos at this stage. Alternatives to *p* represent possible objections to *p* (for there may be arguments supporting those alternatives and thus supporting the falsity of *p*). Hence the more significant alternatives to *p* (or evidence pertaining to such alternatives) one has not considered or thought of, the more unconsidered objections to *p*—and the more strongly negative evidence—may be lurking in the unrecognized evidence. (There is only one way of being right in the claims we make, and ever so many ways of going wrong for finite creatures like us.) And clearly at a certain point we will wish to say that the unrecognized evidence is at least as likely to turn out to be strongly negative in its import as positive (or else that we are completely out of our depth and unable to make relevant probability assessments at all—which leaves us in the same unhappy position vis-à-vis [ii]).

Let me now fill out that expression "at a certain point" by introducing some *general properties* that can jointly add to the number of unconsidered significant alternatives—or the amount of unconsidered evidence pertaining to *considered* significant alternatives—that we must expect there to be in relation to a proposition *p* at any given stage of inquiry in which apparently strong support *E* for *p* of the sort earlier described obtains.[18] It is not at all difficult to identify a handful of such properties, and discussion of them in connection with our five categories of unrecognized evidence will prove illuminating. As just suggested, these are potentially overlapping categories, and as we will see, the more they overlap in the case of any given proposition, the more significant but unconsidered alternatives (or associated evidence) we should expect, because of the nature of the interactions among those categories/properties and the various forms of unrecognized evidence.

So what are the properties? First we have the property of being *precise,* that is, having specific content strictly distinguishable from many other possible contents, being definite and sharply exact (as opposed to being vague or—in that sense—general). An example of such a proposition would be "There is a 1987 Volvo on John Schellenberg's driveway in Chester Basin, Nova Scotia." An example of a proposition lacking this property would be "There is something on someone's driveway somewhere in the world" or "Something exists." There is, second, the property of being *detailed*—by which I mean thorough or full of particulars, and thus complex or multifaceted (as opposed to simple). A detailed proposition tries to give the whole story, to identify all the parts of a certain picture (or aspect of a picture). A large conjunctive proposition describing *everything* on my driveway, whether large or small, would qualify here; and of course the Volvo proposition above would be relatively simple. Third is the property of being *profound,* that is, deep or fundamental, comprehensive in scope, and pregnant with explanatory possibilities (as opposed to local, superficial, and explanatorily barren). The Volvo proposition tells us very little about one extremely small corner of the universe and can be used to explain hardly anything interesting. Propositions with more in the way of profundity would try to say how it is in some or many respects for some large tract of reality or the whole: propositions expressing or seeking to express laws of nature provide examples. Finally, we have the property of being *attractive:* likely to be approved by human beings and liable to draw

---

[18] Though I will be using the points here to support a sufficient condition for the satisfaction of (ii) in the relevant cases, it will be obvious that they provide additional support for the satisfaction of (i) as well.

forth a positive emotional response from them (as opposed to being dry, cold, uninteresting). This property is not as "objective" as others, requiring us to introduce the notion of human cognizers and emoters. It is possessed by propositions that promise what humans are likely to see as good things, and to which humans will tend to respond with positive emotion. An example here would be "There will be peace on earth one day." And we are all only too familiar with examples of unattractive propositions.

So why should we think of these four general properties as indicating—especially in concert—the possible presence of significant and unconsidered alternatives to the proposition in question (or the epistemic possibility of relevant unconsidered evidence)? Well, if we know that a proposition is precise, we can immediately infer that it has many alternatives. A precise proposition commits itself to the world having, in some respect, a very specific character, and, seeing this, we can see as well that its denial must always be logically equivalent to a large disjunction of alternative propositions (each specifying a way the world might be said to be, such that if it really were that way, it would have a different character, and the precise proposition would be false). Now not all these propositions will be very significant. Nevertheless, in other cases of precision there will at any rate be more than no chance at all that one of the many ways in which I could go wrong in believing the precise proposition is a way I *would* go wrong in doing so. And this must prove troubling, for now we will be inclined to ask, "How *big* a chance?" Some significant alternatives will perhaps be less significant than others: it may be less likely that young and vigorous Burton will fail to visit me next week because he dies of a heart attack than because he is too busy to leave the house. But it is not hard to see how the probability of their disjunction—amounting, in the case of such mutually exclusive alternatives, to the *combined* probabilities of the disjuncts—and so of the denial of the precise proposition may quickly become quite high indeed; or, at the very least, it is not hard to see how I might often be in no position to rule out a high probability here. Why? Because I may not be able to rule out, in connection with all or even many of those alternatives, overlooked or neglected or inaccessible or undiscovered or undiscoverable supportive evidence. Where there are many ways I (and others investigating before me, on whom I depend) could go wrong, there are many ways in which the world can conspire against me and my evidence, preventing me from having in view all that bears on the case at hand. (Compare here the concern I should have about future defeat of the proposition "Someday some friend will visit me" with that which should attend "Burton will visit next week.") Now for each such alternative there may also be unconsidered evidence entailing or probabilifying its falsity. But insofar as the possible evidence we are talking about here really is unconsidered, how are we in a position to say that its import should be expected to be of the latter sort rather than the former?

However, that is not the end of the story, and our inclination to (rhetorically) ask the question just mentioned must certainly increase as we add to the story. For suppose the proposition in question is also detailed. In such a case we start to move in a yet more disconcerting direction. A detailed precise proposition can be construed conjunctively, and it will have many more alternatives than a precise proposition that is not detailed. Though it is still possible to have a proposition with few or no significant alternatives, since each of the conjuncts may have this status *in excelsis*, it does seem we should expect fewer propositions in this enlarged category to qualify for that description. And it is easy to see how (except for propositions in the privileged class just mentioned) errors in connection with one or another or various of the alternatives, resulting from their being supported by one or another or various of our forms of unrecognized evidence, must become even more likely in cases of this sort. The chance that one of the ways I could go wrong in believing this proposition would be realized were I to believe it is getting decidedly bigger. (Here compare the Volvo proposition above with the following proposition: "There is a steel gray 1987 Volvo with a four-cylinder engine and rust above the bumper and a tailpipe held in place with twine on Schellenberg's black asphalt driveway in the village of Chester Basin, Nova Scotia." Might it be some *other* sort of gray? Is it perhaps a *six*-cylinder engine? Might the rust be *below* the bumper? Might it be *wire* instead of twine? Might it be *cement* instead of asphalt? Might Chester Basin have recently been incorporated as a *town*? . . .)

Things get much, much more disturbing for one who wishes to avoid doubt about representativeness when a proposition is not just precise and detailed but also profound. (Profundity alone need not be a problem in every case: we might have few worries about the claim that *some* sort of evolution is involved in the correct explanation of the present state of the universe, but when someone starts to talk with greater precision and detail about, say, memetics, the notion that ideas invade and make use of individual minds for purposes of propagation just as viruses and genes make use of individual bodies, we should certainly get restless.) With a profound proposition that is also precise and detailed we have an extremely large number of alternatives, representing the vast store of possibilities incompatible with any proposition that has such wide and also specific ambitions and probes so deeply, in an attempt to learn the basic secrets of the universe. Indeed, the bottom has fallen out of our pot of alternatives: we are now in no position to say that we know what all or even many of them are, or how credible the far-flung possibilities among them might be in relation to the proposition under consideration, or what the evidence pertaining to them might be; so how can we be in a position to say that our evidence is representative? The chance of error here is obviously very high, and must surely be deemed at least as great as the chance of getting things right. And the connection with the history of thought and all the changes we have seen as human intellectual capacities and skills have developed only makes this very high chance of error more evident: these things can be exploited to show with clarity that precise and detailed claims about the fundamental nature of things must often be stumbling around in the dark, for want especially of evidence inaccessible to us or undiscovered, and perhaps even undiscoverable. And here a further point may be added. For if we have reason to expect that a view apparently supported in the present may well be defeated by future discoveries, we also have reason to expect that there may right now be accessible information supporting its mistakenness that we have simply failed to see: if the view may be mistaken, our view to the effect that present evidence supports it may also be mistaken.[19] So the possibility of overlooking evidence is highlighted here as well.

At this point we already have the makings of the sufficient condition we are seeking. But suppose we take one more step and think about a proposition that is not just precise, detailed, and profound but precise, detailed, profound, *and attractive*. The overlapping of all these properties makes things even worse for the one who would avoid doubt about a representativeness claim. Why? Because propositions promising the good and evoking positive emotion, especially in respect of matters deeply implicated in the nature of things and thus liable to be associated with the meaning of human life and perhaps cosmic opportunities, will be ones that anyone might *want* to be true. And so we find ourselves in an arena where *neglect* of alternatives flourishes, and where *past* neglect due to the influence of attractiveness may lead to the relative impoverishment of our present evidence concerning such alternatives, yielding a situation in which much relevant evidence we might otherwise have taken account of is instead inaccessible or undiscovered. (Think here of theories telling us that we are at the center of the universe or that our more sinister tendencies can all be removed through education or that this

---

[19] Here the distinction between examined evidence and accessible evidence is again relevant (see n. 14). One may think that one's present evidence, evidence accessible to one right now, supports a proposition, and perhaps the examined evidence really does support it, but this is compatible with there being important information in evidence accessible to one that has simply been overlooked, and thus not examined and incorporated in the course of one's inquiry.

or that culture, conveniently our own, has it over the rest—all of which have at some time seemed to careful inquirers to be well supported, by comparison with more plausible but humdrum or depressing options that would not always even come to mind.) Conscientious inquirers will of course seek to avoid it, but we have seen how easy it is to fall prey to neglect, and the neglect of the past and its effects we can obviously do little about. Thus when a proposition with all the properties I have listed beckons, apparently supported by good evidence, we must beware of being fooled by virtue of human desires, and take seriously the idea that the proposition may really be too good to be true. When this is added to the fact that it is already too precariously detailed and precise about profound things to be legitimately *thought* true, it becomes evident that representativeness claims in connection with such a proposition have no legitimacy at all.

In general, then, we may say that the more a proposition *p*, apparently supported by *E*, exemplifies the overlapping of these properties and *the more completely* (that is, the more precise and detailed and profound and attractive it is), the more reason we finite creatures have to suppose that the unrecognized evidence relevant to *p* may as well be negative as positive in its import, and (thus) the more reason we have to be in doubt about the representativeness of *E*. And as we near the limit point to be associated with "more" here, there is really nothing that can legitimately bring us to affirm that *E* is representative instead of falling into doubt about this matter, judging both conditions (i) and (ii) to be satisfied and the belief that *p* to be unjustified.

7. *Additional Support for the Strategy*

Now the defender of *p* and *E* against (i) and (ii) might still want to hang on here and insist that, with nothing to go on that *proves* the negative import of unrecognized evidence, we should stick with the belief supported by the recognized evidence in cases of the sort in question. Developing this point a bit (and here there are hints of an argument tried earlier) the critic may say that that if we are not skeptics about induction, then, having examined the evidence available to us, we will take an inductive "leap" and infer that the evidence we have not assessed will support the same conclusion, to the same degree, as the evidence we have assessed.[20]

[20] I am grateful to William Hasker for his suggestion of this objection (and the objection discussed at n. 23) in his comments on a paper of mine presented at the 2004 meetings of the Society for Philosophy of Religion.

Well, there are leaps and then there are leaps. I suggest that even some-one entirely bereft of a general skepticism about induction should resist this particular instance of induction where our four properties are pres-ent. Indeed, they may use induction to do so. The critic appears to be saying that from the fact that at a certain time t1 the *examined* evidence supports or does not support a certain precise, detailed, profound, and attractive proposition *p,* it may be inferred that at t1 the *total* evidence has the same quality. Think here about all the inductions made in the past and similar to the one in question that have straightaway or eventually been overturned. But, it will be protested, t1 is not just any old time: at t1 a *careful* examination has been completed. The protest is ineffectual, for we may simply repeat ourselves: think about all the inductions made in the past and similar to the one in question—that is, grounded in careful examination—that have straightaway or eventually been overturned.

Perhaps the strongest inductive evidence here comes from the *undiscov-ered* evidence that has often been revealed to surprised inquirers in the his-tory of science, which has witnessed one break from the past after another. What historians of science recognize (and what the rest of us often forget) is that, as W. H. Newton-Smith puts it, "all physical theories of the past have had their heyday and have eventually been rejected as false."[21] All once-popular theories of science, from Ptolemaic astronomy to the phlo-giston theory of combustion, however carefully developed and defended against objections available at the time, have been judged by science to be incorrect. Now we are as much in the grip of apparent present success as were people of the past, and just as vulnerable as they to suppose that the "final truth" has been reached. But the odds are that, like them, we are mistaken. Newton-Smith goes on to say: "There is inductive support for a *pessimistic induction:* any theory will be discovered to be false within, say, 200 years of being propounded. We may think of some of our current theories as being true. But modesty requires us to assume that they are not so."[22] And what goes for theories of science goes for other precise, de-tailed, profound, and perhaps attractive views about the nature of things too. Even if we are more modest than Newton-Smith, saying only that cur-rent views may well turn out to be false, we have all that is needed for the skeptical conclusion.

But there is additional inductive evidence that might be adduced here, which links up with other of our five categories of unrecognized evidence.

---

[21] W. H. Newton-Smith, *The Rationality of Science* (London: Routledge & Kegan Paul, 1981), p. 14.
[22] Ibid.

One must surely expect that there may well be neglected or overlooked evidence of *some* sort in connection with propositions of the special kind we are discussing. But what sort? Doesn't experience teach us that neglected and overlooked pieces of evidence tend to have a negative rather than a positive bearing on the justification of the belief in question? Certainly, it is possible to overlook or neglect something that *adds* force to what we are already inclined to believe. But how often does that happen? For well-known psychological reasons, when evidence starts to lean in one direction, we will tend to expect other evidence to fall into the same pattern, and so be more likely to overlook the evidence that does *not* do so. And obviously we are less likely to *neglect* evidence that follows the general and accepted drift of examined information. By its very nature neglected evidence most commonly is evidence that does not fit in with what we have some personal stake in supporting, and thus with what we so conveniently find *to be* supported. Hence, when considering a proposition with our four properties, one can argue as follows. For all we know, there is neglected or overlooked evidence relevant to this proposition; but most commonly, neglected or overlooked evidence is negative rather than positive; so for all we know, there is unrecognized evidence with a negative bearing on belief of this proposition; now we are in no position to rule out that such evidence would have a *strongly* negative bearing; so for all we know, there is unrecognized evidence with a strongly negative bearing on belief of this proposition (which, by argument from the beginning of this section, is to say that belief of this proposition is defeated).

Take inaccessible evidence as well. We all very commonly change our views on matters large and small as new evidence becomes known to us: this is in fact one of the most obvious features of human life. If much new evidence now inaccessible to us became known to us, wouldn't we expect the same thing to occur? But when we change our views, it is because our newly enlarged stock of evidence *no longer supports the view we once held*—in other words, because the previously examined evidence is not representative of the newly enlarged stock. Hence, much as before, if we suppose there may well be inaccessible evidence pertinent to the proposition under inquiry (as surely we must in the case of such ambitious propositions as we are now considering), then we should also suppose that there may well be inaccessible evidence with a negative bearing on belief of that proposition. And if negative, why not strongly negative?

Thus the claim that one must be a skeptic about induction to accept my argument in this chapter is quite implausible; only the most undiscriminating adherent of inductive reasoning—and one who ignores or overlooks all the inductive support *I* can appeal to—will want to make such a claim. Of course, despite all these points, we may in some cases, given practical exigencies, have to take what appears supported at a certain time as a basis for action, but acting on an assumption is something quite different from believing. What we are learning is how audacious *belief* is in circumstances of the sort I have emphasized.[23]

8. *Application of the Strategy to Religious Inquiry*

I turn now to the question of how the arguments of the previous sections may be applied to religious and irreligious belief. The main point connecting religion to our discussion will perhaps be obvious. The propositions at issue here are ultimism and its denial, and they immediately bring us to terrain that is eminently favorable to skeptical arguments concerning our susceptibility as finite creatures to belief on unrepresentative evidence.

To see this, suppose that we have an examined body of evidence, the result of long and careful investigation, that makes one of the many elaborated forms of ultimism probable. Perhaps it is a story of God or gods, with all the qualities of the divine being in full display and the ultimate good to be attained in relation to it evocatively expressed. At once we can see that we have precision, detail, profundity, and attractiveness combined, and very large proportions of each. We have *precision,* because there will always be many other ways the world could be in respect of ultimate reality and ultimate good. (Perhaps instead of a personal creator who in the beginning makes the world from nothing it is a creator who never begins to create but also never ceases, or a force or spiritual essence that makes the *world* divine,

---

[23] I should also address another suggestion: that *counterexamples* to the notion that the four properties I have mentioned should, in combination, inspire doubt can be drawn from science. Bill Hasker, for example, has suggested to me heliocentrism and the large conjunctive proposition that could be distilled from the periodic table of the elements, which propositions, so he says, are clearly and undeniably true. Now I do not in fact find these to be obvious examples of propositions that have all the properties of precision, detail, profundity, and attractiveness, and have these properties in any very high degree. Indeed, the former—heliocentrism—was long resisted precisely because of its unattractiveness, and provides a clear example of how evidence can be neglected on that account. But suppose that one of these two or else some other scientific proposition has the properties in question and is generally and rightly accepted as clearly correct. What would this show? That even where we have the four properties the evident truth of a belief may sometimes be our warrant for saying that evidence is representative? We would still have to say that all the *failures,* all the precise, detailed, profound, and attractive propositions that have turned out to be false despite what was at one time strongly supportive evidence, provide strong inductive support for at least doubt about any such proposition presently supported by evidence, *unless it is as obviously true as our assumed counterexample.* And if anyone wants to claim such obvious truth for the religious and irreligious propositions I now go on to discuss, I will be all ears.

or a glorious profusion of magnificent energies that prevent us from ever legitimately speaking of a unified One—or one of innumerable other possibilities, whether finely or more sharply distinguished from such as have been mentioned. And perhaps instead of a personal relationship with the Divine creator, our ultimate good is to be found in accepting our place in an everlasting process of becoming, or in identifying with the Universe, or in harmonizing the rhythms of our lives with the dance of the divine ones through celebratory rituals—or in what is expressed by one or other of the many remaining conceptions of wholeness or fulfillment.) We have *detail,* because, as is well known, the religious are not reluctant to extend our pithy terms "ultimate reality" and "ultimate good" indefinitely. (Theists, for example, would be inclined to append a glorious profusion of magnificent attributes to our description of the personal creator.) We have *profundity,* because, as is required for anything to be an elaborated version of *ultimism,* the reality referred to is always thought of as being metaphysically *and* axiologically as deep as can be. Here we have indeed *the most profound claims possible*—the most deep and comprehensive, with the most explanatory connections. Together with the mentioned precision and detail, this must, by the arguments previously given, immediately suffice to generate deep worries about representative evidence. (If, as we saw earlier, there is good reason to be skeptical about some of the detailed theories of science, how could we be confident about our ability to formulate reliable detailed claims about what is *beyond* science?)[24] But to this we are still required to add that we have *attractiveness,* and given that the good in question is said to be an ultimate good, an attractiveness as great as any could be.[25] Can

[24] Perhaps some will here be inclined to appeal to Divine revelation, hoping to connect our finite intelligence to one that is infinite and infallible. But claims to the effect that this or that individual or group is hooked up with an infinite intelligence carry a spurious charm: clearly errors in such a judgment are just as possible as in others; and why in any case should we suppose that we would be able to *understand* what we wish to have revealed? More specifically, and applying now the apparatus of this chapter, it should be noted that claims as to the *credentials* of revealers must also fall prey to skeptical arguments of the sort here propounded. For those claims too may be expected to be precise, detailed, profound, and attractive. (Comments on the topic of revelation appear here and there in other chapters as well, especially Chapter 8.)

[25] Here someone may say—as Hasker has suggested to me—that putting any weight on attractiveness in this context and in particular on the related possibility of past neglect reflects a rather low estimate of the efforts of the opponents of religion in the last few centuries in digging up objections to religious belief. But notice that most of those objections have been to conventional *theistic* depictions of the Ultimate and associated existence claims, which advocates and opponents alike find most familiar and immediately attractive, with perhaps countless alternatives to theism even now remaining in the dark as a result. The attractiveness of this or that elaborated ultimism, in short, can prevent *other* elaborations of ultimism (which would on reflection be found attractive too) from being so much as noticed.

anyone deny that when we have all these properties combined, in these massive proportions, at least doubt is demanded of the reasonable inquirer facing the question of whether the evidence accessible to her, apparently strongly supportive, is representative? Can we—to reemphasize what is perhaps the central question—*ever fully map the alternatives* there must be to any elaborated ultimism? Hence the point about insufficient evidence and also the "unrecognized defeater" defeater can here be brought to bear with full effectiveness, and prevent us from saying that the good evidence with which we started is *overall* good evidence.

However, we must now entertain a response that the religious critic, especially one informed by contemporary philosophy of religion, may wish to urge on us. There are, as we saw earlier, some cases or sorts of case where the evident truth of a belief is itself our warrant for saying that no such argument as I have here developed may effectively be applied, and perhaps also others where it might plausibly be thought that past inquiry has turned up all the important evidence. These classes were by no means precisely delimited in that discussion: our lists of relevant cases were by my own admission not fine-tuned. So what is to prevent us from saying that some *religious* propositions appear on one or other of these lists, and so escape my present argument unscathed? More specifically, while complicated probabilistic cases in support of religion like that developed by Richard Swinburne might well fall prey to the argument I have mounted, ontological arguments of the sort associated with Alvin Plantinga represent ways in which even religious propositions can be truths of reason, and arguments appealing to religious experience of the sort put forward by William Alston show how something quite analogous to the sensory experience that was earlier allowed to generate the needed immunity can be brought into play.[26]

But this response, when carefully examined, turns out to be quite weak. Some of the reasoning I would use to show this draws on the full range of arguments in Part 1 and is presented in Part 2, where I offer a detailed discussion of the evidential force of religious experience. But already here we can note several points that, when taken in conjunction, provide a convincing reply. First, even ontological arguers don't claim that the existence of God is a straightforward truth of reason like "2 + 2 = 4." It is, after all, an *argument* that they are putting forward, and its main premise in Plantinga's most plausible version is still the eminently challengeable

---

[26] See Richard Swinburne, *The Existence of God* (Oxford: Clarendon, 1979); Alvin Plantinga, *The Nature of Necessity* (Oxford: Clarendon, 1974); and William P. Alston, *Perceiving God: The Epistemology of Religious Experience* (Ithaca: Cornell University Press, 1991).

claim that unsurpassable greatness is exemplified in some possible world.[27] This claim Plantinga himself shrinks from calling a clear truth of reason. In any case, as many have observed, whatever in *reason* moves us to find plausible claims about the possibility of a necessary God's existence should move us to find equally plausible claims about the possibility of a necessary God's *non*existence, and from such a premise it is not the actual existence of God but the actual nonexistence of God that follows. So the same reason that generates ontological arguments also generates defeaters for the beliefs they are used to defend. (All this must influence the philosopher thinking about which belief types to put forward as justified, even if the occasional religious believer inculpably unaware of what reason shows here may be justified in believing that God exists on the basis of an ontological argument—i.e., even if this or that corresponding belief *token* may be justified.)

As for arguments appealing to religious experience, to these also there are many serious objections—for example, objections pressing problems grounded in religious diversity—which are still being debated.[28] All this leads to something considerably less clear cut and much more subject to doubt than what we find in the case of the carefully examined and most *obvious* sensory beliefs I earlier included in my list of "clear" cases. Furthermore, as Alston himself admits, although religious experience can generate "beliefs full of force and conviction," it is also true that "often the content is very limited, and it doesn't give us by itself a full theoretical characterization." Where, then, do religious believers go to get the full theoretical characterization? Why, to "what they have garnered from their tradition"—which means that the justification for the detailed religious beliefs they seek to uphold, which are the beliefs at issue here, "depends on the credentials of this additional information."[29] So we see that the force of religious experience is reliant on the very claims it was supposed to "clearly" yield. Certainly it cannot function in the way envisaged by the present objection, even on the most optimistic projections of its best defenders.

Perhaps some inquirers into matters religious will respond to all this by suggesting as a candidate for justified religious belief a belief expressible

---

[27] For an interesting example of a challenge to the truth of this premise, see Richard Gale, *On the Nature and Existence of God* (Cambridge: Cambridge University Press, 1991), chap. 6.

[28] My latest contribution to this debate appears in Part 2 (see also the end of Chapter 3). For an earlier one, see my "Religious Experience and Religious Diversity: A Reply to Alston," *Religious Studies* 30 (1994), 151–159.

[29] Alston, *Perceiving God*, pp. 293–294.

by generic ultimism alone, eschewing the extravagances of all elaborated incarnations thereof. Is this an improvement? The skeptic can argue that if it is, it is hardly a noticeable one. Generic ultimism may seem a rather vague and imprecise claim by comparison with the usual religious fare, and indeed it is. But notice that it is still much more precise than other claims that might be made here. It is not just the suggestion that *something* exists or that *something* can better our existence to *some* extent. It is the idea that a reality both metaphysically and axiologically ultimate exists in relation to which an ultimate good can be attained. And although the detail of this claim is not inordinate, so that the number of alternatives might be thought on that account to be fewer, one can see just from its enunciation that they have not exactly become few. As for profundity, this remains as strong as ever and is in the end the reason why alternatives must be many here as well, including, perhaps, such as exceed our powers of understanding or description. And attractiveness is here in equal measure. We tend to be fascinated by the thought of a reality so profound and so magnetic, and this means that we are epistemically vulnerable not only because of metaphysical distance but also because of desire. All in all, then, considerations of the sort developed in the previous section may be applied effectively here too.

But now we must turn to religious disbelief, which involves the *denial* of ultimism in all its forms. How does this fare in the present climate? Not very well, as it turns out, and for similar reasons. Notice that what we have here is actually a rather strong claim, and even more vulnerable to change than the denial of such specific religious propositions as the proposition that there is a personal God. For the truth of any religious claim at all would falsify it whereas a narrower range of possible facts is relevant to the latter denial. And how can we rule out the possibility of unrecognized evidence vindicating one of those religious claims? Since, as we have seen, the farther reaches of religious possibility are not even statable for finite creatures like ourselves, yet must be empty of truth for the denial of ultimism to be correct, the belief that some evidence currently supporting that denial is representative can hardly be justified. In short, the problematic precision and profundity are here as well. As for attractiveness, those who find the denial of ultimism to be supported by present evidence must carefully consider whether their own investigation—or the investigation of like-minded individuals in times past—has not been skewed or limited by the dictates of desire. It is well known that even those who respect the open future of science are often prepared to close the book on religion. This comes perhaps from a failure of imagination, or a lack of interest in exercising it on behalf of religion, perhaps because of devotion to the methods and habits of mind of science, which religion is seen as claiming to transcend. In other words, the denial of religion can have its own seductive charms, and those who find it epistemically appealing must be on their guard against the quiet intervention in their investigations of such non-epistemic influences. In any case, whether such factors are operative or not, the previous points are sufficient to establish that in the irreligious case as much as in the religious, there is no basis for the claim that evidence is representative, as it must be if the belief in question is to be justified.

The Subject Mode of religious skepticism, which reminds us of our finite limitations, is therefore capable of being developed in such a way as to make short work of the claim that religious belief, or that irreligious belief, is justified—*and this even when all examined evidence supports a contrary conclusion.*[30]

9. *Is the Subject Mode Self-Defeating?*

Let me conclude this chapter by blocking a path of objection that—as suggested in the Preface—some will find appealing: the objection that not just religious and irreligious beliefs but also *the belief that my arguments in support of the Subject Mode are sound* must be unjustified if those arguments are correct, which is to say that the latter mode of reasoning is self-defeating. Now this *objection* can be sound only if my arguments do indeed apply to themselves, and it will not take much to see that they do not. One might be led to suppose otherwise because those arguments are, after all, philosophical arguments, arguing for a philosophical conclusion—and is not belief of a philosophical conclusion a prime example of a belief that may turn out to be false on account of unrepresentative evidence? But here we need to make a distinction between bold, ambitious, and risky metaphysical beliefs about what most fundamentally exists together with beliefs to the effect that they are justified, on the one hand, and the belief that some such bold, ambitious, and risky metaphysical belief is *un*justified, on the other. (Notice that the latter sort of belief, though in a sense epistemological, does not seek to answer theoretical questions in epistemology, such as questions about the nature of knowledge—which answers might well be

---

[30] Of course, as our inquiry has shown, if a new discovery in favor of ultimism or its denial as powerful in its results as the "clear" cases earlier mentioned were to emerge in philosophy of religion, religious skepticism would be surmounted. Meanwhile, in the absence of any such thing, skepticism is the justified response—and, indeed, by the argument of this chapter and by virtue of its blocking force, many future arguments that might otherwise be thought to rise to a "clear and obvious" status may instead be seen to fall well short.

bold, ambitious, and risky too.) Items in the former category tell us that the world, at bottom, really has a certain character, and they can be right only if the total evidence bearing on the world fundamentally being that way is in their favor. Though there may be many unrecognized alternatives to their claim (or unrecognized evidence bearing on recognized and examined alternatives), they tell us that active investigation should cease; the truth has been discovered. The item in the latter category, contrariwise, does not purport to discover the fundamental structure of reality but merely judges that beliefs that *do* make such a claim have not successfully made their case; it bids us to *continue* investigation. Now it will be evident that beliefs of the latter sort must be much less difficult to justify within a context in which truth, understanding, and wisdom are prized than beliefs of the former sort, even though both fall under the philosophical umbrella.

But what about *arguments* for such beliefs, like those I have presented? May these not involve premises and inferential claims as controversial and risky as the metaphysical beliefs just mentioned? Let's take a look. Does the Subject Mode include claims as controversial and risky as that? To be more precise, does it include precise, detailed, profound, and attractive claims liable to being overturned because of some conjunction of unrecognized evidences lurking outside the reach of our gaze? What we see here is that the Subject Mode, much like other arguments deployed in this part of the book, specifies certain special conditions that, if satisfied, signal a lack of justification; and its own claims do not satisfy those conditions, for reasons already suggested in the previous paragraph. After all, though perhaps precise and detailed, its claims are not profound in the relevant sense, nor are they particularly attractive, and so the reason I have developed for expecting many significant alternatives to be possibly unrecognized or inadequately assessed in the religious case (and relevantly similar cases) does not apply to them.

Why are the claims of the Subject Mode not particularly attractive? Because skepticism is always a position of last resort in truth-seeking contexts, and we do not like to hear that there may be much that we do not and perhaps cannot know. Having to acknowledge yet more complexities—the four properties—that may make the deepest understanding unavailable to us is not a pleasant experience. Moving from attractiveness to profundity: the unattractive points just mentioned and claims to the effect that they justify nonbelief are, none of them, deep, fundamental, comprehensive, and the like in the way that metaphysical claims would be; rather, *they stand in the way of our making such claims*. And in referring to unrecognized evidence and the impact of the four properties, they do not claim that these represent how things must *always* be for us humans, or even that this is *definitely* how things are at present. Rather, it is modestly claimed that things *may* be thus and so, since this is enough to justify doubt for beings as limited as we are.

Finally, there is no reason to suppose that cognitive limitations of the sort to which I have referred, should we be subject to them, would make it hard for us to correctly identify such limitations and their effects—in this case the experience of being limited helps! All we need is introspection and some humble observations drawn directly from our own experience and simple inductive arguments like those developed above, which no one seriously committed to inquiry will be in a position to challenge.

I suggest, therefore, that the Subject Mode does not apply to itself and so is not self-defeating. Rather, it represents a powerful—and commonly overlooked or neglected—way of justifying categorical religious skepticism.[31]

---

[31] The results of this section apply also, mutatis mutandis, to all the other arguments endorsed in Parts 1 and 2. For there is nothing in the Object Mode to which we might lack access for reasons related to the incomprehensibility of its object, and nothing in the Retrospective Mode to which we might lack access because of a pitiful past record of investigation on matters religious, and nothing in the Prospective Mode to which we might lack access because of unrealized discoveries of centuries to come. (Though we might be rescued from skepticism by certain new discoveries in the near future, there is no relevant reason to expect discoveries showing that we are wrong to be skeptics *now* on the grounds that the Prospective Mode provides.) And so on. For my "proofs" of atheism in Part 3, a somewhat different rationale is needed to deal with the "self-defeat" objection and is there provided.

The Object Mode

The categorical skepticism I am defending, as the name suggests, is a doubt that embraces any and all religious claims. It is natural, therefore, to suspect that its doubting arises because of something *shared* by members of that set of claims. This suspicion is borne out by my arguments in this book, and nowhere more so than in this chapter. Here I focus on how skepticism may be supported by reflection on what we may loosely call the *object* shared by religious claims. All religious claims are, by definition, in some way directed toward there being an ultimate and salvific reality—or, as I shall sometimes say, for convenience brushing aside the distinction between state of affairs and proposition, toward ultimism. The Object Mode of religious skepticism exploits this fact, pointing out difficulties it raises for religious belief and also, by extension, for irreligious belief. As might be expected, it makes use of some of the facts of finitude that put in an appearance in the previous chapter, but it does not start with them, as does the Subject Mode. Instead, it starts with the nature of the Ultimate. As we might put it, the Object Mode starts from *above* rather than from *below*.

So what are the problems connected to the object of religious claims? What is it about the notion of an ultimate and salvific reality that might be thought to raise doubts about whether such a reality exists? Some related points were already mentioned toward the end of Chapter 1, where I made use of the obvious fact that this notion is about as deep as any could be. Here I will develop the point about "profundity" somewhat differently, while also addressing certain problems more specifically related to the features of ultimism. These latter problems prominently include the following: (1) There are reasons supporting the idea that the various known ways of filling out the basic notion involved here—our present conceptions of the

Ultimate—may be completely unworthy of such an exalted reality. Reflection suggests that these conceptions may fall far short of what is required. In such circumstances there is no hope of justifiedly believing that there is an ultimate reality by believing that one of these conceptions is realized, nor of justifiedly believing that there is *no* such reality by believing that *none* is; and not enough evidence to support the generic denial of religious belief either. (2) There are, further, unresolved issues about the *coherence* of the idea of something metaphysically and axiologically ultimate, and also salvific. Perhaps nothing could be both. And this serves to inspire doubt about the affirmation of generic ultimism, which latter claim, as we shall see, is left untouched by the previous difficulty. Together these two difficulties justify categorical religious skepticism. But before coming to them, let me develop the more straightforward argument from the profundity of the Ultimate.

1. *The Ultimate: Knowable or Unknowable?*

Suppose that the religious claim of ultimism is true. What sort of reality has been introduced? Well, as we have seen, ultimism takes the idea of what even a scientist might call the biggest fact there is, namely, the fact that underlies all others, that is metaphysically fundamental, and builds on this to achieve something rather larger, the concept of what we might call the biggest fact there *could be,* something not just metaphysically but also axiologically ultimate. In this transformation we not only find a separate idea added to what the scientist has in mind. Rather, the metaphysically ultimate, which a scientist might in certain circumstances be content to regard as finite and limited in various ways, comes to be thought of as completely unlimited and unbounded—as unsurpassably great in every respect. Religion, by its very nature, invites us to strain our intellect and imagination to the utmost in considering its central axiological notion, and to extend this notion boundlessly in every conceivable direction, in order thus to reach the idea of something *infinitely profound.*

The religious skeptic accepts this invitation and listens carefully to what religion says. The skeptic takes ultimism seriously, arguing that to do so is to arrive at a point that is literally beyond belief—beyond the belief that we finite beings have now, or will ever have, the capacity to discern basic truths about a reality of the sort to which it refers, that is, truths about the details of its nature or as to its existence or nonexistence.[1] In other words,

---

[1] And, of course, also beyond the belief that we will *never* have it.

we have here a straightforward argument for unqualified capacity skepticism. But if capacity skepticism can be made out, then, as indicated in the Introduction, we have a case for *categorical* skepticism as well: the force of any apparently good evidence we might have for or against ultimism is blocked if we discover a reason for doubt as to whether humans possess the capacity we would need to have in order to assess that evidence correctly.

So how can the argument for unqualified capacity skepticism be developed? Its basic claim is that we should be in doubt about whether so exalted a reality as we have conceived here can ever be more fully understood by finite creatures: certainly we can say that we are talking about something metaphysically and axiologically ultimate, and this has some comprehensible content, but when it comes to filling out the idea, we are simply out of our depth—or, at least, this is true for all we know. And it is likewise epistemically possible that we are out of our depth when it comes to determining whether such a reality exists. For suppose we think that it does or must exist. Given the nature of ultimacy, and the infinite gap between ourselves and any ultimate reality there may be, it will *always* be an open possibility that, because of some fact concerning reality or value unavailable to us, it does not or even cannot exist. And suppose we think that it does not or cannot exist. Given the nature of ultimacy, and the infinite gap between ourselves and any ultimate reality there may be, it will *always* be an open possibility that, because of some fact concerning reality or value unavailable to us, it does or indeed must exist. To think otherwise, the skeptic may say, is just not to take seriously the idea we have got hold of here.

Support for this can be found by ruminating more deeply on that idea, in connection with the work both of those who have sought to do so and succeeded and of those who, while apparently sharing this aim, have been less successful. Where serious effort in this direction has been expended, it has led to ideas like those of Spinoza, who, though he identified God with nature, saw nature as infinitely more profound than the nature the typical naturalist envisages, which is linked to physicality alone: the physical represents only *one* of an infinite number of "modes" of Divine Being—of Nature—according to Spinoza.[2] And, of course, Spinoza's God is also infinitely more profound than the traditional theistic God, who is likewise fleshed out in terms of only one of Spinoza's infinite number of modes, this time mentality. Expanding our own mentality with Spinoza, we may find ourselves thinking of not just a unidimensional or even a

---

[2] See *Spinoza: Ethics,* ed. G. H. R. Parkinson (London: Dent & Sons, 1989).

multidimensional ultimate but an *infinite*-dimensional ultimate. Here we may also be reminded of Iris Murdoch, who speaks of "the infinite difficulty of the task of apprehending a magnetic but inexhaustible reality."[3] Surely there is something to this, which it is easy to brush under one or other of our intellectual carpets but which we ought to take much more seriously.

Robert Adams, like many, gives quite eloquent lip service to the sentiments operative here, speaking of what he calls "the transcendence of the divine perfection" as "wonderful in a way that escapes both human understanding and human purposes." Indeed: "We cannot comprehend it. It is fearful to us, and in some ways dangerous." But then he goes on to say this: "We are not the measure of all things, and have at best a very imperfect appreciation of the full dimensions of the good."[4] This still sounds humble, in line with the previous remarks. But notice that it allows that we may have *some* appreciation of the *full* dimensions of the good. And elsewhere Adams suggests what this appreciation might amount to: "If God is the Good itself, then the Good is not an abstract object but a concrete (though not a physical) individual. Indeed, it is a *person,* or importantly like a person."[5] So perhaps we are in a sense the measure of the "full dimensions" of the good after all. What one sees here is the influence of religious tradition but also the demands of Adams's ethical theory, which says that "excellence consists in resembling or imaging a being that is the Good itself." If this is so, he says, then "nothing is more important to the role of the Good itself than that persons and their properties should be able to resemble or image it. That is obviously likelier to be possible if the Good itself is a person or importantly like a person."[6] So if Adams's theory can be sufficiently well defended and requires a personal conception of the Ultimate, we might have adequate support for both his humble admissions and his seemingly audacious assertions—for his attempt to "have it both ways," in opposition to my argument.

There is, however, significant doubt on both counts. Adams is fully aware of the fact that his theory is, for various reasons, quite controversial, and, appropriately developing it as strongly as he can, he puts it forward for continued discussion. Especially in connection with factors already

---

[3] Iris Murdoch, *The Sovereignty of Good* (New York: Schocken Books, 1971), p. 42.
[4] Robert Merrihew Adams, *Finite and Infinite Goods: A Framework for Ethics* (New York: Oxford University Press, 1999), p. 52.
[5] Ibid., p. 42.
[6] Ibid.

discussed in Chapter 1, we can say that there is nothing justifying *belief* of his theory here. Perhaps more to the point, one wants to say things like this in response to his emphasis on the personhood of God: "Isn't it also likelier to be possible that a *flower* resembles or images the Good itself if the Good itself is a flower or importantly like a flower?" In other words, how does the focus on persons end up being more than arbitrary?

I think Adams would answer by referring us to the way in which an appeal to "God's view of things or God's attitude toward things" (notice the personal attributes involved here) helps to solve certain problems about "determining whether the relationship between two things constitutes a resemblance and whether an acknowledged resemblance images God 'faithfully' enough to constitute an excellence" and also "whether in general there are objectively correct answers to these questions."[7] So there may be theoretical benefits to thinking of the admittedly inexhaustible God as personal.[8] But he has hardly considered alternatives, saying instead that "for a theistic theory it is natural to appeal at this point to God's view of things or God's attitude toward things,"[9] which comment displays how an antecedent commitment to theism is active, with Adams attempting to show how theism may be put to work in ethics instead of simply trying to see how best to answer his questions. Of course, seeing how theism may be put to work can be valuable, but whether this is a substantial point in favor of theism will depend on how other ideas—including other "excellence as resemblance" ideas—can be put to work, something that needs to be further discussed in a larger context.

Perhaps the most interesting response to Adams, however, and one that allows me to make my own central point most effectively, is a response that takes an important part of the "humble" Adams as its point of departure, turning it against him, or at least against the idea that any finite conception is adequate to delineate the Ultimate. He writes: "In thinking about the divine perfection, or the attributes of the being that is the standard of value, we should suppose that God's superiority exceeds our cognitive grasp in a positive direction, and is not exhausted by negative or universalizing operations on properties familiar to us. The divine

---

[7] Ibid., pp. 33–34.

[8] As Adams himself says, his theory "relies in various ways on the assumption that the Good itself is a person and, indeed, a lover; and its usefulness in this context may provide an additional argument for the assumption [additional to the aforementioned argument pointing out the desirability of human persons and their properties resembling God]" (*Finite and Infinite Goods*, p. 42).

[9] Ibid., p. 34.

knowledge, love, beauty are not just free from defects we can identify; they contain a richness we can hardly name. To us this richness is bound to be alien in ways we may find uncomfortable."[10] This is intuitively appealing, as far as it goes. But one wants to ask: How uncomfortable are we willing to get? Are we willing to admit not only that analogues of properties familiar to us may be instantiated and in richer ways than we can name, but also that there may be many *properties* in the Ultimate that we cannot name? The passage above is ambiguous on this score, but it seems evident that the intuitions pushing Adams to countenance familiar attributes that exceed our cognitive grasp in a positive direction must also push us to countenance *unfamiliar attributes.* Perhaps they push us all the way to the countenancing of something like the infinite modes of Spinoza—which would of course take us infinitely far beyond personality as we know it. Again, expanding our minds sufficiently might involve thinking of not just a unidimensional or even multidimensional ultimate but an infinite-dimensional ultimate. Where would personality be then? Where would any of our ideas be then?

An interesting way of further supporting the basic claim of this section's argument is suggested by the "mysterian" approach of McGinn and others of like mind, already encountered in Chapter 1. According to their line of thought, certain metaphysical problems puzzled over by philosophers, such as the mind/body problem and the problem of free will, are quite simply too hard for us to solve. And, as we saw, it is epistemically possible that they are right. But the claim whose status we are considering when we consider the status of ultimism is also a metaphysical claim, and not just any metaphysical claim. It is one referring to the *ultimate* metaphysical fact. Now the ultimate metaphysical fact must surely, among other things, contribute to an explanation of the relation of mind and body as well as of free will; so might not whatever difficulties attach to the latter items also attach to (perhaps having been inherited from) the former? I am not suggesting that there is an obvious connection here—that it is quite obvious that if we are incapable of understanding the relation of mind and body or the nature of free will, we are also incapable of understanding the ultimate reality embracing these more limited realities—but I would suggest that the *epistemic possibility* of such a connection *is* obvious. And that is all the religious skeptic needs.

Now it is important to note that the skeptic, in emphasizing such points as I have been making, need not be acquiescing in what is often called "negative theology"—an approach according to which we can say only

---

[10] Ibid., p. 52.

what the Ultimate is *not,* since nothing we can say has any connection to what it is. It could be that the problem is not that nothing positive can be said of the Ultimate, but rather that *too many* of our terms apply, in ways we cannot now and may never conceive. Of course it could also be that much of what is central to the nature of the Ultimate is simply unsayable. But either way, a straightforward and forceful argument for unqualified capacity skepticism, and thus for categorical skepticism, seems available here. If it is epistemically possible that the nature of the ultimate religious reality would be so completely beyond our grasp as this, then, as earlier indicated, it seems clear that it will also be epistemically possible that, because of some pertinent fact concerning reality or value unavailable to us, we have fallen into error in whatever view we hold with respect to its existence or nonexistence.

2. *Religious Conceptions of the Ultimate: Adequate or Inadequate?*

I have argued that to take ultimism seriously is to arrive at a point that is literally beyond belief of either ultimism or its denial. Here I want to develop fresh arguments for a slightly modified and more modest version of this claim—the claim that to take ultimism seriously is to arrive at a point beyond belief *that this or that detailed conception from one of the world's religious traditions corresponds to what would be the case if it were true.* Now traditional religious conceptions may entail that there is such a reality in the sense that somewhere they ascribe to the entity or state (or whatever) to which they refer, whether it be God or gods or Brahman or the Buddha nature or something else again, metaphysical and axiological ultimacy, and also salvific power. But if we look at the latter qualities in themselves and at their implications, abstracting from the details of particular religious accounts, and look also at the verdict of those who, even from a religious point of view, are perhaps best positioned to know any ultimate reality there may be, we will find reason to be in doubt as to whether such realities as are described by ordinary religious conceptions *should* be called metaphysically and axiologically ultimate or salvific. More than one sort of argument is hinted at in the previous sentence. The first is basically a modus tollens move, but we might also refer to it, more specifically, as the strategy of *transcendental reduction:* by carefully considering what would be the case if some presently available religious conception adequately represented what is ultimate and noticing that this is not the case or is in doubt, we find reason to demote all such conceptions to a lesser status, or at least we come to be in doubt as to whether this is not what they deserve.

Let us apply this first strategy. It can be argued that if any extant idea concerning the detailed nature of the Ultimate were on the right track, it would strike all who carefully examined it in the spirit of religion as tremendously impressive and astonishingly beautiful, or, at least, would be endorsed by mystics of the various religious traditions, those individuals who strain after infinite things in truly prodigious ways and are respected in each tradition as possessing knowledge by *acquaintance* of the Divine Beauty. Most of us have become so used to existing propositional formulations—for example, definitions of "God" in the West—that we are only paying lip service to the idea of the Ultimate when we say we are talking about an ultimate reality; we do not feel in our hearts what we are talking about. If instead we consider more carefully and with liberated imaginations what it is to speak of ultimacy, we will see the force in the suggestion just made, that the correct understanding of the Ultimate would have to be aesthetically and intellectually breathtaking for all who encountered it with open hearts and minds. (Other things that at best *reflect* ultimacy have such effects—we have all experienced moments that were aesthetically and/or intellectually breathtaking—so should this not be true a fortiori for something so closely linked to the Ultimate itself?)

But no specific religious idea has had these universal effects. Instead there is unceasing disagreement and controversy over the lineaments of the Divine. And those who spend any serious amount of time contemplating the basic religious idea and then return to the land of ordinary religion, where that idea is filled out in one way or another, often find those fillings thin and vaguely ludicrous. As for the mystics, it is well known that they tend to distance themselves from the details of popular belief, claiming that our "definite descriptions" do not come close to capturing the essence of the Ultimate—do not so much as touch the hem of the Divine garment. Why should all this be so if some extant picture of the Ultimate has got it right? It is tempting to conclude that human imagination has not yet been sufficiently exercised to do justice to the profundity of ultimacy, and that mystics and all who are truly contemplative can see that this is so, without—at least as things stand—finding any way to move further, falling into propositional silence instead.

Perhaps it will be replied that our limitations, the very human limitations I stressed in Chapter 1, can prevent us from seeing the force and beauty of the correct account, even when it is among us. Perhaps many are not properly disposed or have not investigated deeply enough. But the mystics and contemplatives are precisely those we think of as having transcended *these* limitations. Should we then suppose that other, more general human limitations are involved, so that even mystics are prevented from seeing the correct account in our midst? In that case we could hardly avoid doubt about our religious conceptions; for if because of human limitations the correct account cannot be expected to be recognized as such by even the most careful and most well-disposed inquirers, when it is present in their midst, then none of us is in a position to point to it and say with any authority: "There it is."

A philosophical defender of religious belief may now attempt to stake out a more moderate position than either that of the skeptic or that of the previous objection. Perhaps, she may say, due to the greatness of the Ultimate that we have been emphasizing, it is not possible to gain any comprehensive religious knowledge, but we may, for all that, still claim *some* knowledge (or justified belief) about the attributes of the Divine—even central attributes. One does not have to know *everything* about the Ultimate to know *something*. And she may add that the limited truth about the Ultimate that we do know, arrived at through cold reasoning, should not be expected to elicit the same response when it appears in words on paper that express this reasoning or its result in dense philosophical formulations and arguments as when the referent of those words is directly apprehended. Thus, even if one of our accounts has got it right, we should *expect* something less than unanimity among inquirers as to where propositional religious truth is to be found.

But the skeptical argument we have developed cannot be escaped that easily. Why shouldn't even the results of reason produce the effects in question, if the partial knowledge they express is truly central to the nature of the Ultimate? Propositional knowledge of the Ultimate would be expressed in *words,* the words would express *meanings,* and the meanings—if they were of the relevant sort—would penetrate to the heart of an *unsurpassably great reality,* and be apprehended as such by *minds.* Should we really expect the end result, if the minds were clear and well disposed, to be disinterest or impatience? Is there not at least considerable doubt as to whether this is so? If now we insist on degrees of centrality, and seek to distance our philosophical accounts from the heart of the truth, we become vulnerable to the point that we may have hit only on some accidental or dispensable aspect of the Divine—like a garment that is worn and then thrown away—or one so qualified by a much larger and central aspect embracing it but unknown to us as to be completely uninformative, like the single numeral "2" within a complex mathematical theorem.

Our first argument, therefore, appears to have considerable force. Suppose now we introduce another main element of ultimism, the idea that our deepest good is achievable in relation to the Ultimate—that the ultimate reality is not just ultimate but also salvific. If we do, I suggest, we will see that we have the basis for a second skeptical argument from religious conceptions of the Ultimate, an argument related to, but distinct from, the first. To get this argument going, we have to conjoin the idea that a correct conception of an ultimate and salvific reality is in our midst with the idea that it is realized. Having done so, we can also construct a reductio of this conjunction, which runs as follows. If a correct conception of an ultimate and salvific reality is in our midst and realized, then this account is also *spiritually effective* in all those sensitive and open to it, in a manner that entails quite a wide recognition of its beauty and force. For would not a reality the understanding of which *was* in this way spiritually effective be greater than one that was limited to other means of salvific influence? (I do not want to assume that human wholeness and liberation cannot be achieved through the Ultimate *without* our possessing a correct propositional understanding of its nature. But the point here is that if it exists and we *do* have an understanding of it within our grasp, then we might also expect the relevant effects to be forthcoming in the lives of those prepared for them.) However, again, no such effects are forthcoming. Hence we must either admit that there is no ultimate and salvific reality or concede that the correct conception of the Ultimate has not yet been developed. (The latter option will no doubt seem the more appealing to many, especially in the context of the other arguments for that conclusion I am developing in this chapter.)[11]

In answer to the reductio it may be said that our impression as to the greatness of universally effective salvific influence should be qualified by recognition of the value of other states incompatible with it, such as, for example, freely developed investigative dispositions. But this sort of reply simply represents a tempting sort of misconstrual of my argument: the latter is limited to such individuals as are spiritually sensitive and open to the Ultimate, whose dispositions involve just such qualities as the reply refers to. Thus we can preempt the reply. Indeed, *many* factors may be countenanced

---

[11] Notice that, quite apart from the introduction of the salvific element and the more widespread spiritual effects it envisages, this argument does not simply repeat the point of the first argument, since this one works with the assumption that the Ultimate exists and the other does not: the other says that even if there were no ultimate reality, the correct idea of what such a reality would be like, if available to us, would sweep us off our feet, aesthetically, intellectually, and no doubt in other ways too. Notice also that this second argument does not require the assumption that the Ultimate would be a *personal* being who would *act* in such a way as to produce the relevant effects. Such an assumption would be self-defeating in this context, requiring us to fill out the idea of the Ultimate in a specific way—a theistic way. But that is no problem, since the "influence" spoken of here can be understood in perfectly general causal terms: if there is an ultimate and salvific reality, then, because of the requirements of greatness, there will be *something* that brings it about that the effects in question are achieved, perhaps something quite incomprehensible to us.

as representing preconditions of salvific influence, for even when we have all the plausible ones out in the open and consider the set of individuals who satisfy them, we will find it to be a much larger set than the set of those who are affected in the relevant ways by this or that account of the nature of the Ultimate.

Let me now attempt a slightly different and more direct route to the skeptical conclusion about common religious conceptions. What exactly is it that mystics who object to the standard accounts of the Divine *see* when they consider them? My third argument suggests that, if truly perceptive, they will see a kind of *narrowness*. There is, no doubt, a reference to ultimacy, but it is an ultimacy *within parameters*, and so still severely limited. Take, for example, a standard theistic account, rendered precise and filled out by Swinburne when he defines the Ultimate as follows: "There exists necessarily and eternally a person essentially bodiless, omnipresent, creator and sustainer of any universe there may be, perfectly free, omnipotent, omniscient, perfectly good, and a source of moral obligation."[12] Swinburne's account, though impressively developed and accepted by many, is often criticized, even by other philosophers, as excessively anthropomorphic: when it comes right down to it, so it may be said, Swinburne's God, however magnificent, is just a super-person very like the human persons we know. It is true that the references to omnipotence, omniscience, and so on operate as ultimizing references *within a personal frame of reference*, but what we have when all is said and done is still only the ultimate person.[13] Brian Davies levels a criticism of this sort, referring us instead to what he takes to be the more profound account of Aquinas, who thought of God as subsistent being itself.[14] This notion, however, might be said to correct the anthropomorphic tendencies in writers like Swinburne by leading us to the opposite extreme of abstract impersonality, and so again to be limiting. (Adams is thinking along similar—or at least complementary—lines when he says of medieval theological conceptions that they involve a formality whose presence is a sign of "excessive reliance on materials that are only too familiar to our intellect.")[15]

Now, of course, both Aquinas and Swinburne are working within a Christian philosophical context, and this sort of tradition-oriented constraint

---

[12] Richard Swinburne, *The Christian God* (Oxford: Clarendon Press, 1994), p. 125.

[13] Here it may be useful to observe that Anselm's famous formula is "*that* than which a greater cannot be conceived," not "*the person* than which a greater cannot be conceived."

[14] He does this in various places, including his recent *Introduction to the Philosophy of Religion,* 3rd ed. (Oxford: Oxford University Press, 2003).

[15] Adams, *Finite and Infinite Goods,* p. 52 n. 2.

can prevent one from even attempting to conceive not only what would be unsurpassably great within parameters acceptable to Christians (or Hindus or Buddhists or whatever)—perhaps the greatest possible person—but unsurpassably great, *period*. Little effort has been expended on this issue by individuals not similarly constrained (more on this in Chapter 3). Where it has been expended, as we saw in section 1, it has led to ideas like Spinoza's. Perhaps if we took ideas like Spinoza's (or Murdoch's) more seriously, we would see the point of periodically transcending the traditions in attempts to make use of all their insights and also new ideas to formulate conceptions of the Ultimate that may improve on the more limited accounts advanced so far. Perhaps then we would not be so sanguine about these matters in the face of widespread disagreements and the denunciations of mystics and contemplatives. Perhaps then we would see the force of religious skepticism.

An interesting way of moving beyond the "person" emphasis of traditional Western theology in particular involves altering our understanding of how "person" functions here. Instead of thinking *ourselves* to be the paradigm of personhood, as theology often has done, perhaps theists might consider taking the *Ultimate* as an objective paradigm or standard of personhood that we only most dimly reflect. Perhaps we are fragmentary persons at best, only starting out on a long journey of intellectual and spiritual development (more on this in Chapter 4). Perhaps in our exemplification of personhood we are the tip of a wedge that extends infinitely. Thus we might "resemble" God, but God on this view might resemble items unavailable to us in so many ways that we could not at all be sure how deeply personhood in God (where "personhood" means "personhood as we know it") was qualified by other things. As we saw in section 1, our words fall over each other in their attempts to express what a reality unsurpassably great might be like, and while it can be argued, as we argued there, that our words may always fall down, because they are simply incapable of doing what we are asking them to do, it can also (and compatibly) be argued that whether or not they always fall down, we may not *yet* have formed a picture that comes close to being intellectually and spiritually satisfying or accommodating of all that belongs to even a correct sketch of ultimate things. Altering the metaphor, we may say that there is a land on the "other side" of the conceptions we have so far developed, an undiscovered country, which the concept of ultimacy naturally invites us to explore, if only to find that it is barren of life, or incapable of being traversed by explorers as humbly equipped as are we. This, and what must in its light appear as the narrowness of our own present conceptions, is, I think, at least a part of what the mystic sees, and it gives us our third argument for doubting whether any of the realities described by religious conceptions humans have so far devised are worthy of being called ultimate.[16]

So what can we do with the results of our discussion in this section? Just how do these arguments contribute to religious skepticism? It works like this. If we have found reason to be at least in doubt about whether such realities as are described by religious conceptions known to us truly match the content of ultimism, when properly filled out, then we have reason to be in doubt about whether we are able to access the truth about religion *by believing that one of those conceptions is instantiated.* It is obvious that the main ways of believing that the Ultimate exists take the form of believing that some detailed conception of the Ultimate from the religious traditions of the world is instantiated, on the basis of evidence apparently supporting its instantiation. But because my arguments seek to undermine the attribution of ultimacy to any of the realities involved here, anyone who accepts those arguments, even if he thinks that what some such conception delineates exists, will be bereft of any reason to suppose that the *Ultimate* exists. And so to that extent he must fall toward categorical skepticism. (I say "to that extent" and "toward" because it is also possible to be a religious believer by believing generic ultimism alone, leaving aside all forms of elaborated ultimism. Another, related argument made possible by the Object Mode—the one given in the next section—will be offered to deal with this sort of religious belief.) In other words, in the present case we lack what is needed to avoid religious skepticism with respect to any detailed sort of religious claim, namely (see Appendix B), a situation in which we can say that there is sufficient and overall good evidence for the truth of the claim, because we do not have sufficient evidence. Any evidence we *thought* we had, which investigation in times up to and including our own has unearthed, may not really be evidence for the existence of something truly *ultimate.* So more evidence is needed before any detailed religious belief can be justified—new evidence supporting the adequacy

---

[16] There is a response involving the idea of "revelation" that theists at least may be inclined to make to all three of the arguments developed in this section. Have I ignored the possibility that precisely because of its greatness and our ignorance the Divine reveals itself to us? But inasmuch as a Divine revelation must be true, we can say that our arguments against the intellectual adequacy of extant conceptions of the Ultimate are equally arguments against any of them having been Divinely revealed. And, of course, the very idea of a Divine Revealer shares in the problems revealed by these arguments. Thus, to avoid being question-begging and to be all-things-considered successful in this context, theists would need to find arguments stronger than these to support suggestions about a Divine Revealer. Attempts at such arguments are (indirectly) taken into account in the other chapters of this part of the book and also in Part 3.

of some extant understanding or (more hopefully) new evidence that some detailed understanding yet undiscovered is more adequate.

A similar problem faces the belief that there is *no* ultimate and salvific reality. One way of being a religious disbeliever, a way that depends on the assumption that if there is such a reality it is described by some one of the religious conceptions available to us, is to think that none of those conceptions is instantiated. But if the assumption is cast into question, then so is the (dis)belief. Of course another way (the only other way) of being a religious disbeliever is just to disbelieve ultimism directly. And how is *that* challenged by my arguments? Well, if we have no idea how generic ultimism is to be filled out, if we lack so much as a clearly representative set of possibilities here, disbelief of generic ultimism is unjustified, since it may well be that from those possibilities will emerge in time—though perhaps only in future time—more viable forms of religious belief than any disbelievers have so far had the opportunity to encounter or criticize. So here again the available evidence is too thin.

Now it will be said that a disbeliever's denial of ultimism may depend not on any such encounters or criticisms but rather on *naturalism*—the belief that there is nothing beyond the world of physical nature—and on its *entailing* that ultimism is false. But the essential point can simply be rephrased: How can the naturalist rule out as epistemically impossible the idea that her awareness of new ways of conceiving the Ultimate might undermine her reasons for being a naturalist? What we see here is a specific application of a point from the last chapter about possibly unrepresentative evidence: anyone today who is contemplating religious disbelief should be able to see that there may well be unrecognized evidence not just opposing but also supporting religious belief, bound up with new conceptions of the Ultimate so far unconsidered. Anyone presently inclined to find naturalism impressive is likely to be thus impressed, at least in part, because she has been comparing it with a limited and well fleshed-out disjunction of purportedly religious claims that she finds *un*impressive. But if my arguments here are correct, then the further reaches of the *relevant* disjunction fade into the mists of our ignorance, and we are pretty much back at square one, and, in particular, without any good reason to suppose that evidence for naturalism is representative.

There is more on all this in other chapters, but already we can see strong reasons for denying that either religious belief or disbelief is justified, and so for categorical skepticism. All that remains here is to show an additional way in which the Object Mode of religious skepticism may be utilized to undermine *belief* of generic ultimism. That is the task of the next section.

3. *Ultimism: Coherent or Incoherent?*

I say "additional way" since we have already seen, in the first section of this chapter, how the Object Mode provides an argument against generic religious belief. Problems arise when we try to speak convincingly about the detailed nature of the biggest fact there could be, or to defend the view that it obtains or does not obtain. Ultimism, the basic religious claim, introduces the idea of such a fact. It appears in the first half of that claim. But in the second half of the claim we find the idea that the highest or deepest good of human life (an ultimate good) is to be attained in relation to the ultimate reality referred to in the first half. This idea was already mentioned in the previous section, in connection with my second argument there. Here it will be central. As we shall see, introducing this idea considerably complicates matters and raises an additional difficulty so far unmentioned.

What difficulty? Well, with a proper appreciation of the inexhaustible greatness that would go with the truth of the first part of ultimism—and here we may draw on the results of both section 1 and section 2—it appears that we must fall into doubt as to whether an ultimate reality would not be so far out of our league as to be, in the details of its nature, eternally incomprehensible to us in any possible world in which we humans exist. But then we must also fall into doubt as to whether the second part of ultimism could be true in conjunction with the first part, for it is hard to see how our salvation could come from relating ourselves to the Ultimate without more knowledge of it than that being possible for us. Perhaps if the first part of ultimism is true, the second must be false. In other words, perhaps the two parts are incompatible.

Now in the previous section we toyed with the idea that future inquiry might put us in a better position with respect to understanding the Ultimate than we are in at present, and such speculation would have little point if we believed the incompatibility in question to obtain for the reason given. But I will not on that ground be arguing that the incompatibility *obtains* (and so denying what I said or implied in the last section), only that it is unclear that it does not. If an ultimate reality is *not* such as to be eternally incomprehensible to us, then we may indeed come to learn more about it, and it is epistemically possible that it is not. But this epistemic possibility is compatible with its being epistemically possible that it *is* completely and eternally out of our reach; and the latter is the epistemic possibility to be (again) applied in this section.

We have already seen why it is an epistemic possibility, in defending that part of unqualified capacity skepticism concerned with our knowledge of the *nature* of the Divine, in section 1. But we can also approach this matter from the perspective of section 2. For if we are in doubt about the adequacy of any of our conceptions of the Divine, then we are vulnerable to a deeper doubt inspired by the following sorts of questions: *How far* might the Ultimate transcend us? Are we in any position to countenance a *cutoff line?* The point is that once we come to see that our present conceptions may be radically defective as portraits of the Ultimate, there is really no way to limit the skeptical fallout. And if it is true for all we know that we will always lack something needed to discern basic truths about the nature of the Divine, then it is similarly epistemically possible that any belief we do form on such matters will be false, and that a Divine reality would be eternally incomprehensible to us.

Consider now just why eternal incomprehensibility of this sort would arguably be fatal to the salvific claim. The important idea here is that of establishing a *relation* to the Ultimate. It is supposed to be through such a relation that our highest good is realized. And this relation, as clarified in my *Prolegomena* (p. 28), must be construed as an *explicit* relation (otherwise we lose the religious character of ultimism). The claim of ultimism is not just that we will in fact attain our highest good if there is an ultimate reality, perhaps in some way completely disconnected from this notion, but that we will attain it through consciously relating ourselves to it in some way. The first, and weaker, claim could be true even if the idea of an ultimate reality never entered our heads and even if we never developed any sort of intimate connection to it (the greatest fact there is could be anonymously responsible for our salvation). But of course the second claim could not be true under these circumstances. And, more to the point, it is hard to see how it could be true if the Ultimate exists and is necessarily and eternally incomprehensible to us. All we would ever know in that case, even if we knew that it existed, is that something with the general properties of metaphysical and axiological ultimacy existed. We might have lots of ideas about how to make a start at filling this out, though recognizing their limitations, but we would never have a complete and satisfying picture that we knew corresponded to the Divine or anything close to it; in trying to settle this matter we would *always* hit a brick wall.

Now it is tempting to argue as follows: to achieve salvation in relation to the Ultimate, we must at some point, even if only far into the future, be able to improve on our knowledge by acquaintance of its value; but this entails having at least some propositional knowledge of what, more concretely, the unsurpassable value of the Ultimate consists in; hence if the latter is impossible, so is the relevant knowledge by acquaintance and salvation in relation to the Ultimate. The idea is that salvation in relation to the Ultimate would require that the value of the Ultimate be ever more fully communicated to us experientially, and even if we take "communicated" and "experientially" here quite broadly, as suggesting the incorporation of its value at various levels of our lives, surely it is plausible to suppose that the intellectual level is included, and indeed that its inclusion is a necessary condition of the rest of what we have in mind here. For how could someone ever more fully experience the greatness of the Ultimate without coming to *understand* it to at least some extent? Should we not at the very least fall into doubt as to whether this is possible?

But perhaps—or so an objector may now claim—there could be such a thing as salvation explicitly in relation to the Ultimate that did not involve ever more fully experiencing and incorporating its value, at least not in the sense here intended. Perhaps the latter is an idea, again, too influenced by specifically *theistic* models of the Divine and of the Divine-human relationship, according to which God is a person whom we as persons can come to know and experience intimately. In Buddhism, by contrast, there are very different tendencies, with the Buddha himself notoriously associated with an unwillingness to seek precise determinations about the nature of ultimate things, while still championing the Noble Eight-Fold Path as a way of properly relating oneself to them. Why, in connection with this, couldn't there at least conceivably be a revelation of how to live that we have reason to link with a Divine source but that does not divulge any relevant details of the Divine nature? Why, to turn to another possibility, might we not allow that it could be salvific to rest in awe precisely at the incomprehensibility of the Divine, as some mystics can be seen as doing?

Perhaps some of what is mentioned here represents epistemic possibilities, but more than that is needed to defeat the epistemic possibility of a deep logical divide between the two parts of ultimism. In fact, it seems to me that this objection contains the seeds of its own demise, at least when it is construed as an attempt to relieve or preempt doubt about a connection between salvation in relation to the Ultimate and (eventual) knowledge of its nature. For in introducing one religious model that involves a relevant intellectual component and another that allegedly does not, it only suggests that there are various ways things could be here; and this, taken seriously, only leads to another source of doubt.

The point here can be developed as follows. What the objection really supports is the idea that, even if the theistic picture is ultimately inadequate, it illustrates that the Ultimate might be such as to be salvifically linked with us only under certain conditions in which it is not incomprehensible to us; and even if no Buddhist model may be trusted, such models illustrate that the Ultimate might be such as to be salvifically linked with us even when it *is* incomprehensible to us. And although this might seem to leave both alternatives logically possible, and so to leave us without the incoherence in ultimism I am alleging to be epistemically possible and without that epistemic possibility, the result should rather be doubt as to which alternative *is* logically possible because of the following consideration: given the normative and metaphysical elements involved, it is at least strongly plausible to suppose that whatever is true here is *necessarily* true and that whatever is false is *necessarily* false. Because of this, if we are in doubt about the truth of either alternative, we must also be in doubt about its logical possibility. But we ought to be in doubt about the truth of *each* alternative. Hence we can believe in the logical possibility of neither but rather must remain in doubt as to whether the two parts of ultimism are logically compatible.

What about the idea of salvation as resting in awe at the incomprehensibility of the Ultimate? I concede that this might describe something true and important, but depending on what is in fact the nature of the Ultimate (and we might add, depending on our nature), truths about which would appear to be noncontingent, it might also describe only a flailing about in the dark, completely unconnected to the attainment of the deepest good of human life. Once again we are left in doubt as to the compatibility of salvation in relation to the Ultimate and the latter's incomprehensibility.

Might the objector now suggest that the Ultimate would be *greater* if at some time cognitively accessible to every human being? It might be thought that this move has force here if it does in the previous section, where I utilized a similar one in our discussion of whether a propositional understanding of the Ultimate would be spiritually effective. But it must be remembered that my aim there would be satisfied even if all I introduced was doubt, rather than belief, whereas the latter is what the objector needs to justify here if she wants an *antidote* to doubt. And, in any case, the objection simply begs the question, since the Ultimate would be made greater by being cognitively accessible only if the latter state of affairs is logically possible, and that it is logically possible is precisely what the arguments to which the objection seeks to respond are opposing.

I suggest, therefore, that we have reason at least for doubt as to whether attaining our highest good in explicit relation to the Ultimate would not entail cognitive access to the Ultimate of a sort that is ruled out if the basic facts of its nature must be eternally incomprehensible to us. But we have already seen that we have reason for doubt as to whether these facts would not be thus eternally incomprehensible to us even if the Ultimate were to exist. It follows that we have reason to be in doubt about whether the two parts of ultimism—one claiming that an ultimate reality exists and the other that our deepest good lies in appropriately relating ourselves to it—are compatible.

What can we do with *this* result? If we must, on achieving awareness of the relevant facts, be skeptical as to whether the two parts of ultimism are compatible, we must equally be skeptical as to whether ultimism is true, since no internally inconsistent proposition can be true. But then the would-be religious believer who seeks to escape the skeptical results of our previous section by embracing the belief that generic ultimism is true instead of one of the extant elaborated ultimisms has literally nowhere to go. Careful reflection on the object of religious claims reveals that the former sort of religious belief is no more justified than the latter. Combined with the conclusions of the previous section, according to which similar reflection removes justification for religious disbelief as well, and the independently forceful arguments in the first section of this chapter, this result makes very clear how mining the vein of reasoning I have labeled the Object Mode leads ineluctably to categorical religious skepticism.

CHAPTER 3

The Retrospective Mode

It is obvious that in cultures where science is undeveloped we do not expect anyone to be discerning truths in electrodynamics or particle physics. But then perhaps something similar applies where truths about *ultimate* things are concerned. Perhaps many rich layers of development and maturation, of very demanding sorts, requiring much time, need to be laid down before any human being can hope to be able to access such truths. Do we have any reason to think that such growth has already occurred? It certainly seems not: there is plenty of reason to be in doubt about whether the world has so far traveled any great distance along the path of preparation for religious discovery. Indeed, we may well be stuck somewhere far back in the beginning stages of development.

These ideas concerning our past, when permitted into our thinking, can be quite arresting. Carefully developed, they may be seen to cast serious doubt on the idea that we are presently capable of discerning the truth about matters religious, and thus on the idea that any beliefs about such matters are justified—or so says the *Retrospective* Mode of religious skepticism.[1]

---

[1] This is different from what was argued in earlier chapters (notice, in particular, that the capacity skepticism of Chapter 2 was unqualified). The problems cited in those chapters might obtain even if we had done our best as a species to transcend them (for example, even if our past record of development in the areas that will here be discussed were impeccable, we might find that all the conceptions of the Ultimate we could get our hands on proved ultimately unworthy of such a reality). Thus those problems do not depend on what is emphasized here. Nor, for similar reasons, does the problem developed here depend on them (for example, it might reveal a difficulty facing us in our present stage of inquiry even if it could not with any plausibility be argued that, in just *any* stage of inquiry, an "unrecognized defeater" defeater must threaten).

1. *General Preliminaries*

Perhaps the first thing that should strike us when looking into the human past with our ultimate aspirations in mind is its *brevity*. We humans have been around for no more than a few million years, and our civilizations—which mark the time span in which one can find organized intellectual exploration—are only a few thousand years old. Now it may seem to us that a few thousand years should be more than enough time for clever humans to figure out the truth about things, but this is only because we lack the patience of the universe and overlook the fact that our aim here is to unlock its ultimate secrets. Even if those secrets were to include the fact that in certain circumstances they may be revealed to appropriately disposed subjects by some Higher Power responsible for the universe and its workings, we have no a priori reason to suppose that the time scale involved in the delivery or processing of the revelation would be one familiar to us or deemed desirable by us. If there is anything that is evident from both science and ordinary experience imbued with common sense, it is that the universe takes its time.

Looking into our past with those ultimate aspirations in mind, we should be struck not just by its brevity but by how much of that short time has been devoted to *other things:* foraging, breeding, fighting, dominating, coping, playing, and the development of ever more sophisticated technologies to serve the former needs and impulses—things that, apart from the time they steal, are not exactly such as to help us make large strides toward the deepest understanding, with the focus on creative and imaginative activity, a disinterested love of truth, and patient deliberation which that would entail. For most of our history, human minds—those much touted rational and intelligent minds—have been occupied with anything but the needs of the deepest understanding.

But, one may say, what about the thinkers: philosophers, theologians, and the like? Well, consider how small their number has always been relative to the total population, and how little our societies have supported their interests. Our societies and their governments have always been more interested in warriors and technologists than in thinkers, and our systems of education even today are often more focused on depositing facts in brains than on cultivating critical and creative problem-solving tendencies in students—tendencies of a sort that might lead more of them to undertake serious and productive inquiry on matters religious.

Further, such thinkers concerned with religion as the world has seen have decidedly not been immune from surrounding influences—the picture of disembodied minds engaged with ideas in intellectual compartments sealed off from the outside world is flawed in multiple ways—but have often and only too obviously reflected in their work the immaturity of the race and its preoccupations. Witness the ideological constraints under which most of them have labored and which many have actively sanctioned or fostered, and by which, in any case, many of their conclusions have been determined; witness the endless disputation among, for example, Christian or Buddhist or Hindu scholars about the most insignificant matters (the picture of scholars discussing how many angels can dance on the head of a pin is unfortunately not entirely inaccurate); witness the demonizing of opponents and of those outside one's own tradition; witness the extremely narrow and thin body of data concerning religion informing the assessments of so many *anti*-religious thinkers writing in the last few hundred years. (Many, many books on religious subjects have been written, it is true, but to see my point here, consider only how few of those books have sought to set out as wide a range of conceptions of the Ultimate as possible, both ones antecedently found appealing by the writer and ones not, both conceptions actually adhered to in the world of religion and ones previously undiscussed, applying all the tools of human imagination and reason to their analysis and evaluation.) The result is very spotty work, often strikingly brilliant but within strikingly narrow parameters—work which we have no reason to suppose is at all representative of the full range of the religious realm, and which, in particular, leaves much territory involving *relations* among extant conceptions of the Ultimate and also *new* conceptions of the Ultimate unexplored, in its all too common concern with the maintenance or critique of the status quo within a particular tradition.

All this is (or should be) common knowledge, and it furnishes the general background for the skeptical argumentation of this chapter.

2. *The Heart of the Matter: How Religious Investigation Has Suffered*

A much neglected fact is that aspects of ourselves and of our relations with others that may not directly involve thinking can nonetheless affect how well we think. In considering how the past bears on religious skepticism, this is where we come to the heart of the matter. This "heart of the matter" involves, among other things, facts about the moral, psychological, and social aspects of the human condition. We are poorly developed in all these areas, in ways that bear the marks of past beliefs and should give pause to present believers. Because of these limitations, the investigative spirit has not taken us very far in matters of religion and, indeed, has often been choked out by other attitudes actively militating against improvements in religious understanding. In this section I examine these factors.

(1) Moral Factors. Here I will focus on human hubris, greed, dogmatism, hostility, rivalry, and loyalty. These items are related in a variety of ways, as we will soon see.

Let us begin with hubris, or self-importance. Deeply impressed with ourselves and our experiences and our information, inclined to radically overestimate our abilities and the magnitude of what we or individuals in our time have uncovered, we often cannot see with clarity how true understanding may still elude us. Consequently, we are not motivated to seek it further. But, someone may say, surely such factors operate as much in science as in religion, and yet science has been able to develop. This, however, is because, whatever their fallibility, there are in science certain self-correcting mechanisms (involving the verdict of nature and of critical peers) for which no counterpart exists in much religion and even, sad to say, in much religiously and irreligiously motivated philosophy (more on this later). And while no doubt our self-important tendency operates in other areas too, it is easy to see how it may be even more active in relation to religion than elsewhere, given the unrivaled significance and prestige that must naturally come to be attached to the possession of *ultimate* truth.

The point just made suggests that human hubris or self-importance may play a stultifying role in respect of religion-related intellectual development not only because it does so in *all* areas of human intellectual life but also because of the *special content* of religious and irreligious beliefs. Interestingly, a variation on this theme appears in much religious writing (it emerges most strikingly perhaps in Pascal's *Pensées*), where one finds the suggestion that *dis*belief of religious claims has its source in hubris. Disbelievers, so it is said, may find the content of religious belief just too much of a challenge to their autonomy. Surrendering in humility to the Divine requires a degree of self-forgetfulness that many disbelievers simply cannot muster. Hence they dodge the careful attention to things religious that, were they to manifest it, would allow the religious truth to be revealed to them.

Now I would not deny that there might be something to this point were it held to apply only to some disbelievers and phrased less question-beggingly. But it is important to go beyond this concession and in all impartiality to observe that a parallel point applies to religious belief: surrendering the notion that one is the special object of Divine Love or a special instrument of Divine Will—more generally, that one's life is intimately bound up with something of ultimate significance—requires a degree of self-forgetfulness and humility that many a *believer* would find difficult to muster. Thus it may be that the content of both irreligious *and* religious beliefs has, via a connection with self-importance, contributed to keeping humans at a relatively primitive intellectual state where religion is concerned.

Another moral factor to which I want to draw attention here is greed. This is sometimes realized intellectually, with unfortunate consequences. Our thirst for knowledge, ironically, can be an obstacle to its attainment. In the intellectual realm, as notoriously in other areas, humans lack patience and are liable to want immediate gratification. We do not suffer ignorance gladly, even in those cases in which its short-term costs ought to be borne for the sake of long-term intellectual, and perhaps spiritual, good. This may very well be a factor in the proliferation of ill-conceived metaphysical and religious systems (and attendant patterns of belief) with which history is littered, and of which more cautious—and, surely not coincidentally, more skeptical—thinkers like Hume have always complained. Instead of seeing themselves as contributing to a perhaps ages-long cooperative endeavor, humans may feel that the truth—the final truth—must somehow be capable of being embraced in a single lifetime, and the malleable stuff of human experience is hastily shaped accordingly, forced into a mold for which their own tendencies of thought and feeling conveniently provide the form.[2]

We are all vulnerable in this area, even cautious skeptics, who may be tempted grandiosely to argue that *nothing at all* can be known, or, failing that, to suggest that a skeptical attitude can provide a degree of satisfaction par excellence, which can stop for all time the itch that, through inquiry, we are seeking to scratch. And perhaps some aspect of the discussion and defense of religious skepticism on which I am here embarked will somewhere turn out to be flawed in a similar manner. Be that as it may, it also seems to the point, right now, to draw attention to the fact that such arguments as I am making—with their emphasis on putting off present belief because of the deficiencies in our investigative record—are quite rare in the history of thought, and to the support this itself provides for the idea that intellectual greed is often present among us. The rarity of such arguments, as I see it, is testament not to their subtlety, for the facts they cite often stare us in the face, but rather to the tendency that we have

[2] Such tendencies are to be found in every area of human inquiry, including ones that might seem quite "objective." Take, for example, economics. Even in our own day, Amartya Sen finds it necessary to plead for a "many-sided approach to development." (See his *Development as Freedom* [New York: Anchor Books, 1999], p. 126.) The common story is a preoccupation with narrow, one-sided approaches and the need to transcend them.

to want to "figure it all out" now, without waiting for the future. It would be unduly optimistic to think that such a tendency has not contributed to neglect in the area of human religious development (by, for example, contributing to neglect of deep and continuing religious investigation), and dangerous to forget the overhastily formed beliefs to which it must inevitably lead.[3] Indeed, my points here may apply to religious and irreligious beliefs more than to others, since in arriving at or maintaining such beliefs after a modicum of inquiry one is even more likely than in other cases to think that one has contributed to figuring it *all* out.[4]

Intellectual greed, together with self-importance (which makes one think that what one desires can be achieved), represents one way in which a certain quite well-known tendency that we might delicately describe as "the tendency to insist that one is right with insensitivity to the possibility of error" can be generated. (Of course there are many other possible causes of such a tendency as well.) This familiar phenomenon, however generated, I call *dogmatism.* Like the states of mind and character already mentioned, dogmatism is a vice, which is why I consider its operation in human history a moral factor. Dogmatism often leads to or is involved in a fierce resistance of what *others* believe on the same subject: when this is one-sided I shall call it intellectual *hostility;* when it is multi-sided and mutual, we may call what we see intellectual *rivalry.* Here one's focus comes to be placed on zealously guarding and protecting what one believes or on defeating others' beliefs. Since these dispositions and activities are, to a greater or lesser degree, bound up with tendencies toward misrepresentation, ridicule, bitterness, jealousy, possessiveness, or unwarranted resentfulness or indignation, I view them as vices as well.

[3] Perhaps it will be said that we need the fervent believers who try to "put it all together" themselves if the continuing enterprise of human religious inquiry is to be provided with something on which to work. But this we could have even if belief were more wisely seen as inappropriate, and various possibilities, construed as such, were developed by those interested in them and put forward for the consideration of others. And we could have something even better if this were conjoined with a modesty of presentation and true openness to adjusting or abandoning one's thoughts or having them absorbed by the better thoughts of (perhaps future) others: all of which must of course be easier if one's ideas are not *believed,* and—more to the present point—is made quite impossible by intellectual greed. (A similar response is appropriate to a similar point that might be made about the instrumental value of the dogmatism and rivalry to be discussed later.)

[4] As this suggests, intellectual greed of the relevant sort may involve the desire not just to come to know the ultimate truth about things but to be *oneself responsible* for its discovery. Where this latter element is present, the effects discussed immediately below are even more likely to be realized.

Now I think it must be said that religious and irreligious dogmatism, hostility, and rivalry are rather well represented in human history. In the religious world, as we know, much more is at stake than elsewhere, both intellectually and (as we shall see more fully later on) emotionally and socially. Hence the struggles back and forth have been even more protracted and intense here than elsewhere, with individuals and groups for long periods engaged in combating opposed views, and rivals locked in rancorous disputes, and virtually everyone expending huge amounts of energy to defend his or her own view against what are seen as encroaching competitors.

Of course this goes on all the time at the everyday level—think, for example, of what "life as usual" involves even today in many parts of the Middle East, India and Pakistan, Northern Ireland, and both liberal- and conservative-dominated parts of the United States. But what goes on at this level affects and is deeply affected by more "scholarly" disputes. Consider, for instance, the conflicts among Christian scholars through much of Christian history over the meanings of Trinity and Incarnation, about baptism, papal authority, and scripture, and concerning the Eucharist and ecclesiastical structure. And the history of discussion among and between Jewish, Islamic, Buddhist, and other religious scholars prominently features struggles of a similar nature. On the irreligious side, such denunciations of religion as those sponsored by Marxism and scientism are almost as well known.

Conflicts of this sort have dominated religious history and the history of religious discussion, and it must be said that, intellectually speaking, they have often been quite useless. They almost always generate more heat than light, and are more often ended by changes in other parts of the culture or society involved—perhaps an emperor comes into power or a pope dies or democracy flourishes—than by the discovery of an intellectual solution that helps people deal effectively with the disputed matters.[5] Nourished by the vices mentioned above, such conflicts have indeed resulted in a phenomenal amount of wasted time in human history. Where a disinterested concern for the truth might have led to an enlarging of the terms of debate (with thinkers attempting to harmonize apparently conflicting insights or to locate more generous perspectives that rendered the conflict irrelevant or even to identify problem areas where

[5] Or perhaps they will be ended when one party or coalition manages to impose its will successfully on others, as when opposition to Anabaptism in the sixteenth century—"opposition" is too mild a word when one thinks of the widespread torture, murder, and misrepresentation the latter group suffered—sent Anabaptists underground and permitted non-Anabaptist positions to gain preeminence in the public realm.

progress could more swiftly be made), and also to the development of more precise tools for conducting it productively, humans have instead so very often indulged their peculiar penchant for fruitless controversy. This has clouded the issues instead of illuminating them and may well, one is tempted to think, have left us with a poorer capacity to divine the truth about religion than if religious questions had not yet been introduced.[6]

Now I have focused rather strongly and, it may appear, one-sidedly on human traits and activities of the past affecting our capacity to achieve religious understanding which are ultimately rooted in *self-centeredness* or *egoistic concern*. Surely, someone will say, more attractive traits can also be detected in both religion and irreligion. Yes, indeed. But what I want to show is that even when we turn our minds from vice to virtue we bump into something that may quite significantly have held us back in religious discussions of the past.

The main item I am thinking of here is *loyalty*. It is perhaps relatively easy for someone tabulating reasons for religious skepticism to notice such points as I have already mentioned, and also certain others I have not yet developed, bound up with the emotionality that commonly attends religious belief. But the argument from loyalty commonly goes unnoticed, so I want to draw attention to it. First, though, let's remind ourselves that everything else we have said so far in this book underlines the need to engage in at least as searching and diverse forms of inquiry where religious questions are concerned as in science. We saw in Chapter 1 how, despite much creative inquiry of this sort, science still faces serious obstacles where the intellectual reliability of its results are concerned. So, straining ourselves to the utmost, growing in every way possible, exploring with imaginative energy and intellectual rigor might plausibly be considered prerequisites for discovering truths about religion. And it is here that loyalty becomes especially relevant. As we will see, it is not only on account of such vices as were featured above but also and prominently because of a *misplaced* loyalty to which religious believers are especially prone that proper religious inquiry has been and is neglected, and our present capacity to make discoveries about ultimate things placed in doubt.

The basic points to recall here are these: that the reality religious believers take themselves to be in contact with is thought by them to be *ultimate,* and that their concern with this reality is an *ultimate* concern. Because religious belief is all wrapped up with this ultimate concern, it has tended

----

[6] It is indeed *so often,* not always, and this needs to be noted, even though my emphasis is on the rule and not the exceptions. There have always been those who have sought to point us to a better way, but so far their voices have tended to be drowned out by the cries of conflict.

to go hand in hand with a rather *fierce* loyalty. Nothing less than complete devotion is appropriate where such a reality is involved. The development of the believer's moral character has thus typically been one involving a rather generous emphasis on this trait of loyalty (notice here the commonness of themes in religion involving praise of faithfulness and commitment, and the familiar denunciations of apathy and betrayal).[7] And a quite natural extension of this loyalty is of course to religious belief itself. How, for example, can one remain loyal to God if one allows oneself to be seduced by objections to the belief that there *is* a God? My phrasing here is deliberate: a believer often *will* see arguments against her belief as a challenge to moral virtue. (Hence the common and pejorative expression "giving in to doubt.") But what this means is that, once having formed a belief on ultimate things, the religious person is unlikely to be stirred from her position. She may think of herself as loyal to the truth, but the important thing is that she thinks she has *found* it in her present belief; and it is her response to *this* that sets in motion a process making it ever more difficult to view objections to her belief, or different and conflicting conceptions of the Ultimate, as serious candidates for truth. So just when she should be sitting up and taking notice of how the facts may be other than she thought, she is likely to become more deeply invested in her belief instead. Dealing with issues that may be expected to be, of all issues, the most difficult to resolve, and therefore deserving of special care and open-mindedness, she is likely rather to become stubborn and intransigent, because of well-intentioned but misplaced loyalty.

It is important to see how misplaced this loyalty is. Especially given that our intellectual situation in respect of religion is as described in previous chapters, a more generous loyalty beckons—to the truth, *whatever* that may be, and to *all* who seek it. Instead many religious believers are stalled, in large part due to the loyalty we have described, right where they first thought of themselves as coming in contact with the truth about religion. When they notice that others disagree, they tend not to think of this as an opportunity for dialogue and growth toward deeper under-

---

[7] Where the Ultimate is construed as a person (or as something like a person) an emphasis on loyalty is especially likely to be found, for given the nature of our psychology, persons tend to provoke responses of loyalty in us more easily than abstract principles. The theistic believer praying to her God may feel a wide range of responses awakening within her, but given the way that human psychology operates, and given the way that religious traditions in the West—where person-centered religion is well entrenched—have evolved, the deeper her spirituality is in her life, the more likely it is that an especially dominant response will be a sense of the need to be *loyal and faithful* to God, and to ward against all that might prevent this.

standing, but rather feel impelled to insist on fundamental error in the opposing views. Quite independently of careful investigation, they con- sider much of the specific behavior and emotional life of those others to be "wrongheaded," grounded in an inaccurate conception of the way things are. What I would suggest is that such a loyal commitment to not being budged from a certain way of viewing the world has done a great deal to prevent proper investigation of religious matters in the past, and still today may ironically prevent many religious believers from growing in ways required for truly coming to grips with any ultimate and salvific reality there may be.[8]

It is interesting and important to note that among the effects of the religious loyalty I have described is a diminished sense of the importance of religious matters among intellectuals *generally*. Many of those who deny that there is truth in religion have an impoverished sense of what religion is and may be, obviously deeply affected in many cases by the limitations of the actual forms of religion with which they have come in contact.[9] There is a tendency, for example, to infer from the fact that many actual religious persons are fiercely loyal to their beliefs and unwilling to submit them to serious scrutiny, that religion must by its very nature be irrational, and that any commitment to creative and critical inquiry should therefore include a *rejection* of religion. This is a poor inference, itself badly in need of criti- cal scrutiny, but the effect is still such as to make many who might other- wise be interested in religion suspicious of it instead and unconcerned

[8] Those inclined to dispute my conclusions in this and in other parts of this section might consider how religion is so often threatened by the results of science instead of in- terestedly exploring them and actively incorporating them where appropriate. If religion were not usually defensive and conservative, if there were genuine openness to *developing* understanding, then all such information would rather be found *stimulating*.

[9] Many examples might be given, but in our own day three writers have done more than most to represent a nonreligious (sometimes antireligious) perspective in the popu- lar press and in academic works: Daniel Dennett, Richard Dawkins, and Steven Pinker. And it seems that it is almost invariably theism—and a fairly crude theism at that—that these writers have in mind when commenting on religion. Recently, Dennett devoted a whole book to the subject (*Breaking the Spell: Religion as a Natural Phenomenon* [New York: Penguin, 2006]). Full of interesting ideas, the book nonetheless reveals early on that Dennett has devoted far less time to understanding religion than science ("I simply do not know enough about [religions other than Christianity, Judaism, and Islam] to write with any confidence about them" [pp. xiii–xiv]); and it settles on a distressingly narrow definition of religions as "social systems whose participants avow belief in a supernatural agent or agents whose approval is to be sought" (p. 9). Removing all doubt that, despite his earlier admission of ignorance, he really does think of religion as narrowly as this (and is not simply advancing an "operational" definition), Dennett adds, on the same page: "This is, of course, a circuitous way of articulating the idea that a religion without *God* or *gods* is like a vertebrate without a backbone."

about religious inquiry. And thus the dismissal and rejection of religion, so common among today's intellectuals, can be prevented from being any more reliably grounded than the loyal embrace of believing on the part of the religious which may have caused it. More to the present point, because of these facts the irreligious have commonly not been motivated to *dig deep* in their investigations of religion, and so have done no more than the religious to contribute to the advanced state that may well be necessary for the capacity at issue here.

(2) Psychological Factors. Such moral points as we have found to support the idea that religious intellectual development among humans may not be very far advanced are, of course, in many ways intertwined with psychological ones. I already indicated this, at least implicitly, in speaking of individuals as *fiercely* loyal or *zealously* self-protective or *uncomfortable* with ignorance. Here I want to develop the connection between psychology and religious and irreligious belief a little further.

The most obviously relevant psychological phenomenon is emotion. Our often unruly emotions may be, as is often remarked, a large part of what makes us human. Certainly, a complete story of the rise and many falls of our race could hardly be told without a bulky chapter devoted to them. And I do not mean to suggest that their influence is all bad. Many of the glories of human life would be quite impossible without our power of emotional response. It is also hard to imagine how a fully appropriate response to religious realities (if such there be) could be completely bereft of emotion. But there are human emotions—think, for example, of jealousy and envy—that are just regrettable and can cause enormous trouble and grief; and others that, while perhaps admirable in themselves or at least sometimes appropriate, may become devastatingly powerful or connected to inappropriate or unworthy objects—think only of anger or love.

And such emotional states, perhaps together with closely related psychological states like desire, may also hold us back where religious intellectual development is concerned—this we can see from the fact that they *have* done so. It is evident that history is full of cases where individuals and groups become psychologically attached to religious (or to antireligious) beliefs, by which I mean that much agreeable emotion—perhaps including such emotions as go with loyalty or self-importance or self-righteousness, but also loving, trusting, grateful, joyful emotions—comes to be bound up with having those beliefs, and a naturally accompanying psychological need or desire to retain them is (consciously or unconsciously) active. Gripped by such a condition, humans have often been far more reluctant to let go of their beliefs than is compatible with any kind of religious intellectual development—in particular, with persistence in religious inquiry. Attached to this belief instead of that, they have frequently allowed themselves to become "blinkered," no longer open to the diversity of experience and imaginative response that may be required to arrive at a place where the truth about ultimate things can be disclosed to us.[10]

The danger of such an occurrence is rooted partly in the nature of belief and partly in the nature of religious states of affairs and propositions. As mentioned once or twice already in this book, to believe something is to be involuntarily disposed to see the world as embracing a certain state of affairs, to see it as simply part of the way things are. The experience involved in believing is an experience as of my thought *going right out to the world.* One who is disposed to such an experience will, as is often said, find the proposition expressing its content becoming part of their "map of the world," and will tend naturally and spontaneously to respond to their believing experience in thought and word and action.[11] All these things will come to be causally interconnected in complex ways. One's beliefs, in other words, become part of the flow of one's life.

Now it is true that many beliefs are such as *come and go* in the flow of life as new information is acquired or old information discredited. But it is equally true that others are, in their content, closer to the center of what matters to one, what one values or identifies with. And such beliefs, precisely because of the nature of belief, which seems to put one intimately in touch with reality, will have a *tighter* hold on one. If a state of affairs includes something you find to be of great personal importance and value, and you not only entertain it as a possibility or wonder about it or wish it obtained but experience it—*repeatedly* experience it—as belonging to what is real, this will have a psychological effect on you: your belief together with your value judgment will unleash much positive emotion that would otherwise have been held in check, and the thoughts and words and actions that bear the mark of your belief will give that emotion even more room to grow. That emotion will carve a veritable channel through

[10] It is hard not to see such mechanisms at work in some of the current advocacy of "intelligent design" as an alternative to evolutionary theory, as also in that view's less highly evolved ancestor "scientific creationism." On this weakness as well as others, see the fine essays and reviews by H. Allen Orr—for example, his review of William A. Dembski's *No Free Lunch: Why Specified Complexity Cannot Be Purchased without Intelligence* (Lanham, Md.: Rowman & Littlefield, 2001), in the *Boston Review* (summer 2002).

[11] An interesting illustration of the power of belief to shape one's "seeing" is to be found in Peter van Inwagen's essay "Genesis and Evolution," in his *God, Knowledge, and Mystery: Essays in Philosophical Theology* (Ithaca: Cornell University Press, 1995). About his preconversion days he says this: "I can remember having a picture of the cosmos, the physical universe, as a self-subsistent thing, something that is just *there* and requires no explanation," but "it is now impossible for me to represent the world to myself as anything but dependent."

your psyche, you will become used to having it and what it is connected to in your life and more and more resistant to losing it or losing what permitted it to flow in the first place, namely, your *belief.*

Here we might consider as an example what happens when somebody moves from wishing that he might win the lottery to actually believing that he has done so. All sorts of emotions are now released—there is no reason to prevent them if this has *really happened*—and a flurry of thoughts about what he will do with the money, words (shouts) to others about his wonderful experience, and actions of various kinds premised on this having really taken place naturally soon follow, and themselves find an important place in his experience (for example, through memory). Now suppose that evidence is produced to show that the individual's belief that he has won the lottery is false. What are the intellectual effects likely to be? Of course, the evidence may here be undeniable and he may sooner or later have to give in, but if it were possible to question it, to resist it, and to hang on to that belief a little bit longer, don't you think he might be successfully tempted to do so? Wouldn't most of us be?

Now apply all this to religious belief. The religious believer repeatedly experiences as really the case a state of affairs involving an *ultimate* reality and an *ultimate* good, in which she is privileged to be able to participate; and her thoughts and words and deeds, causally interconnected in complex ways, will bear the mark of this experience. Clearly such a belief must be quite close to the center of what matters to her, and thus (in accordance with our reasoning above) may be expected to be a belief to which she is rather deeply attached. If we add that the need to retain a *religious* belief can be fairly easily accommodated, because where ultimate matters are concerned evidence is more easily manipulated than in cases like the lottery example, we can surely see how investigation of religious belief and the project of straining toward possibly higher levels of understanding may suffer.[12]

The nature of religious states of affairs and propositions has another role to play here as well, not yet sufficiently indicated. Because of the ultimate value the religious believer associates with her belief, her religious belief will tend to give shape to much else that matters to her as well: her other beliefs about what is valuable will naturally tend to reflect the influence of her belief about ultimate value, and the former may indeed often be seen to entail the latter.[13] (A monk, for example, who has devoted his whole life to a

---

[12] That religious beliefs are commonly inculcated at a very early age no doubt often contributes to the hold they have on individuals.

[13] The relation might *not* be of this sort, for it might instead be because the religious belief is seen to entail the secondary value belief that the latter is held (this is how the "shaping"

certain kind of meditation may easily see that there would be little point to this if his religious beliefs were false.) But then the independent psychological attachments that may grow up because of these *other* value beliefs (even, perhaps, for meditating monks, seeking to rid themselves of attachment) will have the effect of deepening the religious believer's attachment to her religious belief, since those value beliefs depend on the religious belief. The psychological attachment to religious beliefs, in other words, is deepened by the *additional* attachment to *other* beliefs dependent on them.[14]

A more general but similar point is also relevant here. It arises from the fact that religious beliefs are, as noted in my *Prolegomena* (p. 81), "world-defining." Here, indeed, we find precisely those beliefs that must contribute the most, for those who hold them, to an overall picture of how things are. Now such a world picture, unlike this or that particular belief not intimately bound up with the rest, is something one will get *used* to. In part because it affects so very much of how one thinks and speaks and acts and is intertwined with virtually all the positive emotion in one's life, one finds it hard to imagine being without it—in short, one becomes attached to it. One is *familiar* with it (and in this case familiarity hardly breeds contempt). So again we see how religious beliefs will have a distinct tendency to become psychologically embedded, and hence more resistant to inquiry than other beliefs.

Thus far we have been talking about how religious believers may become psychologically attached to their beliefs because of how facts about religious content interact with facts about the nature of belief. By broadening the scope of our discussion of the nature of belief from propositional belief to what in *Prolegomena* (p. 67) I called *affective* belief—belief-*in* as opposed to belief-*that*—we can discern a further point that deserves mention here. It is natural for persons who hold propositional religious beliefs also to form affective belief. The individual who believes that there is a God,

---

might occur). I am thinking here of value beliefs that can be grounded both religiously and nonreligiously. Many moral beliefs may be like this, entailed by religious beliefs but not entailing them. In such cases there might still be a psychological transfer of attachment from the secondary belief to the religious belief, for the subject might notice only the religious reason for holding the former and so be moved to seek to retain her religious belief. But such a transfer is evidently much more to be expected where the subject sees that her secondary value belief *entails* the religious belief (that in this deeper way the former *depends on* the latter).

[14] Here, and also immediately below, one can apply Plantinga's notion of "depth of ingression." Using his language, one might say that religious beliefs have great depth of ingression into the noetic structures of those who hold them—giving them up would have "extensive reverberations" throughout the rest of a believer's noetic structure. (See Alvin Plantinga, "Reason and Belief in God," in *Faith and Rationality,* ed. Plantinga and Nicholas Wolterstorff [Notre Dame: University of Notre Dame Press, 1983], p. 50.)

for example, reflecting on the content of her belief, may very easily come to believe *in* God: for a person with normal values and a normal emotional life, the positive evaluation and emotions of trust and loyalty belonging to such affective belief could indeed hardly be withheld if she really believes that God—the source of her existence and of a supremely worthwhile good in which she is invited to participate—exists. But if a propositional religious belief whose content is reflected on tends thus to be followed by affective belief, then, given the emotion *entailed* by the latter, we have an independent reason to expect emotional attachment to the former: affective belief has—obviously—an emotional life of its own, and the more it becomes entrenched in the psyche, the more deeply must the associated propositional belief on which it depends become entrenched, for as indicated the two go hand in hand.

A final point on this subject that should be made comes into view when we broaden the scope of our discussion once more, this time to include religious *dis*believers. It is important to see that here too psychological attachment may be expected. For irreligious belief also, though in its own way, is "world-defining": it has deeply significant implications for what else a reflective religious disbeliever can believe. Thus it too will have a tendency to become psychologically embedded and resistant to inquiry. There is even a version of "belief-in" on the disbelieving side that is associated with the disbeliever's disbelief and can have effects similar to those just noted in connection with religious belief. For the religious disbeliever may be caused to positively evaluate *anti*religious symbols, goals, practices, policies, people, and so on—things whose value is bound up with there being no ultimate and salvific reality—and come to experience positive emotions, that is, approving, trusting, loyal emotions, toward them. Such a state would certainly count as belief-in or affective belief, and appears to presuppose propositional religious disbelief. It has also often been realized in human history, especially recently: think here of the attitudes of some Marxists, Freudians, evolutionary naturalists, and others of a similar orientation, who are opposed to religion in general, favoring goals and policies that might allow us to move beyond it. And where it is present, affective irreligious belief, like affective *religious* belief, may be expected to deepen attachment to the associated propositional belief.[15]

---

[15] An interesting variation on the theme of this paragraph is to be found in the recent work of Thomas Nagel, who admits that he hopes there is no God: "I don't want the universe to be like that." Then he adds: "My guess is that this cosmic authority problem is not a rare condition and that it is responsible for much of the scientism and reductionism of our time." (See his *The Last Word* [New York: Oxford University Press, 1997], pp. 130, 131.) More than one of my points is illustrated here: most obviously, that irreligious affective belief rather than careful investigation may have a role in producing and/or maintaining propositional religious disbelief; but also (more subtly) that the prevalence of not very

Points like those I have mentioned here seem clearly to show that—and also to explain why—religious believers and disbelievers commonly are quite attached to their beliefs. But, as we all know, the more attached one becomes to one's beliefs, the more difficult it is to remain open to their falsity and to engage in investigations that might show them to be false. Of course, here as elsewhere, humans have not typically shown themselves to be especially adept at doing what is difficult, and as a result, religious investigation has often been neglected.

Another and perhaps deeper point about our emotions that I want briefly to mention is that we still have *so much to learn about them*, and about the larger psychological world of which they are a part. Obviously, we are affected by both outer and inner realities. The possibility of extending and refining consciousness of both is critical to our development. And yet the inner world remains poorly understood. We are still largely a mystery to ourselves—as is often observed, psychology is still a young science, and startling discoveries about who we are in the inner depths of our being may well lie ahead of us. Given especially the many connections between this area of inquiry and religion, shouldn't religious believers and disbelievers alike take more seriously the limited extent to which psychological understanding has been developed? Perhaps this limitation is linked to a similar limitation in religious understanding, and their joint effect such as to leave us far behind the line when it comes to making basic discoveries about ultimate things. Certainly, acquaintance with recent psychology can make *some* of what religious people have believed about what is ultimate look rather *less* than ultimate—a god made in our own image (and reflecting some of the less desirable aspects of the human image at that), a controlling and dominant, obsessive-compulsive and insecure being who has serious problems with disagreement and projects his own needs on others, and so turns out to be supremely unworthy of worship—a god who is evidently not God! Under the influence of contemporary psychology we find actual examples of such old religious conceptions starting to yield to new ideas. And these may be supplanted in their turn, when their own relative primitiveness is revealed. Such facts should surely give us pause when we reflect on whether we are presently capable of discerning basic truths about religion.   .

(3) Social Factors. I come now to certain points about human society, which are analogous in many ways to factors already discussed, as well as interwoven with them in their operation, and so may be dealt with more briefly. Religion typically occurs in social contexts: it is typically nurtured

---

well-developed religious ideas, such as the idea of a somewhat authoritarian personal God, may put some people off religion, contributing to a failure on *their* part to "dig deep" and do justice to the range of actual and possible religious ideas.

and even shaped by the interaction of individuals in groups; children are brought up in such communities and from an early age taught to see the world in ways sanctioned by them. Here we can as well speak of Buddhist sanghas or Hindu sampradayas or Islamic mosques or Jewish synagogues as of the many Christian churches. And before any of these, as the archaeological evidence suggests, religion may still have been practiced communally.

Now religious communities have always tended to be quite patriarchal and authoritarian in structure, much like (most of) the broader societies in which they have appeared. The result in many quarters has unfortunately been a stifling of creative imagination and critical thought, and this from a very young age. Critical creativity has commonly been replaced by reliance on the word of shaman or elders or pastor or priest or pope or king (or king who is pope, where ingenuity sufficient to bring about such a happy coincidence has been available), with obvious negative consequences for the possibility of any real intellectual development.[16] There has also been a tendency for the loyalty of which we spoke earlier to be extended, in quite an exclusivist manner, to the religious believer's community. All this together produces a system in which *various* factors inimical to creative and critical thinking interact and are mutually reinforcing—each believer's personal loyalty to the Ultimate as she conceives it, her loyalty to various associated beliefs, her loyalty to other members of her community who hold the same beliefs, as well as to authorities within the community who affirm her in those beliefs, and whose word, in conjunction with whatever relevant experiences she may have on her own or with the community (all of course mediated by the same beliefs), is often deemed by her to provide sufficient justification for them. When psychological factors are added to the mix, it is not hard to see how the result can produce and maintain a fairly conservative approach to matters religious (thereby motivating the casual rejection of religion among its detractors, noted earlier), which may be precisely what the world does *not* need if the capacity for religious discernment is to have room to grow.

In recent years, however, certain relevant changes have begun to occur that have had a wide influence and suggest that the conservative system

---

[16] Here it may be said that the word of such authorities has often been informed by thought and discussion concerning the issues involved. I would not care to deny that this is the case. But as any student of history knows, non-intellectual—often social and political—factors have generally been very influential in religious discussion, and (as elaborated below) many voices have not been represented in such discussion. As an acquaintance once said, we know which religious views are correct because they are the ones that "won out." Indeed, one wants to reply, but was it a clean fight?

can be altered. But while this might seem to show that we are capable of more in the arena of religion than I am inclined to allow, it really only exposes how far we have to go. What I have in mind here are such things as the structural changes in our societies, and their ripple effects in religious communities, which have permitted and are permitting women more of a voice where a consideration of intellectual questions is concerned. We have yet to see the full development and the ultimate consequences of this loosening of the patriarchal grip on our individual and collective selves, but indications already available suggest that changes in our thinking about a whole range of issues, including religious ones, may be among the results.[17] It only stands to reason that new ideas about such issues may emerge if the voices of half the race, once largely silent, come to be heard. We have indeed been held back in our intellectual development as a species and as individuals by the fact that this has been prevented from happening until now. More generally, we may certainly say that social factors have had their own generous role to play in producing what looks like a relatively primitive intellectual situation—a situation that plays right into the hands of religious skeptics.

3. *The Skeptical Fallout*

What *can* a skeptic do with all these facts? Perhaps by parading them before us, in conjunction with some of the ideas mentioned at the beginning of this chapter, the skeptic will help us see that there is good reason to question whether we are—at any rate presently—capable of discerning basic truths concerning religion. The human species has been thinking about these things—these *ultimate* things—for only a relatively short time, and our thinking about them has been limited in a variety of ways. It could well be that there has not been *enough* time for the needed development to occur, or perhaps for vital stepping-stones to a capacity for religious discovery to have been traversed. (Of course, as mentioned once or twice before, such a suspicion may be overthrown by new and obvious discoveries, but in their absence, it is surely strongly fueled by such points as have been raised.)

---

[17] For a couple of Christian examples, see Elizabeth Schüssler Fiorenza, *In Memory of Her: A Feminist Theological Reconstruction of Christian Origins* (New York: Crossroads Press, 1992), and Sally McFague, *Models of God: Theology for an Ecological Nuclear Age* (Minneapolis: Fortress Press, 1987).

Here we should remind ourselves again of the challenging idea that supposing us to have already arrived at a capacity for religious understanding might be comparable to expecting someone from the Middle Ages (or perhaps a Neanderthal) to have what it takes to spout truths of particle physics. If so—if that many layers of sophisticated development need to be laid down before humans can be in the right state of mind for religious intellectual discovery—then we are *definitely* not there yet. And who is to say that it isn't so? Notice that we might not be there yet even if we had made the best possible progress in the time that we have had. And now what we see is that this has decidedly *not* been the case—various moral, psychological, and social factors reflecting our immaturity have affected us in ways that may have led us to distorted pictures of reality rather than the truth. Surely these inhibiting conditions need serious and prolonged attention and amelioration before we can be reliably persuaded that they are not obstructing our spiritual view. But this means that capacity skepticism—at any rate, qualified capacity skepticism—together with the categorical skepticism that follows in its wake must be the order of the day.

If in response to this the religious or irreligious believer says that my argument is assuming the falsity of his beliefs and thus begging the question, the proper reply is that here something new has been introduced which *challenges* those beliefs. The believer, confident in the reliability of the circumstances in which his belief was formed, has now been given reason to *question* that reliability. To respond with the same belief that is being questioned in this way is to commit the very offense of which he is accusing my argument.

Let me expand on this a little, in connection with some tendencies in contemporary Christian philosophy of religion, which might seem to give aid and succor to the response we are considering. What I am thinking of is a certain Calvinism-inspired argument according to which the believer is reasonable in taking his belief and the experiences in which it is grounded as authoritative and in interpreting nonbelief and disbelief as manifestations of spiritual blindness or sin.[18] By means of the more general considerations concerning our limited moral, psychological, social (and thus also intellectual and spiritual) development, this sort of argument is hoist on its own petard: the argument from history allows us to turn the "sin" argument back on itself, for now we must ask, have human moral weaknesses (or other factors of the sorts here discussed) made us

---

[18] See, for example, Mark R. Talbot, "Is It Natural to Believe in God?," *Faith and Philosophy* 6 (1989), 155–171. For a more qualified statement of similar views, see Alvin Plantinga, *Warranted Christian Belief* (New York: Oxford University Press, 2000).

too ready to see others as blinded or mired in sin? Have whole systems of religious belief sprung from the influence of such factors? This need not be positively asserted to be effective—all the philosopher needs to do is to urge an extended retrospective glance, and ask whether it does not reveal that we have yet to arrive at a place where the possibilities in question can reliably be ruled out. Our past reflects serious intellectual failure and deep immaturity where religious matters are concerned—a failure and immaturity that affects us all. That we are *im*mature in these ways suggests that religious and irreligious beliefs are *pre*mature.

I conclude this chapter by presenting a particular state of affairs that illustrates the situation we are in—in whose obtaining such factors as I have discussed are no doubt implicated—and then deriving a moral from my story. The state of affairs in question is the present-day situation of religious diversity and its treatment by philosophers. Notice first that because traditional religious propositions are quite specific, there are many different and mutually exclusive ways in which they can be false, and many claims to the effect that one or other of these ways is realized. Call the latter claims *alternatives* to the originals. Now, as it happens, religion has proliferated throughout the world in a variety of forms, and the claims each form has generated show little concern for consistency with those of others. Thus many of the alternatives to this or that traditional religious claim are claims actually made and defended by religious people—that is, they are themselves traditional religious claims. Each defended traditional religious claim, then, faces opposition from various other defended claims of the same sort. This is a basic fact involved in what I am calling religious diversity.[19]

Take, for example, traditional theism. Opposed to it are various other religious claims, including claims according to which the Ultimate is personal but inseparably linked to the universe in an everlasting process of becoming (process theism), internally differentiated in such a way as to permit us to speak of *many* gods (polytheism), nonpersonal and substantial (certain forms of Hinduism), nonpersonal and *in*substantial (certain forms of Buddhism), not a being or state but dispersed among all things (traditional native religion).[20] And of course there are plenty of variations on these themes inconsistent with others, not to mention other defended themes incompatible with all of these. Because these claims are mutually

[19] Most traditional religious believers need not look outside their own tradition to find alternatives to many of their beliefs. Religious sectarianism not only divides the major traditions from each other but also creates many splits and divisions *within* traditions. Here, however, the focus will be on the former divisions.

[20] Since I am focusing on *religious* diversity, I have left out the naturalistic claim that there is nothing transcendent of the physical universe *at all,* but clearly this is an alternative to traditional theism (and to all the other propositions) as well.

exclusive, we must say that opposed to each of them is each of the others (plus of course traditional theism).

So what are advocates of such claims to make of this fact? Surely there are plenty of objections to the truth of any one of their claims lurking in the presence and (articulated or possible) defenses of the others, if the truth of the others entails its falsity. Of course, as will no doubt be observed, it is only *uneliminated* alternatives that need trouble us if we want to endorse one of these claims. For just about any claim you believe, there are plenty of others that entail its falsity (you think the earth is spherical, for example, and so face opposition from as many claims about the earth's shape as there are nonspherical shapes); but this is no reason to worry unless there is reason to suspect that some such claim may be true, and often there is none (there is no reason, for example, to believe that the earth is other than spherical). Fair enough, I would reply, but where individuals are *defending* alternatives to your own views by reference to argument and/or experience to which you could easily pay attention, then you need to listen. Basic respect for those others, as well as intellectual empathy, humility, and a love of the truth, should compel us to do so. These widely accepted moral and epistemic demands—many of which receive support from within traditional religion itself—have obvious consequences for a situation of the difficult sort in question. The problem is that many traditional believers have yet to properly recognize or acknowledge that they are *in* such a situation.

To see this, consider that many traditional believers could tell you little about the meanings of (all but one of) the religious claims referred to above, or about the different forms they can take, or about the contexts in which they have arisen. Even philosophers—indeed, even philosophers of religion—are often outfitted with the barest conception of what most such claims are about. The temptation, of course, especially among analytical philosophers of the West, is to say that certain of these claims and their central terms are congenitally unclear or obviously implausible (or can be shown to be such with a bit of armchair argument) and so may be dismissed; but coming from people who tend to know much less about religion than their colleagues in the philosophy of science know about science, this approach can hardly be taken seriously. *It is just a fact that the serious investigation of religious options other than Christianity has yet to be undertaken by most Western philosophers of religion.* I would suggest that all this must change (and of course it must change not just for philosophers but for anyone interested in religion and guilty of this neglect) if a nonsuperficial assessment of the facts of diversity is to be achieved. Without such change, an adequate assessment really cannot be achieved. For who knows what careful attention to unfamiliar claims may reveal concerning their deepest meanings? And who knows whether our intuitions as to what is plausible and what is not may not be adjusted by serious exposure to ways of thinking radically different from our own?

It is interesting to note here that even those who recognize the importance of this "intellectual empathy," taking a genuine interest in the intellectual life of individuals belonging to unfamiliar religious traditions and seeking to improve their understanding of it, may still reflect in their articulation of that understanding a variety of incomplete or mistaken interpretations. This can be seen, for example, in the discussion between Thomas Merton and the Buddhist scholar Daisetz Suzuki recorded in Merton's *Zen and the Birds of Appetite*.[21] Each writer is able, in turn, as insider, to reveal deficiencies in the other's—the outsider's—understanding. And this is just what we should expect in an area as complex as religion, where we have finite individuals from very different backgrounds trying to come to grips with ultimate things. But if this is so even where there has been some careful study and dialogue and efforts toward sympathetic appreciation, how much more should we expect it where there has been very little study and the attitude is an apathetic or adversarial one? A proper awareness of the various religious alternatives (including their possible formulations, what they do and do not entail, what counts for and against them, what acceptance of them facilitates, and so on) therefore makes some imposing demands on all of us.

This story about religious diversity illustrates how poorly equipped we may presently be to arrive at judgments about religion anyone has reason to trust. The sort of serious work on the explication of extant and possible religious claims and on methods of religious investigation and on the development of attitudes conducive to investigating religion with insight and discernment that may need to be done to make us *better* equipped, though begun in some quarters (for example, in some of the interaction one notes between diverse religious and irreligious groups, and perhaps even in some university departments), has simply not yet been brought anywhere near completion. This state of affairs should feed doubt about the truth of religious claims instead of belief or disbelief, for, as we saw in the last chapter, the force of any apparently good evidence we might have for or against ultimism is blocked if we discover a good reason to question whether humans possess the capacity we would have to have in order to assess that evidence correctly. Now perhaps even after we have done better, problems of the sort discussed in other chapters of this book will still loom, but surely—so the religious skeptic may plausibly claim—we cannot suppose ourselves to be in a position conducive to accurate belief on such matters *without* doing better. And this generates its own problem, and a distinguishable mode of reasoning in support of religious skepticism.

---

[21] New York: McLelland & Stewart, 1968.

CHAPTER 4

The Prospective Mode

The fourth distinctive mode of reasoning on behalf of a generalized religious skepticism I shall develop looks into the future instead of the past; it considers what may lie ahead rather than what lies behind us. It is the *Prospective* Mode. We human beings pay considerable attention to the past (though not—as the last chapter suggests—always the right sort of attention), some attention to the present, and much attention to the immediate future. But the more distant future receives very little consideration: it is a gray haze. And yet it is certain that there will be some sort of future (whether we will be in it or not), and we know quite a lot, in a general way, about what it may contain, both for the universe as a whole and for our species in particular. We need to take this into account in our philosophizing, but often we do not. And our failure to do so has, among other things, obscured from us an important way of arguing against the justification of religious and irreligious belief.

So how might such a future-oriented form of religious skepticism be developed? No doubt there are many ways. Perhaps we should expect a development of points from Chapter 1, where we saw that inaccessible and undiscovered evidence may become accessible or be discovered, and turn out to contain defeaters of religious or irreligious beliefs supported by the examined evidence of the present. But in Chapter 1 we were talking in a general way about the consequences of finitude and developing an argument that might be utilized in *any* present, in reference to *any* future. The Prospective Mode, to exploit other possibilities of reasoning and retain its distinctiveness, might be expected to emphasize instead certain more particular facts about what may occur when a transition is made from *this* present—the first decades of the twenty-first century—to *our* future, and the connections between such facts and the justification of religious or irreligious belief in our time. Even someone who did not accept the argument of our first chapter might have reason to accept this one, and so the latter is not dependent on the former.[1]

Now it may seem that the Prospective Mode, thus construed, must still be dependent on the Retrospective Mode, bringing us into direct contact with facts emphasized in the previous chapter. For will it not focus on what needs to occur in order for us to leave behind the impoverished moral, psychological, and social conditions there discussed? To this I reply that our undistinguished past (or one similar in the relevant respects) does indeed represent a necessary condition for the truth of some of what I say here. Thus certain parts of the present argument might be said to presuppose the truth of (and in that sense to depend on) a *premise* of the Retrospective Mode. But the Prospective Mode as a whole still does not presuppose the success of the Retrospective Mode itself, both because it could be developed without any reference at all to the past and because, even though facts about the past sometimes appear in my own interpretation of it, that interpretation does not require that we may presently be *incapable* of discerning the truth about religion. Even if this is not so and the contrary claim of the Retrospective Mode is false, the Prospective Mode may retain its force—and thus the latter is distinct from the former. The Prospective Mode, as we will see, is concerned to advance the idea that, whatever might be true of other futures, in our future there may be enormous changes in the intellectual and religious realms. Because of this we have good reason to suspect that any views on ultimism that seem plausible to us now may well turn out to be false, or appear false to more fully informed individuals of the future, and hence to be in doubt about whether any evidence so far examined for and against religious claims is *representative* of the total evidence. This strongly suggests that the evidence humans have so far gathered is radically insufficient. And, moreover, when the possibility of unrepresentativeness is itself taken into account, we are again left with a situation in which even the available evidence, whatever its force might otherwise appear to be, is, overall, less than *good* evidence for the claim that ultimism, or its denial, is true.

---

[1] And this even though—as we will see in a moment—the two arguments share (as an interim conclusion/premise) the claim that evidence in this present may be unrepresentative, for in the argument of Chapter 1 this is inferred from more general facts of finitude whereas here it will be inferred from facts *about* this present.

1. *Why the Future Matters Now*

It is very hard for us, as human beings, to take the long view required to put present concerns into proper perspective. We may wonder at the way we once were under the spell of certain fashions in music or clothing. But we forget that *then* those things seemed just as interesting and attractive as various quite different things seem to us now. It is obvious to reflection that whatever clothes or cars or popular musicians may presently appeal to us will very likely one day seem just as dated and antiquated as those we loved and left in the past. And to have a proper, mature perspective we need to take this into account. We need to be less dazzled by the present and to take ourselves and our present concerns less seriously.

Something similar is true at the intellectual level. It is also hard to put present *evidence* into proper perspective and to recognize how—due this time (one hopes) to more weighty and objective considerations—one may well come to think differently about a matter that seems now to admit of but one conclusion. By analogy, then, we might argue that one ought to take what seems presently plausible where some intellectual question is concerned less seriously—to seek to be less dazzled by the present in this way as well, and more open to the possibility that present intellectual resources and what one has garnered by means of them may not suffice to make a full and reliable answer possible. We need to be ready to see things in a different light, in a completely new way, if we are to become aware of all that may need to be considered to arrive at the truth about such questions.

This is all the more pertinent if an *especially long* future may stretch before us and investigation so far has been *less than impressive*. And that such is the case is clear (the last chapter's discussion should help us to see this). Having been around for at most a few million years, with our civilization only a few thousand years old, we live on a planet that science tells us will—assuming it is not the victim of cosmic accident or human folly—remain habitable for much, much longer, perhaps another *billion* years, in which time many further and interesting but, at present, largely unpredictable changes will no doubt occur, affecting the development of our species in significant ways.

These facts are certainly cause for pause. Reflecting on them, it may occur to us that, by comparison with future variations on the human theme that may well come to exist, we might be found to have, at present, about the degree of comprehension of the "bigger" facts that a dog has, when compared with our present selves, of the nature and intended function of such things as stop signs and fire hydrants. Aware of this, most scientists and philosophers of science have indeed tended to be fairly modest, and sometimes even pessimistic, with regard to how far detailed results of human intellectual inquiry are "established" and how much of the universe and its ways is presently within our grasp.[2] Recognizing that we have been around and thinking about religious questions for only a short while, and that we are part of a process of development and change that may well continue for an extremely long time, it might likewise occur to us that by settling into religious or irreligious belief, we may be cutting off original inquiry about such profound matters prematurely and completely missing the truth about ultimate things.

For we have no way of ruling out that what emerges may not appropriately change our ways of thinking quite radically. Even in our short history there are examples of this in other areas, as the history of science and of philosophy illustrates. And the work of scientific innovators like complexity theorist Stephen Wolfram, whatever its merits may turn out to be, at least provides an especially vivid example of what is *possible*.[3] Here we might also consider what may happen if and when such obstacles to religious inquiry as we discussed in the last chapter begin to be decisively overcome. Perhaps there will be a flood of new work and new results that no one previously expected—a period of "theological inflation" analogous to the sudden jump in the size of the physical universe shortly after its birth hypothesized by the so-called inflationary-universe scenario of cosmology. (The inflation of the universe is credited by cosmologists with smoothing out certain initial regularities. Perhaps something analogous will occur in an inflation of religious consciousness.)

It is not hard to see how such considerations might lead someone working in philosophy today in the direction of skepticism about ultimate things. Of course it may be that some particular formulation involving

---

[2] Even the greatest scientists and philosophers of science belong to this group. Einstein somewhere compares his work to that of a person who has entered a vast library of books in a foreign language, taken down one volume, and translated one passage on a single page. Of his theory of relativity he said, "It will have to yield to another one, for reasons which at present we do not yet surmise. I believe that the process of deepening the theory has no limits." (This remark can be found in John Barrow, *Theories of Everything* [Oxford: Clarendon Press, 1991], p. 88.) And here is the famous philosopher of science Karl Popper: "If the progress that has been made is great, then the new problems will be of a character undreamt of before. There will be deeper problems; and besides, there will be more of them. The further we progress in knowledge, the more clearly we can discern the vastness of our ignorance" ("The Rationality of Scientific Revolutions," in *Scientific Revolutions*, ed. Ian Hacking [Oxford: Oxford University Press, 1981], pp. 83–84). In this sentiment, these thinkers of course only echo Socrates, who said that his sole claim to knowledge concerned an awareness of how little he really knew.

[3] See Stephen Wolfram, *A New Kind of Science* (Champaign, Ill.: Wolfram Media, 2002).

a personal God or a nonpersonal Absolute or the absence of any such thing appears plausible, but knowing what we do about our developmental nature and the alluring present, about how little we have so far accomplished in the world of religious investigation and the incredibly long and winding road that may still lie ahead of us, it could hardly be reasonable to take such a formulation very seriously. The likelihood of a relevant future change in our information base and in our thinking is just too great. Or, at least, *given proper intellectual vigilance* such changes are likely. People who are alert and think hard tend to be constantly bumping into considerations that put things into a new perspective—not being fully informed at the start and developing in all manner of ways and acquiring new information continually, how could it be otherwise? One wonders how many more instructive changes one might undergo if one lived robustly to the age of two hundred or three hundred. And when one thinks more generally, of the species, it is hard to avoid the conclusion that, given a few thousand years more, we might just come up with some new ideas about ultimate things. We are only at the beginning of what may be a long process of human development. Should we not expect that our ideas about such things may well seem to an enlightened human of the year 4000 or 40,000 CE as antiquated and inadequate as many of the ideas of the ancient Egyptians or Babylonians or Greeks appear to us today?[4] It seems a huge mistake to form beliefs about ultimate things on the basis of even apparently quite strong evidence pro or con available in our time, given such an awareness.

We can approach this matter in a slightly different way. How long should we investigate—how much evidence do we need—before it would be appropriate to make a definite judgment, yea or nay, on the basis of the evidence we have? I have deliberately left this ambiguous: Does the question refer to individual investigators or the race? We are so used to thinking of things individualistically, using the span of our own lives as the relevant time frame, that probably most of us would immediately assume the former. As C. S. Peirce noted, doubt can be agitating, and we typically want to turn it into belief as soon as we can—we certainly tend to assume that somehow before our individual lives are over, a determination permitting the formation of belief should be possible.

But especially given our track record as humans, the "big" questions invite us to consider an *alternative* way of looking at things—a more

---

[4] Any resistance to the idea of thousands or millions of years of development potentially lying ahead of us might instructively be compared to early (and, in some quarters, continuing) resistance to the idea of millions of years in our past. Given how we experience the passage of time, we find it mind-boggling to work with such large figures, but, again, the universe takes its time.

expansive, less temporally fixed attitude that unites us to the species as a whole in an ongoing process of inquiry that may continue to produce interesting new results for thousands or millions of years more, if zealously pursued. If we back up and give this view of things a try, we may see more clearly how shortsighted it would be to assume that "all the evidence we need is in," no matter how long *as individuals* we have been pursuing religious inquiry. As a *species* we have hardly begun, and this fact should influence the philosopher wondering what response to religious claims is justified, as well as anyone who listens carefully to what he or she has to say. For a close look at this fact will tell you that much new evidence, giving a completely different complexion to the religious picture, may well emerge long after you are dead and gone. If as individuals we want to make the best response to religious claims possible for us, and, as part of this, to hold religious or irreligious *beliefs* only insofar as there is good reason to think them *true*, not simply fitting ourselves into the best belief available as soon as we can, then we will recognize that, at least from the most informed present perspective, it cannot be expected that the available evidence will be sufficient in our lifetime. Then we will recognize the imperative of religious skepticism.

But how, it may now be asked, is it even possible to avoid belief, given the plausibility with which this view or that may strike us in the present, and belief's involuntariness? Here the other way of arguing against justification for belief, which focuses on how even our *available* evidence may be affected by the awareness in question, becomes relevant. If our intellectual vigilance involves, as it should, an attempt to ingrain that awareness deeply in our psyches, we will have ready access to a consideration that *defeats* such beliefs concerning matters of the sort in question as might otherwise have seemed well evidenced. If we recognize that we are at only some rudimentary stage of an evolutionary process potentially involving much more cognitive and spiritual development, we may see the need to take *this* fact into account along with the evidence concerning ultimate realities presently available and how it looks to us *now*, when considering what stance to take up with regard to propositions referring to such realities; and doing so will block the force of such evidence. Even if one does not infer on the basis of this new consideration that the seemingly plausible view will definitely turn out to be false (and thus that it *is* false), one could because of it hardly *deny* that this will occur (or, at least, that that view is quite likely someday to *appear* false to a *more fully informed individual*, whether oneself or someone else); and if such a denial is unjustified, then so is belief that the view is correct. Put otherwise, if doubt about the proposition "It is not the case that *p* [some apparently plausible view about ultimate things] will turn out to be false" is justified, then so is doubt with respect to "*p* is true." And any intellectually scrupulous individual who sees this may be expected to be influenced by it in the appropriate manner.

Sometimes, of course, one will still find oneself in effect denying that the view in question will turn out to be false. Then, I would say, an awareness of human limitations and of the fickle present is not yet deeply enough entrenched. And it is indeed difficult to arrive at the place where it is. We are so easily seduced by the apparent sophistication of present arguments and modes of discussion and analysis—which, as we are sure to think, supersede everything seen before—that it is easy to think of ourselves as having arrived at the final truth (or at the definitive justification of our views) about the ultimate nature of things. At the pinnacle of human thought *so far,* we take ourselves also to be at the pinnacle *period.* In this state it is hard to give much more than a moment's reflection to the very real possibility that we know *nothing* yet about ultimate things. Deeply impressed with ourselves and our experiences and our information, caught up in the most recent "advances," we often cannot see this possibility with the clarity that true understanding may require. Thus we may indeed find it hard to resist the plausibilities of the present. But when we really see that possibility clearly, it will instead, I suggest, be hard to avoid a response of skepticism.

2. *How the Evidence May Change*

We can, of course, hardly expect to have so much as a clue as to what enlightened humans of the year 4000 or 40,000 or 40,000,000 CE might think about ultimate things, or just how they might get there; and it is indeed one of the strengths of the Prospective Mode that we cannot. But we can still open our minds a little further—make it a little harder to be seduced by the fickle present—if we spend some time imagining specific changes of various kinds and thinking about their relevance to the world of religious investigation. I will begin here by indulging in what I freely admit is a bit of science (and religion) fiction with dubious literary merit—fiction that may nonetheless have the merit of making certain facts about the dubiousness of present evidence more clear.

Suppose, then, that as the twenty-first century unfolds, the world is ever more filled with violence, with more and more money diverted from scientific investigation to help manage various "wars on terrorism" that are spiraling out of control. In the midst of this deepening chaos on earth, attention to observing the skies diminishes, and—you guessed it—a large meteorite that might in better days have been noticed and averted finds its way to earth, leaving much of it in ruin. The human costs are huge.

Nearly everything is lost. But through luck and enormous effort, some few humans beings and some significant traces of past culture and knowledge are enabled to survive. After many millennia of struggle and adaptation in the midst of greatly altered circumstances, a period that features an eclectic mix of old knowledge developed in novel directions and cooperative survival skills turned into traditions of greater intellectual flexibility and interdependence, a sort of "golden age" arrives, in which, experiencing relative stability, the world is able to turn its attention more fully to science and art and the pursuit of knowledge about ultimate things for its own sake. Despite lapses into aggressive and competitive behavior, inquirers in every part of the planet manage to incorporate into their activities something of the cooperative ethos created by their unique history and, despite a natural ebb and flow, succeed in retaining the support of their broader communities in a manner that is in striking contrast to what had been the norm prior to—what is now called—the Catastrophe, with the result of, among other things, an unprecedented flowering of intellectual life. In particular, scientific and religious forms of thought come to be interwoven in creative ways, and new conceptions of the Ultimate, derived by (for example) metaphorizing key elements of new scientific ideas (which have long since eclipsed both Newton and Einstein), emerge. Institutes for the study of religion and psychology, and of religion and politics, and of religion and art, and many similar institutes, dot the landscape in every populated region, with various levels of parent institutes and partnering institutes connecting the dots in diverse ways. And their ideas, together with the ideas of other cultural institutes and organizations, dot the mental landscape, so that an enormous synergy is created.

I suggest two alternative endings to this story: (1) Over a period of many thousands of years which, while seeing countless other changes, preserves unbroken a strand, sometimes thicker, sometimes thinner, of intense communitarian intellectual inquiry, the various possible construals of the Ultimate that arise from the aforementioned synergy and its consequences are one by one shown to be in some deep way *confused* or *incoherent*, or else proven to correspond to nothing in reality. After a further thousand years in which, despite much concerted effort, no new religious ideas are discovered and a great deal of "experimental religion" yields ever diminishing returns, with scholars and nonscholars alike concluding that nothing of distinctive or enduring value is to be found in religious practice, religious thinking gradually dissolves into a holistic morality, which the human beings of this advanced age take with them into their future. (2) Over a period of many thousands of years which, while seeing countless other changes, preserves unbroken a strand, sometimes thicker, sometimes thinner, of intense communitarian intellectual inquiry, the thinking of people of the earth concerning religion gradually converges on a single idea, which scholars and nonscholars alike declare to be an idea of unparalleled beauty and richness. It is an idea that gives a finer and fuller texture to the notion of ultimacy than any previously encountered, while admitting of indefinite extension and application in theory, practice, and both individual and communal experience. After a further thousand years in which, despite much concerted effort, no defects are discovered in the Idea, and sophisticated arguments provide untarnished good evidence that it is realized, and also much "experimental religion" confirms its multidimensional potency in practice, life on earth, influenced by these results, has come to be transformed in innumerable positive ways; and—needless to say—the human beings of this advanced age take the Idea with them into their future.

About these two stories (generated by the one story, given its two endings) I have four things to say. First, nothing like the scrupulosity of investigation featured here has ever yet occurred: what we actually find in the history of the species right up to the first decade of the twenty-first century does not come *anywhere close* to matching in quality and results what we see in either of these stories. Second, *both* stories, and innumerable variations on their themes, represent epistemic possibilities: nothing the philosophy of religion community has before it at present justifies the judgment that such things will not occur, or tells us *which* will occur, if any does. Third, if something like what we see in the first story were to be realized, religious belief of the present would be defeated; and if something like what we see in the second story were to be realized, *ir*religious belief of the present would be defeated. It follows, by arguments previously given, that the beliefs in question are *already* defeated, since the epistemic possibility of such defeat is in this context itself a defeater, showing as it does that we have no basis for judging that the evidence so far examined by the human species is representative of the total relevant evidence. Fourth, and pursuing now the other line available to us here, it seems that our stories show the need for more evidence. Even if we do not say that religious investigation exactly matching in quality and results what we have here is *necessary* for religious or irreligious belief to be justified, simply by knowing that these stories and others like them about the results of more advanced investigation are epistemically possible, we come to be in a situation where we would have to say, should our investigation be *much less* advanced, that the possibility of a relevant future change in our information base and in our thinking is just too obvious to allow us to rest content with presently available evidence: we need to have *more and better* evidence. All things considered, then, it seems clear that we can use our stories about the open future to justify religious skepticism.

Now it may be that, influenced by the individualistic mentality that marks our time, we will find it tempting to respond to the argument just made by saying that its claim is simply too strong. New evidence can *always* be introduced; what I have generated is really a recipe for *never* forming beliefs on religious matters and it is accordingly to be rejected. But I remind the reader of how a suitably expanded, more communitarian vision and also due respect for the truth (in connection with an awareness of how much one is *claiming* when one expresses a belief) require us to resist any such conclusion. And, more specifically, what I want now to do, in order to make the point about a "communitarian vision" and the epistemic possibilities associated therewith a bit more sharply, is to provide some discussion in aid of a very important recognition: namely, that we may right now be on the cusp of discovering and employing qualitatively new and immensely more powerful means of gathering and processing evidence which allow us as a species to radically deepen the degree of relevant communication between various sectors of our cultures and make a bold new advance on the truth about matters religious. To get us in the right frame of mind and thinking in the right direction, I will preface what I have to say here with an observation about the coming "universal library" drawn from a recent article in the *New York Times:*

> From the days of Sumerian clay tablets until now, humans have "published" at least 32 million books, 750 million articles and essays, 25 million songs, 500 million images, 500,000 movies, 3 million videos, TV shows and short films and 100 billion public Web pages. When fully digitized [a process already begun] . . . it will all fit onto your iPod. . . . The real magic will come in the second act, as each word . . . is cross-linked, clustered, cited, extracted, indexed, analyzed, annotated, remixed, reassembled and woven deeper into the culture than ever before. . . . Once text is digital, books seep out of their bindings and weave themselves together. The collective intelligence of a library allows us to see things we can't see in a single isolated book. . . . If you can truly incorporate all texts—past and present, multilingual—on a particular subject, then you can have a clearer sense of what we as a civilization, a species, do know and don't know. The white spaces of our collective ignorance are highlighted, while the golden peaks of our knowledge are drawn with completeness. This degree of authority is only rarely achieved in scholarship today, but it will become routine.[5]

[5] Kevin Kelly, "Scan This Book!" *New York Times Magazine,* May 14, 2006, p. 43.

With this interesting expectation to fire our imaginations, let us turn our attention to some more general developments in human culture that we might hope soon to see.

It seems possible, first, that in various formal and informal ways, the many strands of religiosity in our world should come into closer contact one with another. Call this a deepening of communication between (and concerning) *religion and religion*. We may find more careful study, at many levels in many religious traditions, of the most important literature from other traditions. There may also be an increase, for many religious people, in the sort of knowledge by acquaintance that can come only by in some way associating with members of other traditions, observing and perhaps participating in their practices, discussing their beliefs and experiences with them, truly befriending them, and thus learning in more of a "first-hand" way what their religion is about. (There is a tendency toward misinterpretation that can remain even after a fair amount of academic study of religion, and a strong temptation, when one is aloof from personal contact with unfamiliar others, to in subtle ways uncharitably evaluate their behavior and claims; and in time more and more conscientious religious persons may come to recognize this, and accordingly come to value more highly "knowledge by acquaintance" of the sort just mentioned. It may also be that more of them simply come to desire a way of deepening their understanding of others, recognizing this as intrinsically valuable.) It is not hard to see how the number and quality and diversity of interreligious events and initiatives—whether practical or festive or academic in nature—would increase if such were to be the case, and how interreligious knowledge would in many ways be improved. It is not hard to see, either, how each tradition's *self*-understanding, and the substance and details of its intellectual products, might be correspondingly altered. We might even find entirely new religious traditions coming into being.[6]

---

[6] Those who really make the acquaintance of other traditions and their adherents, exercising intellectual empathy and openness as well as humility and respect as they go, are going to broaden their circle and quite naturally become more inclusive. Learning to see the often attractive personal qualities of persons they meet, and noticing that many who think very differently from themselves are nonetheless their equals in intelligence and virtue, they will find it much more difficult to accept that the truth is recognized only in their own camp. For the latter view suggests that many such individuals are *inadequate* epistemically and/or morally. Coming to love and even more deeply respect many of these people in the course of time, they will quite naturally find desirable an understanding of ultimate things that more fully includes them and at least partially validates their insights, and so be disposed to *notice* and *develop* such support for views of this kind as is accessible to them. And some of the loyalty they formerly felt only or largely toward their own tradition and the individuals, experiences, and beliefs most intimately associated with it will therefore quite naturally come to be transferred to the religious world at large.

It seems possible, second, that there should at the same time be a deepening of communication between (and concerning) *religion and science.* In various formal and informal ways, the consequences of science for our understanding of the world may come to be more fully discussed by and among religiously interested and scientifically minded individuals of the future, and within the organizations to which they belong, with "trickle down" effects in religious institutions, religious thought, and popular religious consciousness. Perhaps the scientific investigation of ideas that have their origin within a religious context—for example, ideas about physical and/or psychological healing—will produce more interesting results and discussions as well, and lead, on the one hand, to a new understanding of the extent of scientific resources and, on the other, to a deepened appreciation of the nature of religious insight. Future science may involve new theories even more strange (and, one hopes, more obviously amenable to testing) than the string theory of early-twenty-first-century physics; and whatever their reliability as indicators of how things are, such developments in scientific thought may feed the imagination of religious persons and result in new models and metaphors for depicting the Divine which take human minds to spiritual regions previously unexplored. Developments in neuroscience and in the social sciences—especially psychology—may illuminate the human substrata of religious experience, revealing facts about us and our beliefs either worthy or unworthy of an ultimate, salvific reality, and either consistent or inconsistent with our present ideas concerning human fulfillment.

It seems possible, third, that there should be, in the near future, a deepening of communication between (and concerning) *religion and art.* At various times in the past and in various places, artists and art have been recognized as possessing or potentially possessing spiritual power, but humans are very far from fully exploiting this insight. The *persons* of art, that is, artists themselves, may come to play a more important role in religious communities as their unique ability to express and deepen a community's self-understanding and worldview, and also to represent—literally to expose—in arresting ways the needs and the views of minorities within the group, comes to be more fully appreciated. The *processes* of art, which require ways of seeing and feeling one's environment very different from the norm, indeed, ones akin to the mystic's, may come to inform more fully the spiritual disciplines of religious individuals and groups, and—together with the aforementioned influence of the artists themselves—generate alternative and so far unconsidered understandings of the Divine. Here it is especially pertinent to notice how doing art can open humans to the creative power of apparent chaos and generate an understanding of new forms of order, where, uninfluenced by art, we might carry on in more conventional paths instead, overly influ-

.enced by preconceptions, not even noticing the alternative construals of our environment available to us. Finally, there are the *products* of art which evolve through such processes, from visual images to forms of creative movement, which may in the future more commonly mediate and perhaps also alter the nature of religious experience, as they are given a more prominent place in religious communities and as members of religious communities learn to engage them with a more sensitive understanding. It is easy to see how, as such understanding grows, the *study* of relationships between religion and art may grow as well and have its own effects.

It seems possible, fourth, that there should be a deepening of communication between (and concerning) *religion and philosophy.* (It might seem odd that this is the *last* area of change I, a philosopher, have chosen to discuss, but I think it is important to notice how *various* changes, in *various* areas of human life, may have effects relevant to religious investigation.) The day can certainly not be far away when philosophers—especially Western philosophers—take to heart such commentary on the limited extent of their awareness of religion as appears at the end of the previous chapter. The deepened understanding of unfamiliar ideas and the richer networks of interconnected ideas to which they would then have access might be expected to influence the arguments they develop and the conclusions they endorse. Here it should be noted that philosophers concerned with traditional *Western* religious claims, fully informed about the *millennia-long* history of their discussion, are *still* digging up new and interesting interpretations of them and arguments for them. Set this alongside the breezily dismissive attitude often taken toward other religious claims hardly known at all, or even the dedicated research of a few years into their nature and justification, and you can see how much Western philosophical discussion may yet have to learn and how it may be enriched through a deeper and wider familiarity with non-Western forms of religion. Of course even without this observation we can see how further discussion in philosophy may yield interesting and important new distinctions and arguments with relevance to the truth of religious claims.

This gives us a taste of what some aspects pertinent to religious discussion of our future—and, in particular, the near future—may turn out to involve. Now I want to add a couple of further dimensions. For, first, if such developments as I have outlined in respect of religion and religion, religion and science, religion and art, and religion and philosophy come to be, it may also be that complex relationships *between* them emerge, as individuals and groups seek to make use of all available resources for determining whether there is an ultimate reality and, if so, what it is like. These lines of interpenetration and mutual influence can be represented visually (Figure 2).

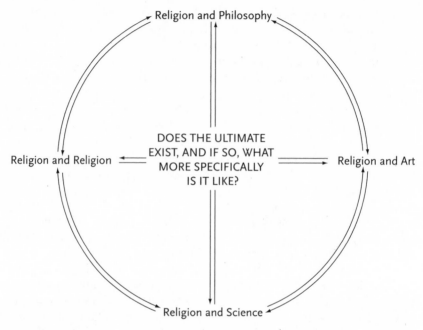

Figure 2

I suspect that if anything like this begins to develop, it may quickly become much more complicated still—that is, perhaps as an outgrowth of what *is* represented on the "wheel" in the figure, other centers of discussion *not* thus represented may spring up and call for their own place along its circumference. But even without that, the possibilities of mutual influence (and extension of influence) are virtually endless. Thus religious persons and groups who improve their understanding of unfamiliar religious traditions and practitioners may have new arguments to discuss and, when they do philosophy, new insights to apply, and what they learn from philosophy may influence their decisions as to which forms of religion to investigate or the conclusions reached in their discussions with other religious practitioners. They may also have a broader and sturdier base on which to build their understanding of the compatibility or otherwise of religious and scientific attitudes, and what they glean from studying unfamiliar ideas in science may help them tolerate unfamiliar ones in other religious traditions. They may, further, have a wider familiarity with examples of religious art to bring to their study of how art can express and expand religious ideas, and what they learn about the processes of art may help them understand the significance of diverse religious phenomena involving similar processes, such as the activities of contemplatives. These are only a few examples. Similar stories could easily be told about relations between the other centers of interaction and study.

The second extra dimension is this. Out of all that has already been described may evolve higher-level *centers of synthetic discussion,* which seek to draw together and integrate the threads of knowledge represented by Figure 2 (or the much more complex representation that might well be needed to express what actually transpires) into a larger and more comprehensive tapestry of understanding. And such activity might very well enlarge rather dramatically—and all the more so the longer it is pursued—the store of information relevant to ultimate questions that human beings possess.

Now on the basis of this outline of possible future changes relevant to the world of religious investigation, I reason as follows. (1) These changes are indeed epistemically possible (some have already begun to occur). (2) On reflection and as investigators we would have to say that many of them would represent *vast improvements* over what we have at present: in particular, the level of wide communal involvement, the democratization of research, and the deep integration of results referred to represent something radically new and important in the history of religious investigation. And it only stands to reason that (3) such changes, when they occur, may well generate important new evidence relevant to the truth of religious claims, forcing adjustments in our present views on that subject. And in that case, regardless of what might be true at *other* times in human history, (4) *we* ought not to rest content with the position we are in right now and the evidence we have right now in support of religious or irreligious belief, but rather should advocate *getting more evidence of the sort described in the imagined scenario:* it would indeed be *intellectually reckless* to do otherwise. Which is to say that (5) the evidence presently available must be deemed *insufficient* to provide a reliable basis for religious or irreligious belief, and thus cannot justify such belief. As before, we can also go further and suggest that the epistemic possibility uncovered here, when added to the available evidence, provides a defeater for any religious or irreligious belief we might be inclined to form on its basis. It seems, therefore, that the Prospective Mode can be powerfully mobilized in support of religious skepticism.

3. *Does the Prospective Mode Underwrite Irresponsible Generalization?*

In objection to what I have said, it may be argued that the Prospective Mode (or an argument like it) can similarly be applied to a whole swath of beliefs we rightly take for granted, and so must be setting out conditions for justification that are too strong. Furthermore, my approach, just because it may thus be generalized, must leave us "frozen," unable to act. We need to form beliefs if we are to act in one way as opposed to another—for we act *on* our beliefs. The approach I am recommending is most unsuited to the perils of life; it is quite unhelpful when we are seeking to navigate smoothly into the brighter future I am holding before us. Here decisions need *constantly* to be taken on less than perfect evidence.[7]

But what are the beliefs ruled out by my approach that we rightly take for granted? To retain plausibility, any answer to this question would need to emphasize such beliefs as were mentioned in a similar context in Chapter 1: certain beliefs of immediate experience and relationship, and concerning necessary truths, including certain truths of morality, and also the most general and long-standing and well-evidenced beliefs of science. But as we saw there, such beliefs are apparently not subject to arguments raising the specter of unrepresentative evidence: because they are so obviously true, we may infer that any unrecognized evidence required for this to be the case must indeed exist. It is, for the same reason, not epistemically possible—even if logically possible—that such beliefs should be overturned by future evidence. Hence the first objection here seems simply irrelevant to my argument.

The second objection raises issues that will be more fully discussed in Chapter 6. But it will be good to say something about it here, given how obvious its claim may seem to some readers of this chapter. What I would say, first, is that we are quite able to negotiate our way through life without religious or irreligious beliefs. Indeed, given the points outlined above and the manner in which such beliefs may inhibit the sort of richer and fuller investigation those points represent, our intellectual future may be much brighter without them. What about other beliefs? As mentioned above, clearly many of the most important have immunity here. But what about beliefs *at other levels of serious intellectual inquiry?* Here I would respond with what I think is the most important point I can make in this connection:

---

[7] At the end of his *Is There a God?* (Oxford: Oxford University Press, 1996), Richard Swinburne expresses a similar sentiment: "Argument and counter-argument, qualification and amplification, can go on forever. But religion is not exceptional in this respect. . . . New experiments can always be done to test Quantum Theory, new interpretations can be proposed for old experiments, forever. And the same goes for interpretations of history or theories of politics. But life is short and we have to act on the basis of what such evidence as we have had time to investigate shows on balance to be probably true" (p. 140). No doubt this is correct. But it in no way follows from it that we should *believe* what our limited investigations support. (Indeed, Swinburne himself is committed to this, given what he says about related matters in his *Faith and Reason* [Oxford: Clarendon Press, 1981]).

that the objection is mistaken in supposing we *need* beliefs (of the relevant kind) in order to act. If some matter—say, in quantum physics or theoretical ethics—is complex, requiring many difficult and subtle questions to be dealt with, concerning which our views are likely to change, either it will be action-relevant (i.e., such as needs to be resolved if we are to negotiate our way through an important part of life) or it will not. If, as must typically be the case, it is *not* action-relevant, no difficulty arises. If, on the other hand, it *is* action-relevant, then we will have to choose the view that seems most probable given present information and act on *it;* and this we can do *even if we do not believe that view.* Indeed, we *often* find ourselves in circumstances where we have to go with what seems most likely, even when it cannot (for whatever reason) be said to be more likely than not on the total evidence (think, for example, of decisions made in response to terrorist threats, or when lost in a cave, or when one is betting on some specific outcome in a horse race), and thus even when it is not plausible enough to inspire belief. We can go further here and point out that we also sometimes have to act when the probabilities are *quite unclear,* and so when we do not have obvious support of *any* kind in favor of one judgment over another. (When lost in a cave you may not have a clue as to which of several tunnels—if any—leads out, but you may still pick one.)[8] That's just life. Given the arguments presented in this chapter, we need to accept that, for us, and perhaps also for many of our descendants, life just is going to be like this where the deepest of our intellectual interests are concerned. Here we may still act, if action is required, but we should leave positive belief for another day, when our vision is clearer and the unconsidered or uneliminated alternatives to be reckoned with fewer.

---

[8] To connect with a central theme of *Prolegomena,* one mentioned in the Introduction, we may add that it is in some such situations that *faith,* as distinct from belief, comes into its own.

CHAPTER 5

The Modes Combined
Limitation, Immaturity, Presumption

The four modes of religious skepticism developed in previous chapters—Subject, Object, Retrospective, and Prospective—can be represented schematically (Figure 3).

1. SUBJECT	3. RETROSPECTIVE
2. OBJECT	4. PROSPECTIVE

Figure 3

Each of these modes of reasoning, I have argued, is quite capable of justifying categorical religious skepticism on its own. But having seen this, we may now rather swiftly come to see something else as well: these modes (more exactly, certain prominent elements therefrom) may be *combined* to create *additional* modes, each distinct from the others and even more powerful than the others. There are various ways of doing this. Here we will start by thinking about combining 1 and 2, noticing the emergence of the *Limitation* Mode, a mode of reasoning more powerful than either 1 or 2 alone. Then we will combine elements from 3 and 4 to realize the *Immaturity* Mode, which surpasses in force both 3 and 4. Finally, we will

bring *these* two modes together, thus achieving the most powerful mode
of all, which emphasizes what must now appear as the huge *presumption* of
religious and irreligious belief. All things considered, then, a slightly more
complicated representation of our modes is called for (Figure 4).

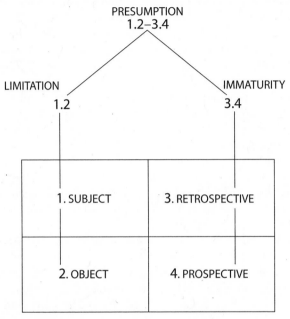

Figure 4

The remainder of this chapter is mostly given over to the explication of
these additional modes of religious skepticism, thus completing the construction of our edifice of doubt.

1. *Combinatorial Reasoning*

But before getting to that, let me say a little more about the nature of
the combinatorial argumentation instantiated here. How exactly is my
suggestion about increasing forcefulness or power from mode to mode
to be understood?

The details may be quite different in different cases of such reasoning.
One of my reasons for speaking of *modes* is indeed that I wish to invite
recognition of how quite a number of closely related arguments are lurking about in each case: there are various *tokens* of each *type* of argumentation that I employ (with correspondingly various ways of linking up tokens
from one type with tokens of another), and I make no claim to having

discovered them all. So what I have to say must be left, in a certain sense, open-ended. Moreover, I will be using the same combinatorial approach in Part 3 when arguing against theism; thus what I say here must be broad enough to accommodate those arguments too.

Having said that, I would still suggest that certain general unifying features of all such arguments—features marking the meaning of "increased forcefulness" in this connection—can be discerned. First, there is the fact that *each time a combinatorial move is made, the result is a more plausible premise (or premise-set) from which a shared conclusion can be inferred.*[1] Though sometimes this premise (or premise-set) is the same in both of the arguments involved in the combination and is being made more plausible simply through being supported from both sides (or through having one of its members thus supported), sometimes it appears in only one of the arguments and sometimes it is a new premise (or premise-set) formed by conjoining considerations from the two arguments. And though at times the shared conclusion is the final conclusion (in the present chapter, that religious skepticism is justified; in Part 3, that theism is false), at other times it is only an interim conclusion from which a shared final conclusion is to be inferred. Finally, the increased plausibility of the premise (or premise-set) may result from distinct inductive considerations derived from different arguments each adding to its probability (or to the probability of one of its members); from a combination of inductive and deductive considerations; or from a combination of purely deductive ones. Notice that where the arguments combined are both deductive—the same point could be made where one is deductive and the other inductive—and are each developed using already highly plausible premises, perhaps made the more so by previous combinations, it remains possible for a yet more plausible premise to be found through appropriate further combinations. As we will see in a few moments, I may rightly believe, separately, the principle that a certain form of human immaturity removes justification for supposing humans capable of religious understanding and the principle that a certain other form of immaturity does the same, but rightly believe with yet more confidence the principle that *the two forms of immaturity together* have the mentioned effect. And in such circumstances it is appropriate to think of the argument in which the third principle appears as the more forceful, even if all these arguments are deductively valid with premises that we are justified in believing.

---

[1] Modestly, I assume that no mode prior to the seventh is maximally forceful—such as cannot in the manner I here describe be made *more* forceful. (If it is concluded that this is a mistake, I will not be greatly perturbed: in that case, the added forcefulness of the new modes may be interpreted in terms of the second feature—shortly to be discussed—alone.)

But a second, quite different, unifying feature is this: *each time a combinatorial move is made, the result is potentially capable of convincing a wider range of responsible inquirers, and thus of doing more to contribute to a consensus about the worth of responses to religious claims.*[2] Such a consensus, as argued in the Introduction, is an appropriate goal for philosophy of religion, and if an argument or mode of argumentation A potentially does more to contribute to it than another argument or mode of argumentation B, then it is natural and appropriate for someone with that goal to think of A as more forceful, more powerful, than B.

Now these two features, though quite distinct, are of course linked: the first concerns how additional considerations bring with them more justification (ultimately) for believing the final conclusion of the arguments involved; the second how, *because of this,* we may expect more who carefully consider the arguments in which the additional considerations are incorporated to be convinced. Yet another feature that might be thought important here can be discerned by noting how each time a combinatorial move is made, we arguably have even more scope than we did previously for *elaboration of arguments.* That is, while in every case we have a type of argumentation of which there is more than one token, in each of the last, combined cases more diverse material is incorporated than in the previous one, and so in each such case we might expect to have more potential for elaboration—*more* tokens of the type. In a certain very loose sense this point itself (if correct) might be thought to generate a reason for considering each of these last types of argument more "forceful" or "powerful" than the previous one, but the better word might be "fecund" or "resourceful," and I will not emphasize this aspect of the situation except to say that it may contribute to the wider effect described above. (If there are more ways for a type of argumentation to be elaborated, there are more ways for responsible inquirers to be convinced.) In other words, this feature, insofar as it is linked to increased forcefulness, is not independent but subordinate to the second unifying feature just mentioned.

In the present chapter, modes 1 and 2 (Subject and Object) are combined to form 1.2 (Limitation); 3 and 4 (Retrospective and Prospective) to form 3.4 (Immaturity); and 1.2 and 3.4 to form 1.2–3.4 (Presumption). Each of these combinations, I suggest, displays the two features I have

---

[2] This feature might be thought more "subjective" than the first, but notice the qualifier "responsible" used when describing those whose agreement may be won, and the assumption of a context of inquiry. We refer here to how persons respond to the modes instead of to the objective plausibility of the moves made by the latter, but I am not talking *only* about how the later modes might, more than the earlier, make it hard for someone to resist being persuaded. In the latter sense an argument or pattern of reasoning could have its forcefulness increased even if it were, objectively, quite *lacking* in force.

described. I turn now to the details of these additional moves available to the religious skeptic.

2. *The Limitation Mode*

Reasoning that unites considerations from the Subject Mode and the Object Mode might proceed as follows. Given human finitude, we are required sometimes to say that critical evidence, evidence required for an accurate picture of how things are with regard to the matters we are investigating, may well have been missed—this is a limitation we must simply accept. And the matters we are investigating need not be inordinately deep and complicated for such to be the case: detail, precision, some degree of profundity and attractiveness will do quite nicely. But given the nature of the object of religious belief, *religious* investigation concerns matters about as deep and potentially complicated *as any could be*, and there is reason to think that the truth here might go unrecognized even by much more sophisticated finite inquirers than we. These facts, together with the former ones, throw our limitations in respect of successful religious investigation into even sharper relief. We can now argue that our general limitations as finite subjects, taken together with the specific limitations pertinent to religious investigation (which presents the spectacle of finite beings probing the infinite), must make it very plausible to suppose that critical evidence may have been missed. And, more to the point, these combined considerations provide even stronger grounds for the claim that such is the case than the Subject Mode is able to generate on its own.

In the Limitation Mode, doubt about representativeness and doubt about whether we are capable of discerning truths about ultimate things— forms of doubt central to the Subject Mode and the Object Mode, respectively—come together. As we have just seen, the latter sort of doubt can be taken as supporting the former. But the emphasis can also be reversed, and so we can say that, in the Limitation Mode, these two sorts of doubt are mutually reinforcing.

How may the emphasis be reversed? As we saw in developing the Subject Mode, sometimes—in the most troubling cases—we have to allow that there may be evidence pertinent to our investigation that is undiscovered or undiscoverable, and especially the latter notion can be put to use in connection with the idea that we may simply be incapable of discerning truths about ultimate things. Just by considering our limitations as finite subjects, without any reference to religion at all, we can already see that there may be, and indeed must be, many matters on which we cannot expect to *be able* to recognize critical evidence, simply because we would not understand it even if it were presented to us. Now suppose the theme of religion and ultimate things to be introduced. Will there not naturally be an inclination to suspect that precisely *this* theme may be one of those that concerns inscrutable facts of the sort in question? In this way we can start with the limitations emphasized by the Subject Mode, using them to add force to the premise about our possible incapacity generated in connection with our limitations by the Object Mode, instead of simply moving in the other direction, as above.

There is another way in which we can do this as well. The strategy of the Subject Mode—the strategy involving reference to detail, precision, profundity, and attractiveness—already permits us to bring into stark contrast the poverty of human awareness and the huge ambitions of religious and irreligious belief. Suppose, then, that we begin with these points of the Subject Mode, pretty much as they stand. Onto them may yet be grafted what we learned from the Object Mode, when we were considering the possible narrowness and unworthiness of extant conceptions of the Ultimate, concerning the limits of our *imagination,* and also the unspeakable value- or greatness- or (most vividly) *awesomeness*-differential that must be noticed by anyone who sets the notion of a human being alongside that of an axiologically ultimate reality. In developing the aforementioned strategy of the Subject Mode, we spoke of how the bottom falls out of our pot of alternatives when the proposition for which we are seeking evidence is profound, and of how we cannot ever fully map the alternatives there must be to any elaborated ultimism. This is indeed a limitation. But by reference to the limits of our imagination and our limited greatness, we generate much added support for the point that even if the correct alternative were to come before us, we might not be able to recognize it *as* correct. With this combination of support, we again have a more forceful premise by means of which to contribute to a defense of capacity skepticism than the Object Mode by itself can generate.

Taking all these matters together—the limitations of the Subject Mode with those of the Object Mode, considerations concerning representativeness with those about capacity—we therefore arrive at a new mode of religious skepticism, one more productive of plausible premises from which to defend that stance and richer in resources than either of the modes it exploits.

3. *The Immaturity Mode*

Here again we will find both considerations concerning unrepresentativeness, this time from the Prospective Mode, and considerations concerning incapacity, from the Retrospective Mode, and again we will discover them to be mutually reinforcing. But before getting to that, let's consider how both those modes yield points that can be expressed in terms of human immaturity. Sometimes when we say of someone that she is immature, what we mean is simply that she is not yet fully developed or grown. But sometimes we mean more—we mean that the individual in question is not sensible or appropriate in behavior or in the management of her emotions, that she is *less mature than might be expected.* In the one case we make only a negative point, about something being absent, and do not pass judgment. But in the other we make a positive point, about the presence of certain habits or dispositions that *account* for the absence, which here too will be noticeable even if it is not our first concern—habits or dispositions that we consider to reflect badly on their possessors. Now what we see about our species when looking into the past with the Retrospective Mode is, I suggest, the latter sort of immaturity; and what we see when thinking with the Prospective Mode, so I would say, is the former. And together these insights provide a powerful argument indeed for religious skepticism, more powerful than either can summon alone. That the human race has just begun its journey of development, and has, potentially, so much farther to go, is already very significant. But when we add to this that what it has accomplished with its time thus far has little advanced the cause of religious understanding, and may indeed have set it back, producing a distorted picture of things sustained by bad intellectual and emotional and social habits, then we have a powerful reason indeed to be more than a little suspicious of any suggestion that the truth about ultimate things has already been arrived at. Again, and now in this *combined* sense of "immature," we can say that the *im*maturity of our race shows that religious and irreligious belief are *pre*mature.

This idea it is natural to flesh out in terms of a possible incapacity and also in terms of possibly unrepresentative evidence. Whereas each of the two modes on which we are drawing emphasized only one of these, here we can refer to either or both. Starting with the former notion: the argument for present incapacity, already strongly supported when we consider our poor track record, gains ground when we see that thousands and perhaps millions of years of development lie ahead of us. By contrast with what we may *become,* what we are *now* will seem that much more likely to be lacking some of those layers of refinement that, as we saw in Chapter 3, may stand between us and the place where truths about ultimate things would be discernible by us. In light of this contrast we will seem that much more likely, in our ultimate beliefs, to be comparable to prehistoric individuals making confident pronouncements on the inner nature of material reality, or to the Greek, Parmenides, discoursing on being and nothingness.

We all know what assessment is appropriate to prehistoric thinkers and Parmenides: critical and relevant developments in (for example) atomic theory and grammar had not yet occurred, and so these individuals were simply not in a *position* to get at the truth on matters with which they were concerned. If we see that we have squandered many relevant intellectual opportunities in the past and, *on top of that,* are only in the early childhood of the race, perhaps it will occur to us that things may be similar where our present capacity to discern the truth about ultimate things is concerned.

We can also come at this from the direction of unrepresentativeness (as to some extent we were already doing in Chapter 4). It will seem to us all the more likely that future changes will bring profound evidential surprises, overturning any beliefs that might previously have seemed well supported, the more we consider and emphasize that the story of our intellectual past is *not* one of beings alert and eager and open to the truth about religion engaging in fair-minded and diligent and cooperative inquiry concerning it, whose dominant disposition as parents and community leaders is to nurture a critical and creative spirit in their children, but rather a sorry tale of greed, dogmatism, rivalry, and the suppression of independent thought. In such conditions, to say the least, it cannot be expected that a huge amount of relevant evidence will be uncovered, or that such evidence as is uncovered will be impeccably assessed. Instead it will seem all the more likely that completely new understandings of ultimate things, which inspire such responses as "Now why didn't we ever think of *that* before?" are lurking around one of the many corners along the path that will take us further into maturity as a species.

Just as in the case of the Limitation Mode, then, we find in the Immaturity Mode both unrepresentativeness and incapacity considerations, and find them to be mutually reinforcing. More generally, it is clear that by combining the two forms of immaturity in one argument we generate a stronger mode of reasoning in support of religious skepticism than we could otherwise have achieved.

4. *The Presumption Mode*

And so we come to the Presumption Mode, which builds on everything that has come before. It makes the higher-level move of combining the two combined modes just discussed, creating from these yet another mode of reasoning. This utilizes the strengths of each of its already venerable antecedents, leaving us with the most powerful mode of all. (Tapping into the mother lode of skeptical reasoning as it does, perhaps we should call our new way of reasoning the Mother Mode.)

It will not take long to see how it does so (or, at least, how it does so on the interpretation of this new mode that I shall defend). I begin by underlining the central insight of the Limitation Mode: that for various overlapping reasons, in seeking to arrive at truths about ultimate things, we may very well have bitten off more than we can chew or—to exchange one apt metaphor for another—be completely out of our depth. This already provides good grounds for skepticism. But what the skeptic can say to enhance still further the strength of his case is this: *given* what the Limitation Mode reveals (and in the absence of some obvious religious or irreligious breakthrough of the sort we have mentioned from time to time), we must at the very least admit that it is a *necessary condition* of the justification of either religious or irreligious belief that human beings have engaged in a long process of very high-quality (i.e., wide-ranging and open-minded and systematic and detailed) investigation into religious questions and into the requirements of religious understanding such as might allow them to *transcend* their limitations, and have also gone some distance toward *applying the results.* Even the most optimistic inquirer into things religious must be moved to make *some* concession on recognizing and taking to heart the limitations under which we labor. And surely anything weaker than this would not come close to taking the measure of those limitations.

To see this, consider an analogy. Suppose we wish to put through an intellectual examination a child who seems somewhat unintelligent, who, in particular, finds the subject of the examination very difficult. Would there be justification for *believing*—for thinking it to be *the case*—that this child has what it takes to recognize the right answers and the proper techniques for arriving at them, or that he is correct when, early into the exam, he declares that he has discovered all the solutions to the problems set before him, if we have not even taken the time to *prepare* him both attitudinally and intellectually, training him and grilling him repeatedly, or—if the subject is one we ourselves find difficult—making sure that his trainers are reliable and the techniques he is taught likely to be successful? Another analogy. Suppose that I wish to run and *win* a race in which it may be that many runners much more competent than myself are entered. Would there be any justification for me to *believe* that I will win if I have done little to get myself into shape or to train for the competition—if, perhaps, I have instead been lying around on the couch watching television and drinking beer or indulging my appetite for junk food? The correct answer to these questions is presumably obvious, and so, the skeptic may say, is the correct answer to the question whether his necessary condition for the justification of religious or irreligious belief is really necessary.

This point about a "necessary condition" is of course the pivot on which the Presumption Mode turns. For now we may add to our premise-set that, given the information supplied by the Immaturity Mode, the necessary condition in question is very evidently not fulfilled. *Human beings are both profoundly limited and profoundly immature.* Even with our limitations—though here one waxes optimistic—a present capacity to discern the truth about ultimate things and the present availability of representative evidence concerning them might not seem incredible, if that present had been preceded by a long process of development in which the relevant skills and intellectual habits, and other dispositions underlying them, were scrupulously sought and diligently applied. But to say that such commodities have been procured by this time given both our limitations AND our immaturity betrays serious overconfidence and invites a charge of presumption. (This is a massive understatement.) Thus even were the previous powerful modes of religious skepticism to be judged insufficient on their own to complete the task I have assigned them, with the present mode victory would be assured.

CHAPTER 6

The Bearing of Pragmatic Considerations

To the conclusion of the previous chapter, a proviso must now be added: *provided that there are no non-truth-oriented, pragmatic considerations with sufficient countervailing force.* Everything we have said so far in the book has been said on the assumption that only truth-oriented or epistemic considerations are relevant to the justification of believing, disbelieving, and skeptical responses to ultimism. This is in line with the procedure for evaluating such responses outlined at the end of my *Prolegomena* (p. 217). After having identified various problems facing a non-truth-oriented or pragmatic or justificationally pluralist approach, I stated there that philosophers should *begin* by applying a truth-oriented criterion. But I also noted that out of respect for the deepest pluralist idea, which urges sensitivity to goodness in all its forms, and to ensure that no mistake is made in dealing with this important matter, philosophers might be expected at least to entertain the possibility that whatever conclusion truth-oriented considerations support—whether a conclusion in some way affirming a believing response, or a disbelieving one, or else some form of skepticism—should be altered in light of non-truth-oriented considerations pointing to a better or equally good alternative response. With respect to a defense of skepticism in particular, it was suggested that the following principles, which refer not just to the weakness of evidence but also to the non-applicability of pragmatic considerations, should be utilized.

P20. A skeptical response is *negatively* justified if (1) available information does not permit a judgment of sufficient and overall good evidence for either the truth of the proposition that would be believed in a believing response or the truth of the proposition that would be believed in a disbelieving response; and (2) there are no non-truth-oriented considerations with sufficient force to show some alternative response to be better, and thus preferable in the circumstances.

P21. A skeptical response is *positively* justified if (1) it is negatively justified, and (2) there are no non-truth-oriented considerations with sufficient force to show some alternative response to be as good, and thus equally worthy of being made in the circumstances. (*Prolegomena*, p. 219)

It will be evident that I have so far been arguing in support of the view that, where the proposition at issue is ultimism or its denial, condition (1) of P20 is satisfied: our modes of religious skepticism have in various ways sought to show that available information does *not* permit a judgment of sufficient and overall good evidence for the truth of either of these propositions. But now, taking to heart my own advice, I will consider the bearing of pragmatic considerations on this skeptical conclusion, asking whether the second condition of each of these principles is also satisfied. My answer will in each case be an affirmative one. Indeed, I will be arguing that, so far from disturbing our skepticism, pragmatic considerations actually *strengthen* it. Religious skepticism, in other words, faces no threat from religious pragmatism, but can make of it an ally.

1. *The Benefits of Belief*

I shall begin by considering what non-truth-oriented considerations might be marshaled in support of the alternative response to ultimism involving *belief*, and assessing their force. As a preface, though, let me offer a small clarification concerning "non-truth-oriented considerations." It would be natural to understand this phrase as referring to considerations suggesting ways in which a believing response might be thought good that do not involve its conduciveness to an awareness of the truth of any proposition. But this is a somewhat more strict interpretation than the one I shall adopt. It is true that most of the prima facie good-making properties that would be mentioned in this connection apparently have nothing to do with the truth of ultimism. In *Prolegomena* (p. 210) the sample list looked like this: "being conducive to the fulfillment of moral obligation or the development or expression of moral virtue, being conducive to psychologically healthy functioning, to an interesting life, to understanding, to wisdom, to consciousness (as opposed to ignorance and gullibility, especially about oneself), to creativity, to the general happiness, to communal or cultural enrichment or growth of one sort or another." Any of these properties might, given the broad sense of the term applicable here, be thought to represent a pragmatic "benefit" of belief or, for that matter, of one of the other responses one might make to ultimism. But—and here is my central point—I will also treat conduciveness to contact with truth *elsewhere* (i.e., in respect of propositions other than ultimism or claims entailing it) and conduciveness to contact with truth *down the road* or *in the long run* (whether in respect of ultimism or claims entailing it, or other propositions) as such benefits.[1] All that I will here count as a *truth*-oriented consideration is the sort of *evidential* consideration purportedly putting one *directly* in touch with the truth of *ultimism* (or its denial), or contributing to such a result, that we have been talking about in previous chapters.

So the religious pragmatist has quite a wide assortment of "non-truth-oriented benefits" to choose from in seeking to show that, despite the fact that truth-oriented considerations (as I am understanding them) have come out decidedly in favor of skepticism, a believing response to ultimism is as good as or superior to a skeptical response. How might her argument proceed? She might claim, to begin, that by believing there to be an ultimate and salvific reality and acting on this belief we will discover important psychological support for the business of living, and also for our development into properly functioning and useful moral agents with a deep sense of moral order and purpose. A very general belief like this functions as a *framework attitude,* which provides a way of looking at and making sense of the *whole* of things. Given its content and the psychological power of propositional belief, including the latter's tendency to be joined by affective belief (features used to argue *against* religious belief in Chapter 3), this particular framework attitude would surely help us retain our zest for life: if I believe that something of unlimited value is at the heart of things, I will be disposed to see signs of that value in all aspects of my experience and will find it easier to think that life is worth living, as well as to pursue my goals with dedication. Furthermore, if we believe that in the final analysis all shall be well, we may find it easier to trust reality in the face of terrible things that happen to us and to others—and as part of this we may find it easier to trust that part of reality *constituting* ourselves, in the face of all the stubborn problems involved in becoming more deeply mature. We may also be more strongly motivated to find a

---

[1] Clearly contact with truth may *itself* be construed as a benefit that we have reason to pursue, in which case anything helping us to do so effectively may be thought to have (in the broadest sense) practical or pragmatic value.

like-minded community and to work with its members in the forwarding of moral goals that, precisely because of the content of our shared belief, are likely to be more *ambitious* than the moral goals we might otherwise pursue, possibly resulting in a wider range of benefits for humankind.

The religious pragmatist can develop her argument in support of a believing response to ultimism in another way too. A believing response to ultimism could remain very general, focused on *generic* ultimism alone. (Though it might be through believing some elaborated form of ultimism that someone believes there to be an ultimate and salvific reality, this need not be the case.) Because it remains general, such belief is capable of motivating inquiry into the *deeper* nature of the Divine—into the question of which elaborated ultimism, whether one already thought of or one as yet completely unknown, has got it right. The pragmatist can go further as well and suggest that, if one possesses belief of generic ultimism, one's motivation to investigate must be much stronger than it could otherwise be, for now one will sense that there is indeed something to be discovered, and that it is not all just a wild goose chase. Thus our understanding of ultimate things might well be considerably improved over time. (Here we see a way in which "truth in the long run" might be the result of belief now.) What this shows, the pragmatist may conclude, is that on top of everything else, a believing response would also have important *intellectual* benefits, contrary to what we might have been inclined to suppose when we saw available truth-oriented information pointing in another direction.[2]

What is the force of such considerations? Do they cumulatively have sufficient weight to show the believing response to be *better than* or at least *as good as* the skeptical response to ultimism, despite the tendency of truth-oriented considerations to support skepticism? I think not, and here is why. First, it is clear that any philosopher recommending a believing response on grounds such as these in the face of what truth-oriented information shows would be sponsoring *self-deception;* and this itself entails great *disvalue*—perhaps enough to outweigh or trump any combination of positive points of the sort we are considering. Why self-deception? Because, given the involuntariness of belief (on this see *Prolegomena,* Chapter 2, section 4), no one aware of the relevant evidential facts would be able to act on the philosopher's recommendation without coming to change her

---

[2] By developing her argument as suggested in this paragraph, the religious pragmatist may avoid what would otherwise surely be a powerful pragmatic point *against* religious belief—that without religious belief there would be a great deal less violence and hatred in the world. A generic ultimistic believer would presumably not be caught up in such sectarian fervor as, in the actual world, consistently leads to hatred and violence.

view of those facts—without coming to believe that the available evidence does after all clearly support ultimism, contrary to what she has seen to be the case. The religious inquirer, to follow such a recommendation, must foster in herself a belief about truth or probability which she knows the evidence alone, correctly viewed, would never give her; she must develop a belief and act on it, and thus must come to think certain propositions to be true or probably true, when (at least initially) she knows perfectly well that this is not the case. Such self-deception and dishonesty seems clearly to go against virtue, and—as part of this—to strike at the heart of a concern for wisdom, with its love of truth; it seems to be such as could not be entered into without irresponsibility. Accordingly, it appears that one who engaged in such behavior, aware of the pertinent information, could never be in circumstances where it was true of her that her response was justified. Such a response, it appears, should rather be *avoided* by anyone properly aware and is *un*justified.

Perhaps it will be argued that if the non-truth-oriented benefits were very great, and could not be achieved in any other way, self-deception would, all things considered, be permissible in this case. But now we must note that neither of these conditions is satisfied. The pragmatist rightly does not claim that psychological support for facing life with courage and for moral development and intellectual inquiry is *completely unobtainable* in the absence of religious belief, only that *more* of this is to be expected where it is present. And so the benefits she is in a position to draw to our attention are not as great as we need them to be to warrant the subversion of our intellectual faculties. As it happens, there are *other* beliefs, nonreligious beliefs better supported by *evidence*, that may do the job of providing at least some such support—beliefs about the intrinsic value of courage, moral development, and understanding, for example. Thus we are not completely bereft of assistance in this regard even if we lack religious belief.

But the more important point here is that even the seemingly "extra" value that appears to require religious belief in fact does not: it is available to skeptics as well, and is even in a certain sense available *through* skepticism—here we start to see how the non-truth-oriented benefits of *skepticism* come into play. For given the relevant analyses from *Prolegomena*, whose results are summarized in the Introduction, religious skepticism is quite compatible with religious faith: indeed, propositional faith *requires* skepticism and is *incompatible* with belief. And when the religious skeptic decides to be skeptically religious, mobilizing what I have called the *faith response* to ultimism, he brings within reach certain extra psychological resources very like what the religious pragmatist associates exclusively with religious belief. Such faith too involves a "framework attitude"

that organizes one's experience in a positive manner, and it too provides an impetus for pursuit of moral goals with like-minded others and for religious investigation. Indeed, it may be for just such reasons as these that it is taken up.

And this last point tells us something else about faith: that it permits considerable scope for *responsibility*—unlike propositional belief, which is in itself involuntary and could be produced over time only through self-deception, propositional faith *can* be taken up, can immediately be chosen without self-deception, and so even in the *pursuit* of faith opportunities for the advancement of virtue naturally arise. As just suggested, faith also, because it coincides with skepticism, is able to remain more *clear-sighted* about what the available evidence really shows (the person of faith realizes that the available evidence is weak while imagining—though perhaps with some difficulty—that the total evidence is strong) and, further, can avoid the *complacency* that belief with its sense of reality and (typically) assuredness threatens to generate. (Is not a believer, for example, in greater danger of assuming that the deepest moral goals will be taken care of—after all, there exists an ultimate salvific reality—and basking in the warmth of fellowship with other believers and in their shared sense of Divine privilege rather than diligently pursuing those goals?) In another place I will have much more to say about the faith response, but what I have said here already suggests that when wed to faith, religious skepticism has access to non-truth-oriented benefits at least as great as those alleged by the pragmatist to be associated with belief.

But we can go further. Not only is equally great pragmatic value realizable through skepticism, but overall it is clearly *greater:* given the nature and consequences of skeptical faith, the skeptic has resources for dealing with the pragmatist appeal on behalf of belief which unexpectedly lead to a decided *advantage* for her side in the debate. For, notice, the faith response does about as well in respect of non-truth-oriented benefits as the belief response *while not vulnerable, as belief is, when acquired on non-truth-oriented grounds alone, to accusations of self-deception.* Because the problem of self-deception represents a serious non-truth-oriented *deficit* for belief, if the faith response can bring us about as much in the way of benefit without incurring that deficit, it must, all things considered, be judged *preferable* to the belief response where non-truth-oriented grounds alone are considered.

Since the religious pragmatist must thus favor skepticism over belief, we may conclude not only that there are no non-truth-oriented considerations with sufficient force to show a believing response to be better than a skeptical one, but that there are not even non-truth-oriented considerations with sufficient force to show such a response to be *as good as* a skeptical response. Thus, at least as far as the *believing* alternative is concerned, the second condition of both principles stated earlier can be affirmed, and we are on our way to the conclusion that religious skepticism is both negatively and positively justified.

2. *The Benefits of Disbelief*

"On our way" is indeed the operative phrase: there is another alternative to the skeptical response to ultimism as well, namely, the *dis*believing response, and if it were to be supported by strong enough pragmatic considerations, it would stop us in our tracks and prevent us from declaring religious skepticism all things considered both negatively and positively justified. Many inquirers will have some imaginative connection with religious belief, simply because so many human beings have experienced it at one time or another, but fewer are thus acquainted with disbelief, and consequently it does not loom so large in the public consciousness, intellectually, morally, emotionally. Precisely for that reason we should take some care in getting acquainted with what it is like—or, at any rate, could be like—to be a disbeliever; otherwise we will not be able to form an accurate assessment of what this perspective has to offer.

Now because of the strength of ultimism's claim, it is in theory possible to find among religious disbelievers both philosophical naturalists and individuals holding that there is a limited supernatural reality in relation to which some limited good can be achieved—for the latter view too can be combined with the claim that there is no *ultimate* reality and no *ultimate* human good. That being said, a fully naturalistic orientation very commonly goes hand in hand with a denial of ultimism, and few actually identify themselves with the intermediate option that a limited supernaturalism might represent. Because of this, the pragmatic benefits to be associated with a fully naturalistic form of religious disbelief are the ones most likely to be extolled in discussions of the justification of disbelief taking place in our time. In any case, they are clearly the most *distinctive,* and perhaps they are also the most easily *underrated.* Hence I will focus on them in what follows, understanding "disbeliever" as "naturalistic disbeliever."

So what are the benefits that might be claimed here? Perhaps it could be argued that becoming a disbeliever would have the effect of taking a huge load off our minds: instead of carting around those very heavy ideas involved in ultimism, we would be freed to enter more completely into the here and now, and to appreciate exclusively for its own sake the beauty and wonder of our marvelously intricate planet and universe—a natural system to which we would now consider ourselves fully to belong.[3] We might see the natural world more for what it is, instead of thinking of it as a showpiece of Divine creativity or the medium of a transcendent spiritual energy or an illusion that we need to see *through* in order to find a reality yet more ultimate. Viewing the spring green of trees and the undulating hills awash in sunset, feeling the bite of the wind and tasting the salty sweat of hard work, we could say, "Yes, this is *it*," and truly enter into the experience of *being* this natural spark of consciousness, however briefly lit, recognizing that every moment counts—for *itself.* Accepting a humble place in the universe, we would not only—as my adjective suggests—be less vulnerable to self-conceit, already a great benefit from the standpoint of virtue, but might also, at least in time, find ourselves more able to *relax* metaphysically, and so experience a deeper mental calm and emotional peace. Surely these are impressive benefits.

At the same time, appreciating *other sentient beings* for what they are— alive to *their* natural beauty, unhindered by the distorting effects of religious ideology—we might, as disbelievers, be able to enter with deeper sympathy and dedication into the task of creating justice in the world. If we really believed that no one and nothing else is responsible, that it is all up to us, and that the only beauty to be experienced is what is here right now and in the future, and what we, as part of that, can create, might we not be moved actually to *do* something about suffering where we find it? Freed from metaphysical angst and transcendent aspirations, perhaps we would be more able to open ourselves to fellow travelers and the world during the short time we share the latter with the former, and then simply let it all go as our spark is extinguished, recognizing that we are making room for others to experience the marvel of consciousness—who will appear like a new crop of dandelions or butterflies in the spring, just as beautiful as those, now vanished, that we saw before.

There is an undeniable attractiveness in the disbeliever's perspective, charitably and sympathetically construed. Non-truth-oriented considerations can appear to give it a considerable boost—looking carefully at this perspective one might be inclined to say, "Well, why should we want anything more?" But do such considerations have sufficient force to show this response to ultimism to be better than or at least as good as the response of religious skepticism, given what we have already seen

---

[3] And this even if, say, some form of property dualism turned out to be the correct solution to the mind-body problem: should our existence introduce both physical and nonphysical properties into the world, we could still "fully belong" to the natural world so long as those nonphysical properties are generated naturally (more on this in the next chapter).

about which way truth-oriented considerations point? I would say no. It is important here to remind ourselves again that our assessment *must* be carried out under the shadow of that truth-oriented verdict: we are asking whether the philosopher looking to determine which is the best response to ultimism we can make, *and realizing that the evidence does not support disbelief,* should be moved by such considerations as we have outlined to *nonetheless* recommend a disbelieving response. The interesting thing here is not just that once again we have the problems of self-deception, which must prove as much a deficit for a disbelieving as for a believing response, but, in connection with this, that if disbelief is recommended in the face of truth-oriented considerations that do not support it, it cannot claim some of the most important merits its proponents do claim for it, namely, a distinctively tough-minded realism and willingness to look the truth in the face, and all the virtues—for example, courage—bound up with that. Here we find a turning *away* from the truth instead. Thus insofar as any of the "benefits" outlined above depends on *actual* realism or *earnest* truth-seeking, it is a chimera; and even if those benefits do not depend on an authentic truth-seeking attitude, we can now see that we have to lay alongside them the deficit of its absence, which must prove a special embarrassment for anyone implicated in it who is influenced by the usual picture of disbelief as distinguished by intellectual high-mindedness.

There are other difficulties for the pragmatic disbeliever as well. Obviously much is given up. And here I mean not only the extra support for living and for moral commitment and community which religious belief or faith can provide and which we would be naive to say we could never benefit from being able to access. Significant too is what I call a reduced sense of the mystery of the world (here we see what many would identify as a certain "blandness" or "thinness" or "flatness" in the disbeliever's metaphysical outlook). Though he will no doubt see many exciting discoveries in science and philosophy as still lying ahead of us, the religious disbeliever will not be inclined to look very carefully into the possibility of realities deeper and more profound and more valuable than the natural world could represent. And any intimations in his experience of such realities will be suppressed, and explained in terms of familiar this-worldly categories (e.g., wishful thinking). When his mind encounters the thought of limitless value, the disbeliever must always pull back: for him there *can be nothing* of truly limitless value. And so the spark of human consciousness and goodness, which is brightened by such thoughts (at least where the latter are not ruled out by truth-oriented inquiry), by the perhaps absurd but nonetheless inimitably human desire to burst into an infinite flame, glows more dimly in the disbeliever's universe.

As just suggested, any person who denies the truth of all religious claims will also see radically less in the way of possibilities for *good* in the world than he would if he were a religious believer or even a skeptic; and the good of which he thinks we are capable and which he thinks it appropriate to pursue, while perhaps still great, will be something less than an *ultimate* good. Religious disbelievers may of course seek in many ways to improve the world and themselves within those limits. But their worldview is necessarily less *optimistic* than that of others and holds open no possibility of redress for most of the fruitless suffering and unfulfilled human potential that the world has seen. Of course in the *future* the human condition may be better than it is now, if we work hard enough to advance the cause of justice. But the unredeemed suffering of past and present will always remain unredeemed.

And here we come, I think, to the deepest difficulty for pragmatic religious disbelief that can be advanced on similarly non-truth-oriented grounds. It hinges, again, on the fact that our *truth*-oriented information supports no more than religious skepticism. This leaves open the distinct possibility that the suffering of past and present need *not* remain unredeemed: that there is a power for good not our own capable of ensuring—in the words of Julian of Norwich—that all shall be well, and all manner of thing shall be well. So long as that possibility remains open, and thinking not of future bliss for ourselves but of a real chance at peace and fulfillment for those whose hopes this world has dashed, should we not live by the little light it sheds instead of closing it off for such pragmatic reasons as were sketched above? Though he may speak of universal justice, the disbeliever's vision, *where not demanded by truth-oriented investigation*, must ultimately be seen as turning away from truly *universal* justice. Indeed, a pragmatic move of the sort that the philosopher is here asked to endorse can itself come to seem egoistic and also more than a little elitist—a move in the direction of peace of mind for those of us, who, due to the ease of our affluent lifestyles, can call nature friend, and one that requires us to turn our backs on all those whom it has destroyed. Again, were available truth-oriented considerations to decisively support a disbelieving stance, we would reluctantly embrace it and make of it the best we could. But such is not the case. And in these circumstances, such non-truth-oriented value as is cited above cannot suffice to bring a disbelieving response up to the level of religious skepticism, which not only is more sensitive to truth but can realize great pragmatic value of its own as a guardian and friend of redemption and of the unredeemed.[4]

---

[4] This it may more easily do if wed to faith, but even without that connection, religious skepticism clearly comes out ahead of the competition where non-truth-oriented grounds are concerned.

I therefore find that here too nothing stands in the way of affirming that the second condition of each of the principles with which we began is satisfied. Religious skepticism can indeed make of religious pragmatism an ally. But in that case we are *all* the way to the conclusion that religious skepticism is both negatively and positively justified. Which is to say that religious skepticism is not only, rationally speaking, at least as good a response to ultimism as any other, but, for our time if not for all time, *the best response that can be made.*

3. *Passive or Active Skepticism?*

What sort of skepticism have we thus defended as rationally preferable, all things considered, to any alternative state? We know it is religious skepticism, and *categorical* religious skepticism, and remembering certain other conclusions from previous chapters, we will see as well the *capacity* skepticism lurking only a little below the surface, providing a basis for categorical skepticism and yielding what I have called *complete* religious skepticism. But one question remains unanswered. When we say that complete religious skepticism is positively justified, are we talking about passive or active skepticism, or both?

In the first instance it seems we only have reason to speak about passive skepticism, for the whole emphasis has been on how neither religious nor irreligious belief is justified, which is to say that one should lack both those beliefs—which beliefless state is precisely what I have labeled a passively skeptical one. There is nothing to show that a person who instantiates passive religious skepticism must always be actively skeptical as well. But a slightly more complicated situation is also possible, in which active skepticism *does* have a role and inherits whatever positive justification may attach to passive skepticism.

Let me explain. If I am right about the force of my arguments in this and previous chapters, then anyone starting out as a religious or irreligious believer who responsibly examines all available information—including now my arguments—will avoid both religious and irreligious belief, instantiating *or pursuing* a passive religious skepticism about ultimism instead. And it is the "pursuing" part of that sentence which I want to focus on here. Because of the psychological power of belief, together with various related phenomena such as the power of loyalty, addressed in Chapter 3, passive skepticism may not always immediately be engendered by what are seen as powerful counterarguments. One may be in a state where one recognizes the force of arguments but finds *elusive* the state they would naturally produce in someone completely impartial. The believing disposition may remain, in however weakened a form. Now in this sort of quandary, if indeed at some level she *recognizes* that the best response is a doubting one, the religious believer or disbeliever who follows the justified course will seek to bring it about that she instantiates that response—and this is where active skepticism has a role to play. In the Introduction such skepticism is defined as a complex *stance* or *cultivated* disposition, a kind of "coming out on the side of skepticism" that involves the resistance of mental affirmation on either side of the relevant issue, together with reinforcing behavioral dispositions. The point is that one need not remain a victim of conditioning but even in intellectual matters can take some responsibility for the state one is in. When we employ such terms as "withholding judgment," we suggest that this is the case. "Withholding" certainly sounds active and voluntary. It refers to something one *does,* and takes us beyond mere doubt—to something we can do even when we are *not yet* in doubt. Withholding judgment about ultimism—and we may think here not only of a one-off or once-and-for-all decision or action but also of a policy initiated by a decision—involves seeking to avoid or to counter mental or oral affirmation of either ultimism or its denial, expressing a desire to look further into the issue when asked about it, better acquainting oneself with evidence contrary to the view one finds (intellectually or otherwise) most attractive, and so on.

When such an attitude is taken on, passive religious skepticism may, in time, be engendered. But since passive skepticism about ultimism is positively justified, so must be anything that is needed to engender it, in circumstances where it is not naturally forthcoming. Saying that active skepticism about ultimism is positively justified in such circumstances is indeed *part* of saying that passive skepticism about it is positively justified. If at some level she recognizes the appropriateness of doubt and thus the preferability of a passively skeptical state where ultimism is concerned, the religious believer or disbeliever who does not find herself naturally falling into doubt should take responsibility for seeking to induce it and thus should adopt active religious skepticism. This conditional role for active skepticism, then, should be understood as *included* whenever we say—as, at the end of our discussion of the modes of religious skepticism, we now may and must do—that complete religious skepticism is positively justified.

PART II

CRADLES OF CONVICTION
The Modes Applied and Fortified

THE COLLECTION OF ARGUMENTS developed in Part 1 itself illustrates the human limitations and immaturity of which some members of the collection spoke, since fairly obvious and elementary and commonsensical in many of its contentions, and yet revealing much that has not been adequately considered to date. In the next part of this book I draw on what we have learned from those arguments to address what must be among the central sources of this oversight or neglect: the psychological and social force of *religious experience,* and the psychological, social, and intellectual force of *philosophical naturalism.*

Religious experience of one sort or another has appeared in the role of familiar and virtually unquestioned justifier of religious belief for about as long as humans have been thinking about ultimate things. The powerful influence of naturalism is a more recent phenomenon; the latter owes much of the easy familiarity and comfortable plausibility it enjoys among the nonreligious to the very high status accorded to science—especially natural science—in contemporary intellectual life. Clearly, many people, including certain contemporary philosophers of religion, would be inclined to say that religious experience can justify belief of ultimism—a number of sophisticated new arguments whose conclusions imply as much have recently appeared in the literature. Many other people, including many other philosophers, would be inclined to say that because of the support available for naturalism we should infer the *denial* of ultimism—indeed, this view (or a view entailing it) is so widely accepted in the intellectual realm that it is rarely thought to need serious argument. But, drawing on the results of Part 1, I will claim that both sides are mistaken: if we are willing to look past familiarity and carefully consider, in the light of what we have already seen, arguments that can be given in support of religious experience or naturalism, we will find that these sources of religious and irreligious belief do not have it in them to justify such belief. And this new result will, in turn, allow us to fortify each of the results of Part 1, the forcefulness of any one of which the influence of either naturalism or religious experience might have led one to question.

What I have just said gives an indication of how the various results in this book are interwoven. There are many mutually supportive threads of argument. But the conclusion that religious skepticism is positively justified is a conclusion that *everything* in the book is, directly or indirectly, aiming at. My arguments in Part 2, though involved in a kind of feedback loop with arguments of Part 1, have a critical role to play in connection with that desired result. So let the games continue. As its title indicates, in the first chapter of Part 2 the spotlight is on naturalism.

CHAPTER 7

An Answer to Naturalism

1. *The Nature of Naturalism*

What *is* naturalism? Earlier in the book I referred to it as the thesis that there is nothing beyond the world of nature. This interpretation has many adherents in the literature. According to Sterling P. Lamprecht, for example, naturalism "regards everything that exists or occurs to be conditioned in its existence or occurrence by causal factors within one all-encompassing system of nature."[1] And as John Herman Randall, Jr., nicely puts it: "[Naturalism] can be defined negatively as the refusal to take 'nature' or 'the natural' as a term of distinction."[2]

But this is rather vague. Spinoza would have accepted the stance referred to by Lamprecht and Randall, while (as we saw in Chapter 2) giving it a religious twist—Nature, not just nature. And if there is anything that is evident, it is that we are looking for a view incapable of being religiously twisted. It is at this point that one tends to hear references to *science*. As Richard Fumerton puts it, a natural property is "a property with which science feels comfortable."[3] This is echoed by many other writers, old and new. Roy Wood Sellars, for example, writes that naturalism is "the view of

---

[1] Sterling P. Lamprecht, *The Metaphysics of Naturalism* (New York: Appleton-Century-Crofts, 1967), p. 160.
[2] John Herman Randall, Jr., "Epilogue: The Nature of Naturalism," in *Naturalism and the Human Spirit,* ed. Yervant H. Krikorian (New York: Columbia University Press, 1944), p. 357.
[3] Richard Fumerton, "Skepticism and Naturalistic Epistemology," *Midwest Studies in Philosophy, Vol. XIX: Philosophical Naturalism,* ed. Peter A. French, Theodore E. Uehling, Jr., and Howard K. Wettstein (Notre Dame, Ind.: University of Notre Dame Press, 1994), p. 321.

133

the world which founds itself upon the results of science."[4] And according to Hilary Kornblith, "the task of the naturalistic metaphysician . . . is simply to draw out the metaphysical implications of contemporary science."[5]

But this is still rather vague. Does what we are talking about now coincide with old-fashioned materialism and its claim that everything is or is reducible to *matter* (whatever that is)? This certainly seems to be something that someone whose metaphysical leanings are dictated by science might say. Is the claim instead that everything is or is reducible to the *physical* (again, whatever that is)? And how might these notions be related? If, as has been suggested, the objects or methods of natural science are to be taken as in some way providing a guide to the boundaries of what is material or what is physical or what is natural, or, more generally, to the nature of naturalism, do we mean *actual* science or *ideal* science, whatever the latter may turn out to be? And if ideal, how are we ever to make this standard usable?

These are just some of the questions that emerge when we try to settle on a more precise understanding of what the claim of naturalism amounts to. As Jeffrey C. King puts it, "if you ask *n* philosophers what naturalism is, you receive *at least n* different answers."[6] Indeed, given the multiple layers and slippery concepts to be found in what those say who apply this label to themselves, one can these days even write a fairly plausible treatise premised on the view that naturalism is not a thesis or claim at all but rather a scientifically oriented "program" of some sort![7] However, for our purposes it would be useful to find in this tangle a claim—and I suggest that, all things considered, this should be a claim satisfying the following four conditions: (1) a popular metaphysical claim that is (2) rooted in contemporary science and (3) incompatible with any religious claim while also (4) the weakest claim (weakest in terms of how *much* it claims) that satisfies the previous three conditions. (The fourth condition is included so

---

[4] Roy Wood Sellars, *Evolutionary Naturalism* (New York: Russell & Russell, 1922), p. 18.

[5] Hilary Kornblith, "Naturalism: Both Metaphysical and Epistemological," *Midwest Studies in Philosophy, Vol. XIX: Philosophical Naturalism,* p. 40.

[6] Jeffrey C. King, "Can Propositions Be Naturalistically Acceptable?" *Midwest Studies in Philosophy, Vol. XIX: Philosophical Naturalism,* p. 53. Consider also Kornblith, who in "Naturalism" (p. 39) says, "The motivations which attract philosophers to naturalism are many, and the views which arise from those motivations are no less diverse." And this is not a recent discovery. In his 1922 work *Evolutionary Naturalism* Sellars writes (p. i): "We are all naturalists now. But, even so, this common naturalism is of a very vague and general sort, capable of covering an immense diversity of opinion."

[7] As has Michael C. Rea. See his *World without Design: The Ontological Consequences of Naturalism* (Oxford: Clarendon Press, 2002). After all, even Sellars, while calling naturalism a view, is driven to say that naturalism is "an admission of a direction more than a clearly formulated belief" (*Evolutionary Naturalism,* p. i).

that we do not run the risk, in our criticisms, of simply prompting a scaled-back and more plausible formulation of naturalism, which is immune to our criticisms but still incompatible with ultimism.) Though the problem of unclarity we have found already reveals a sort of preemptive answer to naturalism, which advises it to get its house in order (we need more investigation not only into the large disjunction of ignored religious possibilities but also into the large disjunction of possible interpretations of naturalism), let us not be deterred by this problem but rather seek an understanding that satisfies the above desiderata. After all, if what those who might question religious skepticism on naturalistic grounds tend to think has any weight, then we should be able to find a strong challenge to religion in this vicinity fairly swiftly, without entering too far into the tangle of debated possibilities.

A good candidate for such an understanding is to be found in Paul Draper's recent article "God, Science, and Naturalism."[8] Draper's account is developed with sensitivity to the history of relevant discussion in both science and philosophy. Since his aim is to arrive at the most plausible formulation of naturalism, Draper also seeks to avoid incorporating unnecessary or extraneous claims into his interpretation of it. So let us consider what he has to say.

According to Draper, the *non*-natural should be distinguished from the *super*natural. He defines the natural as including what is physical in the narrow but also fairly common sense of what is directly studied by contemporary physical science (e.g., atoms and gravitational fields), together with whatever is physically composed (a bacterium is his example here) or caused (here many would mention conscious states)—that is, whatever is *ontologically or causally reducible* to physical entities. The non-natural therefore turns out to be that which is neither physical in his narrow sense nor ontologically or causally reducible to the physical. But the *super*natural is given the crucial extra property of *causally affecting* nature: it is of course non-natural but also interacts causally with natural entities (Draper's example of a supernatural item is a Cartesian soul), unlike other non-natural entities one might believe in, such as propositions or the number 2. Naturalism is then defined *negatively* as the claim that *there are no supernatural entities.*

This appears to be a useful formulation since it articulates a popular sentiment among academics, one ruling out (as surely any naturalist would

---

[8] In William Wainwright, ed., *Oxford Handbook of Philosophy of Religion* (Oxford: Oxford University Press, 2004). See also Draper, "Seeking but Not Believing: Confessions of a Practicing Agnostic," in *Divine Hiddenness: New Essays*, ed. Daniel Howard-Snyder and Paul K. Moser (Cambridge: Cambridge University Press, 2002). The arguments defending the relatively high prior probability of naturalism that are discussed in the early going of the next section are based on arguments found in Draper's work.

want to do) non-natural causation affecting the natural world and with that apparently any religious claim—an ultimate and *salvific* reality would presumably have to causally affect that in us which is part of nature, even if only through a part of *ourselves* that was supernatural, such as a nonphysical soul. And it manages all this without ruling out non-natural entities that do *not* causally affect the natural, such as (on a common construal) abstract objects, thus avoiding a possibly controversial commitment for the naturalist. Naturalism, so defined, also appears to be easier to support with such arguments from the success of science as are standardly utilized by naturalists in defense of their claim than a wholesale denial of the non-natural would be. And though clearly tied in its definition of the physical to such entities as are identified by modern physical science, it is able to accommodate very different entities so long as they are ontologically or causally *traceable* to the former. (Hence the compatibility of naturalism as Draper construes it with dual-aspect theory in the philosophy of mind.)

Now it may be thought that Draper's narrow understanding of "physical" is *overly* narrow and, in particular, contrary to our ordinary use of the term. After all, as he himself admits, his interpretation separates the physical from the biological, and surely the latter would be thought by all of us to belong to the physical realm. But the idea here is to start with what is most venerable and most influential in modern science, and to allow for other things insofar as they bear an appropriate relation to that, either ontologically or causally. Notice that with the latter concession, we permit into the realm of the natural everything that on other, perhaps more common, uses of the term would count as physical, and so no real harm is done—popular sentiments are not finally contravened but simply relocated. A related and more serious problem with Draper's definition, also recognized by him, is that it appears to assume that there will be no development *beyond* contemporary science, no revolutions casting into doubt all or much of what it has to say about the physical realm. But here we must remember that naturalists who challenge religion (and, indirectly, religious skepticism) typically have a very high degree of confidence in the results of today's scientific theories. So it is perhaps not inappropriate to define their view accordingly. Having said that, let me also indicate that after discussing the prospects of naturalism on this construal of it, I will briefly entertain certain revised understandings by which it might be replaced, relating them to our discussion.

2. Arguments for Naturalism

What, then, *are* the prospects of naturalism, as we are conceiving it? Is there a forceful case here against religious skepticism that we have so far overlooked or neglected, or will closer attention only allow us more decisively to block the support for a denial of ultimism that support for naturalism represents?

"There are no supernatural entities." This, we said, is how naturalism may be formulated. And it is no coincidence or matter of indifference that what we see here is a negative claim. Rather, in the hands of the naturalist or the defender of naturalism such a formulation is purposeful, designed to give the naturalist an edge going into the debate. For, so the naturalist will say, by only *denying* the existence of a *specific sort of entity,* she does not claim very much, and this should contribute to our readiness to grant her claim a higher intrinsic probability—and thus a higher *prior* probability— than supernaturalism, which makes a positive existential claim.

But apart from the murkiness of the probability terrain into which she is here venturing, we should draw the attention of the naturalist to the fact that her "specific sort of entity" really breaks down into a *disjunction* of possibilities: a disjunction of possibilities that may—as discussion in previous chapters confirms—be huge. (Naturalism is not simply denying the existence of the entity put forward by *theism,* as is often casually assumed.) Reading each possibility as a positive claim, we may say that naturalism denies the disjunction while supernaturalism affirms it. Naturalism says that *none* of the claims incompatible with only natural causes affecting nature is true; supernaturalism says that *one* of them is. Presented more graphically: where the relevant disjunction is "Either $p1$ or $p2$ or $p3$ . . . or pn," supernaturalism says that *one* of the disjuncts is true whereas naturalism denies them all, thus affirming "It is not the case that $p1$ and it is not the case that $p2$ and it is not the case that $p3$ . . . and it is not the case that pn." A close look at this assertion may be sufficient to remove our readiness to say that naturalism "is not claiming very much."[9]

But the naturalist may develop her point in another way, one more explicitly connected to the notion centrally at work here, namely, that of *simplicity.* We get a simpler and thus intrinsically more *probable* hypothesis, she may say, by supposing there to be *only one type of cause* at work in nature than if, as with (at any rate any sensible, nonidealist) supernaturalism, we suppose there to be two.

Now the bearing of simplicity on probability is also controversial. But quite apart from this, we may observe that this argument, as it stands, is

[9] An inclination to say that the disjunction in question is huge might for some derive from the fact that it has to include not just religious possibilities and other possibilities standardly viewed as supernaturalist but also all those many possibilities presupposing *alternative construals of nature.* I do not want my point here to rest on that. Even if we subtract the latter set of possibilities, a huge number of disjuncts may remain, stemming from all the different ways in which what would be supernatural on *any* relevant understanding of nature might be realized.

no more than a piece of sophistry. It counts on our neglecting to remember that *two quite distinct sorts of phenomena* are covered by that one word "nature": both physical entities *and* entities ontologically distinct from but causally reducible to the physical, if such there be. It is strategically important for the naturalist to countenance both of these, as we have seen in connection with the diversity of views about our mental life. But then, assuming that both might have causal powers, there may be two irreducibly distinct forms of causation within the one world of nature, even if naturalism is true. Now when we consider the disjuncts composing the disjunction that is supernaturalism, what we often see is that they detach the mental both ontologically and causally from the physical, claiming in one way or another that the mental is active in nature without being in any way reducible to it. (Traditional theism would be an example of such a disjunct.) Reading natural causation as one type of causation, we would have to say that according to any such supernaturalist disjunct there are two types of causation in nature, both natural and non-natural. But remembering that two forms of causation are allowed *within* our concept of nature, we will also see that this does not make such a disjunct less simple than naturalism. Seeing further that the truth of any such supernaturalist disjunct would be a sufficient condition for the truth of supernaturalism (only one disjunct need be true for the disjunction to be true), we will rightly conclude that there is nothing here to show that *supernaturalism* is any less simple than naturalism.

But the naturalist has another argument waiting in the wings. The denial of a particular existential claim, so she may say, is intrinsically *more* probable than the claim that *nothing* exists, while such an existential claim (in this case, supernaturalism) is intrinsically *less* probable than the claim that *something* exists; so assuming that the intrinsic probability of the claim that nothing exists is roughly equivalent to that of the claim that something exists, naturalism must have a higher prior probability than supernaturalism (or any claim entailing supernaturalism, such as ultimism).

Draper is inclined to say, because of the possibility of arguments like this one, that it is "far from clear" that naturalism is not ahead of the competition going into this game;[10] but it is equally far from clear that it *is* ahead. For one thing, it is time to observe that while her purely negative "There are no supernatural entities" may not entail it, there is a *positive* claim in the neighborhood to which any naturalist is also committed. Defining "exclusively natural world" as "world including our universe in which all causation is natural causation," we may put this as follows: an exclusively

[10] "Seeking but Not Believing," pp. 207, 213 n. 17.

natural world exists. (This claim the naturalist may not call by the name of naturalism, or incorporate into what she does call by that name, but just watch her try to get by without it!) And, given this definition, we can also see that the supernaturalist could easily give her claim a *negative* formulation: there is no exclusively natural world. So it is hard to see why we should think any especially impressive argumentative benefit or deficit to follow from the fact that the naturalist's claim can be formulated negatively and the supernaturalist's positively, even if we accept the assumption that the intrinsic probability of the claim that nothing exists is equal to that of the claim that something exists.

More important, though, is the fact that that assumption is, to say the least, highly questionable. Why should we suppose the existence of something and the existence of nothing to be equally probable prior to considering any evidence? When the proper understanding of *probability* is, notoriously, still being debated, and when other less fundamental probabilities, such as the probability of theism on a certain piece of evidence relative to the probability of atheism on another, are very difficult to determine, it seems optimistic in the extreme to suppose that something as abstract and abstruse as the intrinsic probability of there being nothing relative to that of there being something should be within our grasp.

But we can offer another point here as well. Think of the claim that the concept of a perfect and thus necessarily existing reality is exemplified in every possible world. Given standard moves discussed in connection with the ontological argument (and using the possibility terminology as indicated in Chapter 1), if this is so much as logically possible, then it is true. But if it is true, then it is *logically impossible for there to be nothing*. Now even if we are not prepared to grant that the proposition in question *is* logically possible and thus true, it does seem epistemically possible that it is. But then it is epistemically possible that it is logically *impossible* that there should be nothing at all. And in these circumstances any confidence we might have had as to the existence of nothing being as intrinsically probable as the existence of something must surely be removed.

On the basis of such points, then, I would suggest that there is no justification for believing that naturalism's prior probability is higher than that of supernaturalism; and so the tantalizing prospect of a quick head start for naturalism may quickly be put to rest.

This represents an obstacle for many *other* arguments for naturalism that might be advanced: without knowing where we start, probability-wise, it may also be difficult to tell where we end up when the relevant evidence has been assessed. But, for now, let us suppose for the sake of argument that naturalism and supernaturalism start out even—that is, equally probable. In that case, the availability of evidence strongly favoring naturalism would at least have a *better* chance of forcing the conclusion that naturalism is, overall, very probable. Is such evidence available?

In this connection defenders of naturalism will speak with one voice: *the success of science,* they will say, provides strong evidence for the truth of their view. What they appear to be referring to here is that scientific theories have successfully *explained* so very much that goes on in our world. Barbara Forrest, whose view is typical in this connection, suggests that because of this explanatory success of science there is an "asymptotic decrease in the existential possibility of the supernatural to the point at which it is wholly negligible." Because of science's success in explaining how things go purely in terms of natural causes, we have reason to think that no non-natural entities causally affect nature. As we might put it, the explanatory success of science is itself explained at the philosophical level in terms of the truth of naturalism. As Forrest puts it, naturalism is "a generalization of the cumulative results of scientific inquiry."[11]

Before assessing this argument, let me make two quick points about it to forestall certain easy misinterpretations to which its advocates and its enemies, respectively, are susceptible. The first point is this. Any such argument can gain specious support from the ambiguity of that phrase "success of science": the latter phrase may bring to mind science's *predictive and technological prowess* instead of or in addition to science's alleged capacity to explain why things happen as they do in the world, which is the only relevant "success" here. (The mistake I have in mind is suggested by Fumerton when he says that naturalists are inclined to argue as follows: "Whatever they are doing, scientists are doing it effectively. The terms they employ in their scientific reasoning must unproblematically refer to kinds of things that really exist.")[12] Although it might be thought that predictive and technological prowess and explanatory prowess go hand in hand, that is hardly a foregone conclusion given the disputes in philosophy of science over whether science is slowly enlarging our store of truths about the world or should perhaps be understood in a nonrealist way. A scientific

---

[11] Barbara Forrest, "Methodological Naturalism and Philosophical Naturalism: Clarifying the Connection," *Philo* 3 (2000), 25. A slightly different point, though still about the power of science, is made by Kornblith ("Naturalism," p. 40): "A metaphysic which goes beyond the commitments of science is simply unsupported by the best available evidence. . . . For the naturalist there is simply no extrascientific route to metaphysical understanding." But to get an argument for naturalistic belief out of this, one would have to assume not only that science provides the best available evidence for metaphysicians to use (which in this context could be deemed question-begging), but also—implausibly—that *some metaphysic or other must be developed by us* (that suspense of judgment on metaphysical matters is not an option) and that, if we develop and utilize a metaphysic, we must also *believe* it (that beliefless acceptance is not an option).

[12] Fumerton, "Skepticism," p. 322.

nonrealist—for example, an instrumentalist—will accept science's great success in generating predictions that actually come off, which we can exploit to achieve our ends. But he will deny that science has successfully *explained* anything going on in the world. And whether nonrealism is correct or not, its assumption that science can be successful in the one way even if not in the other is surely correct. False statements can have true implications, and in a similar way science's theories, even if not literally true, might still generate predictions that are fulfilled. So we must be careful not to obscure the issue by focusing uncritically on science's predictive success and technological innovations: the question here is whether science is successful in the sense of *successfully telling us why things happen as they do.* Are scientific *explanations* generally *true?*

Now for the second point. The form of the argument from science's explanatory success seems sometimes to be missed by religious opponents of naturalism, who think that, because there may be non-natural entities that slip through the net of science, any argument from the explanatory success of science is really irrelevant to the defense of naturalism, revealing at most science's ability to handle the natural realm and leaving the supernatural untouched.[13] The point the naturalist can be seen as trying to make, however, is that in "handling the natural realm" science provides us with strong grounds for concluding that *only natural causes operate in the universe,* and so any non-natural entities that slip through its net would also have to be *causally impotent,* or at least causally isolated from us; whereas things must be otherwise—at least some of what happens to *us* must have *non*-natural causes—if supernaturalist claims are true. Again, supernaturalism requires not just the non-natural but the causal influence on us of the non-natural. This suggests that the argument from the explanatory success of science is at least relevant.

Is it more than that? I myself think the argument is highly overrated. Science's being explanatorily successful—the obtaining of the datum from which the truth of naturalism is here inferred—depends on all or most currently accepted scientific theories being *true.* (If they are not true, why should we suppose ourselves able to learn anything from them about what sorts of causes operate in the universe?) But there is good reason to be in doubt over whether this is the case. Here we are returned to a discussion touched on in Chapter 1 and in Chapter 4, concerning the rather poor performance of *past* scientific theories. We saw there how Newton-Smith speaks of a "pessimistic induction" based on that performance as yielding the conclusion that all currently accepted theories will turn out

---

[13] Huston Smith suggests such a move in many places, for example, in *Why Religion Matters* (New York: HarperCollins, 2001).

to be *false* within two hundred years or so. And similar points are made by many respected writers in philosophy of science. Consider, for example, Brian Skyrms:

> When we look back over the history of science we see a pattern of laws being confirmed and accepted, serving well for a time, but eventually breaking down when confronted with new domains of experiment and observation and finally being superseded and replaced by more adequate laws. . . . Accordingly, when we accept a law now, we do so with the expectation that it will eventually be superseded, that we will eventually uncover a domain of experiment and observation where there are counterinstances to it. . . . [But if] we believe that there *are* counterinstances to the law, whether they have been discovered yet or not, we must believe that the law is false! . . . In fact, I think that we are living in such a time now. Near the end of the nineteenth century, most scientists may have believed that truth had been attained. But at present most physicists regard even our best scientific theories as transitional.[14]

In response to this it may be tempting to protest that crucial facts are being ignored. Aren't many scientific theories of the past now regarded as facts that new theories must accommodate? And don't many scientific theories that have been supplanted by new theories remain correct within a restricted domain (e.g., Galileo's law is still roughly correct for freely falling bodies near the surface of the earth). But then the alleged inductive evidence for the falsity of our current scientific theories falls apart when the total available evidence is considered.[15]

I would suggest that these facts concerning the history and development of science fail to block the force of the sort of argument Skyrms is developing when the general and modest nature of its central claim is properly appreciated. Here is Skyrms again:

> The generalization about the history of science with which I started is not very controversial. Simply put, it is this: "Time after time we had a law or theory that worked very well, and then new considerations led us to believe that it was wrong." This modest observation in no way depends on radical skepticism regarding comparability of scientific theories and progress in science. It is quite consistent with

---

[14] Brian Skyrms, *Causal Necessity* (New Haven, Conn.: Yale University Press, 1980), pp. 37–39.

[15] Draper has pressed such points in correspondence.

a belief in the principle of correspondence, with the view that there *is* progress in science and that the old rejected theory is regarded from the vantage point of the new as a reasonable approximation within some limited domain (but note that it may be *wildly* inaccurate outside that domain). The historical claim is there solely to persuade you that it is reasonable, when we accept a law now, to accept it with the expectation that it will eventually be superseded.[16]

Especially in the context of observations of the sort put forward in Chapters 1 and 4, Skyrms's point may seem mild indeed. I suggest that information about our limitations as finite subjects, which so commonly obscure from us vital considerations bearing on claims supported by our present evidence, and about the incredibly long way science, like other areas of human inquiry, may yet have to go, *together with* Skyrms's modest historical observation, should at the very least put us in doubt as to whether all or most of today's scientific theories are true. But then it is the evidence utilized by the argument from the explanatory success of science for naturalism that falls apart when the total available evidence is considered.

There are other problems for this argument too. One is that even if all current scientific theories *are* true, we should be tempted to explain this fact in terms of naturalism only if we have reason to think that those theories and their subject matter are, as I will say, *comprehensive*—that no phenomena of experience fall *outside* their range. Otherwise, for all we know, along with the truth of current scientific theories and scientific success in *this* respect, we will someday be forced to accept the existence of facts for which only a supernatural account will do—for example, maybe we will need to postulate non-natural causation of one sort or another to account for the facts (whatever they are; no one today knows) associated with consciousness or intentional action—and in that case we cannot *now* demand an explanation of the explanatory success of science in naturalistic terms. But, as my examples here already suggest, there are some difficulties in the way of supposing that scientific theories *are* comprehensive. At the very least, there is reason for doubt on this score.

It is interesting that phenomena involving consciousness should represent one of the difficult areas for science in its attempt to offer a truly comprehensive account of nature, given that religious effects, of an experiential and transformational nature, are supposed to occur in the "inward parts." It is not as though the only sort of effect that could be associated with non-natural causation is the more obvious or "surface" sort of effect exemplified by the fact that things outdoors appear in a variety of bright

---

[16] Skyrms, *Causal Necessity*, p. 38.

colors on a warm summer's day. Suppose that, given the relevant definitions, the miraculous appearance of such colors were the only possible
sign of a supernatural reality. Then a decisive disproof of supernaturalism would be generated by science's physical explanation of colors. But
things are rather different. A sensitive religious supernaturalism, in particular, will settle precisely where contemporary science cannot reach—and
this not to *escape* its reach but because that is where sensitive religiosity
has always settled. And (enlisting Blake) if the doors of perception were
cleansed, perhaps we would see much more that scientific accounts are
incapable of touching. We in the modern world tend to be completely
preoccupied with things that can be provided with natural causes. In our
finite way, this has become "everything." Perhaps it really *is* everything;
but, equally, perhaps we are simply in a phase where we are draining dry
the scientific approach, seeing nature only from the peculiar slant our
preoccupation affords.

A third problem for the argument from the explanatory success of science should also be noted. As we have seen, that argument centers on
an explanation of science's alleged explanatory success given in terms of
naturalism—which is to say given in terms of only natural causes affecting nature. But how, really, is this arrived at? To see how more clearly
and without the distraction of details, let us take the naturalist's best-case
scenario, in which she can straightforwardly be assured of both the truth
and comprehensiveness of current scientific theories. This would suggest
more strongly, and indeed entail, what naturalists will take to be suggested
by the evidence even in less favorable circumstances. And what is that?
Well, surely, that *all the phenomena of experience have natural causes.* And now
an important move is made: because all such phenomena have natural
causes, *non-natural ones are excluded;* and so we form the hypothesis that *no
non-natural causes affect nature,* which is to say that there are no supernatural entities or that naturalism is true.

This, I suggest, reveals how the naturalist arguing from the explanatory
success of science will most naturally arrive at her position, but the central
move here is fatally flawed. For the inference from "All the phenomena
of experience have natural causes" to "Non-natural causes are excluded"
is fallacious. To make the latter proposition follow in the manner apparently intended here we would have to read the former as "All the causes of
phenomena of experience are natural." But this introduces content not
at all entailed by the former proposition. It is quite compatible with the
truth of that proposition—that is, with all such phenomena having natural
causes—that there be, in some case where a true natural explanation has
been produced, yet *deeper* causal factors or causal factors *further back* in the
causal web that affect us but are non-natural—think here, for example, of

the traditional theist's God or David Bohm's "implicate order."[17] To support the view that "non-natural causes are excluded" in the stronger sense of "*wherever* causes are at work in a manner affecting us, those causes are natural causes," which is what the naturalist requires, she would need to be in a position to say more than just that all the phenomena of experience have natural causes, namely, the causes referred to by current scientific theories; she would also need to be able to say that all those phenomena have *only* natural causes—that current scientific theories *explain everything natural as deeply as explanation goes*. And this is far from obvious. For one thing, to say this with any confidence the naturalist would first have to defeat independent attempts to prove the presence or epistemic possibility of such deeper supernatural factors as are mentioned above, and this is just what her argument was supposed to allow her to avoid. And when that other discussion is entered into, it is rather easy to arrive at doubt, especially when the range of supernaturalist possibilities we may not yet have encountered is brought into play. Since the way to her hypothesis is thus blocked, we may say that even if current scientific theories are true *and also comprehensive* in the above sense, the naturalist has no justification for her naturalism.

Suppose, however, that an attempt to explain the availability of true and comprehensive scientific theories in terms of the truth of naturalism can be legitimate even without independent evidence that there are no deeper supernatural causal factors of the sort mentioned above, perhaps because some other route to this hypothesis can be found—say, one appealing to the relative simplicity (in some sense other than the one earlier entertained) of the hypothesis that only natural causes are to be found affecting nature. Now we must notice a fourth problem: that the naturalist owes us an assessment that leads to the elimination of specific *alternative* explanations of science's power, ones consistent with the *denial* of naturalism. And here again, though in a slightly different way, we bump into the possibly huge disjunction that the denial of naturalism amounts to—all the different ways in which supernaturalism might be true. Draper discusses one of them, the one represented by traditional theism, and argues that the probability that naturalism should be true given the explanatory success of science is higher than the corresponding probability for theism (while also inclined to hold that when independent factors are introduced, no clear case for naturalism can be made out).[18] However that may be—Draper's probability assignments are controversial—it seems clear that the

---

[17] See David Bohm, *Wholeness and the Implicate Order* (New York: Routledge, 1983).

[18] Draper, "God, Science, and Naturalism," esp. pp. 38–39.

naturalist needs to identify *other* detailed supernatural hypotheses as well and determine how probable the explanatory success of science is on *them*. But how can she be sure she has completed this task when it is possible to argue, in the manner of Chapters 1 and 4, that many such alternatives may be undiscovered or even undiscoverable? Of course this is all very bothersome. Intellectual greed might lead us to be impatient with the demands of investigation as time-consuming as that recommended here and also in the previous paragraph: we would like to have an understanding of the world about which we may be confident in our own lifetime. However, if our concern is not just for *an* understanding but for *understanding,* then we will resist the temptation to foreclose such investigation.

I suggest, therefore, that the argument for naturalism from the explanatory success of science faces overwhelming difficulties, which make it *undeservedly* popular. Summarizing in reverse order: even if the reasoning that provokes the naturalistic hypothesis is not fatally flawed, we are not in a position to rule out *alternatives* to the hypothesis that need to be ruled out; and it seems that it *is* fatally flawed because the inference from "All the phenomena of experience have natural causes" to "Non-natural causes are excluded" is fallacious. Furthermore, it may be that scientific theories are *not comprehensive* in a sense in which they would need clearly to be comprehensive if the hypothesis of naturalism is to suggest itself at all persuasively. Moreover, it appears that many scientific theories currently on offer may not be so much as *true*. And, finally, it may be added that we do not really even know how probable naturalism is by comparison with its (disjunctively expressible) denial *before* any of this evidence from the alleged explanatory success of science is introduced, and so would not be in a position to render a judgment as to how likely that evidence makes naturalism by comparison with supernaturalism *even if it were good evidence.* In the face of these problems and the reasons I have given for supposing them to be unresolved and perhaps unresolvable, it appears quite evident that the argument in question does not justify the belief that naturalism is true.

Now earlier we saw that what exactly a naturalist means by the phrase "the success of science" can vary. Is there any *other* way of understanding it that might seem to lend itself to an argument for naturalism? I think there is. For one may think of the success of science not just in absolute terms but also relatively or comparatively: specifically, the naturalist may think—and I suspect many naturalists do think—that science has been *more* successful than has any *non*scientific source of explanations (in particular, religion) at making sense of certain significant events of human experience and orienting us in everyday life. Scientific explanations have displaced the formerly regnant religious explanations of such things as storms, earthquakes, comets, and physical and mental diseases, and nowadays we all trust science to tell us how to handle the practical problems with which we are presented by these and other phenomena. Notice that this point is not just comparative instead of absolute; it is also *narrower* than the claim we were earlier examining, for it suggests not that all or most scientific theories are true but only that certain scientific explanations specially impinging on human experience (perhaps ones belonging to the "restricted domains" in which even older theories still count as correct) are preferable to nonscientific alternatives. And many a naturalist will take this more qualified explanatory success of science—call it the *comparative and orientational* explanatory success of science—as providing a good reason to accept naturalism instead of supernaturalism.[19]

But why should the situation be viewed thus? Surely an assumption being made in this argument is that if supernaturalism were true, one or other of the ways in which it has manifested itself in human history would have generated explanations of such phenomena as have been mentioned, rendering scientific explanations of them unnecessary or mistaken, and thus would have generated indispensable resources for physically negotiating our way through our environment. Somehow it is supposed to be supernaturalism's *job* to do this, or one of its jobs. But why accept this assumption? Indeed, is it not clearly false? Especially given our results in the first part of the book, it can fairly be said that what we have here is a lamentably limited and undeveloped understanding of supernaturalism and in particular of religion, which links the latter and any sign of the latter's unique causal contribution to nature solely to something like a miracle-working God or gods. Alternative forms of religiosity and alternative construals of the Divine in nature are not so much as recognized. Naturalists who find arguments like the one we have here appealing will be inclined to look for evidence of the supernatural in some startling event—stars forming themselves into words?—that resists any and all scientific forms of explanation, instead of realizing, as indicated earlier, that the causal influence of a truly ultimate and salvific reality might be expected in our "inward parts" or in depths of reality *supporting* nature, where no current scientific theory and perhaps no scientific theory at all can expect to set foot.

This sort of move will, I am sure, strike some naturalists as an evasion. It may seem that my suggestion is dishonest, replacing what *really* belongs to religion with some warmed-over and elusive alternative. Why doesn't religion come right out into the open and show itself for what it is? But

---

[19] Compare Kornblith, "Naturalism," p. 40: "[Theories postulating] occult entities are poor rivals for scientific theories; they are useless, or worse, in prediction, explanation, and technological application."

I suggest that what we see in such a response—in addition, possibly, to a nonrational preference for what is tangible and "out in the open"—is how naturalists tend to be overly influenced by the least mature forms of religion, which in their doctrinal manifestations can be spiritually unimaginative and psychologically naive. If this is all one has encountered, then one may indeed think that the truth of supernaturalism requires there to be non-natural causes for the phenomena of everyday life—droughts, earthquakes, sunny days, the loss or discovery of one's keys, and so on. But what goes unnoticed is that the alleged warmed-over alternative is represented too in the history of religion (though admittedly more rarely than others), through the ideas of mystics and communitarians and other spiritually sensitive types, whose spirit is in fact often the *originating* spirit of a religious movement but equally often suffers the fate of being turned into a stone-cold corpse by later "adherents." And there is neglect also of the fact that we need to be thinking not just about what religion has been but also about what it *might* be. (Would we insist that *science* be understood purely in terms of the forms it took in the Middle Ages?) There is no reason to suppose that any enlightened critique of religion should function under similar restrictions to those found here—indeed, quite the contrary. Thus the argument from the comparative and orientational explanatory success of science also fails to justify the belief that naturalism is true.[20]

There is at least one more way in which "the success of science" can be construed, leading to an independent argument for naturalism. Call this the comparative *methodological* success of science. Instead of focusing on the explanatory results of science, the naturalist here draws our attention to its *methods* and, in particular, to what would appear to be their vastly superior quality and effectiveness, in connection with not only the aforementioned explanatory results but also the technological innovations earlier mentioned. Scientists, she may say, have highly refined and sophisticated techniques for pursuing human goals, which are sensitive to the most subtle alterations in sensory experience (take, for example, various measuring instruments they have devised) and capable of fulfilling very difficult tasks (for example, in the application of medical technology) with exact precision. What do advocates of the various supernaturalisms

---

[20] It is interesting to see how even the most sophisticated naturalists may exemplify a limiting preoccupation with crude forms of religion, and this even when seeking to generate natural explanations of religion. See, for example, Steven Pinker, "The Evolutionary Psychology of Religion," presented at the 2004 annual meeting of the Freedom from Religion Foundation, available at http://pinker.wjh.harvard.edu/articles/media/2004_10_29_religion.htm.

have to lay alongside this? Nothing of significance. And yet, surely, if there were anything to supernaturalism, things would be otherwise.

Now the naturalist we are dealing with here need not be as religiously insensitive as the one associated with the previous argument. She may recognize that the goals pursued in religion are quite other than the goals of science, and admit that we would not expect to find similar forms of technology there. But she will nonetheless say that we should expect to find *comparably effective* techniques and goal-related processes in the religious camp. Suppose that experience of the Ultimate and some sort of personal transformation are, as I have suggested, among the goals of the religious. Why, if there is anything to religion, are the means of achieving these goals not more impressive? While it may be replied that the Ultimate is free to be revealed or concealed, and also that human wickedness is great, this seems weak and evasive, and only casts into bold relief one of the problems here: that there is much confusion among the religious over exactly how goals related to the supernatural are to be understood and over what may further or frustrate them. Some construe the Ultimate in personal terms and so as capable of intentionally withdrawing; others not. Some think wickedness stands in the way of transformation; others ignorance, or something else again. And no one has such clear success in achieving religious goals pursuing their own methods—none of the religious seem to be much distinguished from the nonreligious in respect of moral character, for example—that the others are strongly drawn to them and to the further development of those methods. Altogether the disanalogy with science is striking and cannot fail to lead us to reject the supernatural on methodological grounds alone.[21]

I have spent some time developing this line of reasoning because I think it represents thoughts that are, as we say, "out there" in the public consciousness and thus need to be addressed. But it will not take long to show that this argument, like its predecessors, is lacking in force. The critical assumption is clearly that, if there were anything to supernaturalism, and in particular religion, religious methods of achieving religious goals as powerful as methods we see in science *would already have been developed.*[22]

---

[21] Hints of such arguments are to be found in Daniel Dennett, *Breaking the Spell: Religion as a Natural Phenomenon* (New York: Penguin, 2006) and also in Kai Nielsen, *Naturalism and Religion* (Amherst, N.Y.: Prometheus Books, 2001).

[22] I will focus on this assumption, but another problem is that the argument, contrary to my suggestion in developing it, may depend on an appropriate sort of link between recent technological sophistication and scientific truth. As we saw earlier, that there is such a link in the scientific case is contestable.

Setting aside worries about how connections between the object of religion and the difficulty of developing a "religious technology" might have been pressed more convincingly, we may answer this assumption by reference to the results of Chapter 3, where we saw how various factors have contrived to keep religious forms of investigation at a much more primitive stage of development than scientific ones. It is only when more of the right kinds of efforts toward rectifying this state of affairs have been made that we will be in a position to judge the methodological power of religion. Again, to judge it now would be like assessing the potential of science based on what had been achieved, scientifically, by the Middle Ages. It could be—just for example—that one of the things that will come with time is clearer and more universal and less conflicting instances of religious experience, which lead to clearer and more universal and more distinctive sorts of character development. If such were to occur, then supernaturalism might be better supported—or, at least, it would not be liable to *this* objection. Thus any rejection of religion on methodological grounds is at best premature.

As we have seen, the argument just discussed and also its predecessors are quite weak. A question that may occur to us now is why they are still persuasive to so many. Faulty reasoning in related areas may of course be part of the problem. For example, a distaste for fuzzy and wishful thinking and authoritarian ideas, conjoined with the mistaken assumption that extant religious (perhaps, more narrowly, theistic) views apparently involving such thinking and ideas are the only relevant religious alternatives, could predispose one to accept such arguments. One might also unthinkingly generalize from the fact that what one has encountered has so often turned out to have a natural cause to the conclusion not just that the *next* events *of those kinds* one encounters may be *expected* to have natural causes as well but that all events whatever actually and exclusively *do*.

But here I think we need also to notice some possible causes that are not reasons, which a *social* science of the future may make more clear. In connection with the last point of the previous paragraph there arises the possibility that our deep familiarity with natural causes might lead to a kind of intellectual and/or imaginative "shrinkage," in which our conception of what is possible, causally speaking, becomes commensurately restricted and constricted. Also operative might be a desire for control and a fear of heteronomy: this would suffice to make science and technology attractive and religion unattractive, especially where the latter is interpreted exclusively and unimaginatively in terms of a dictatorial personal God. Where the last two arguments we considered are found to flourish, at least part of what is going on might involve another sort of ego-based dynamic. Liable to inferiority feelings, which respond well to signs of accomplishment, and also (and relatedly) to superiority feelings, which may be directed both to our past selves and to earlier stages of human history, human beings are liable to be strongly affected by the advancements of science. Flushed with the success of technology, which has dug us out of so many ignoble holes, we may cast a disparaging glance in the direction of the ignorance of the past, *with which religion can so easily become enmeshed in our thinking.* Our egos may whisper in our ears that "it would be just like us" to fall for something as unworthy of intellectual respect as religion and that we are well rid of it. In circumstances like these, arguments for naturalism as flawed as those we have considered may nonetheless come to have a grip on us.

The moral of the story is that we should beware of falling for tricks of reasoning or of custom or of the ego that may win such results. In particular, when developing a critical assessment of religion we must pay as much attention to its future as to its past, and pay the *right sort* of attention to its past. As we have seen, a very different picture of our situation, religiously speaking, emerges when we do. And then also naturalism, as we have been construing it so far, turns out to be unsupported.[23]

3. *A More Plausible Naturalism?*

At the beginning of this chapter, I suggested that we should pick a formulation of naturalism that would not make us run the risk, in our criticisms, of simply prompting a scaled-back and more plausible formulation of that view, one immune to our criticisms but still incompatible with ultimism. It may now be suggested that by focusing on Draper's formulation we have

---

[23] A different sort of argument against naturalistic belief (where "naturalistic belief" is construed roughly as we have construed it so far) from any I have utilized is Alvin Plantinga's evolutionary argument. (See, for example, James K. Beilby, ed. *Naturalism Defeated? Essays on Plantinga's Evolutionary Argument against Naturalism* [Ithaca: Cornell University Press, 2002].) According to this argument, the evolutionary naturalist—and what science-respecting naturalist will not accept evolution?—has a view that is self-refuting: if evolutionary naturalism is correct, then, because we have no reason to suppose that the truth of the content of a belief matters to unguided natural selection, we have no reason to regard our cognitive faculties as reliable, and so we have no reason to regard *naturalistic belief* (an output of those faculties) as reliable either. One who accepts the religious skepticism defended in this book of course need not be disturbed by this argument. But neither, I suggest, should he endorse it in defense of that skepticism. For if certain arguments in the Preface and in Chapter 8 are correct, then for all of us, including naturalists, the claim that our cognitive faculties are reliable should function not as a vulnerable *result* of inquiry, capable of being *impugned* by inquiry, but more like a *presupposition* of inquiry. Now if one of the theories developed on that presupposition really contradicted it, then, no doubt, we would expect the rational inquirer to revise that theory or—in an extreme case—to give it up. But, as discussion of Plantinga's argument already reveals, it is far from clear that evolutionary naturalism implies the unreliability of our cognitive faculties.

done just that. For immediately on recognizing the shaky and perhaps transitional results of contemporary physical science, we can see that there are problems with defining the physical *in terms of* contemporary physical science. Draper recognizes this. As he puts it:

> One limitation of this definition is that it assumes that the current word of the physical sciences on which lower level entities exist is the last. History has shown that this is a very dangerous assumption. For example, when physics was forced to accommodate electromagnetic phenomena, it could not do so with the repertoire of entities that made up Newton's universe. Thus, radically new entities were posited, specifically electromagnetic fields, which could not be given a mechanical explanation. . . . Similarly, there may be one or more revolutions yet in store for physics, in which case new sorts of entities may be discovered that, because of their nomological and historical connections to atoms, fields, etc., we will want to call physical and natural. . . . If such revolutions will indeed occur, then our definition of nature in reality only captures nature *as currently understood.*[24]

Indeed, given this sort of point and *given Draper's definitions of the relevant terms,* we have a new way of arguing that, for all we know, there are supernatural entities and naturalism is false, for it *follows* from their conjunction that there may well be entities causally active in the universe that are completely non-natural and nonphysical! (After all, here the supernatural must include the natural as defined in the future.) And this certainly is not an attractive position to be in.

But can the naturalist do better, in a manner that ought to be convincing for us? I would suggest that she cannot, for it does not seem that there is any alternative formulation of her view that *both* avoids this problem *and* leaves the naturalist with a religion-excluding view that she and we have good reason to regard as true. Perhaps the most natural alteration to naturalism as we have understood it would be one that takes its cue from the passage just quoted from Draper and redefines the natural realm in terms of entities recognized by contemporary physical science *and/or entities yet to be discovered that, because of their nomological and historical connections to entities recognized by contemporary physical science, we will want to call physical,* together with any entities ontologically or causally reducible to the physical thus understood. The supernatural now includes those entities, if any, which are non-natural by this definition but which causally

---

[24] Draper, "God, Science, and Naturalism," p. 41.

affect nature (and apparently it still includes any religious entity there may be, since, although we are being less definite about the nature of the physical, we know it includes our bodies and our earthly environment and other such things that we are assuming a salvific reality would in some way causally affect). And of course the new naturalism is the claim that the supernatural, thus construed, does not exist.

Why should we suppose *this* claim to be true? Although we have answered one objection to the earlier argument from the explanatory success of science by not tying the physical to what contemporary scientists say it is, we have not exactly cleared the way for a rehabilitation of that argument. Indeed, in answering that objection—really, giving in to it—we have conceded that no such argument can be successful. For now we have to say that we have no idea whether all or most current scientific theories *are* successful in the relevant sense. Perhaps they will be superseded by future theories, perhaps not. (And—so we should add—even if they are not superseded by future theories, it does not follow that they are correct, for there are also various social and political conditions necessary for the development of science, ones that may cease to obtain in the future and whose ceasing to obtain may prevent us from moving further and *discovering* the correct theories.)[25] Thus perhaps current theories are successful, perhaps future theories will be successful, and perhaps we will never have what we want in this regard. A lot of "perhapses"—certainly too many for there to be here any basis for an argument convincingly supporting naturalism.

In this connection we must also note that already developments in science—for example, string theory—suggest that the "physical" entities of the future may be very strange indeed. It may turn out that in certain critical respects longstanding theories of the physical are very wrong. And if we might thus be wrong about *what* the physical is, we might at the same time turn out to be wrong about *what causally affects it,* having missed crucial information about supernatural causes along with the correct understanding of physical ones. I suggest, therefore, that the proposed alteration to "naturalism" does not leave the position that goes by that name in any better shape than it was in before.

Let's try one more alteration, or set of alterations. Perhaps we could frame our understanding of nature quite generally so as to include *all nomic (lawlike) regularities, and anything exhibiting in its behavior nomic (lawlike) regularities, insofar as it does exhibit them.* ("Behavior" should be construed broadly, so as to include origination, where it occurs in accordance with law. And the qualification "insofar . . . " is there to indicate that if

---

[25] See John Horgan, *The End of Science* (New York: Broadway Books, 1996).

something at some times exhibits nomic behavior and at other times not, only at the former times is it to be considered part of nature.)[26] This would seem to avoid the whole mess about what is physical while still connecting us to what, intuitively, is central to the natural. For it appears that the natural must be whatever is (successfully or unsuccessfully) investigated by science as it seeks to chart the regularities that obtain in and around us, as far as these may extend, and thereby to control the behavior of what is subject to them in service of human ends. Of course on this view rather a lot will potentially belong to nature. What would usually be called "supernatural" entities could belong to it, insofar as their behavior is *its* behavior—the outworking of its rules. After all, we with our consciousness and intentionality are commonly thought to be law-governed, so why not gods? Perhaps this is what John Searle, a prominent naturalist, had in mind when he wrote the following: "For us, if it should turn out that God exists, that would have to be a fact of nature like any other. To the four basic forces in the universe—gravity, electromagnetism, weak and strong nuclear forces—we would add a fifth, the divine force. Or more likely, we would see the other forces as forms of the divine force. But it would still be all physics, albeit divine physics. If the supernatural existed, it too would have to be natural."[27]

Now I think that there may remain, on the view I am developing, a niche for the supernatural, and also that the God that Searle refers to would have to belong to it (more on this later), but he is right in suggesting that nothing need prevent many items we would commonly think of as nonphysical or immaterial and so as supernatural from belonging to nature, on a fairly plausible understanding of the latter. They could even causally affect other parts of it, so long as this behavior of theirs was capable of being brought under lawlike regularities. Thus immortal souls also, which we were inclined to exclude from nature before, could belong to it, so long as they functioned according to rules we could seek to discern and manipulate. If there are many universes, they can all belong to nature, as seems intuitively appropriate, insofar as nomic regularities—however odd they may be—rule there as well as here.

---

[26] This may seem too restrictive. Shouldn't we say that items that sometimes display the regularities in question continue to be part of nature when they don't? But this assumes that nature is some sort of "container" that you are either entirely inside or outside, whereas the apparent conceptual connection, mentioned immediately below, between nature and what can at least in principle be studied by science suggests otherwise.

[27] John Searle, *Mind, Language, and Society* (New York: Basic Books, 1998), p. 35.

All these things displaying lawlike behavior may belong to nature on the generous but intuitively attractive picture we are developing. And the *non*-natural, therefore, would have to include whatever is *independent* of law—all non-lawlike behavior and anything whose behavior does *not* exhibit nomic regularities, insofar as it does not do so. Here we might think of abstract objects, if such there be, as well as events that occur purely by chance. Chance events we might want to think of as occurring *in* nature, but they would not *belong* to nature: they would be interlopers. Events destroying natural order or causing chaos might seem non-natural but would not need to be so long as the destruction or chaos were itself explicable in terms of nomic regularities (however, if events created chaos and this had no explanation in terms of order elsewhere, they would count as non-natural, and certainly if the whole of nature suddenly ceased to exist, that would not be an event *within* nature). God presumably would be a non-natural entity on this construal, since, at least as traditionally conceived, not subject to any such thing as nomic regularities or manipulation by those who come to understand them, but rather their free originator—this is where Searle goes wrong in what he says about God. (God's status would still leave open the possibility of science *discovering* God, for it is one thing to discover an entity and another to be capable of manipulating it.) We ourselves could be non-natural in at least one respect, if we possessed free will of a sort incompatible with determinism, while we would remain natural in others.

As for the *super*natural, here we might begin in a familiar fashion by thinking of the supernatural as non-natural but causally affecting nature, which, given our present definitions, yields the following formula: the supernatural is anything that is independent of law but *causally affects what is produced according to law.* However, this might seem too narrow, for it apparently rules out a paradigm of supernatural activity, namely, *violations* of natural law. If violations of natural law occur, what we have is behavior of a type that normally reflects the influence of law occurring without it (e.g., rain out of the blue in response to prayer), or behavior such as is *never* the outcome of the operation of law exhibited by *things* that *are* normally subject in their behavior to law (e.g., the resuscitation of a corpse). But while this might seem to cause trouble, it really doesn't. For if such things occur, there will be a ripple effect within the realm of the natural (rain in response to prayer may fall on crops whose rate of yield is improved because of the operation of laws, and the resuscitated corpse may eat a meal that is processed in accordance with the same), and so the supernatural is still, indirectly, causally affecting what is produced according to law. (It is still exhibiting what makes it so little loved by naturalists: the power to break up what might otherwise be a seamless system of regularities.) Thus no qualification to our present understanding of the supernatural seems necessary.

Two final points about that understanding. Arguably, any ultimate and salvific reality, whether construed as a personal God or not, would continue to count as supernatural on it—on the one hand because of axiological perfection, which seems incompatible with the constraints represented by being subject to nomic regularities and manipulation, and on the other because of what is involved in being salvific, which, as before, I assume to include some sort of causal contact between the Ultimate and ourselves, insofar as we belong to nature and perhaps also outside that sphere. And presumably any naturalist looking for a useful construal of her position who has followed us this far will again wish to use our understanding of the supernatural, rather than the much broader category of the non-natural, to define her position: naturalism is the view that *there are no supernatural realities*—which now means "there are no realities independent of law that ever causally affect what is subject to it." Thus the central point of naturalism is no longer that all causes affecting things within nature are natural in Draper's sense, but rather that all causes affecting things within nature are natural in the sense that *they are all law-governed*. (Draper's earlier understanding of "natural cause" entails this idea of being law-governed, but clearly the converse does not hold.)

So what should we say about naturalism thus understood? Now that we have before us a fairly plausible understanding of nature and the associated notions—as plausible an understanding, perhaps, as we could design, given the assumption that Draper's earlier construal would not do—can we also hold out any hope of a *plausible naturalism?* I think not. For why should we suppose that all the causes affecting nature operate exclusively according to nomic regularities? This would seem to rule out many *chance* events, for chance events are non-natural on our understanding but clearly might have natural effects (if the law-governed universe came into existence by chance, *all of nature* would be an effect of chance). It would also rule out our own ability to establish lawlike regularities through acts of libertarian or incompatibilist free will. Perhaps such wrinkles can be ironed out, but already we see how "rationally unmotivated" the new naturalism must appear to be.

As for arguments from the success of science, it is hard to see how these can be any more successful than before. Indeed, they must face more difficult challenges now, for nature is potentially a much "larger" reality on the present construal than on either of the others, and thus much more is being claimed on the basis of science's alleged success than before. Science is indeed the domain of endeavor focused on understanding and manipulating nature as far as we can, but there is no guarantee that it will succeed or fully succeed; and with the much larger task it now faces comes an even stronger possibility that its efforts and their results will be too puny to warrant the hypothesis that no causes *not* subject to the lawlike regularities it is apparently capable of mapping will ever be encountered. Contrary claims must now have about them a whiff of possessiveness or perhaps of confusion—the latter if the naturalist has fallen into the notion that whatever marks natural causes must mark *their* causes as well; the former if she wishes, through science, to have *exclusive* control of the lawlike regularities that obtain.

I suggest, therefore, that the present construal of naturalism also fails to yield a claim about the fundamental nature of things that we have reason to believe true.[28]

4. *Conclusions*

I have tried to give naturalism a good run for its money, but, as we have seen, its money does not add up to much: certainly a justified belief about nature that excludes the existence of an ultimate and salvific reality cannot be purchased with it. What naturalists have to say regularly *over*estimates the *accomplishments* of science and *under*estimates the *potential* of religion. Ironically, by prematurely thinking with naturalists that we are forging ahead (that science can accommodate and transcend the facts about religion), we would, intellectually, stay behind. Reliance on this way of thinking would only perpetuate our intellectual infancy where religious matters are concerned.

Let me now add a few points that draw some threads together. As just suggested, here and there throughout this chapter I have been drawing on the results of Part 1 to buttress the case against naturalistic arguments. It is pretty clear that if those results concerning our limitations and immaturity

---

[28] In considering this conclusion and the relative ease with which it, and other conclusions like it, have been reached in this chapter, one is tempted to think that part of the trouble—a similar problem is found in much religion—is that naturalists have moved far too swiftly from all the impressive features and sober commitments of natural science to an endorsement of naturalistic *belief* (cf. n. 11). The construals of naturalism I have been considering, I have said, fail to yield anything that we have reason to *believe* true, so perhaps naturalists should think instead of *accepting* the naturalistic claim (in the beliefless sense of acceptance) or of taking it on board by *faith*. I myself think that such endorsements of naturalism would be no more successful than a believing one (part of my reason for this assessment is given near the end of the previous chapter), but they would at any rate be more plausible than the claim that naturalistic belief is justified, which our investigation suggests is very sorely lacking in plausibility.

hold, naturalism must be unsupported, but it has been useful to see just how they come to bear when the details of naturalistic argumentation are examined. Now that we have seen this we can flesh out one of the connections between Part 1 and this chapter. It is the following. Attempts to refute my earlier arguments by reference to the support for naturalism, which we entertained once or twice in Part 1, turn out in fact to be *question-begging,* since that support for naturalism, as we have now seen, would be there only if the most general considerations advanced by each of the various modes of reasoning utilized in Part 1 are without force (if any of them have force, they block that support). The points raised in Part 1, if forceful at all, count as much against the support for naturalism as against anything. So one cannot introduce the available arguments for naturalism as a basis for rejecting those points without assuming precisely what one is setting out to prove. More fully aware of this, we are now in a position to embrace the skeptical results of Part 1 with even greater confidence than before: that is why in this chapter the results of Part 1 are both applied and fortified.

Even if one concluded that, since we have been drawing on various considerations from Part 1, sometimes in concert, it is only when the *full* skeptical case Part 1 represents is brought to bear that support for naturalism is blocked, and thus that the support for naturalism is not question-begging in relation to *each* of the modes of reasoning in Part 1 but only in relation to their conjunction,[29] one would still now be in a position to fortify *each* of those modes of reasoning. (One would tell the story this way: with the question of individual force initially left on one side, we have shown how jointly these considerations vanquish naturalism; and now, having cleared the way together, each can also advance in greater confidence alone.) This is just a special instance of a familiar phenomenon: the strengths of a collective winning benefits for each of its members.

So religious skepticism is now further ahead. In the next chapter a similar examination of a very different source of opposition to such skepticism will be examined—that deriving from the alleged evidential force of religious experience. In an interesting way that has not yet been brought out, these two discussions will also turn out to be mutually supportive. For although we have declared available arguments for naturalism (under various construals) inadequate, we have not sought to show that (under every one of those construals, or every possible relevant construal) it is *false,* and indeed, a fair assessment of this chapter would reveal that, for all I have said, it is still epistemically possible that a plausible notion of

---

[29] And I do not think this conclusion is warranted, since the full case, when it was brought to bear, represented a sufficient but not a necessary condition for the defeat of naturalistic belief.

naturalism will turn out to be realized. This, together with some more particular natural possibilities we will soon be mentioning, which are realized for all we know, helps to blunt the force of arguments appealing to religious experience. And likewise, the latter arguments are able to marshal considerations not *entirely* without force, and so must remain something of a thorn in the side of naturalism, which would be more plausible if no religious experiences had ever occurred. But to see all this we must now direct the spotlight entirely to those arguments.

CHAPTER 8

The Questionableness of Religious Experience

From time immemorial, human beings have had *experiences* that produced or sustained religious beliefs. Any such experience—even the experience of intellectually sensing that a religious conclusion follows from a set of apparently true premises—qualifies as a religious experience in the broadest sense and might be linked to justificatory concerns. But in the literature, a certain distinctive sort of experience has time and again been viewed as representing a distinctive justifier of religious belief. This is the sort of religious experience on which I will be focusing. The unifying thread that runs through experiences of this type is just this: that each of them—whether it be an overwhelming experience apparently of a Divine reality, or a more humble though insistent sense of a Divine presence, or even just a strong inclination to take some natural phenomenon (e.g., a sunset or a delicate flower) as mediating a supernatural power and beauty—purports to bring the experient into an *encounter* with, or to facilitate a *perception* of, an ultimate and salvific reality.

Two sorts of reasoning in support of religious belief might be thought relevant here. For religious experience has the property of generating both belief-justifications that are available only to individual experients, who, in making use of the justification, refer to their *own* experiences (call these "first-person" justifications), and justifications that can be made public as forms of reasoning and utilized by anyone at all, even persons who have not themselves had any religious experience and must rely on the experiences of others (call these "third-person" justifications). Third-person justifications are arguments to the effect that the occurrence of religious experience throughout the world is best *explained* by reference to a Divine source, or that in some other way the public fact that religious experiences occur provides good evidence supporting religious belief. This sort of justification will not be central to our inquiry: it has rarely been found impressive by either disbelieving or believing philosophers and is not at all naturally linked to what I am most concerned to deal with here—namely, a familiar way of supporting the claim that religious belief is justified which leads many to overlook or neglect skeptical arguments like those developed in Part 1, and represents a perspective from which the forcefulness of such arguments might be questioned.[1] For this we need to turn to first-person justifications.

These justifications, though long neglected in philosophy of religion, have recently been brought into prominence by Richard Swinburne, through his application of a "principle of credulity"; by Alvin Plantinga, through his defense of "basic" religious beliefs grounded in a sense of the Divine presence; and by William Alston, through his advocacy of an analogy between ordinary, accepted (e.g., sensory) modes of belief formation and religious experiential belief formation.[2] I wish to assess the force of such justifications. Accordingly, I plan to narrow our focus to the type of circumstances in which they become relevant, asking whether our judgment concerning the justification of religious belief should be more favorable when its alleged advantages are introduced. (Of course if our answer were yes, we would still not have shown that religious belief is justified for *everyone,* only for those who have the experiential evidence in question. But we *would* have shown that religious skepticism is *not* justified for everyone, which is the denial of the general conclusion I am supporting in this book.) I will consider whether, where one has not only the general circumstances common to humankind but *also* special *experiential* circumstances of the sort in question, the religious belief response is worthy of being

---

[1] Having said that, I hasten to add that what I have to say in response to first-person justification will also, mutatis mutandis, suffice to answer any third-person justification grounded in religious experience that may be lurking around the edges of this discussion.

[2] See Richard Swinburne, *The Existence of God* (Oxford: Clarendon Press, 1979); Alvin Plantinga, *Warranted Christian Belief* (Oxford: Oxford University Press, 2000); and William Alston, *Perceiving God: The Epistemology of Religious Experience* (Ithaca: Cornell University Press, 1991). Other writers who have argued in a similar vein include William Wainwright, *Mysticism* (Madison: University of Wisconsin Press, 1981); Caroline Franks Davis, *The Evidential Force of Religious Experience* (Oxford: Clarendon Press, 1989); Keith Yandell, *The Epistemology of Religious Experience* (New York: Cambridge University Press, 1993); and Jerome I. Gellman, *Experience of God and the Rationality of Theistic Belief* (Ithaca: Cornell University Press, 1997). Swinburne, it may be noted, emphasizes not only a principle of credulity but also a principle of testimony, the combined effect of which, he thinks, permits us to turn first-person justifications *into* third-person ones. I will not be considering this move directly, since the failure of first-person justifications, for which I will be arguing, entails its failure as well.

made.[3] My answer is no. Religious experience affords no immunity to religious skepticism, and this because considerations of the sort advanced in Part 1 suffice to block the peculiar form of support it is said to provide just as effectively as any other.

1. *First-Person Justification: Variations on the Theme*

To avoid advancing to that conclusion overhastily, let us consider more closely why it might be thought that religious experience can put its recipients in a privileged epistemic position. Suppose we begin with the most natural and uncomplicated extrapolation from what has already been said. This can perhaps best be accomplished by means of a simple analogy. If you feel that you have been misled by the design of the ballot in your county to indicate a vote for someone you had not intended to vote for, then the fact that lots of reputable people out there are coming up with evidence that your vote did reflect your intention will not—and rightly will not—affect *your* belief about what has happened. This is because you have a powerful source of epistemic support for your belief— your own experience—that is independent of any support it may get or fail to get by virtue of its relation to the public evidence. Similarly, or so the defender of a first-person approach may suggest, someone need not worry about the public evidence that seems to count against religious belief if he has been favored with *religious* experience—apparent encounters with the Ultimate that occur when he is contemplating the wonders of nature or listening to great music or reading Scripture, or that come out of the blue, with no sensory mediation, jolting him into apparent nonsensory awareness of a Divine reality. Such experience may rightly cause him to become quite sure that there is a God or that we are reconciled to God through Christ or that Brahman is all and in all or that the Quran is a miracle or that some other religious proposition is true, and also cause him to *remain* so after all objections have been duly considered. For how can he doubt what, so to speak, he has come to see for himself? The upshot is that an investigator of religious belief cannot rightly

---

[3] It would be sufficient in this context (sufficient for a rebuttal of skeptical arguments) if *in some such experiential situation or other* a belief response was worthy: the critic of skepticism need not argue that given just *any* religious experience we have justification for belief. This will be relevant later on, when we see how overriding considerations can prevent a belief response in certain circumstances from being justified, even when the practice of belief formation and revision it represents is properly engaged in. If the latter is the case, then a belief response in *certain other* experiential circumstances will still be justified.

declare such belief to be unjustified *in just any circumstances.* Given the relevant *experiential* circumstances, it would surely be justified, much like the corresponding belief in the analogue.

Arguments like this one are commonly made by religious people and have recently been championed by Plantinga—indeed, my analogy is modeled on some of his.[4] Toward the end of his apologia for orthodox Christianity, *Warranted Christian Belief,* it is very clear that the central Plantingian claim is that God may just seem evident to the believer: more exactly, God may just seem evidently *close* to the believer in her experience (this he interprets in terms of a *sensus divinitatis*). And even after difficult objections such as those based on the horrible suffering some human beings experience have been carefully considered, this sense of God's closeness may not be dislodged.[5] What Plantinga invariably goes on to suggest after such observations is that there is nothing unworthy about the believer's belief response if it occurs in such circumstances and is held in a *basic* way, not on the basis of any public evidence reported by other of one's beliefs.

And here we may agree that the question whether there are successful defeaters of the alleged experiential evidence is indeed the important one. Plantinga, as we have seen, will say that even after looking into all available defeaters, the religious person's sureness that her religious experience is guiding her aright may not be shaken, and so she may remain justified in her belief. But, again, we must be careful not to confuse our own concern—whether religious belief as a *type* is justified in the relevant circumstances—with the question whether various belief *tokens*—the individual beliefs of many religious believers who have had religious experiences—are justified, that is to say, whether such believers may be *responsible* in their belief. Perhaps many are. Perhaps many responsibly continue to believe even after considering the various objections known to them, including those canvassed by Plantinga. Our concern, as indicated in the Introduction, is not with that issue but with one requiring us to assess the actual force of defeaters against the worthiness of a certain experiential belief type. How powerful are they, really? And might there be some that Plantinga has overlooked?

Consider again the voting analogy. Some important points appear to have been missed or misassessed here. For one thing, many of the religious experiences had by, say, a traditional theist are not as *forceful* as the experience cited in the analogy. There is a tendency to think of religious experience as always overwhelmingly powerful and inevitably bringing a

---

[4] See, for example, Plantinga, *Warranted Christian Belief,* p. 442.
[5] See especially ibid., pp. 485–498.

sense of obviousness and firm conviction in its train (which is what I shall mean by "forceful" in this context), but this oversimplifies the nature of such experience. There are, as noted earlier, many different forms of it, ranging all the way from a sense of what just might be a Divine presence to the dazzling experiences of some mystics. Even this oversimplifies, of course, but we can already see that not just any religious belief that can call on experiential support will be grounded in something as generative of a sense of obviousness as the experience cited by the analogy of *right now making this mark and intending it to indicate a vote for person X*. And it is not at all clear that experiences less forceful than this can be justifying in the relevant sense. At any rate, experiences less forceful than this cannot be said to be justifying on the basis of the sort of analogy argument here appealed to, which clearly seeks to benefit from the apparent obviousness and undeniability of the experience (and of the attendant belief) cited in the analogue.

Consider now another point: in the analogue it is obvious what the experience is *of* and what it does *not* concern; its content can be quite clearly delineated, and differentiation between what it involves and what it does not involve is clearly possible. For example, it is clearly possible to determine that it is an experience of placing a mark over here and not over there, of intending to vote for person *X* and not for person *Y*, and so on. Given the content of this experience, it will be immensely difficult to get you to back down to the claim that you just intended to vote for *someone or other*. You would find this absurd. But religious experience tends by its very nature to be much more fluid and malleable. It would not be nearly as striking to hear of someone backing down from the conviction that she experienced the God of traditional theism, complete with all the relevant attributes, to the assertion that *something* supernatural or transcendent was present to her. Thus even where religious experience is forceful,[6] it may not be sufficiently *discriminating* to support the traditional believer's *specific* claim.

And should the believer hang on to the idea that her experience suggests *its* content as against others, we have not so much solved our problems as introduced a new one. For now we have to face the fact that religious experiences thus narrowly interpreted are reported by persons in all traditions and not just in one. This was already implicit in my earlier statement of the Plantinga-style analogy argument: we have not only Christians forming beliefs about the saving power of Christ because of

[6] Indeed, perhaps *especially* here, given that the forceful experiences of mystics at any rate often lead to more, rather than less, reticence to articulate what has been experienced in tight, precise, and exclusivistic terms.

religious experience, but also individuals led by their experiences to believe that Brahman is all, or that the Quran is a miracle, or that Buddhist teaching on Emptiness is correct, or that some other such religious proposition is true. As suggested in Chapter 3, if we explore the entailments of these beliefs, we will find them to be mutually incompatible.

Our simple analogy is quite incapable of handling these complicating features. The true situation of someone who has had one of these religious experiences and is wondering whether it will allow her to escape the clutches of religious skepticism after all other avenues of attempted justification for belief have proven to be dead ends is not at all like that of the voter earlier described, who has only his own experience to take into account. It is rather more like that of someone who has a different story to tell from several others—her equals in respect of intelligence, alertness, and the like—about what could be read on a sign giving voting instructions at the voting station, as becomes apparent when they get together to compare notes sometime after the election. (I assume that there is no reason to doubt that any of the apparent perceptions here are correctly remembered.) Suppose that the beliefs she and these other individuals have formed are mutually incompatible. Suppose also that there is no independent way of tracking down the facts about the sign, or that every suggested independent way has fallen under the pall of skepticism. Whatever someone in such a situation might actually do, or (responsibly or otherwise) suppose it appropriate to think, it seems evident that a wise external adjudicator would have to conclude that a worthy response to the facts available in it for those involved would not include a belief about what was on the sign.

For consider: it is always appropriate in such a situation to remember the possibility of misperception; although perceptual experience apparently gives us a most direct access to things and can seem undeniable, we all know that it can get things wrong. Facts about other perceivers and conflicting perceptual experience of the sort we have here only accentuate that possibility. Now we have a *challenge* to what experience has apparently shown us, which suggests that we may indeed be mistaken. For the experience to be taken as undefeated evidence, that challenge must be turned aside. But in circumstances of the sort here described there is no effective way of responding to the challenge represented by each of the other beliefs—or, for that matter, by the disjunction of those challenges and the suggestion that perhaps, due to the hubbub and distractions at the station, *each* of the conflicting beliefs was incorrectly formed. Of course one might insist in the face of all this that one's own experience was veridical and all the others unveridical and misleading, but this only brings to mind the child who, presented with evidence contrary to his apparent perception, stubbornly repeats that he "heard what he heard" or "saw what he saw," completely unwilling to admit that he could well be mistaken, not recognizing that he is responding with the very evidence that has been challenged. I suppose the application of all this to an argument appealing to religious experience in the face of religious experiential diversity is obvious.

Such points as these, as thus far developed, should already put a major crimp in the style of those who wish to move in a straightforward, uncomplicated manner from religious experience to the justification of religious belief. Especially given the messy facts of experiential diversity, which turn our attention back again to *other* evidence, we already begin to see how appeals to religious experience may be hindered by the very skeptical considerations they were supposed to help us transcend (more on this presently). The situation here is not quite as simple as what one finds in everyday cases in which having the appropriate sensory or introspective experience can "trump" contrary public considerations.

But perhaps a more sophisticated, mediating position is possible. This, I suggest, we may find in the work of Swinburne and also of Alston. What each of these writers in his own way can be seen as proposing is that a belief response grounded in religious experience is *innocent until proven guilty*. Certainly (we might read them as saying) there are ways in which the justificational force of religious experience can be canceled: not just any sort of religious experience, even if powerful, can elude such a negative response forever, given only sufficient dialectical ingenuity, as Plantinga seems sometimes to suggest. But neither is it as easy to turn aside that force as critics like me tend to suppose, who put forward a few critical remarks—perhaps a disanalogy or two—and then move on, obviously influenced by a prejudice in favor of ordinary, nonreligious forms of experience. There is, for *any* sort of experience, a standing presumption that it is veridical, and this needs to be *defeated*—our experience needs to be *shown* to be unveridical or unreliable—by anyone who wishes to deny its justificational force. Thus the onus here is not on the defender of religious experience, as I suggest above, but rather on the critic.

Swinburne expresses this sort of view in terms of his "principle of credulity": "I suggest that it is a principle of rationality that (in the absence of special considerations) if it seems (epistemically) to a subject that x is present, then probably x is present: what one seems to perceive is probably so."[7] And he applies this to religious experience: "From this it would follow that, in the absence of special considerations, all religious experiences ought to be taken by their subjects as genuine, and hence as substantial grounds for belief in the existence of their apparent object—God, or Mary,

[7] Swinburne, *Existence of God*, p. 254.

or Ultimate Reality, or Poseidon."[8] The "special considerations" are problems about the subject or apparent object of the experience that yield a successful challenge to the claim that the latter is veridical—for example, clear evidence that the subject's perceptual apparatus is not functioning properly or that the apparent object of her experience does not exist. In the *absence* of such considerations, on this view, we must take the content of any experience to be in conformity with how things are. Why? If we do not do so, says Swinburne, we cannot avoid landing in a "skeptical bog." Our experience provides our sole access to mind-independent objects, and attempts to provide a proof of its reliability have notoriously been unsuccessful. Thus if we did not grant our experience some initial credibility, we could never get any claim about the world off the ground: we would be waiting for a proof of its reliability that never comes, finding every purported proof picked apart by skeptics.

Alston likewise has an "innocent until proven guilty" approach. But his sophisticated book-length treatment includes a number of moves that substantially enlarge on the work of Swinburne. The central Alstonian notion is that of a "socially established doxastic practice." A doxastic practice, according to Alston, is "the exercise of a system or constellation of belief-forming habits or mechanisms, each realizing a function that yields beliefs with a certain kind of content from inputs of a certain type." Such a practice also involves "distinctive ways of assessing and correcting the beliefs so formed"—in particular, an "overrider system" of background beliefs and investigative procedures that can be used in determining whether the beliefs so formed ought ultimately to be accepted as true. To say a practice of this sort is socially established is to say that it is "socially organized, reinforced, monitored, and shared." (Here we might pause to notice the relation between these ideas and my notion of a belief type: to describe one of Alston's practices is to describe a *way* of believing and of revising beliefs, and so appears to *entail* reference to a belief type—the sensory belief-forming practice, for example, involves a *sensory* way of forming beliefs, or the formation of beliefs of a sensory *type*. Thus we can also say that if a doxastic practice is properly engaged in, the corresponding belief response is a worthy one.)[9] Evidently, there are socially established sensory, introspective, memorial,

---

[8] Ibid.

[9] Though remembering the point of n. 3—that this does not imply that it must be worthy in just *any* of the experiential circumstances that constitute the "inputs" of that practice. Consider the sensory analogue: if the sensory belief-forming practice is properly engaged in, then a sensory belief response is worthy *in certain circumstances* (it is, for example, worthy when a bird is apparently seen, and nothing overrides the force of this visual experience), even though it might not be in others (suppose it is shown that the "bird" has been hallucinated).

and inferential doxastic practices. To these Alston would add what he calls the "mystical experience belief forming practice," the practice of acquiring and revising religious experiential beliefs of the sort at issue in this discussion, which he regards as taking a variety of distinct forms: "We have as many different [mystical practices] as there are importantly different doctrinal systems."[10]

The next point to note is that all our doxastic practices are according to Alston infected with what he calls "epistemic circularity": our best attempts to show that sense perception and also memory, introspection, and deductive and inductive reasoning are *reliable,* that is, that they can be relied on to produce mostly true beliefs, "will make use of premises derived from the practice under consideration." Given this fact, he says, "we should draw the conclusion that there is no appeal beyond the practices we find firmly established, psychologically and socially." As Alston repeatedly argues, we must employ *some* doxastic practice in investigating issues, and epistemic circularity is inevitable; so what else can we do than to apply results from the practices we find ourselves using, with which we are intimately familiar, and which we could hardly imagine ourselves doing without? Behaving in this way, he says, is *practically rational.* Of course such practices can be criticized, and it may be that one or other of them is shown to be unreliable by bringing to bear "the total output of all our firmly established doxastic practices." To accommodate this we should say that the previously mentioned considerations show only that it is prima facie rational to engage in any firmly established doxastic practice.[11] (Again, innocent until proven guilty—though now we can see that this notion operates on two levels for Alston: belief outputs of a practice are innocent until proven guilty in the sense of justified unless overridden, and the practice itself is innocent until proven guilty in the sense of being rationally engaged in and properly taken as reliable unless proven to be unreliable.)

"Any" here of course includes, for Alston, the mystical experiential practices. Arguing that there is no good reason to suppose that all experience-able truths will be equally accessible to everyone, he claims that it would be arbitrary to exclude any (non-universal) practice of forming beliefs on the basis of religious experience from the aforementioned status. "Provided that [it] is firmly rooted in its devotees from early in life, interconnected with other practices in a form of life, and socially established, there will

---

[10] For Alston's points in this paragraph, see *Perceiving God,* pp. 182, 155, 158, 159, 163, 184–185, 191.

[11] Alston, *Perceiving God,* pp. 146, 149, 149–150, 168, 175, 168.

be the same argument against abandoning it as there is for more widely distributed practices."[12]

This is an interesting and resourceful set of arguments, clearly among the most substantial of those that have yet been put forward on our topic. We will need to take it, and its Swinburnian counterpart (which it effectively absorbs),[13] very seriously. Such a more sophisticated, mediating position tries to get to the bottom of the epistemology of the issue, and to set out a reasonable stance concerning the epistemic status of religious experience within that context, while avoiding the extremes of easy affirmation and equally easy criticism. I shall follow it in this aim, nonetheless arguing that criticism retains the upper hand when all is said and done. My points arise naturally from previous chapters (and also build on some ideas first broached in the Preface) and permit, I think, a more effective response to this contemporary emphasis in philosophy of religion than can otherwise be mounted. What we will see in their light is, first of all, that religious practices are *not* to be taken as innocent until proven guilty, and then also that the messy problem of religious diversity and the possibility of natural accounts of religious experience combine to provide strong grounds for regarding such practices as eminently dubious instead.

2. *Innocent until Proven Guilty?*

Assume with Alston and Swinburne (and despite the occasional whiff of non-truth-oriented considerations in the case of Alston) that *truth is the goal* in all our doxastic dealings: that our aim is not to hang on to cherished or useful beliefs, whatever the cost, but to have *correct* beliefs and thus to enlarge our understanding of the world. (The meaning of "practical" in the term "practical rationality," as used in this discussion, should be clearly articulated in terms of *this* aim.) Assume as well that Alston is right about epistemic circularity and the "human cognitive condition": there is no noncircular proof of this or that belief-forming practice's reliability, and since we cannot investigate any issue whatever without utilizing some way of forming and evaluating beliefs, there is no alternative to employing practices we find ourselves using and regarding their outputs as potentially justified if we want to get started in inquiry at all. If this is so, shouldn't would-be investigators extend to religious experiential belief-forming practices, along with all the rest, an initial credibility? Isn't this

---

[12] Ibid., p. 169.
[13] For what Alston himself has to say about this, see ibid., p. 195.

practically rational? And wouldn't we otherwise, to revert to Swinburne's point, simply find ourselves in a "skeptical bog"?

In a word, no. Although we must utilize some practice to get going in inquiry, there is clearly still a question as to which one(s). It seems natural and appropriate—and has seemed so to others on whom Alston draws, like Thomas Reid[14]—to go with what is universal and unavoidable here, and thus to restrict ourselves, at least initially, to such practices as those we call sensory, introspective, memorial, and (rationally) intuitive. But how can we prevent this restriction from being arbitrary? I would argue that it is *precisely because of* the requirements of an investigative stance and an investigative aim that it is non-arbitrary. If we really are would-be investigators, concerned for the truth and seeking understanding, then we will ascribe epistemic innocence—even an initial innocence—*only where we have to:* assuming that we have to pick certain belief-forming practices as innocent until proven guilty to get started, we will still pick only what we have to pick, in order to minimize the extent to which non-inquiry-based factors influence the direction of inquiry. (After all, if we are inquirers, we want as much as possible of what we believe and do to be *grounded* in inquiry: as the principles of justification I have been utilizing have it, we want sufficient and overall good *evidence*.)

But here it will already be objected that when we choose to go with our doxastic practices (subject, of course, to the requirement that no proof of their unreliability presents itself), we are not choosing blindly in the dark—not "just picking something," as I have suggested. We will instead be sensitive to certain discriminating features, such as social establishment and self-support; *and religious practices are as socially established and self-supporting as any others*. Here again is Alston on this subject: "It is a reasonable supposition that a practice would not have persisted over large segments of the population unless it was putting people into effective touch with some aspect(s) of reality and proving itself as such by its fruits."[15]

This seems somewhat over-optimistic, however, and even when understood as simply part of a cautious defense of initial innocence. There are ever so many ways in which a doxastic practice could be socially established and yet also the purveyor of utterly false beliefs. Indeed, plenty of actual patterns of belief formation from the world's history that have persisted for generations over large segments of the population and been deeply entrenched, both psychologically and socially, could be called on to make this point. One need only think about false beliefs concerning

---

[14] See Alston, *Perceiving God*, p. 169.
[15] Ibid., p. 170.

the shape of the earth, or the alleged inferiority of women, or claimed conspiracies and plots engineered by Jews or other minority groups. (We could also add a reference to "significant self-support": think about how many of a medieval flat-earther's experiences are just as they would be if the earth were flat!) And, of course, religion itself presents an obvious and uncontroversial example since the outputs of religious experiential belief-forming practices conflict, and thus not all such practices can be reliable: in virtue of this fact we *know* that *right now* there are socially established religious practices purveying mostly false beliefs, failing to put anyone in effective touch with reality, regardless of their fruits. Thus an appropriately cautious—and also curious and exploratory—investigator, when deciding how to proceed, has a reason to discriminate more sharply and sensitively than Alston, choosing to accept certain socially established practices as initially credible, but ones that do not raise such credibility-threatening and investigation-worthy issues and that are in any case universal and unavoidable.

But what about skepticism? An investigator *will* be moved by whatever is needed to get past the most general skepticism, and as we have seen, some defenders of religious experience try to make use of this fact. But an answer to global skepticism does not require a global acceptance of all (including religious) experiences as innocent until proven guilty. Indeed, a close look at this issue only confirms the perspective on universal and unavoidable practices already suggested. For if we think properly about our intellectual goals, we will realize that the only way we are able to get started toward them—if indeed any progress is possible for us—is by trusting those most basic and unavoidable belief-forming and revising mechanisms and processes and taking it that good evidence of truth can be found within them and by means of them. It is not imaginable that we should make a beginning in investigation, even an investigation that eventually takes us beyond some of their deliverances, *except* by means of them. *Precisely because they are unavoidable, we are stuck with whatever beginning is thus made possible.* (If a correct understanding of the world is *not* thus approachable, it will inevitably pass us by.) Hence if *we human beings* are to access the truth, we *must* begin by trusting these mechanisms and processes.[16] This is important, for

---

[16] Here we also have an answer to any who suggest that—in line with what I say elsewhere—I ought to recommend *acceptance or faith* (as distinct from belief) on even the most fundamental matters; that I ought to seek to persuade us to turn even those basic belief-forming practices into (nonbelieving) acceptance practices or faith practices. We are simply unable to do so. For us, the relevant practices unavoidably involve belief, and so in assuming their reliability, we have to assume belief's reliability. (A way of filling out this answer, of making it deeper, is suggested immediately below.)

it seems to generate an immediate practical reason to accept them all as reliable for the sake of investigation (at least in the absence of a convincing proof of unreliability—which, as Alston argues, is going to be hard to come by in these cases).[17] But notice as well that to move forward in inquiry we do not need *more* than these unavoidable mechanisms and processes. So although we have an answer to a completely general skepticism and a good reason to make use of our basic and unavoidable belief-forming and revising mechanisms—to have any chance of knowing the truth and arriving at understanding we must assume they are reliable and move outward from there, forming beliefs on the basis of what they tell us counts as evidence— it is not one that at any stage involves a reference to religion. Thus even an *initial* trust in religious belief-forming practices is not rationalized by the need for an answer to skepticism, contrary to what Swinburne—and, in some moods, Alston—suggests.

It is worth noting that in examining this "universality and unavoidability" restriction I have been defending, we can travel in more than one direction. One might want to say, as intimated above, that universality and unavoidability are required because only where they are present is one forced by the human cognitive condition to go along: we would like to substantiate more fully even such belief-forming practices if we could, but because we cannot, and because to do so is a necessary condition of arriving at any truth and understanding that might be possible for us, we concede defeat and settle for what is basically a naked assumption instead.

But there is something else here too, already suggested by all this talk of what we "want," which puts things in a somewhat different perspective. Because we find ourselves unable to *not* form and revise beliefs on the basis of sense perception, introspection, memory, and rational intuition, a certain basic picture of the world has been generated involving birth and conscious experience and physical objects and relations with other conscious beings and the reality of things past and death and also the appropriateness of *valuation* (presupposed by the humblest desires, and sanctioned by intuition). This picture appears to be our common inheritance. It becomes part of the very fabric of a human being, affecting one's sense of identity and of connectedness to others and of value and thus also of the appropriate goals, *including intellectual goals*. What we can see here—and some of what Alston says about the psychological and social establishment of our basic belief-forming practices is in accord with this—is that we are not independent, truth-registering machines that care not what the truth is and would question everything if we could, but rather

---

[17] Alston, *Perceiving God*, pp. 170–172.

deeply *human* inquirers, whose humanity and the basic picture with which it is intertwined do much to shape the nature of our inquiring impulse. Indeed, that very impulse itself, whatever shape it takes, is deeply conditioned by aspects of our "basic picture"; in particular, it is inextricably interwoven with valuation—how could one desire truth or nobly determine to seek the truth, whatever it may be, without thinking it *good* to do so? Thus just to formulate intellectual goals and to engage in inquiry of any sort, we must already rule out some possibilities (e.g., the possibility that it is true that there is nothing good).[18] Inquiry is not some amorphous thing, ready to be shaped in just any way at all, but has a decidedly human shape, determined by our basic picture of the world.

The upshot is that what we want to know as inquirers is not whether our basic picture is correct: we will acquiesce in our beliefs about birth and conscious experience and physical objects and relations with others and the reality of the past and death and also the appropriateness of valuation and any other very general shared and unavoidable feature of a human worldview. We will not do so grudgingly—not just because we have to. Or perhaps we should say that we will do so because we "have to" in a deeper, richer sense than has been utilized so far: the belief-forming practices underlying the basic picture may be inescapable, but the picture itself has also become inescapable: now we find ourselves *in* the world, *shaped* by the picture, and insatiably curious about how *it* is to be filled out. (And if the true picture is of a very different sort, we will simply pass our lives in the grip of illusion.)

In response to this direction of thought it may be suggested that we can follow it all the way to religion—surely little is more human than religiosity! But just at this point we need our reflections to be balanced by the other direction of thought I have said is inviting here, which reminds us of the value of investigatively substantiated results and of a certain "doxastic minimalism" that will influence the investigator. We want to fill out our basic picture. When reminded by the most radical skeptics that it might be fundamentally flawed, we are still willing to take the plunge. But we want to maximize our chances of filling it out *correctly*, recognizing the

---

[18] It may be said that the inquiry begun through the value assumption at work here might conceivably lead to the latter's demise: perhaps the truth of *nihilism* is something we will discover if we press the inquiry far enough. But even if inquiry seemed to lead in that direction, no normal goal-directed human being would be capable of intellectually absorbing and acting on its impact. That some things matter (and perhaps also, more specifically, that such things as beauty and justice and love matter and are worth pursuing) will seem to any healthy, properly functioning human to be obvious. And if nihilism *were* in some manner taken on board, it seems clear that not just the assumption about value but inquiry too would meet its demise—which is the basic point being made in the text.

myriad ways we could go wrong in the details even if we are lucky enough to be right about the basics, and so we decide to proceed with the greatest investigative care. It is, after all, truth and real understanding that we want. And though some of us grow up experiencing the world religiously, we may also come to wonder whether this experience tells the truth about the world. Further, many people evidently can and do deny the truth of religious beliefs, even when they have been quite certain about such beliefs before. Religious belief-forming practices are by no means universal or unavoidable. So while it is correct to say that we have our basic, unavoidable picture of the world, and while it functions in the manner indicated above, it is equally clear that the deliverances of religious belief-forming practices are not a part of it. Indeed, with a proper awareness of the nature of that picture, and proper investigative sensitivities, we can see that if we are to embrace religious belief at all, it should be because investigation suggests that we need to do so in order to *properly extend* or *accurately fill out* the picture. In this connection we may benefit from noticing that such belief not only purports to take our understanding further some distance or in some respect, but rather purports to tell the *ultimate* truth about things, in terms of which *everything* else must be understood. Furthermore, its influences can be sharply investigation-inhibiting, as we saw in Chapter 3. Thus one might well ask: Since they claim so much and are so psychologically powerful and are not at all unavoidable, should not religious belief-forming practices be required to *earn* our approval?

What all this suggests is that there is a proper division of labor here: the basic picture gets us going, and other ideas, whatever their origin, are candidates for its development that investigators consider, without making any initial assumption as to their credibility. Notice that there is nothing arbitrary about this approach. On the contrary, it seems both sensitive to the widest range of relevant considerations and sensible. But if we adopt it, evidently we will have no reason to regard religious experiential belief-forming practices as innocent until proven guilty.

Thus when we look closely at the most general epistemological issues involved with religious experience, we seem to find ourselves with an alternative approach that grounds a plausible response to the claims of Alston and Swinburne about the initial epistemic innocence of religious experience, without falling into the traps their critics customarily step into. Alston usually takes himself to be able to turn aside criticisms on this score by pointing out what he calls "epistemic imperialism" or else an "arbitrary double standard."[19] But no such complaints seem relevant here. We have

---

[19] See, for example, *Perceiving God*, p. 199.

already seen this with regard to the claim of arbitrariness. What about imperialism? On this matter Alston is inclined to say that his critics err by unwarrantedly supposing that standards satisfied by certain *commonly accepted* belief-forming practices must also be satisfied by all others. Why should we suppose, we hear him ask, that just *any* experienceable fact will be equally accessible to all, or vividly and forcefully and continually presented to us in rich detail as is the case with much sense experience? But any objection to my own account couched in these terms is a red herring. In mounting such objections Alston merely exploits the excessive negativity of most of his critics, who do not leave the matter of religion's status to investigation but enthusiastically deny that its credentials are any good. A critic of religious experience need not fall into such traps. In particular, given our own approach, there is no need to affirm that only a universally accessible experience or a clear and detailed experience can possibly reveal truth. In fact we can deny this. We can concede that perhaps other experiences, including religious experiences, will in time be shown to reveal truth. But still we may refuse to regard the belief-forming practices presently based on them as innocent until proven guilty on the very general methodological grounds I have advanced.

3. *The Problem of Religious Diversity Revisited*

The issue of religious diversity is already touched on above, in connection with Plantinga's approach. Here I want to take the argument further, in conversation with Plantinga and also Alston, who has a fair bit to say on the subject. As it seems to me, the more closely we examine this matter of religious diversity, the more dubious religious experiential belief must come to appear.

Suppose there were but a single experiential belief-forming practice with religious outputs (however widely engaged in). Philosophers of religion, taking account of it, would never be required to consider the complicating issue of whether *one* sort of religious experience to which humans testified should or could be viewed as more reliable than *other, competing* sorts. But given our actual situation of religious diversity, any investigator is faced with just such a question, in relation to any particular religious experiential belief-forming practice she may be considering. Aware that the practice before her, *whichever it may be,* is simply one from among many with incompatible outputs, at most one of which is reliable, she is faced with the following challenge: If so many religious experiential practices are unreliable, then why not *this* one? If powerful experiences full of apparent meaningfulness and illumination may come to persons of intelligence and virtue and yet be *completely delusive,* then what reason do you have to suppose that such is not the case *here?* Or (giving the question a slightly different slant) how do you know that the truth about ultimate things has not been apprehended in one of those *other* practices? Or (yet another slant) might *all* these practices be getting it wrong, for lack of the fuller understanding that only a completely different religious or nonreligious approach could bring?

Such questions must have a profoundly cautionary effect, highlighting our fallibility and the possibility of mistake as they do; and they require a response from anyone who wishes nonetheless to use the practice in question as an antidote to skepticism—a response that vindicates it over all the others. But when the investigator looks around to see if such a response is available, what will she see? Well, the results of Part 1, naturally, and, in particular, our bad track record as humans in respect of religious exploration, which leaves us no clear way of supporting one religious experiential practice's superiority to another, but only an *agenda*—a long list of tasks to perform which may at some point in the future get us to the place where such judgments *can* be made. Thus the investigator faced with the facts of religious experiential diversity has no choice but to plow into deeper levels of inquiry and to put off any endorsement of one experiential tradition over another until she has become much better acquainted with the total religious picture.

But why, a Plantingian might now be inclined to reply, would anyone who really takes the first-person stance seriously be bothered by any of this? An assumption made here, and also earlier in this chapter, is that an investigator has to say that the various experiences are (at least initially) *all on a level* in respect of epistemic force, and that *new* information is needed to (non-question-beggingly) discriminate among them. But—a Plantingian might continue—while from the *outside* the various conflicting experiences may seem to be on an equal footing given various facts one can note from that perspective (similarities in respect of apparent meaningfulness and illumination, etc.), things are very different from the *inside;* and we are of course asking about what response is appropriate for one who is privileged enough to be able to approach things from the latter perspective. One who has had such an experience and for whom it is sufficient to generate a certain specific sort of religious belief will see, when facts about religious diversity are presented to him, that if his experiences are reliable the others must be unreliable. But this will not and should not lead to doubt as to whose experiences are reliable; it rather leads to the view that he must have something—something importantly truth-related—that the others do not possess! This may seem arbitrary, but notice that his position is not now and never was grounded in an appeal to *facts about* his experience, against which various similar facts about others' experiences can be set, but in *the experience itself.* Since this is so, the experiential believer cannot rightly be accused of treating similar cases differently: he never held that they were similar in the first place![20] Nor does his attitude reduce to that of the stubborn child referred to earlier when the issue of religious diversity first came up: he should be viewed not as stubborn but rather as sensitively responsive to his experience.

This will not do, however. We can readily admit that for the experient his own experience, apprehended from the inside, is a different *sort* of evidence than the information about others' experiences brought against it. But this takes nothing away from the fact that the latter is evidence too. And that information is still evidence highlighting the possibility of error, presenting a challenge, which needs somehow to be answered. Furthermore, responding to such a challenge in terms of one's own experience is still an ineffective, question-begging route to take. We might leave the matter there, but there is something else that the Plantinga-style response brings vividly into view which really ought to be taken more seriously. This is a tendency toward a rather myopic, defensive, and isolationist attitude, an *incurious* attitude, which is surely something that an *investigator* has reason to seek to transcend. If we are in any sense curious about how things are, taking the investigative stance and making truth our goal, our attitude might be expected to be a different one. (After all, consider the possibility of an enlarged understanding that comes with fuller exploration of the religious world, given our poor track record in this respect so far.) Loyalty might lead elsewhere—though, as is clear, we might argue for the superiority of a larger, more inclusive loyalty in which all are embraced—but if it is *truth and understanding* that we want, then a problem of experiential diversity like this must provoke serious questions about the veridicality of any individual experience and an associated interest in probing the frontiers beyond convention, which have now been revealed as vast indeed.

But this is just the point at which Alston's answer to the problem of religious diversity can be brought to bear. Notice first that he says, in connection with it, that exploration of other religious options and a search for common ground should *continue* even among those who—he thinks appropriately—form sectarian religious beliefs grounded in religious experience. As he puts it: "I do not take [my position] to imply that the proper procedure for the Christian, or the member of any religious community, is to shut herself up within the boundaries of her own community and ignore the rest of the world. . . . She should do whatever seems

[20] See Plantinga, *Warranted Christian Belief,* pp. 451, 453.

feasible to search for common ground on which to adjudicate the crucial differences between the world religions."[21] So what *is* the position referred to? In brief, that where there is no common procedure for settling disputes among the truth-claims of various religious practices, and where the religious practice in question can claim "significant self-support," the appropriate thing for the religious practitioner to do in the face of uneliminated alternatives is to "sit tight" with the practice of which she is a master and which serves her so well.[22]

Alston uses a variety of analogies to buttress his point. He seeks to show that in cases where it is clear that the presence of uneliminated alternatives marks a problem, *the competitors confront each other within the same doxastic practice,* and *noncircular grounds* for supposing one to be superior in respect of reliability are accessible; and also that where such grounds are *absent,* we do not see a difficulty in continuing belief. Think, for example, of the dispute between psychoanalysts and behaviorists in psychology (on the diagnosis and treatment of neurosis) or between compatibilists and incompatibilists in philosophy (on the nature of free will). As Alston puts his point, specifically with regard to the second of these two disciplines: "In philosophy we notoriously lack neutral ways of determining which party to fundamental debates . . . is in the right, is more likely to be right, or is in a better epistemic position to get the truth. Does it follow that no one is rational in forming views on these matters in the way that they do? If so, we philosophers had better pack our bags and move to an activity in which we can more honestly engage."[23] But if a belief response *can* be worthy in such contexts despite unresolved conflicts, then surely the same conclusion follows for any of the religious experiential belief-forming practices.

Putting all these points together, we can imagine an Alstonian saying that the investigative program must indeed continue, but that the assumption that we have to lay our particular beliefs aside until it is over is false. Indeed, our beliefs keep us "in the game," providing incentive for the continuing quest. Applying her position, the Alstonian might look at the various conflicting religious practices, notice that noncircular grounds for

---

[21] Alston, *Perceiving God,* p. 278. Though it may be that arguing from within one's own camp for the truth of its beliefs on grounds one thinks all the disputants should accept would be a sufficient condition of not "ignoring the rest of the world," on Alston's view. In this connection see what he says on p. 270.

[22] Alston, *Perceiving God,* pp. 270–276.

[23] Ibid., p. 273 n. 16. A similar point is defended in the Introduction to *The Philosophical Challenge of Religious Diversity,* ed. Philip L. Quinn and Kevin Meeker (New York: Oxford University Press, 2000), pp. 21–22, and in David Basinger, *Religious Diversity: A Philosophical Assessment* (Burlington, Vt.: Ashgate, 2002), chap. 3.

arbitrating the disputes between them apparently can't be had at present while also detecting significant self-support in each such practice, and declare religious experiential belief of *all* these forms to be justified (while also recommending ongoing conversation between the parties). Of course, she would have to say that this holds for *various incompatible* experientially grounded beliefs, but, following Alston, she may point out that this is just a special case of the general point that incompatible beliefs "can each be justified for different people if what they have to go on is suitably different."[24]

How should we respond to this Alstonian position? I think we should judge it unconvincing. A first difficulty here is that, as we saw in Chapter 3, religious belief can easily be an impediment instead of a help where broader investigation is concerned. It is all well and good to talk about continuing investigation, but the fact is that sectarian believers notoriously are often led by the content of the propositions they believe and the psychological results of *believing* them to *avoid* this, and the pursuit of truth and understanding suffers as a result. Thus any hope the Alstonian might harbor that the force of the objection from diversity will be dissipated by the possibility of investigation *with belief* seems unfounded.

But there is an interesting and very important additional point to be made here. As our principles tell us (see Appendix B), religious belief is justified only if there is no *better* response, and given the results of *Prolegomena*, even a religious person should say that there *is* a better response to the deliverances of religious experience than belief—namely, the faith response.[25] The faith response is quite capable of embodying religious commitment; it too provides incentive for "staying in the game"; it is more accommodating of the investigative imperative than belief since not as likely to be "blinkered" by a psychological sense of sureness and conviction; and, indeed, it is quite compatible with religious skepticism. The complex consisting of propositional and operational faith can draw on a wider range of good-related considerations to defend itself, and obviously circumvents altogether the objection to continued belief represented by diversity since not itself a species of the belief response. Thus such faith seems tailor-made for someone who wishes to persist in a religious commitment while recognizing the force of skepticism, and particularly the question mark placed against the truth of any particular religious experiential claim by the facts of religious diversity. This is why I say it must be deemed superior

---

[24] Alston, *Perceiving God,* p. 275.

[25] Whatever Alstonians may say, Alston himself should be a good target for this point, since as is shown in *Prolegomena* (see esp. chap. 6), he has recently done important pioneering work toward the development of a nondoxastic conception of religious faith.

to religious belief in this connection. But then, by our principles, religious experiential *belief* is unjustified. Now a religious faith response might itself turn out to be unjustified on other grounds, at least in its sectarian forms, but that need not prevent us from using its availability to show, for now and in this context, that religious belief is unjustified.

This point about faith might have been saved for the end of the chapter, but I have introduced it here because it is so obviously pertinent to the specific Alstonian points being dealt with at this stage, and also to the unspoken assumption of Alton's *Perceiving God*, especially evident in this connection, that belief is the only positive religious response to religious experience—that if one is impressed with a religious experiential tradition's "self-support" or has found it helpful in negotiating one's way through life and wants to defend a religious stance in response to religious diversity, there is no alternative to a defense of *continued belief*. Clearly there is an alternative. However, this point about beliefless faith will be *much confirmed* by the problems for belief and for the Alstonian defense of belief we have yet to outline, and will therefore reemerge at the end, considerably strengthened. For now I continue with the outlining of those problems.

Take, for example, the fact that the central Alstonian emphasis on the unavailability of non-question-begging grounds for discrimination seems irrelevant as an answer to *our* worries, once again because of the type/token difference. Perhaps, since "ought" implies "can," this unavailability would mean that there can be no *duty* to have uncovered such grounds, and so that no one can irresponsibly be *violating* such a duty in continuing to believe despite the unresolved problem of religious diversity. But it is hard to see how it should affect the clear-eyed *investigator* in philosophy of religion, concerned to assess the worthiness of a belief response in experiential circumstances, since in the absence of such grounds there is *still no basis for a reply to the challenge presented by religious diversity,* and thus the evidence of religious experience must still be deemed to be successfully blocked.

But what about the analogies Alston and others have been inclined to introduce at this point? Don't we rightly consider belief a worthy response in precisely similar situations of conflict elsewhere? I would suggest that the analogies face serious difficulties of their own. For one thing, a similar insight to the one that brings faith into view in this context may remind us that philosophers need not—contrary to what Alston suggests—be prevented from further investigation or even from taking certain views on board and defending them by the absence of belief: only an overly narrow understanding of "forming views" that ignores acceptance and acting on assumption (and, yes, also faith) could lead us to suppose otherwise. Thus we may agree on the proposed rationality of forming philosophical views without agreeing that it follows from this that the formation of *belief* is, in the mentioned circumstances, rational.

A second problem here is that only where there has been *protracted discussion and intense intellectual interaction* between behaviorists and psychoanalysts, or between compatibilists and incompatibilists, should we be at all inclined to say that belief one way or the other can be justified despite an unresolved dispute between these parties. (Notice that I am saying only that this is a necessary condition; I am not saying it is sufficient.) There must be serious attempts to resolve the dispute, serious attempts to find common ground from which a resolution or new intellectual possibilities might spring; and this of course implies *getting to know the other side* very well. Where this has not taken place, we would surely want to say that (whatever individuals may actually do) a belief response is precipitous and premature, since in the available information not yet accessed there might well be relevant evidence, which could tilt either way. Thus for the analogy argument being utilized here to get off the ground, we need the assumption that representatives of the various religious experiential practices (or investigators thereof) who wish to say that religious experiential belief is worthy despite the unresolved interpractice conflict *have made such serious attempts to find common ground and know each other and each other's practices that well.* But for reasons drawn from Chapters 3 and 4 which should by now be familiar, we must conclude that this is not the case.[26]

To see a third problem, notice that there is considerable imprecision in the articulation of that idea of the absence of neutral grounds which is central to the analogies Alston and others have deployed: sometimes it is said that there is no *common procedure* for resolving the dispute; sometimes that there are no grounds possessed by those on one side that will *persuade or convince* those on the other; at other times we hear that there are no noncircular, non-question-begging *reasons for discriminating* between the different beliefs available to any of those involved in the conflict. Though the commodities mentioned here are often treated interchangeably, they are not the same. Suppose we have a compatibilist who appropriately thinks he has reasons to suppose that incompatibilism and incompatibilist arguments are wrongheaded. This certainly *could* be the case even if he cannot convince any incompatibilist and even if there is no common procedure he can utilize to make his case. And now the important point: we would not consider compatibilist belief to be worthy in such a situation of conflict in the *absence* of such reasons. Imagine that you are presented with a

---

[26] This suggests, by the way, that the Alstonian's assumption of an *unavailability* of grounds for discrimination, which appears to presuppose that a thorough search has been undertaken and turned out to be fruitless, is unsupported.

battery of incompatibilist arguments but can think of no adequate reply to them. And suppose that you cannot think of any stronger arguments for compatibilism. Would you still confidently declare compatibilist belief to be a worthy option? Surely not. Where it *is* thought to be a worthy option, despite conflict, the other side's arguments are thought to be inadequate in some identifiable way the other side does not properly appreciate, or one's own arguments are thought to be stronger than the others' arguments in an identifiable manner similarly unappreciated by them. This latter state, as we have seen, is quite compatible with the absence of a *common procedure* or *universally convincing* grounds, and represents non-question-begging reasons for discrimination (even if ones that won't persuade the others).

These different things are often not sufficiently well distinguished by the Alstonian: one finds the suggestion that even if *all* of them are absent, there is no problem. But there *would* be a problem if such were the case, and it is, as we have seen, precisely because these things are *not* all absent in the nonreligious cases that we think belief may still be justified there. *However, in the religious case contemplated by Alston every one of them is absent.* The dispute there concerns the force of private religious experiences, and although one may think that one's own experiences are epistemically superior to those on the other sides, one cannot non-question-beggingly identify what it is that makes them so or (therefore) make it available to the others for assessment, and, more important, for the same reasons of privacy one does not really know or understand what the *other* sides have got and so is not in a position to pronounce on its merits.[27]

This point can be developed. Though privacy considerations are often taken to *strengthen* the claim of religious experience (when I experience something for myself in a way that is not accessible to you, I appear to have more *direct* access to it, and direct access certainly seems less liable to error), in fact they lead to the *downfall* of justifications grounded in religious experience, given religious diversity. For who *knows* what I would think if I could have *your* experience? A Christian might be inclined to say to members of other traditions: "You would understand my reticence to give up my belief if you could only see what I see." But a better thought

---

[27] It might be said that *other* analogies Alston presents, which feature conflict between different basic ways of perceiving the physical environment, instead of disputes to which argument is relevant, are better able to handle the religious case, which is after all perceptual in nature. (See *Perceiving God*, pp. 273–274.) But these other analogies are inapplicable precisely because in them experiential practices *are* presented as basic and unavoidable, which suggests the appropriateness of a treatment like that defended in the previous section for our actual basic and unavoidable practices. If the practices in question were not of this sort, they would be subject to the same difficulties I am here developing.

here is this: "What if the Christian (or the Hindu or the Buddhist ...) could see from the inside what *all* religious experients have seen, perhaps in sequence, with a clear memory afterward of what she had seen—would her belief be affected *then?*" Presumably the answer is "perhaps yes, perhaps no." But that is just the point. Who *knows* what would result if one could see from the inside what everyone else has seen? Perhaps one would conclude that one's own experience was the most illuminating and likely to be reliable, but then again perhaps one would notice that the clouds were thicker on one's own side. Who could say? Certainly one's own experience can provide no grounds for going one way or the other on *this* matter. (That I have a powerful experience apparently of Christ may entail, at least for that moment, that I form a religious belief about Christ, and this belief may entail the falsity of incompatible beliefs from other traditions; but neither of these things entails that, *should I experience the world as does a Hindu or a Buddhist, I would not conclude that their experience was more illuminating and convincing than mine.*) But then it could well be that one would judge someone else's experience at least as epistemically impressive as one's own were one's evidential situation suitably enlarged, as in the imagined situation. (That it *cannot* be thus enlarged—at least as things stand at present—is irrelevant here: as we learned in Chapter 1, evidence unavailable to us may still have a bearing on the worthiness of belief.) Indeed, it could well be that one would think *all of a number of different experiences* to be equally convincing and apparently illuminating.

Recognizing all this, an investigator considering a particular religious experiential practice has *right now* insufficient reason to suppose that the unveridical experiences are all to be associated with other practices. He must rather conclude that it is epistemically possible that, were he privy to all the evidence that exists in his situation, he would have exactly the same sort of experiential support for *each* of the conflicting views. Which is to say that, *right now,* the force of the experiential evidence offered by the particular practice in question (whichever it is) is effectively blocked and incapable of justifying religious belief.

I suggest that this argument helps us to see why the analogies to which Alston and others appeal in this connection must be unsuccessful: in those other cases we can always have access to the evidence the others have and form an impression as to its worth, perhaps finding reasons for rejecting it; in the religious experiential case we cannot. This argument also provides a more direct route to the conclusion that the challenge of religious diversity is insurmountable—and, incidentally, puts the last nail in the coffin for that Plantinga-style maneuver which insists on the special privilege afforded by one's own experience and the believer's unassailable right to take refuge in what *she* sees "from the inside."

4. *The Problem of Natural Explanation Introduced*

We have been talking about quite specific religious beliefs, beliefs that can readily be identified as belonging to this tradition or sect *as opposed to* that. Someone might now say that the problem of religious diversity we have discussed can be dealt with by thinking more generically—to put this in our terms, perhaps religious experience can support belief of *generic* ultimism even if not any elaborated ultimism (or any claim entailing an elaborated version of ultimism).[28]

I am doubtful about the prospects of such a move. We would need, for one thing, to explain why we should be confident that the Ultimate was really present to experients even though misleadingly or completely inaccurately represented in most if not all cases. But what I want to emphasize here is that there is another way of defeating first-person experiential justifications of religious belief that applies as much to generic experiential beliefs as to specific ones. This defeater is generated by the present availability or epistemic possibility of *natural explanations* for every religious experience, explanations of religious experience referring solely to natural factors (see the previous chapter for a discussion of "natural": I will be thinking in terms of the disjunction of possible meanings cited there). Though it tends to be naturalists who put forward such explanations, for our purposes it will be appropriate to distinguish between "natural explanation" and "naturalistic explanation." A naturalistic explanation of religious experience would, I suppose, have to be a natural explanation of such experience together with the claim that there are no other, non-natural factors causally involved in its production. As we shall see, the defeater in question, though it may be said to support the epistemic possibility of naturalistic explanations, is more appropriately expressed in terms of natural ones.[29]

[28] Something like this is attempted by Franks Davis in her stimulating and sensitive book. See *Evidential Force*, chap. 7.

[29] One way of trying to prop up such a defeater is by supporting the very general claim that it is epistemically possible that naturalism is true, for if the latter position is correct then natural—and indeed naturalistic—explanations will *always* be right. And this is not an unpromising tack: as we saw in the previous chapter, the truth of naturalism, while not likely to be established by any arguments available today, cannot exactly be ruled out either. When we look out at the physical universe and consider its awesome extent and untold secrets, and when we consider the universe of *thought*, with so many of *its* galaxies unknown or unexplored, the idea that we should be in a position right now to confidently declare that naturalism is false must surely strike us as dubious—just as dubious as the similar idea about its truth. But another way of defending the defeater in question involves focusing on proffered and possible natural explanations specifically of religious experiences. And this is the way that I shall utilize here.

Now an obvious and much discussed natural factor of relevance to our subject is wish fulfillment. (This factor may seem old-fashioned and a bit crude given the most up-to-date neurophysiological and pharmacological developments, but a little reflection on the content of "ultimacy" suffices to show why it must remain pertinent.) We may use this example to identify what is or should be troubling about purported natural explanations of religious experience. It is important that we see this, since such natural explanations are often shrugged off with some comment to the effect that, even if they are successful, nothing has ruled out supernatural activity *further back* in the causal chain of events leading up to the experience in question. The latter is indeed a possibility in many cases, but it is the other possibility—the possibility that nature produced the experience all on its own—that can do the most work in the present context. For suppose we know that wish fulfillment can produce religious experiences. Then we know that people could be having religious experiences *whether anything supernatural is there or not*. If, moreover, we know that wish fulfillment frequently *does* lead to unveridical experiences—the sense that something is there when in fact it is not—then the reason for doubt will be much strengthened.[30] It is obvious that people are often led by their hopes and wishes to "perceive" what is not in fact present. This would be acknowledged even in religious traditions, where what is "experienced" at a lower, less mature level of development is often reconceived or shunted aside at higher levels—and are we not *always* at some "lower than possible" level of development? Even though in dealing with first-person as opposed to third-person justifications we will not think of ourselves as producing a naturalistic *hypothesis* to set alongside a religious *hypothesis*, if we are able to make use of wish fulfillment in this way, we are obviously raising doubt as to whether the supernatural was perceived in the experiences in question (which must affect even the advocate of first-person justifications). For now the reflective experient will rightly be led to wonder whether this factor has not in her own case, as in so many others, led to an apparent perception of a Divine reality when no such reality was in fact perceived. That supernatural activity *could* be involved further back in the causal chain does nothing (or should do nothing) to assuage the doubt thus produced.

As already suggested, quite a number of candidates for natural explanations of religious experience have been put forward: wish fulfillment is only the most notorious. (These may of course be understood as doing the explaining between them—no single explanation need be construed as

---

[30] Franks Davis recognizes the importance of this point. See *Evidential Force*, pp. 192–193.

seeking to account for *each and every* religious experience.) Caroline Franks Davis has a fairly long list, which she discusses in detail: on the pathological side we have hypersuggestibility, deprivation and maladjustment, mental illness, and abnormal physiological states; on the nonpathological side, cognitive need, social learning, compensation, father projection, society projection, attribution in accordance with a religious set or setting, and subliminal activity.[31] Franks Davis concedes that among them, these explanations may account for many kinds of religious experience, but argues that they leave pretty much untouched "senses of a presence, numinous experiences, and introvertive mystical experiences of healthy individuals."[32]

Other writers—for example, I. M. Lewis, Susan Blackmore, and Evan Fales—are much less optimistic, however; and they also suggest many additional explanations.[33] Here, for example, is Fales: "[Mystical] experiences, it turns out, are associated with micro-seizures of the temporal lobes of the brain. When these seizures are severe, they result in temporal lobe epilepsy. But mild seizures, which can even be artificially induced during brain surgery, can result in powerful mystical experiences. A substantial portion of the general population has a disposition to such mild seizures, and there is some circumstantial evidence that they can be provoked by techniques traditionally used to induce mystical states."[34] If this is correct, then it is clearly possible for mystical experiences to occur even when they are unveridical. Indeed, given the possibility of deliberate induction, we would have to say—if Fales's suggestion is correct—that mystical experiences *do* occur even when they are unveridical. (Are we to suppose that the Ultimate is at the mercy of a brain probe?) But then how—barring some *independent* indication that the Ultimate is known in this way, which is not available to us here—could we avoid doubt as to whether this or that mystical experience was veridical? Thus if explanations of the sort in

---

[31] See *Evidential Force,* chap. 8.

[32] Ibid., p. 233.

[33] See I. M. Lewis, *Ecstatic Religion,* 2nd ed. (London: Routledge, 1989); Susan Blackmore, *Dying to Live: Near Death Experiences* (Buffalo, N.Y.: Prometheus, 1993); and Evan Fales, "Scientific Explanations of Mystical Experience, Part I: The Case of St. Teresa" and "Scientific Explanations of Mystical Experience, Part II: The Challenge to Theism," *Religious Studies* 32 (1996), 143–163 and 297–313. For a number of ideas that might generate natural explanations of religious experiences, see Daniel Dennett, *Breaking the Spell: Religion as a Natural Phenomenon* (New York: Penguin, 2006), pt. 2.

[34] Evan Fales, "Do Mystics See God?" in *Contemporary Debates in Philosophy of Religion,* ed. Michael L. Peterson and Raymond J. VanArragon (Oxford: Blackwell, 2004), p. 154. For an interesting discussion of this and other neurophysiological accounts, see John Horgan, *Rational Mysticism* (New York: Houghton Mifflin, 2003).

question are available, then with respect to the experiences and associated beliefs to which they apply we have a defeater: it is epistemically possible that the experients involved are deceived, and so doubt is in order instead of belief.[35] (Recall here that since we have been able to support no initial presumption of innocence for religious experiential belief-forming practices, we do not need to *prove* guilt in order to have a defeater. The appropriateness of doubt about the reliability of religious experience is enough to defeat the justification of religious experiential belief.)

It is hard to say how many religious experiences would be impugned through an attempt to apply this sort of argument universally and in every instance *categorically* instead of hypothetically. As Alston notes, the study of natural explanations of religious experience is "not a popular research field for social and behavioral scientists."[36] But this lacuna only serves to set up the next stage of my argument. In the first stage we saw how natural explanations can threaten religious experiential belief. Now what we see is that even if a thorough and clearly comprehensive natural account of religious experience is not yet available, even if there are many gaps in the story, it is quite possible that this is because *insufficient attention has been given to telling it.* This is a subject area that is really only beginning to get serious attention from scientists, as we can see from the relatively small amount of research that has been done and as is indirectly confirmed by the arguments of Chapters 3 and 4. But even so a great variety of candidates for natural explanations of religious experience can already be identified.[37] Thus this area specially invites a response that emphasizes the epistemic possibility of "unrecognized defeaters" that will be uncovered in the future through the discovery of more powerful natural explanations.

---

[35] It may be difficult to determine in some cases to which experiences this or that natural explanation applies: the range of "mystical," for example, is notoriously fuzzy in many instances of its use. But while this might stand in the way of a *clearly* comprehensive account, I cannot see that it undermines doubt. Indeed, it apparently contributes to it.

[36] Alston, *Perceiving God,* p. 230.

[37] To get a sense of this, see Horgan, *Rational Mysticism.* An interesting candidate that has been in the news lately is the drug psilocybin. According to a study published by a reputable team of John Hopkins scientists (R. R. Griffiths et al.), under appropriate conditions, the use of psilocybin results in experiences very similar to spontaneously occurring religious experiences of a mystical type. (See "Psilocybin can occasion mystical-type experiences having substantial and sustained personal meaning and spiritual significance," *Pharmacology* 187 [2006], 268–283). According to a press release (www.hopkinsmedicine.org/Press_releases/2006/07_11_06.html), Griffiths, the leader of the study, said that "a vast gap exists between what we know of these drugs—mostly from descriptive anthropology—and what we believe we can understand using modern clinical pharmacology techniques. That gap is large because, as a reaction to the excesses of the 1960s, human research with hallucinogens has been basically frozen in time these past forty years."

But if we see that it is epistemically possible that a defeater will emerge in future evidence, then by the argument of Chapter 1 we have a defeater *now,* and again doubt is in order.

The moral, emotional, and social factors mentioned in Chapter 3 provide a context quite favorable to such suspicions about the future. For example, we *know* children can grow up experiencing things in a certain well-defined manner when they have been embedded in a social matrix that engenders the relevant expectations (this is one way in which Alston's emphasis on a socially reinforced practice surely cannot help his case). Perhaps many more natural factors of a similar nature will emerge from further inquiry. Here we also need again to think about the unique nature of the object of any religious practice as *ultimate.* Even the most humble religious experiences purport to be experiences of an inconceivably wonderful reality, promising an inconceivably wonderful good—which for more than one writer has brought to mind the well-established effect of desire on perception.[38] This familiar phenomenon of wish fulfillment may reveal new and unexpected facets of itself to further study. The neurophysiological possibilities are especially intriguing. The study of them is still at a primitive stage, but if it turned out that experiences phenomenologically indistinguishable from the main types of religious experience could be (re)produced at the whim of a scientist simply through appropriate stimulation of the brain, surely this would count strongly against religious experiential belief. For one thing, we would be able to say, as indicated earlier, that it is clearly possible for any religious experience to occur even when no Divine reality is specially present in it—indeed, even if no Divine reality exists! So why suppose, for any given occurrence of religious experience, that this is not one of those times? For another thing, it is widely agreed that to be religiously significant, religious experience must occur in a *spiritually appropriate context,* where, for example, there is need for illumination or support and the experience provides it. Suppose, then, that one never or rarely has such an experience when one might expect it for religious reasons but that the scientist can produce it at will. This would surely augur a lack of genuine contact with the Divine in the religious cases. But given the neurophysiological developments that have already occurred and those that may well occur in the future, we simply cannot rule out that such should turn out to be the case when all these things have been more fully and successfully investigated. Thus we clearly have an "unrecognized defeater" defeater here.

---

[38] See, for example, Nicholas Everitt, *The Nonexistence of God* (London: Routledge, 2004), p. 171.

As I pointed out earlier, in response to natural explanations, religious writers often draw our attention to the fact that God or the Ultimate might be present "further back" in the causal chain, making *use* of the natural processes cited to engender the experience. Alston, for one, can often be found making this point.[39] There are various problems with it, but here, where all we need is doubt, the appropriate reply is as follows. If you want to counter the claim that God *is not* causally involved in the production of the experience, then it is indeed enough to point out how God *could be* involved. But if you need—as here—to counter the claim that God *very well might not* be involved, or *for all we know is not* involved, then such a response is not enough. For it is quite compatible with the claim that God could be involved, that God might not be. Again, one may point out, as Alston repeatedly does,[40] how *weak* present research is and how *nothing at present* allows for a comprehensive natural account of religious experience, and this may suffice to defeat the claim that such a comprehensive account *is* available to us right now; but the point in question does nothing to refute the claim that it is epistemically possible that new defeaters along these lines will emerge in the future—indeed, it plays into its hands.

5. *Final Thoughts*

I suggest, therefore, that through appropriate reflection on natural explanations of religious experience we find another way of showing that, at our present stage of development, religious experience cannot be taken by a careful investigator to provide justification for religious belief. But is this perhaps too quick, given the framework within which we are operating? Might it be said that even if the truth-oriented approach to a defense of religious experiential belief fails, a pragmatic one can succeed? Religious experience (and the beliefs grounded in it) may be very important psychologically, socially, and so on in the life of the believer. So why not let it have its way?

But as we have seen, there are also various deficits that come with letting it "have its way," harmless though it may seem to do so. And, of course, all the more general considerations developed in Chapter 6 against a pragmatic defense of religious belief apply here too. In particular, I remind the reader of the alternative *faith* response, which especially after the various difficulties we have added to the list begun earlier in this

---

[39] See, for example, his "Does Religious Experience Justify Religious Belief?" in *Contemporary Debates*, ed. Peterson and VanArragon, pp. 140–142.

[40] See, for example, *Perceiving God*, p. 233.

chapter, where that attitude was first mentioned, must now seem clearly preferable to belief as a response to religious experience (whatever else we may say about it), from either the truth-oriented or the pragmatic perspective. Thus, all things considered, we seem to be in a position to conclude that a careful investigator has no basis for endorsing religious experiential belief.

Just as in the previous chapter, so here certain results of Part 1 have been central to the argument. If those results hold, beliefs grounded in religious experience are inadequately supported. What this means, of course, is that attempts to refute the arguments of Part 1 by reference to religious experience turn out to be just as question-begging as similar attempts drawing on apparent support for naturalism. The relevant points raised in Part 1, if forceful at all, count as much against the epistemic force of religious experience as against anything. More fully aware of this, we are again in a position to embrace the skeptical results of Part 1 with greater confidence than before: in this chapter, just as in the previous one, the results of Part 1 have been both applied and fortified.

So religious skepticism is once again further ahead. But despite the criticisms of religious experiential belief that I have here advanced in its behalf, it is important to recognize that nothing I have said suggests that we are justified in *disbelieving* that some religious experiences are veridical: Alston's main critics, who enthusiastically opt for outright disbelief instead of doubt, are just as wrong as he is. There is a positive role for religious experience. Grasping this, as it seems to me, involves thinking of religious experience as providing what we may call *intimations* of an ultimate reality, suggestions of what *might be*, even if not good evidence of what *is*. Such experience can help to keep the religious possibility alive, nurturing sympathetic and creative imagination about how it might be realized. It can, as suggested at the end of the previous chapter, help to keep naturalism in check.[41] Ideally, and viewed from a broader and more reflective perspective than a sectarian believer or perhaps any believer can muster, religious experience might even bring us closer to that further and fuller understanding of ultimate things which in the actual world *thus* far it has largely served to hinder.

---

[41] One is reminded of this when reading Dennett's *Breaking the Spell*, which succeeds in making religion appear somewhat immature and unattractive by focusing on immature and unattractive religion and almost entirely ignoring religious experience (the book has but three explicit references to it). Earlier writers such as William James in his famous *Varieties of Religious Experience* were more deeply sensitive and perceptive, recognizing that although such experience may be entirely delusive, if there is a reality *anything like* what appears to be apprehended in it, the most glowing accounts of nature's wonders (of the sort that writers like Dennett wish to substitute for religion) must fade by comparison.

PART III

GOD AND THE GAPS
The Modes Illustrated and Vindicated

LET US TAKE STOCK of where we are. I have been urging us to be *skeptics*
about ultimism. Various modes of reasoning in support of such skepticism
were developed in Part 1. In Part 2, the most general and widely influential sources of nonskeptical complacency were identified, examined, and
shown to be lacking in force. Thus we already have before us a complete
justification of religious skepticism.

But the present climate in philosophy of religion is one in which such
skeptical voices may still be hard to hear. I refer to the very powerful influence of *traditional theism*—the claim that there is a personal God. This
elaboration of ultimism, already encountered many times over in this
book, looms large in all contemporary discussion. Now philosophers
concerned with religion (whether believers or not) have always devoted
a disproportionately large amount of attention to matters theistic. But at
the present time the popularity of theism has moved to another level:
what one will find is that the most influential philosophers of religion in
the West are themselves theists, believing that God exists and defending this
belief in their work. And most other writers in the field today seem to be
following in their footsteps.

In these circumstances—given the cultural and psychological force
and the present intellectual influence of theistic belief—it may be worth
spending some extra time defending the view that this religious belief in

particular is unjustified, so as to remove all doubt for theists that doubt about ultimism is rationally required. Holding on to the idea that theistic belief is justified, and noticing that theism entails ultimism, even philosophers might be inclined to give the modes short shrift (thus here too there is the danger of complacency—a more specific sort of complacency than we observed in Part 2). Accordingly, there may be benefit in such additional arguments. Notice that the support I here provide for religious skepticism *is extra*. That explains why I am not undertaking separate discussions of *each* main concrete and extant form of religious belief, both theistic and nontheistic: the arguments already given suffice to show a lack of justification for all such beliefs, and the discussion of theism is here entered into for special reasons not applicable in the other cases.

So how will I proceed? Well, if my reasoning thus far in the book has been along the right lines, if what I have said at a more general level about our limitations and immaturity and presumption—about gaps in our investigative record and (consequently) in our understanding—is grounded in fact, then at the more specific level of thinking about theism we might expect to find that various interesting and important ideas and arguments have, to date, gone unnoticed. With new questions and the questioning of old assumptions, we might expect to unearth some previously unrecognized vindicators or defeaters—perhaps even some views "clear" in themselves (I allude to the notion of clarity and obviousness prominent in Chapter 1) which have so far been unclear to us.

Just this, I shall argue, is what we find. And the results do not favor theistic belief, for a variety of new arguments against theism can be developed. Whatever one might think of the force of these arguments, their *very existence,* in the argumentative context I have outlined, suffices to provide strong extra support for religious skepticism—and, in particular, at least skepticism as to whether present theistic discussion is on the right track. We have already seen how the earlier arguments—my modes—illustrate their own contentions. In these new atheistic arguments we find fresh illustrations of our limitations and immaturity and presumption, developed specifically in relation to theism. With previous results thus underlined in colors that will catch the eye of a theist, there is perhaps more reason to think that the force of the modes will be brought home even to believers in God, and claims about their force vindicated even in the present climate of philosophical discussion.

But of course I want to do more here than simply trot out some new arguments for atheism. I want to show that these arguments are *forceful* and *powerful,* threatening to *prove* the truth of their conclusion—that many of the claims on which they depend will appear to us as strong candidates for the status of "clear cases" when we rip the veil of tradition and convention from our eyes. If I am right about this, then my arguments justify not just doubt but *disbelief* with respect to theism. (Notice that even if theism is false and justifiedly believed false, the more general proposition of ultimism remains at most doubtful.) At the very least, so I shall claim, we may—when those arguments are set against their best theistic counterparts—justify *doubt* about theism. Hence, by noticing the force of these arguments, the theist is barred from using his theism to resist the modes. (Concerning specifically theistic religious experience, I have nothing to say beyond what I have already said in the previous chapter. I shall simply point to that chapter as evidence that theists are in no position to fall back on religious experience when arguments fail.)

Many connections appear among my arguments against theism. But some central threads binding these arguments together are (1) the idea of personal relationship with God and (2) an emphasis on neglected aspects and implications of the moral character of God. As we see in Chapter 9, a relationship with God is the deepest good for humans, if God exists. And given the relational *love* of God, a problem of *nonresistant nonbelief* emerges. But that is only the beginning. In addition to the general argument about nonresistant nonbelief, there is a collection of independent hiddenness arguments focusing, more particularly, on the different *ways* in which nonresistant nonbelief is realized in the world and on certain aspects of the Divine moral character other than love to which we might appeal in developing the view that these ways *would not* be realized if there were a God. These arguments are discussed in Chapter 10. There follows, in Chapter 11, an argument from instances of horrific suffering (horrors), which highlights the notion of relationship with God just as much as do its hiddenness siblings—though in a different way and with a slightly different moral emphasis. What it claims is that if the deepest good of relationship with God can be achieved without the permission of horrors, then a loving and *empathetic* God would never permit them. This leads directly into a fourth line of reasoning, involving free will. Having dealt with certain free-will defenses in previous chapters, I next, in Chapter 12, develop a free-will *offense*, which shows how free will, if it exists, is a *problem* for theism rather than a solution.

These arguments from hiddenness, horrors, and free will, though internally related one to another, can each stand alone as persuasive grounds for atheism. But—much as in Part 1—we may also combine results from these arguments in various interesting ways and thereby produce independently forceful arguments for atheism. First we bring together results from Chapters 9 and 10, then results from Chapters 11 and 12; and to create the strongest argument of all, we bring together elements of *those* results. How this may be achieved is shown in Chapter 13. And finally, how our results in Part 3 may be applied to yield at least skepticism about theism (and thus to provide the needed vindication of doubt about ultimism), given various assumptions concerning the force of those results, is shown in Chapter 14.

CHAPTER 9

Hiddenness Arguments I

1. *Parameters of the Discussion*

My central purpose in this chapter is to develop the first, more general sort of hiddenness argument. But in order to establish a context from which the central hiddenness claim can naturally and persuasively be extracted, let me start by exposing some central parameters—a modest framework of concept and precept—for responsible thought and talk about God.

The idea of God we will be working with is that of a personal and perfect creator of any universe there may be: omnipotent, omniscient, and perfectly good and loving. That we are speaking of something thought of as "perfect" in some sense follows from the fact that we are dealing with an elaboration of ultimism.[1] The elaboration appears in the qualification of "perfect" by "personal." Together, these two notions yield a particular view of the nature of the ultimate emphasizing certain omni-properties naturally associated with the perfection of personal being—God has *all* power, *all* knowledge, *all* goodness, *all* creative responsibility, and so on. With a different qualifier (a different elaboration) we might find ourselves thinking of different things, but in this case it is ultimized versions of properties appropriate to persons, which certainly include such things as power, knowledge, and creativity.

---

[1] In Chapter 2 we raised some doubts about whether a traditional personalist conception could really be *worthy* of the label "ultimate," and so we might here be led to ask whether any exclusively personal being (where the parameters of "personal" are as narrowly drawn as is customary in theistic religion and philosophy) *could* be *unsurpassably* great. But there is no denying that the personal God is thought of as ultimate, and for the purposes of this discussion I will set aside those doubts.

Now it is important to note that what we see here *is* the traditional *idea* of God. A multitude of *images* swirl about this notion, many of them potentially productive of assumptions about God not at all entailed by that idea. An important and topical example is the image of a human *male*—more specifically, that of a human *father*. Much of what is said about God assumes that the personal being who is God is male and a father, or more like a male and a father than like a female and a mother. But there is nothing in the idea of a perfect and personal creator to support such assumptions, and much to oppose them. Indeed, when we consider the perfections of moral character, which include such things as caring and compassion and empathy, it is obvious that much of what is called feminine must be exemplified in the highest possible degree by any personal God there may be. (Here we see one of the ways in which the idea of God is "ahead" of many of its adherents and critics, still waiting to be properly understood.)

Because of such facts, we ought not burden the traditional concept of God with patriarchal assumptions. That should mean a commitment to the avoidance of masculine language when referring to God. It also means that apt criticisms of traditional belief in God will not rest on its often alleged entanglements with patriarchy. That is to say, it is unreasonable to argue that the traditional idea of God should be rejected because it is one-sidedly masculine "all the way down." (Though it would be in line with my emphasis on growing beyond our limited past to do the former if I went along with the latter, I do not go along with it. I think the belief among many of today's cultural elite that theism suffers from an irremediably one-sided masculinity rests on a confusion of concept and image.)[2] The deepest problems for theistic belief have nothing to do with patriarchal entanglements. Indeed, it is on account of facets of the nature of a perfect personal being that a feminist sensibility enables us to see most clearly and appreciate most adequately that the really serious problems arise.

It is the exercise of imagination that will be of most use to us here, both in seeing that what some common interpretations and criticisms of the God-concept suppose to be entailed by it is not at all thus entailed, and in seeing that certain other things, commonly unnoticed or unthinkingly denied, are—or at any rate may well be—entailed by it. (I shall claim that there are necessary truths in this vicinity that we are only now discovering.) The imagination can loosen the grip of conventional viewpoints and open us up to new ideas, which may be much better supported than conventional ones.

---

[2] In works written for a general readership this confusion is especially evident—see, e.g., Karen Armstrong, *A History of God* (New York: Random House, 1994), and Marcus Borg, *The God We Never Knew* (San Francisco: Harper, 1998).

We are in very great need of such "loosening up" or "shaking up" in the theological domain. Because of the way our thinking is so often shaped from early on by *belief* in God (even those who today are *former* believers are included here), we rarely get used to thinking freely about what this big concept we've got hold of actually implies. Even when our conception of the world is suitably enlarged to include the whole universe, we don't consider carefully enough, for example, whether there would really be a physical universe at all, if there were a God, or think hard about all the other forms the created order might take, on the assumption that God creates.[3] Instead we keep the thought of God tied to thoughts of the actual world (or possible worlds very close thereto), as though there would be something wrong if we were to conclude that a God could never have created a world anything like this one. (A typical symptom: God is commonly described as creator of the universe—that is, of *our* universe—instead of, more correctly, as the creator of any universe there may be.) Even critics of theism commonly assume that a God would create a material universe like ours or would create *human* beings and give them *free will*, and so on, when these are only the most familiar of the scenarios available to thought.[4] If we want to move beyond the limitations of the past, we must become much more comfortable with an expanded imagination on matters of this kind.

There is a potential confusion of theology and philosophy lurking in this neighborhood that it is important to avoid and, therefore, important to point out. We have—all of us—been influenced by the many attempts of theology to make God fit the actual world. Theology starts off by accepting that God exists and so *has* to make God fit the world: in a way, that is its job. But our job as philosophers, faced with the question of God's existence, is to fight free from the distractions of local and historical contingency, to let the voice of authority grow dim in our ears, and to think for ourselves about what a God and a God-created world would be like.[5] When we think at the most fundamental level about the idea of God, we cannot assume

---

[3] An important recent exception, at least on the matter of whether God would create, is William Rowe. See his *Can God Be Free?* (Oxford: Clarendon Press, 1994).

[4] One might reasonably think that *if* God is the greatest possible being and a purely spiritual and nonphysical reality, and *if* the greatest good of creatures lies in relationship with God, then there is a priori reason to expect that any world God creates will be purely spiritual and nonphysical in nature. What we as material beings embedded in a material world *think* it would be good for God to create may be both entirely expectable and—given the content of the antecedent of the aforementioned conditional—entirely mistaken.

[5] Certainly there are relevant insights about such matters to be gleaned from extant views and traditions of religious practice and reflection. But in other cases one sees centuries of rationalization—layer on layer of obfuscatory thought that can almost lead one to lose sight of the fact that if theism is correct, there is *another center of consciousness* in reality, and

that probably God's nature is in accord with the actual world, *and so we cannot take as our guide a picture of God fashioned by theology over the centuries on that assumption.* We must be open to the possibility that the world would be *completely different* than it is if there were a God. For the properties we ascribe to God have implications, and these place constraints on what the *world* could be like if there were a being with those properties.

In this and succeeding chapters, I will be suggesting that if we are truly open and reflectively imaginative in this way about the traditional conception of God, we will be forced to conclude that the aforementioned possibility may well be realized. Many gaps in our understanding of the Divine have been left by the hardening of historical positions formed for no good reason and on the assumptions of theology just mentioned, together with psychological and other factors that have caused such positions to be inordinately influential and prevented the freeing of our imaginations with respect to the issues they concern. I will be exposing some of these gaps and seeking to fill others, and in both of these ways, so I shall argue, the cause of skepticism is advanced, whether we like it or not. I begin with the long-ignored problem of Divine hiddenness.[6]

2. *God, Creation, and Divine-Creature Relationship*

If God exists and is a truly ultimate reality, then before or at any rate independently of creation, unsurpassable metaphysical goodness is already realized in God. That is one reason why it might be (and sometimes has been) wondered whether we should expect there to be in concrete reality anything *other* than God, if God exists. How can unsurpassable greatness be improved on, and mustn't the total value of things indeed in some sense diminish if something is added to God? Clearly, any way of turning that wondering into justified assertion (the assertion that there would *not* be something other than God, if God existed) must leave us with atheism, for if anything is obvious it is that there is something other than God! But

---

indeed the greatest possible such being, with all power and all compassion and love. In any case, for philosophers, the nature of their source can provide no advance recommendation for ideas rooted in religious tradition: the latter will have to prove their merits within the larger context of openness and reflective imagination that I am emphasizing here.

[6] My main previous discussions of this problem are *Divine Hiddenness and Human Reason* (Ithaca: Cornell University Press, 1993) and "The Hiddenness Argument Revisited I" and "The Hiddenness Argument Revisited II," *Religious Studies* 41 (2005), 201–215, and *Religious Studies* 41 (2005), 287–303, respectively. The latter two works respond to the various replies to my hiddenness argument appearing in *Divine Hiddenness: New Essays*, ed. Daniel Howard-Snyder and Paul K. Moser (Cambridge: Cambridge University Press, 2002).

let us suppose that God brings into existence (or everlastingly sustains in existence) an ontologically independent concrete reality (a concrete reality other than God). What might motivate such creativity? Surely, at least in part, the delight of creativity itself, whose wonders all of us have at least in some small measure experienced—a delight instantiating a kind of love. But in the Divine case we must certainly fill this out and also say "creativity exercised in the pursuit of value," or some such thing. For it is inconceivable that a perfect personal God would exercise creativity purely for its own sake and with wild abandon, uncaring about whether the results were good or bad.[7]

Now suppose that a God's creative activity would include the production of finite personal creatures—again, this might be denied or questioned, but for the sake of discussion, which could not even get seriously started otherwise, I suggest we make this assumption. Doing so in conjunction with the immediately preceding reflections yields the following thoughts: (A) that the Divine creation must express not just the love involved in creative delight and the love involved in valuing other good things created but a *relational-personal* love as well, for now the creator has elected to make available to *other* personal beings an experience of reality, and in a perfect personal being contact with other personal beings would necessarily express whatever belongs to relational-personal love (it would be the greater for doing so); (B) that God's relational-personal love must indeed be the most perfect possible; and (C) that the creativity God exercises in producing finite personal creatures must itself be expressed in pursuit of value realizable in and through and by them. This last follows from the earlier point about the direction of Divine creativity but also from that element of the best relational-personal love we call benevolence, which clearly entails the seeking of value for the loved one.

But what value does (C) refer to? Well, perhaps at least in part it is value borrowed from (deriving from some connection with) the value that we have seen must be embodied in the *rest* of a Divine creation, in what I will call nature. But nature itself does not have any value that is not a reflection of value in God if God is *ultimate* and embodies the *greatest possible* value (a being than which none greater can be conceived would have to be such that no value could exist that did not reflect *its* value—else a greater being could be conceived, the value of whose life, otherwise the same, in some way *was* reflected by the value in nature). And the experience of nature

---

[7] Notice that one can be creative for its own sake and *also* for the sake of value to which one sees the relevant exercise of creativity may lead: our motives need not be one-dimensional.

would be richer and fuller if it were experienced *as* the creation of God and *as* reflecting the fullest and richest value of all, existing in God. It would, moreover, be immensely richer and fuller if recognized as the generous *gift* of a God willing to *share* with finite personal beings the wonders of creation. And of course the next insight must be that if there could be *direct*—subject to Subject—experience of an unsurpassably rich and wondrous God, leading the finite subject to ever more fully apprehend and to be progressively transformed in the direction of the life of the infinite Subject, the opportunity to have such experience would be the greatest gift of all, and the surest and deepest way for God to realize value in and through and for created personal beings.

All in all, then, it seems that a God would certainly make available to finite personal creatures who are capable of experiencing it the gift of conscious apprehension of God.[8] Indeed, reflection on the issue with which we began (the issue of how the total value of things could fail to diminish if something is added to God) might have led us to expect this. For what could provide for a total state of affairs as good as one in which only God exists apart from a creation in every corpuscle aflame with the presence of God? (By this means, we see, among other things, how the whole idea of God pursuing external, perhaps unknown, goods for the good of creatures—an idea often used against such arguments as I will be mounting for atheism—is unacceptably anthropomorphic and just out of place, suitable only in relation to more limited beings who do not realize all goodness in themselves: in a very real sense, if God exists, God *is* the good.)

Thus simply through reflection on (C) above, we already see how God would make conscious awareness of the Divine available to every finite personal creature. And this support is only strengthened when we notice how every possible token experience of the kinds at issue here—experience of nature as the creature of God; of nature as deeply reflecting the unsurpassably great value existing in God; of the value thus received as the gift of God; and of God without intermediary—exists somewhere

---

[8] Filling out this use of the term "available" properly might be thought to require some reference to *free will*—by which is in this book meant *incompatibilist* (or libertarian) free will. (An action's being a result of the exercise of free will in this sense is incompatible with its being determined by prior conditions outside the agent's control.) Perhaps God must allow creatures to have this great good of awareness of the Divine if (but only if) they freely choose to have it, in a context of temptations militating against such choice. But so far as we have found no reason to introduce this notion—does God have free will? Perhaps, indeed, awareness of God would be the "natural lot" of creatures, and growth toward God their inevitable trajectory. Now some will say that free will is essential to the sort of *personal* relationship with God we have already begun to discuss, but in Chapter 12 I shall argue that it is not.

along a continuum stretching from early, elementary forms of awareness that have only begun to be filled out, to much richer forms of experience that reflect more of the richness in God, to *infinity* (because both a God-created nature and God must be so complex and wonderful as to be inexhaustible and never completely penetrable by finite personal creatures). When we notice all this, we see how natural it is to affirm that all capable creatures would at all times have available to them *some* form of conscious awareness of God, if there were a God. For then experience of God need not be—as so often it is in the actual world—construed as the exclusive preserve of the spiritually elite; the notion thereof can instead be radically democratized. And would it not be the greater, the more worthy of a truly Divine reality, if construed as fully inclusive in this way?[9]

But that was just (C). Turning now to (A) and (B), we find much more reason to believe the proposition in question. (A) and (B), recall, derived from the most general considerations with which we began that the motive behind creation must include a relational-personal love as well as other loves, and that God's relational-personal love would have to be the most perfect possible. In discussing these points I introduce the notion of *(positively) meaningful conscious relationship with God,* or rather, explicitly introduce, since it was implicit in what was said in discussing (C). Suppose (as implicitly we did before) that there are creatures in the world God creates who are *capable* of this sort of relationship with God. To be more precise: suppose there are individuals whose process of maturation has seen the development of such general cognitive and affective faculties as are required to, in some measure, consciously experience the presence of God and respond positively thereto—the cognitive and affective equipment required, for example, to believe that God is lovingly present and make a response expressing gratitude or one that involves seeking a deepening of the experience of God.

What I want now to suggest is that there is something remarkably odd and indeed incoherent about the idea that, supposing there really is a God whose relational-personal love is unsurpassably perfect, such creatures should ever be unable to *exercise* their capacity for meaningful relationship with God—at least so long as they have not got themselves into that state through in some way over time *resisting* the Divine (for example, emotionally or behaviorally opposing belief in God in a manner stemming ultimately from their own choices) and thus arriving at a place where they

---

[9] One might observe here that the hypothesis that experience of God is available to *all* capable creatures at *all* times (and in a degree limited only by their capacity) is also the *simpler.*

have shut themselves off from God.[10] What sense can we make of the idea that there should exist capable creatures open to positive and explicit relationship with a perfectly loving God, not resisting it in the slightest, but not in a place where they can have such a relationship—and all this in a world in which there exists a God whose relational-personal love is the *most perfect possible?* I suggest that if we look carefully at the matter, we will not be able to make any sense of that at all. A perfectly loving God—if those words mean anything—would ensure that some form of conscious and meaningful relationship with herself was always possible for capable and nonresistant finite persons. For suppose she did not. Then she would be electing to make available to other personal beings an experience of reality—in that sense *sharing* reality with them—and doing so in a manner that expresses the most perfect relational-personal love but at some or many times failing to share *God* with them! This way lies inconsistency: if we say that God shares reality with other persons in a manner that always expresses the deepest love for them but sometimes is unavailable to them (where what is unavailable is understood in terms of the continuum of innumerable possible experiences of the Divine mentioned above), we imply that at some time God does not love them most deeply—which generates the contradiction.

Notice also how our everyday understanding of the language of love pushes us in this direction. By appealing to it I am not arguing from analogy for a probabilistic conclusion, but as the previous sentence suggests, I am really making a conceptual point: various examples can be used to motivate realization of the fact that when we use the word "loving" *discriminatingly*—not just as a synonym for "good"—and also *admiringly* of person *A* who loves person *B*, it is part of the very meaning of what we say that *A* does whatever she can to ensure that *B* is always able, just by trying, to engage in meaningful conscious relationship with *A*. One way in which doing "whatever she can" might not be enough to facilitate a meaningful relationship—which, as indicated, I am supposing to be possibly applicable also in the case of God and finite creatures—would involve *B*'s resisting and ultimately shutting herself off from *A*. (And perhaps among finite creatures there will sometimes also be difficulties deriving from *A*'s previous deficiencies as a lover or from some other negative feature associated with *A* that—as later discussion will confirm—must be inapplicable or remediable where *A* is God, which lead *A* to recognize that whatever

---

[10] This point assumes that the creatures would have free will. Perhaps they would not (cf. n. 8). However, for the remainder of this discussion we may go along with this assumption, so natural in the context of contemporary philosophy of religion, if only to show that the development of a problem of Divine hiddenness does not depend on denying it.

she could do would still not be enough.) But insofar as she can do so, *A* will ensure, if *A* admirably loves *B*, that *B* is—as I will say—*in a position* to have a meaningful conscious relationship with *A*. This is just *part* of love for any admirably loving mother or husband or brother or friend.

Now a loving person might, to be sure, occasionally stand to one side and let the loved one take some responsibility for the relationship's development, and would want to avoid suffocating the loved one with attention, and now and then might even withdraw for a time to make a point. Further, she might not always be *immediately* present to the loved one (I may love you perfectly well but be off in Africa where for a time you can't contact me). But it is important to notice that these are still moments *within* a love relationship, which only reveal the diversity of ways in which someone's presence can be positively experienced and positive responses thereto can be made. (While I am in Africa your life may still be infused with the positive features of our relationship—you may, for example, feel emotionally supported in a way you otherwise wouldn't—and you may be called on to trust in my promise to return.) A loving person might also, as we have seen, reluctantly accept the fact that her loved one is (at least for the moment) unwilling to participate in relationship or else has taken deliberate steps that (at least until his attitudes change) put any kind of relationship out of reach for him, respecting the decisions that led him to that state.

All this we can acknowledge. But what we cannot say is that insofar as we are truly and properly loving parents or spouses or siblings or friends, we will ever take steps to put meaningful relationship out of reach *ourselves*, and thus, if the object of our love takes no such steps, he will always (insofar as we are able to ensure it) be in a position to relate to us positively. The possibility of some form of meaningful conscious relationship will always be there for him. Surely this is overwhelmingly plausible. What loving mother or husband or brother or friend would ever allow this possibility to be taken completely away, if he or she could help it? And to this we must surely add, given that God's love for us would have to be far more unremitting and indefectible than the best love of human persons (and given that "if she can help it" has no application to the Divine): What *perfectly loving God* would ever allow this possibility to be taken completely away?

Now here we need to recur briefly to some points made in section 1 (or to a specific application thereof). Perhaps many of us are not fully comfortable with applying what I have said about love to God due to features of our environment and of the religious teaching to which we have been exposed, all of which make it easy for us to go along with the idea of a God who is more detached and aloof. There are indeed many factors that may cause us to underestimate the force of love-based arguments like the one I am developing. We have, for example, as we have seen, a tendency to image God as male and father, and it is still easy in our culture to think of males and fathers as forgivably distant. Moreover, we have been influenced by the attempts of theology to make God fit the actual world, in which, of course, the Divine presence is far less than obvious (more on this below). But if we stand back from all this for a moment and seek to think for ourselves about what a truly ultimate reality that was fully personal and really was perfectly loving in relation to finite personal creatures would be like, a somewhat different picture of God from the one we are used to will emerge. Then what I have said about Divine love and the availability, for all, of relationship with God, though quite foreign to the actual world, may come to seem perfectly natural and appropriate to us.

So what do we have at this point? I suggest that on the basis of previous argumentation involving (A), (B), and (C), we have more than sufficient reason to affirm that

> (1) Necessarily, if God exists, anyone who is (i) not resisting God and (ii) capable of meaningful conscious relationship with God is also (iii) in a position to participate in such relationship (able to do so just by trying).

And that first premise of the hiddenness argument is the critical one. If you accept it, you will find it easy to go the rest of the way with the argument. For *the belief that God exists* is obviously and necessarily one of the conditions of being in a position to exercise one's capacity for meaningful conscious relationship with God—how can I experience nature as the creature of God or hear God speak to me (interpreting it as God speaking) or consciously experience Divine forgiveness and support or feel grateful to God or experience God's loving and inspiring presence and respond thereto in love and obedience and worship if I do not believe that there is a God? That gets us the next premise:

> (2) Necessarily, one is at a time in a position to participate in meaningful conscious relationship with God only if at that time one believes that God exists.

And because belief *is* one of those conditions and because God in willing a certain state must obviously will all its conditions, we may quickly infer from the conjunction of (1) and (2) the further claim that

> (3) Necessarily, if God exists, anyone who is (i) not resisting God and (ii) capable of meaningful conscious relationship with God also (iii) believes that God exists.

The presence of God will be for such creatures like a light that—however much the degree of its brightness may fluctuate—remains on unless they close their eyes.

But just by looking around us with *our* eyes open, we can see that this state of affairs does not actually obtain. (As I shall often put it, there is much *nonresistant nonbelief,* or, in a proposition here treated synonymously, God is *hidden.*)[11] Consider, for example, those who have always believed in God and who would love to go on believing in God but who have found, as adults, that serious and honest examination of all the evidence of experience and argument they can lay their hands on has unexpectedly had the result of eroding their belief away. These are individuals who were happy and morally committed believers and who remain morally committed but are no longer happy because of the emotional effects of an intellectual reorganization involving the removal of theistic belief. Perhaps they will be happy again, but the point is that for the time being, it is the *removal* of theistic belief that they are inclined to resist, if anything. For they were still on friendly terms with God and benefiting in a variety of ways from what they took to be contact with God when their belief in the existence of such a being was whisked away.[12] Consider also all those—both at the present time and throughout the past—in whom theistic belief has *never* been a live option. In some such individuals, quite other beliefs, supported by authority or tradition or experience, have held sway instead of theism. In others, the basic conceptual conditions of so much as *entertaining* the idea of a being separate from a created physical universe who is all-powerful, all-knowing, and perfectly good and loving in relation to it have never been satisfied. Hence there is overwhelming support for the claim that

---

[11] In previous writing I have spoken of *reasonable* or *inculpable* nonbelief, nonbelief that arises through no fault of one's own, construing this as representing a sufficient condition of nonresistant nonbelief whose occurrence is fairly easy to establish. But as I have been (mis)understood to suggest that a general inculpability is not just sufficient but necessary for a situation in which God would—according to the argument here developed—be revealed to someone, I now speak otherwise.

[12] Notice that I am introducing the unhappiness of these individuals not as evidence that something *bad* has occurred (which might be turned into a variant of the argument from evil—more on this below), but only as evidence that they are not resisting God or belief in God. Notice also that since by "belief" I understand an involuntary tendency to see the world a certain way—a "seeing" that involves being passively *represented to* instead of actively *representing the world to oneself* by imagining or picturing it a certain way—what we are talking about here is something that *can* be "whisked away" when the evidence no longer seems to support it. For much more on the nature of belief and of related attitudes, see my *Prolegomena to a Philosophy of Religion* (Ithaca: Cornell University Press, 2005).

(4) There are (and often have been) people who are (i) not resisting
God and (ii) capable of meaningful conscious relationship with
God *without* also (iii) believing that God exists.[13]

And from the conjunction of (3) and (4) it clearly follows that

(5) God does not exist.

What we find, then, through careful reasoning and consideration of
the heart and soul of love, in the context of more general considerations
about God and creation and the need for thinking unrestricted by traditional theology, is that the existence of nonresistant nonbelief shows the
nonexistence of God.

3. *Objections to the Hiddenness Argument*

How forceful, all things considered, should a philosopher consider the
hiddenness argument to be? An answer requires consideration of objections.[14] Most critics contest (1) and/or (3), usually by putting forward
considerations that, it is alleged, should put us (at least) in doubt about

---

[13] Given the different forms of support I have cited, it would take something like willful blindness to fail to affirm that not *all* nonbelief is the product of willful blindness (or
some other resistant state), even if some of it is. Being a generous sort, I will assume that
none of my readers is willfully blind and accordingly take it as having been established to
everyone's satisfaction that there is nonresistant nonbelief. (Those who want more on this
may consult my " 'Breaking Down the Walls That Divide': Virtue and Warrant, Belief and
Nonbelief," *Faith and Philosophy* 21 [2004], 195–213.) A different sort of objection to premise 4 might question my assumption that nonresistant nonbelievers are in fact *capable* of
positive relationship with God. As Paul Draper has suggested in correspondence, we need
to be open to the possibility that, given the huge distance between an unsurpassably great
God and ourselves, this *cannot* be the case, on account of our just not having what it takes to
understand anything a God might want to tell us or to experience anything of such a God's
reality in a meaningful and non-overwhelming fashion. I reply that if we were talking about
the *generic* idea of ultimacy, unqualified by personhood as commonly understood, some
such point might be forceful (see Chapter 2 on this). But theists bring the Ultimate within
range by saying that what is ultimized are qualities much like ours. And so the present objection is committed to saying that the maximally great *person* might possibly be unable to
communicate with other *persons*—with (to some extent) ontologically similar beings. And
how persuasive is that? If God is maximally intelligent and has maximally great "know-how"
and is a person is *some* way like us, wouldn't God be able to figure out how to communicate
with lowly me and transmit enough of the Divine glory down the line to get me moving in
the right direction? If this weren't the case, wouldn't God be rather like a stuffy professor
incapable of extricating himself from his circle of sophistication and communicating in a
simple manner with simple folk about profound things—and thus somewhat *less* than an
unsurpassably great person?

[14] For a more detailed consideration of certain objections to the hiddenness argument,
see the sources cited in n. 6.

whether what the argument says God would do is so much as true. (They are well-advised to do so, for otherwise the hiddenness argument might be recast in terms of what God would do in the actual world even if not necessarily—more on this later.) I will start with such objections, but at the end of the chapter I will also address an objection that contests, more specifically and exclusively, my presentation of (3) as a *necessary* truth.

Some objections, reflecting less than a serious engagement with the argument, can be dealt with swiftly. It has been said, for example, that a God shouldn't be expected to entertain us with spectacular cosmic performances or overwhelm us with miracles. But it doesn't take much imagination to see how nonresistant nonbelief in its various forms might be prevented through the provision of more subtle and interesting forms of evidence, such as religious experiences whose character and force are modulated according to our intellectual and moral needs. It has also been said that God would not force us into relationship or coerce our love. But even a cursory glance at the argument should reveal that I have not suggested that God would *bring us into* Divine-human relationship; rather I have made the heavily qualified claim that God would put in place the conditions necessary for us to be *able* to *bring ourselves* into such relationship, *insofar as we have not already made choices leaving us in a contrary position.*

Another less than serious attempt to deal with the hiddenness problem involves sweeping it under the rug of the problem of evil. The suggestion here is that since the problematic nature of Divine hiddenness consists in the *suffering* that uncertainty or the loss of theistic belief may sometimes involve, and since there are far worse forms of suffering than that, which discussion of the problem of evil has shown can be handled by theists, the so-called problem of hiddenness may safely be ignored. I hope it will be obvious that this approach is misguided; the severity of the problem posed by hiddenness cannot be judged by the severity of the suffering it may occasion. For one thing, as suggested above, there are types of nonresistant nonbelief that do not involve regretted *doubt* or *loss* of belief. But more fundamentally, even if doubt *were* the only thing at issue, it is not the anguish of (some) doubt and the empathy of God that, in the first instance, should lead us to wonder why there are nonresistant doubters. It is rather the disposition of a Creator to share the value involving conscious awareness of God and the natural inclination of any loving parent (and so of any loving Parent) to make meaningful relationship with herself possible for her children—for their sake, certainly, but also for its own sake, *and even where there would be no pain and suffering if it were not made available.* The Divine Creator/Parent's motivation to make Divine-creature relationship possible therefore includes much more than do the motives to which we appeal when we argue, if we do, that God would prevent pain and suffering.[15]

A more serious (though still misguided) objection conflates what my argument claims—that if God exists, nonresistant nonbelief does not occur—with "If God exists, nonresistant nonbelievers receive evidence sufficient for belief," and argues that nonresistant nonbelievers might, for one reason or another, not be *ready* for such evidence. But what the claim of my argument actually means is that if God exists, there is *never* a time when someone nonresistantly fails to believe (belief is made available as soon as there is a capacity for relationship with God). In other words, if there is a God, *there are no nonresistant nonbelievers who may be treated in the imagined fashion.* It is no use showing that God would not or might not interrupt the lives of nonresistant nonbelievers with evidence when what we need is a way of understanding how God could have permitted someone to become a nonresistant nonbeliever in the first place.

Yet a further objection seeks to convince us that a perfectly good relationship with God can be had even if one simply *accepts* that God exists in a manner compatible with nonbelief (or has faith that God exists in the beliefless sense I myself have delineated in *Prolegomena*),[16] and that, despite insufficient evidence for belief, there is plenty of reason to accept that God exists (or to have faith that God exists), because of the pragmatic benefits of such acceptance (or faith).[17] But even if *we* might be satisfied under certain circumstances with such an acceptance-based relation to God, an important point here is surely that nothing has been presented to show that *a perfectly loving God* would rest content with it: all the points

---

[15] Perhaps the suggestion will instead be that the hiddenness argument is reducible to the argument from evil because the former, like the latter, is arguing from things *bad*. But even if we were to suppose that in some sense the hiddenness argument can be said to be arguing from what is bad (and this is questionable—certainly atheists would disagree), to say because of this that the hiddenness argument is reducible to the argument from evil would be like saying that because the theistic teleological argument, like the cosmological argument, argues from things contingent, the teleological argument is reducible to the cosmological argument; or that because the argument for God's existence from religious experience, like the argument from miracles, is concerned with apparent terrestrial manifestations of Divine action, the argument from religious experience is reducible to the argument from miracles. Such claims are manifestly unconvincing, and so—for the same reason—is the reductionist claim about the relation between the hiddenness argument and the argument from evil. Whatever one's view of the latter, the former will require independent consideration.

[16] See *Prolegomena*, chap. 6.

[17] Jeff Jordan develops this objection in terms of acceptance in the course of his response to my argument in a forthcoming Internet debate, moderated by Paul Draper, to be developed as an e-book: *God or Blind Nature? Philosophers Debate the Evidence.*

about how love entails making available the fuller sort of relationship involving belief remain untouched (notice, for example, how to consciously experience the presence of God and to respond gratefully thereto and be comforted by God or feel forgiven, and the like, all presuppose *believing* that God exists and not just accepting that proposition).

Now perhaps one might say—as does Jeff Jordan, the author of this objection—that acceptance is preferable because it is not subject to the waxing and waning, ebbing and flowing, properties of involuntary belief, or because it permits one to choose whether one will interact with God. But the latter point only ignores again the distinction between *being in* a relationship with God and *being in a position to enter (or remain in) such a relationship through one's free choice to do so*. Even if one believes in God, one is not necessarily in the first of these states, only the second. And the second state is (by definition) compatible with just the sort of choice Jordan values. As for Jordan's former point: this ignores how God could easily see to it that our evidence for belief was adjusted according to the vicissitudes of life and kept always causally sufficient for the belief that God exists. Perhaps Jordan is here influenced by the ebbing and flowing to which theistic belief appears to be subject in the *actual* world. But then he is in danger of question-beggingly assuming that religious effects in the actual world are indicative of what the effects of God's behavior in self-revelation would really be. Why suppose that the actual world reflects all that God could produce in the way of stable belief unless you are assuming that its instances of theistic belief *are* produced by God—and thus assuming that God actually exists?[18]

Quite apart from the points I have just been making, I must also observe, in response to Jordan, that anyone who has read the first two parts of this book has reason to deny that pragmatic arguments could support acceptance of the existence of God: even if something like this might be true for generic ultimism, human ignorance of the range of religious options undermines the rationality of plumping, in either belief *or* acceptance, specifically for theism. (Writers like Jordan tend to ignore or without much investigation to disparage nontheistic forms of religion in the actual world—and to overlook entirely that many forms of ultimism may not yet have been encountered.) If it is presently to be the case that some

---

[18] The mistake referred to here is a tempting one and can be realized in a variety of ways. One might, for example, argue that the experiences of those who in the actual world struggle with doubt show the benefits of such a state, unrealized in any other way. But who is to say that they would not be realizable in other ways if there really were a God? (More on such "other ways" later.) We must think of various possible things a God might do, not just the possibilities suggested by actual experience. Otherwise, again, we are in danger of assuming that God actually exists and begging the question.

kind of relationship *with God* is the clear rational choice, evidence sufficient for theistic belief *as opposed to other forms of religious belief* will need to
be provided (and then of course the fuller relationship referred to above,
which we have independent reason to suppose a loving God would make
available, will also be possible).

Many serious objections to the hiddenness argument (including, in
an inchoate form, one or two of the points already mentioned) have this
in common: they concede that God has reason to make some sort of
relationship with the Divine available but refer us to some additional reason they suppose to be available to God—usually expressed in terms of
some great good God would or might seek to realize—in virtue of which
God might permit nonresistant nonbelief for some time for some or all
created persons, *despite* the Divine motivation to make Divine-human relationship at all times available to individuals. Let us now consider this
type of objection more closely. Various goods we know of might be enu-
merated and considered in doing so—such goods, for example, as moral
freedom, serious responsibility (both intellectual and non-intellectual),
the cultivation of character, a choice of destiny, cooperation with others,
spiritually efficacious revelation of moral/spiritual deficiencies, nurturance of a deeper spiritual maturity, and occasions for meaningful investigation and intellectual debate. But discussing all the issues that arise in
connection with such goods would obviously take a great deal of time.
Fortunately, there is a way around that. First, let's notice that if the most
fundamental spiritual reality is a personal God, then all serious spiritual
development must begin in what I have emphasized, namely, personal
relationship with God. Second, such relationship with an infinitely rich
personal reality would have to be the greatest good any human being
could possibly experience, if God exists. But then, one wants to ask, why
this talk of some *other* good, for the sake of which God might *sacrifice* such
relationship?

Consider also, in this connection, the infinite *resourcefulness* of God, and
again—but in a slightly different way—the infinite depth and richness of
God. If God indeed possesses these attributes, then there must at any point
in time *after* the beginning of relationship with God be literally an infinite
number of ways of *developing* in relationship with God and experiencing
wonderful new goods (here we see again the point from section 2 about
experiences of God existing on a continuum). Given the richness and
multileveled nature of any personal relationship with God, there must
always be more to discover and overcome. Indeed, at virtually any stage
along the way, there can be new opportunities for the exercise of moral
freedom and responsibility, the cultivation of character, choices affecting
one's destiny, cooperation with others, and meaningful investigation and

intellectual development, not to mention the need for awareness of one's moral/spiritual deficiencies and for the nurturance of a deeper spiritual maturity. In light of this fact, it seems extremely odd that anyone should think that, on account of some such reason as has been mentioned, some creatures might be prevented by God from so much as *beginning* a conscious relationship with God. And yet this is what the defenders of Divine distance must make intelligible to us.

In other writing, I have called the strategy for defeating objections to the hiddenness argument suggested here an "accommodationist" strategy, since in employing it we show how goods emphasized by the critic can be accommodated *within* a properly commodious and subtle view of Divine-creature relationship, and so would not be viewed by a loving God as providing reasons for leaving creatures without it. Given what we have seen must be the natural disposition of Divine creative love to express itself—what even someone unconvinced by my conceptual arguments about love would have to call the Divine *bias* in favor of relationship—the critic must surely concede that any reason God found appealing as a reason for remaining hidden from finite personal creatures would have to be one whose dominant concern *could not* be met within the framework of Divine-creature interaction over time envisaged by the argument. For otherwise God would not be convinced by it in the relevant way—after all, then God would be able to achieve both the relevant desiderata, but only by *not* being hidden. And even our own meager imagination can provide powerful reasons for supposing that an infinitely resourceful God *would* be able to procure all the relevant desiderata without being hidden.

To see how this "accommodationist" strategy works, consider part of Swinburne's response to my argument, in his recent *Providence and the Problem of Evil.*[19] Having outlined what he takes to be the great goods of individual and cooperative investigation of the question whether God exists (being able to find out for ourselves the "ultimate truth about the Universe")[20] and of helping others who are ignorant to discover the answer to this question, he writes as follows: "[Not everyone will] have that opportunity [to learn of God's existence] until after death, but I see no adequate grounds for supposing that God would ensure that they have it at every moment of time, in view of the benefits that flow from their not having it for some time."[21] Is there some way in which the goods Swinburne mentions can be accommodated (satisfactorily achieved or made up for) by

---

[19] Richard Swinburne, *Providence and the Problem of Evil* (Oxford: Clarendon Press, 1998).
[20] Ibid., 210.
[21] Ibid., 257–258.

God in a scenario involving the banishment of nonresistant nonbelief? The answer is clearly yes.

Let us see how this answer can be developed specifically in relation to the alleged distinctively great value of the discovery, through investigation, that theism is true.[22] It is not at all clear why we should suppose that this question is intellectually the *most* significant, and so represents a possibility of intellectual attainment greater than all others. Swinburne says that, given theism, the ultimate truth about the universe is that God exists, and that it is a great privilege to be able to discover this ultimate truth for ourselves. The suggestion is that the privilege of being able to discover—to come to know—this ultimate truth is the greatest privilege of intellectual discovery we can have. If God does not give us this, we can only have what is intellectually second-best. But surely there is an important sense in which the ultimate (in the sense of greatest) intellectual discovery possible is not the discovery of the ultimate truth, where this is a lone proposition like "God exists." The ultimate discovery given theism would be discovery of just exactly what belongs to a huge—perhaps infinitely large—conjunction, of which the proposition "God exists" is but one conjunct. This conjunction of propositions, including propositions about the nature of God and God's creative and revelatory activity and the nature of the universe and ourselves and about the relations among all these things, will perhaps never be known by any creature, even if God exists; but creatures might nonetheless come to know ever larger significant subsets of the set of conjuncts that make it up—and let us think of a significant subset here as one that generates a unified picture of its subject matter, with all the connections among parts filled in. Surely it is coming to know *such* things, which really amounts to achieving ever deeper levels of *understanding*, as opposed to just individual, unconnected bits of knowledge, that should be a religious investigator's central intellectual goal—a goal that a God concerned for our intellectual well-being would certainly wish to help us forward.

And now notice that this is a goal that is quite compatible with, and indeed most generously supported by, having knowledge of the existence of God from the beginning. If we have this knowledge, then the understanding we achieve at any stage along the way will be far richer than it could be otherwise, for the fact of the existence of God, if it is the ultimate fact, is woven into all the others. Now the state one is in when one is able to move into any of those deeper and richer levels of understanding seems at least as valuable, intellectually, as is one's state when, so far

---

[22] I address the other details of Swinburne's points in "Hiddenness Argument Revisited II."

bereft of that opportunity, one discovers a single truth that is involved in them, even if it is the central or—in that sense—the ultimate truth. Hence there would appear to be a rather large number of intellectual attainments (and indeed no end to their number) at least as great as that of discovering that God exists which it must be open to us to pursue even if we have achieved knowledge of that proposition. Indeed, these particular attainments are possible *only* if we have discovered that God exists. Accordingly, there is no reason here to think that a God who, because of the link between love and meaningful relationship, is looking for something as good, intellectually, to offer us as the opportunity of discovering God's existence might be disappointed in the quest.

This particular application of the accommodationist strategy is, as it were, a prototype of what we can do in many other cases, for other criticisms succumb to that strategy in much the same way. Consider, for example, the suggestion that, unless God gives us much weaker desires for the good and much stronger desires for the bad, ruling out nonresistant nonbelief would have the consequence of introducing such strong incentives to choose the good (deriving from desires to avoid punishment and/ or to please God and/or to ensure our future well-being) that we would no longer be free to choose the bad instead, and so would be unable to participate in the sort of "soul-making" that theist and nontheist alike will say God has abundant reason to facilitate. This argument is discussed in connection with Swinburne's work in Chapter 5 of my *Divine Hiddenness and Human Reason*. Since that book was published, Swinburne has refurbished the argument and responded to some of my criticisms of it.[23] And he has been joined by Michael J. Murray, who agrees with Swinburne that there is a successful defeater for the hiddenness argument in this line of reasoning.[24]

Now the first thing to be said here, before pointing out how the accommodationist strategy can be brought to bear, is that just by considering the main things said about this appeal to moral freedom in my book on hiddenness, we can see that there are serious problems in the way of any attempt to apply it not only to a situation in which God appears *evidently and forcefully present on a continual basis* but also to a situation in which God only provides evidence causally sufficient for belief in the absence of resistance. Some of those points already apply something like the accommodationist strategy (take, for example, the suggestion that God can tailor the force of religious experience to our moral needs), but here I want

[23] See Swinburne, *Providence*, chap. 11.

[24] See Michael J. Murray, "Deus Absconditus," in *Divine Hiddenness: New Essays*, ed. Howard-Snyder and Moser, 62–82.

to develop that strategy more explicitly and in another direction. What I want to show is that even if everything I have said about their argument so far is inadequate and Swinburne and Murray are right when they claim that—at least without the aforementioned adjustment in the strength of human desires for good and for bad states of affairs, itself objectionable— the removal of nonresistant nonbelief would remove the ability to make sufficiently serious bad choices, their argument is *still* in trouble because of what is revealed by sufficiently serious attention to the moral freedom it does not remove (and certain new forms of its exercise that are facilitated by theistic belief).

To see the main point here, notice that although it may seem that, in order to engage in the sort of difficult-soul-making-resulting-in-good-character-for-which-one-is-responsible so emphasized in contemporary philosophy of religion, one must choose what is good for the sake of the good in the face of serious temptation to choose the bad, a more accurate indication of what is needed would be given by something more general: choosing the good for its own sake in the face of an inclination or propensity to *not* choose the good for its own sake. Now one way of not choosing the good for its own sake involves not choosing it at all and instead giving in to temptation to do the bad. The opportunity to do this, we are supposing with Swinburne and Murray, would, in the absence of objectionable changes to the strength of human desires for good and for evil, be lost if God were not hidden. But another way of not choosing the good for its own sake involves *choosing it for some other reason,* under the influence of a contrary motive. And the opportunity to do this would *not* be lost if Swinburne and Murray are right. For if they are right, then evidence sufficient for belief would remove our ability to do serious wrong *by giving us strong prudential desires.* Individuals, they say, would inevitably do what is right because they would see that it was obviously in their interest to do so. But in that case individuals would face a new challenge, and new choices: they would have the opportunity to grow *beyond* the purely self-interested motives and to cultivate a love of the good for its own sake. This might be difficult to do, in light of (what we are supposing would be) obvious prudential reasons to choose the good. Perhaps the influence of such motives would never disappear, at least to the extent that they would continue to emerge if wrong actions were suggested or thought about. But that would not make impossible the *addition* of non-self-interested motives to an individual's character, and growth toward a situation in which more and more often she does the good for its own sake, and (if there are truths about such matters) would do so even if the special considerations encouraging prudence were absent.

If such growth were to occur, the individual would in a very deep way be responsible for her character, and all without ever being in a position to make seriously wrong choices. Although she cannot fail to choose what is good, she can fail to choose the good for a morally admirable reason, and she can make the higher-level choices required to ensure that this situation is avoided (that is, required to ensure that the lower-level choices are of the appropriate sort, motive-wise). We might even say that what we see here is the possibility of an individual choosing the good in a deeper sense than is realized simply by choosing *what* is good. The phrase "choosing the good" or "coming out on the side of the good," to continue this thought, might be said to be ambiguous: in a first sense that—if Swinburne and Murray are right—requires hiddenness to be realized, it means "choosing what is good instead of what is bad," but in another, deeper, sense it means "choosing what is good for its own sake instead of for (purely) self-interested reasons"; and this does *not* require hiddenness to be realized but rather refers to a sort of freedom that flourishes in its absence.

Perhaps someone will reply to this by saying that while what we have here is a genuine and serious form of moral freedom, what the scenario I have described still lacks is a serious possibility of *self-determination*. For in it individuals one and all, through an inability to do seriously wrong actions, are unable to determine what their ultimate future will be. By preventing them from being able to do seriously bad things and move in the direction of total corruption, God has taken that choice out of their hands. But insofar as a genuine "determination of ultimate fate" *can* be available to us, it is available to us in the scenario I have described as well as in the critic's. Perhaps in the former scenario one could never make choices leading to hell (whether literally or figuratively construed), but one could still fail to "go to heaven," that is, to achieve good character and all the deeper goods that require a love of the good for its own sake; and *someone with the right values* would surely see this as at least as significant a loss as the loss of well-being involved in "going to hell." So the contrast between a will that is firmly set on the good through one's own efforts and a will that is heteronomously determined also allows us to speak sensibly of "self-determination." I conclude that there is nothing in the Swinburne/Murray moral freedom argument that should prevent us from holding that a perfectly loving God would put the existence of God beyond nonresistant nonbelief, and this *even if* my original replies to that argument are unsuccessful and (as I do not in fact believe) its proponents are right in their claim that removing hiddenness would remove our freedom to do seriously bad things.

I hope it will be obvious that a general pattern is emerging in our discussion of the "greater good" type of objection. Infinite resourcefulness, as even we finite beings can see, would provide many ways for a perfectly loving God to make explicit Divine-creature relationship a genuine possibility at all times without failing to meet the dominant concern of any of the reasons for God to remain hidden that have been advanced, or seem likely to be advanced. Moral freedom, serious responsibility (both intellectual and non-intellectual), the cultivation of character, a choice of destiny, cooperation with others, spiritually efficacious revelation of moral/spiritual deficiencies, nurturance of a deeper spiritual maturity, occasions for meaningful investigation and intellectual debate—all these goods and many more can be provided *within* the context of a relationship-conducive set of conditions, with creatures left free to decide how to respond to God (indeed, as we have seen, with a *larger* set of options than they would otherwise have). If God exists, then there must at any stage along the way be literally an infinite number of ways of developing in relationship with God that God could facilitate, despite obstacles to continuing relationship of the sort to which reasons for hiddenness often make reference. To say less than this would apparently be to contradict obvious points, emphasized by the theist, concerning the greatness of God. It follows, given that it is a necessary condition for the existence of a reason for God to remain hidden that it *not* be thus capable of being accommodated within a relationship-conducive set of conditions, that theistic replies to the hiddenness argument of the sort we have considered do not provide us with such a reason.[25]

Now I have, in my defense so far of the hiddenness argument, emphasized the resourcefulness of God. But one particular—and important— form the exercise of God's resourcefulness might take has not yet been highlighted. Strange as it may seem, there is an important form of "hiddenness" that is quite compatible with—and indeed *requires*—a situation in which there is no nonresistant nonbelief.

To see this, suppose that God exists and that there are no nonresistant nonbelievers. Indeed, go further and suppose that every capable creature responds to her belief by entering into personal relationship with God,

---

[25] In his recent book *The Problem of Evil* (Oxford: Oxford University Press, 2006), Peter van Inwagen devotes a chapter (chap. 8) to the hiddenness problem, but his treatment is vitiated by the fact that he ignores the strongest versions of the hiddenness argument, which can absorb most of the points he makes about (for example) the limited spiritual role of theistic belief. In particular, van Inwagen's persistent representation of the hiddenness arguer as seeking "signs and wonders" fails to put the hiddenness argument in the best light—indeed, in relation to the most discussed version of the hiddenness argument, what he has to say must appear as a rather large red herring. However that may be, it is clear on inspection that van Inwagen's response to the hiddenness argument depends on his more general response to the argument from evil, which, as we will see in the next chapter, faces serious problems.

"conversing" with God in prayer, feeling God's presence, living her whole life in the context of Divine-human communion. (Notice that we need not suppose that these "capable creatures" include the human beings who actually exist: there is no reason to suppose that a God would antecedently find *our* existence preferable to the existence of any of an infinite number of collections of other creatures.) Suppose also that subsequently one or other of the goods that have been mentioned as providing reasons for Divine hiddenness becomes a Divine desideratum in relation to those creatures. What can God do?

Well, there is still the possibility of a sort of Divine withdrawal *within* relationship. What I have in mind here is analogous to what has traditionally been called "the dark night of the soul," a state in which there is evidence for God's existence on which the believer may rely, but in which God is not felt as directly present to her experience, and may indeed feel absent (what I have in mind is *only* analogous to the "dark night" of the actual world: how it is realized might well be different in various ways from what is experienced in the actual world—for example, in the manner in which evidence causally sufficient for belief in the absence of resistance persists through the "dark night"). While not removing the conditions of relationship, such a "withdrawal" would severely test the believer's faith, and clearly would provide an occasion for the realization of any goods (if such there be) that are easier to acquire given such a withdrawal. In other words, it would be capable of accomplishing everything that theists sometimes say the *other* sort of hiddenness is designed to do. But if this sort of hiddenness can produce the goods in question and is compatible with God having been revealed to the nonresistant, what reason could we have for insisting that God would leave anyone in *doubt and nonbelief* in order to further those goods?

This point, in conjunction with all that came before, can be compressed into a sort of summary statement. The choice we face here is essentially between (i) a picture in which the self-revelation of God is basic—God's existence is beyond nonresistant nonbelief—and God withdraws if and when such withdrawal is needed to facilitate hiddenness-related goods but without ever removing the possibility of relationship with God, and (ii) a picture in which *withdrawal* is basic—God's existence is *not* beyond nonresistant nonbelief—and God is selectively revealed to some individuals or to none at all, leaving many in a position where they are unable to enter into meaningful relationship with God even if they should wish to do so.

To which picture should we be drawn, intellectually speaking, in light of the Divine bias toward relationship that any inquirer must acknowledge and the Divine resourcefulness? If you were thinking about some other possible world in a manner uninfluenced by religious tradition, and were handed the description of the being we have been talking about (*all-*powerful, *all-*knowing, *perfectly* good, and *perfectly loving*) as well as the two pictures, and asked which picture best represents what that world would include should the being in question exist in it, which picture would you choose? Clearly it is (i). Surely this is, in light of all we know about love and the greatness and the creative aspirations of any God there may be, a more adequate picture than one in which a personal God is presented to us as not naturally loving in the first place—too much of a "distant father" to relate easily with children—or as suspicious and controlling or insufficiently equipped to satisfy *both* the impulse to make relationship possible and the desire to nurture the growth and flourishing of creatures. Indeed, the second picture has nothing going for it at all. But if so, then it seems we must also conclude that objections to the hiddenness argument, requiring as they do a different answer, are unsuccessful, and that the nonresistant nonbelief of the actual world provides a powerful basis for believing theism false. Weak theistic evidence, in other words, is strong atheistic proof.

4. *The Free-Will Defense against the Problem of Hiddenness*

To this conclusion, certainly when supported by means of the necessitarian claims I have introduced into the hiddenness argument, there is a way of responding that we have not yet considered, which borrows from Plantinga's famous free-will defense against the problem of evil. Here there is no attempt (as in most of the objections previously considered) to show that God would or might *actually* be hidden from creatures, only an attempt to prove that this state of affairs is *logically possible*. A possibility proof of this sort may appear unduly modest in its aspirations, but, if successful, it would suffice to show that I am mistaken in my bold assertion that hiddenness is *conceptually* ruled out.

How might this new objection most forcefully be developed? I suggest as follows. First define "unqualifiedly free creatures" as creatures whose freedom is never interrupted or suspended by God. Then argue that it is logically possible that, given the distribution of truth-values on the relevant sets of counterfactuals of creaturely freedom,[26] what God saw when contemplating creative options is that not as much could be done toward realizing free positive responses to the Divine in any of the worlds that include the good of unqualifiedly free creatures but exclude nonresistant nonbelief (call these free believer worlds) as could be done in worlds like

---

[26] Counterfactuals of creaturely freedom are propositions of the form "If *S* existed and were in circumstances *C*, *S* would freely do *A*."

ours, with the same sort of freedom but also nonresistant nonbelief (call these free nonbeliever worlds).[27] Why is this possible? Because it is possible that the counterfactuals of freedom for creatures in free believer worlds have antecedents and consequents such that *regardless of which antecedents were caused to be true,* free acts of resistance would be performed sufficient in number and character to make those worlds inferior in the relevant respect to free nonbeliever worlds. According to this argument, what is possible is that *no matter what God might do, no matter how long Divine resourcefulness of the sort emphasized in the previous section might be brought to bear,* a result in respect of freely chosen relationship with God inferior to what is achieved in free nonbeliever worlds would be realized in free believer worlds, because of the resistance free creatures happen to put up in the latter worlds.[28]

Suppose all this were to be established. Would we have enough to reach the conclusion that, possibly, God exists and permits nonresistant nonbelief (and thus that proposition 3 of the hiddenness argument is false)? Not yet. What we need to add is a premise stating that it is possible that God would, despite the consequence of nonresistant nonbelief and regardless of what might be achievable in *other* worlds excluding nonresistant nonbelief, *decide to aim for* the better result in respect of freely chosen relationship represented by free nonbeliever worlds (call this the nonbelief acceptance claim). And as we will see in a moment, this premise, despite its apparent plausibility, is vulnerable to refutation. But for now let's simply recognize that this second stage of the argument is needed and turn back for a moment to consider some of the vulnerabilities of the first stage.

Prominent among these is the Molinist assumption that God would possess *middle knowledge:* knowledge, for each possible person and each situation in which that person might exist and be free, of what that person would freely do in that situation—exhaustive knowledge, in other words, of the truth-values for counterfactuals of creaturely freedom. Actually, several assumptions are buried in this vicinity, and each is seriously controversial: (1) that counterfactuals of freedom *have* truth-values; (2) that

---

[27] This point could be generalized in such a way as to include *any and all* freedom-involving Divine goals, including such particular goods (e.g., freely developed good character or free cooperation) as were discussed in the previous section. But since the answer I shall give to the free-will defense may similarly be generalized, I will not introduce this complication.

[28] If this is possible, then, ironically, it is possible that by making belief universally available, God would only guarantee that fewer would freely choose to act on it appropriately. (Even if more of those who in our world or worlds like it are nonresistant nonbelievers would be choosing in favor of relationship with God, the *overall* distribution of choices would be such as to make the rate of free and positive response lower than it is in free nonbeliever worlds.)

God *could know* what they are; and (3) that God *would choose to exercise* such knowledge in relating to free creatures. All these claims are sharply disputed in the literature today, and not just by nontheists.[29]

In response to this reminder, I think the free-will defender's best strategy is to insist that despite of—and indeed precisely because of—the abstruse metaphysical issues involved here and significant controversy concerning them, I should be willing to grant at least *epistemic possibility* to his three assumptions. That is, I should be willing to concede that it is epistemically possible that what is described by those assumptions is logically possible (more simply: that it is possible for all we know). And since the conclusion defended by means of them (that a result in respect of freely chosen relationship inferior to that of free nonbeliever worlds would possibly be realized in free believer worlds) is so *persuasively* defended, I should also grant that what this conclusion describes is at least epistemically possible.

Suppose I grant all this. I would still wish to point out two things. First, even if, for the time being, it served to undermine the hiddenness argument, that would be a very modest result, for the free-will defender would now himself be required to concede that the hiddenness argument might yet escape his points: future inquiry and discussion may—I would guess, will—clearly reveal the falsehood of the disjunction of his assumptions (1)–(3). Second (and more important), the concession in question *does not* undermine the hiddenness argument, even for the time being—to suppose otherwise is to ignore the critical second stage of the argument, which involves the nonbelief acceptance claim. If we can show that *this* claim is false, then the *conjunction* of possibility claims needed by the free-will defense against the hiddenness argument is false and that defense is unsuccessful, even if a number of its conjuncts must be said to be epistemically possible. I think this can be shown, and proceed now to defend this assessment.

My key point is that *both* free believer worlds *and* free nonbeliever worlds would, in the possible situation of Divine deliberation we are asked to

[29] It is tempting to think that in their claims about middle knowledge, writers like Plantinga (another is Thomas P. Flint: see his *Divine Providence: The Molinist Account* [Ithaca: Cornell University Press, 1998]) underestimate the depth of the notion of free will so important to them. (For arguments that can be taken as developing this point, see Robert Merrihew Adams, "Middle Knowledge and the Problem of Evil," *American Philosophical Quarterly* 14 [1977], 109–117; William Hasker, *God, Time, and Knowledge* [Ithaca: Cornell University Press, 1989], pp. 29–52; Swinburne, *Providence*, pp. 127–133; and Peter van Inwagen, "Against Middle Knowledge," *Midwest Studies in Philosophy* 21 [1997], 225–236.) And it is tempting also to think that if God *can* know such propositions as are here at issue but is going to give real independence and autonomy to creatures and actively participate in a style of relationship with them colored by that fact, God must become vulnerable in ways that require *not using* such knowledge. For discussion relevant to this point, see William Hasker, *Providence, Evil, and the Openness of God* (London: Routledge, 2004), and Scott A. Davison, "Privacy and Control," *Faith and Philosophy* 14 (1997), 137–151.

imagine, be viewed by God as inferior to certain yet unconsidered and indeed neglected *alternative* states of affairs, in which God prevents nonresistant nonbelief and does not preserve, unbroken, the free will of resistant creatures forever. (Because of the qualification of freedom to be found in them, call these free* believer worlds.)[30] If this point is correct, then we have reason to *deny* that the nonbelief acceptance claim is true for all we know.

To see that it *is* correct, consider some prominent features of free* believer worlds. Such worlds have initial segments that resemble those of free believer worlds, for in them we find the undesirable pattern of positive creaturely response to the Divine characteristic of the latter. However, at a certain stage of their history, free* believer worlds take on a life of their own, inaugurated as follows: despite their belligerent condition, the beauty and glory of God is made so clear to creatures that the contrary desires and false beliefs supporting and enabling their previous resistance fade away and are replaced by beliefs and desires appropriate to the nature of God, as a result of which a positive response to God inevitably ensues. Here there is in the end no *free* choice of relationship, but there are still many prior free choices, including choices *against* it, that retain their value and are woven into a beautiful denouement in which the love of God is made poignantly evident. And the free resistance of creatures is not simply overridden; rather their *information is filled out through the introduction of missing propositional knowledge and knowledge by acquaintance.* At a certain point in this process of having their information filled out, the creatures in question no longer find themselves with any inclination to resist (infinite attractiveness must at some point melt even the most hardened finite being). They long only to know God more fully, recognizing the infinite shortsightedness of their previous resistance; so there is no free resistance to override.[31] (Even though freedom is here suspended, God therefore does not "force" the desirable response—that is rather the natural reaction to a revelation that washes both freedom and resistance

---

[30] We shouldn't call these worlds *un*free believer worlds, for, as we will see, there is no need to assert that their creatures are *never* free. Another point to note here is that if what I am about to argue is correct, then it may be that free believer worlds are not so much as possible—at least if we assume that God is active in them. Perhaps it could be argued, on grounds similar to those I shall be utilizing, that a loving God would not even possibly allow the free resistance that distinguishes free believer worlds from free nonbeliever worlds to continue forever. But for the sake of (relative) simplicity of discussion, I leave this issue aside.

[31] What I have described here may seem incompatible with what I said early in the chapter about creatures being free to resistantly shut God out of their lives, thus preventing *themselves* from being able to enter into relationship with God. But there is nothing in the latter point to suggest that the resistant state in question is one that God would in any possible world tolerate *permanently*. Hence there is in fact no incompatibility.

away not by fiat but in a display of "information" to which the response must be: "I was obtuse . . . ") And the life thereafter of creatures in free* believer worlds is as bright as it is possible to imagine, for they are permitted to move ever more deeply into the infinite richness represented by knowledge of God and of God's creation.

On the basis of this description, I would claim, first, that free* believer worlds would be seen by a gracious and loving God to be *more worthy of actualization than their free believer counterparts.* If there is a reason for doubting this, it is provided by the suggestion that it might be better to leave freely resistant creatures to their own devices, even if that involves the eternal dissipation of their potential for communion with the Divine. But why think that? Of course it is a *familiar* view—woven as it is into many of the scriptures, theologies, even hymns that have helped to shape the dominant Western view of God's relation to creatures. But does it have any chance of being *correct?* A philosopher might wish to defend it by arguing, with Swinburne, that "to give us the choice to reject God, but never to allow that choice to be permanently executed, is not to give us a real choice at all."[32] But this argument seems to presuppose that in a "real choice" to reject God, someone says no to God in a completely general and thoroughgoing sense, intending to get rid of God once and for all, whereas it might instead be a no to God *in this or that respect* (e.g., in respect of a particular Divine overture or imperative) and a decision concerning only *this or that occasion* (e.g., concerning only what is to be done about the particular Divine overture or urging in question).

Perhaps someone will say that possible persons who go on resisting or rejecting God at many times and in many representative situations of life, despite the fullest and most persuasive revelations of God compatible with freedom (as the free-will defense requires us to imagine), can be taken as indicating the more serious and thoroughgoing choice in question. But this hardly follows, for we have still not transcended particularity (no matter how many and diverse the situations and times we postulate, they still do not support a general assessment embracing a creature's whole life, including future situations and times). Furthermore, to make sense of such persistent resistance—at least if we are imagining significant freedom tested by temptation and not, incoherently, thinking of free will as only a matter of chance—we have to imagine the persistent influence of (and persistent capitulation in the face of) contrary desires and beliefs that pull creatures away from God. And this reveals its own way of arguing that there can be no thoroughgoing decision to reject God in free believer worlds, one that puts a new twist on the idea of a "real choice." For such contrary desires

---

[32] Swinburne, *Providence,* p. 257.

and beliefs, with the distractions they represent and the distorted or incomplete picture of God they must inevitably involve, can hardly form a basis for *facing the issue of God head-on and making a clear-headed decision about it*—something that even the critic will regard as necessary for God justifiedly to leave resistant creatures "to their own devices" forever.

Perhaps the critic will now wish to remind us that we must imagine these creatures as the recipients of frequent and increasingly powerful instances of *Divine self-revelation,* and to suggest that this surely gives them everything they need for a real decision of the sort in question. In response to such self-revelation, they have nevertheless persistently rejected God, and thus are themselves responsible for the distorted or incomplete picture of God that now holds them back.

But contrary desires and beliefs sufficiently influential to undergird resistance of *God* must necessarily at *any* stage be distorting or distracting, preventing an accurate picture of God from properly coming into focus. And if instances of God's self-revelation are here to be viewed as increasingly powerful, it is only because such is needed to match the ever-deepening resistance of creatures—the latter never have any *more* reason to yield than they did at the beginning if God is, *all along,* really doing *all that God can do,* compatibly with free will, to prompt a desirable response.

Furthermore, at this stage of the discussion we only encounter another side of the problem I am developing. For even the most persuasive revelation of God compatible with free will must still be somewhat limited, *precisely because* of the "compatible with free will" proviso. Certainly evidence causally sufficient for correct propositional belief with respect to the existence of God can be provided, and especially if this comes in the form of religious experience, one can see how, as I argued earlier, it could constitute an invitation to relationship and provide that all-important *access* to meaningful conscious relationship with God, and do so compatibly with the preservation of free will. But even in that earlier discussion there was also a reference to religious experience being modulated according to our moral and other needs. Clearly, too evident or full a Divine self-revelation would remove freedom. (This point, it is important once again to emphasize, does not touch the hiddenness argument, which requires only that a *beginning* of conscious relationship should be made available to all who become capable of responding to God and can point to how even *elementary* forms of explicit awareness of God are often lacking.)

What can be built out of the various sides of the problem I have been developing? What we have is an interesting dilemma. If persons are to have a "real choice" as to whether they will—in a thoroughgoing manner—reject God or not, they should surely have a full and clear idea of what they are rejecting. And these individuals we are imagining, as just noted, must be construed as *lacking* such information. Now suppose that information sufficient to give them a clear and undistorted and undistracted idea of what they are rejecting—a real sense of the beauty and glory of God—were to be provided for them. It would only take away their free will, for according to what we are imagining, they have already been given *the fullest revelation compatible with free will.* So these creatures must either lack the proper information or else lack free will. And *either* way, no "real choice" is even possible for them. If such a choice *could* be made, perhaps it ought to be respected in the way Swinburne suggests. But given what we have to say instead, no such result follows. ("Forgive them, for they know not what they do" must always apply.) Indeed, now, I suggest, we have reason to say that the best thing God can do is to suspend free will in the manner described above and institute a new style of relationship, of the sort also there described. For the possibility of such relationship with God is just so evidently of more worth than the persistence of choices to resist God influenced by seriously deficient information—that is, the persistence of choices that are, in the sense I have been presupposing, less than "real."

As support for this view, consider the following parallel case. Suppose that your daughter, whom you dearly love, is in the grip of an erroneous picture as to what sort of person you are and what you intend in relation to her. No matter what you do in seeking to facilitate real contact with the truth and a choice in favor of a full and meaningful relationship with you, the response is only fresh resistance. And you correctly conclude that very likely nothing else of the same sort will work in the future. Now suppose that some way of instantaneously transforming her perspective is made available to you: if you press this button she will see you for who you really are and all the snagged and tangled and distorted beliefs will rearrange themselves into a clear perception of the truth. Surely you will use this means of cutting through that mess, for it represents only an abbreviated version of what you have already been seeking. But suppose also that in facilitating a correct picture of who you are and what you intend in this way, you will render it inevitable that your daughter make at least an initial choice in favor of meaningful relationship with you—that is, her choice to do so will not be free in the sense we have been emphasizing. (She will say, "Oh, what a fool I've been," and immediately be prompted to seek to make up for lost time.) Surely you will still do it, for you see that a free choice, yea or nay, in favor of meaningful relationship with you of the sort that would have *real* value and that you ought never to take lightly *isn't threatened thereby:* given the deficient information available to your daughter about who you are, even if you leave her alone she will not have been able to make such a choice. And you will also see that what you and your daughter would have to give up in order to keep in place the possibility of such limited free choices as *are* possible is far more valuable than they are. (Wouldn't any parent make the correct view available, even if the choice facing the child is then so obvious and attractive as not to be free, rather than have the child persist forever in her misunderstanding-based free choice? And what would be chosen by a perfectly loving God, the one who according to spiritual geniuses like Jesus of Nazareth never ceases to seek the lost sheep and to reveal to it a shepherd?)

So much for my defense of the view that God would prefer free* believer worlds to their free believer counterparts. Would God also prefer the former to free *non*believer worlds like ours? In the latter worlds, recall, we are imagining more free and positive decisions in respect of relationship with God on the part of creatures than in either free believer *or* free* believer worlds. And that might seem to be a decisive point in their favor: one might think a free response to God is massively more desirable than an unfree (or free*) one.

But again it is only neglect or oversight that might lead us to that conclusion. For the Divine-creature drama and the possibilities of Divine-creature relationship to be found in free* believer worlds are just *different* from what one might find in free nonbeliever worlds; they are not inferior. Notice that if the background to God's fuller self-revelation in free* believer worlds is of the sort that I have described, then God's suspension of freedom so that relationship is chosen can be fully meaningful, and much of the richness of relationship that *is* freely chosen can be preserved. For here creatures still have had the opportunity to form themselves over a long period of time and are able to integrate all that they have learned and become into the larger perspective provided by deep knowledge of God. (Interestingly, their choice of relationship with God, though strictly speaking unfree, is therefore still in a sense very much *their own,* for it is woven into their overall dispositional set, which is strongly shaped by other exercises of free will.) They are, moreover, able to express heartfelt gratitude to God, reflecting on the path along which they have come and God's generous redemptive acts which brought them to see the error of their ways. For the same reason, their love of God can be genuine—as we shall see in subsequent chapters, love does not need to be such as can be relinquished to be genuine—and their service of God a gift they gladly give in return for all they have received. And as they move ever deeper into the knowledge of God and of God's creation, how can they fail to achieve ever more fully a good as great as any that a relationship with God has ever been said to represent?

The central point here (more fully defended in Chapter 12) is that a style of relationship with God that involves much less free will than we are (or think we are) familiar with from our experience of the actual world cannot be inferior to other styles of relationship, for every one of them, after all, is a way of ever more fully and deeply coming to know an unsurpassably great and infinitely rich reality.[33] And if one adds to this that free nonbeliever worlds include *nonresistant nonbelief and its attendant deficits* (or what would be viewed by a perfectly loving God as deficits), which are absent from free* believer worlds, we must surely conclude that the latter worlds would, all things considered, be viewed as the more worthy of actualization. (If a perfectly good and loving God is able to choose between a scenario whose value is very great but requires the permission of nonresistant nonbelief and a scenario with value *equally* great and *no* need for the permission of nonresistant nonbelief, how might we suppose the Divine choice will be made?)

It seems clear, then, that God would prefer free* believer worlds to both free believer and free nonbeliever worlds. But in that case we may draw the following conclusion: the nonbelief acceptance claim is not epistemically possible but rather false. Although there may be a possible world in which God sees what the free-will defense says God might see and in which certain freedom-related states cannot be achieved without permitting nonresistant nonbelief, there is no possible world in which these things are so *and God goes ahead and permits nonresistant nonbelief*. But, as we have seen, *all* these things must be epistemically possible if the free-will defense against the argument from hiddenness is to succeed in even the attenuated sense that we have been considering. It follows that it does not succeed, any more than the other objections to the hiddenness argument I have discussed, in which case my original conclusion about the force of that argument stands.[34]

[33] Free will, if given at all, might be viewed as only level 1 of perhaps an infinite series of styles of relationship God might try, instead of leaving creatures to their own devices or with nonresistant nonbelief. (There will be more on the many styles of relationship in the next chapter.)

[34] Anyone who, despite my arguments, thinks that something like the free-will defense shows my necessitarian claims about hiddenness to be implausible should observe that the hiddenness arguer can always retreat, if need be, to a non-necessitarian formulation. For, as has often been noted, there is no reason at all to think that the claims of the free-will defense might be *true* (as opposed to logically possible, for all we know). Perhaps it will be replied that the premises of the hiddenness argument could receive strong support only from reasons appealing to what is necessarily true of God, and thus are defensible as necessary truths or not at all. But although reasons of the sort in question commonly refer to properties that a God would necessarily possess, they can be *differentially applicable:* forceful and undefeated in some worlds though not in others. And so we can have—as I suggest we here do have—good reason to accept the premises in question as true even if they turn out not to be necessarily true. It follows that multiple avenues of response present themselves to the hiddenness arguer who is faced with a free-will defense.

CHAPTER 10

Hiddenness Arguments II

It is a familiar observation in philosophy of religion that someone wishing to develop an argument from evil can argue not only from evil in general but more narrowly from this or that *type* of evil. The most commonly mentioned types are natural and moral evil, and recently there has also been discussion of *horrific* or *horrendous* evil (I will have much more to say about this last category in the next chapter). Similarly—and here we are venturing into unexplored territory—what I am calling hiddenness falls into several interesting types.

Now it is important to realize that I am not just saying that we can see various types of hiddenness by *relaxing the meaning of the term,* by allowing that term "Divine hiddenness" to range over more than just nonresistant nonbelief.[1] What I am saying instead is that *nonresistant nonbelief* comes in various types. In this chapter I seek to bring some four of these to light and to develop the "other layer" of atheistic hiddenness argumentation that is permitted by awareness of their details, in conjunction with certain new claims about the moral character of God (i.e., ones other than the perfectly general claims concerning creative love and relationship emphasized in the previous chapter). That these types are instantiated is—or should be—common knowledge and as uncontroversial as

---

[1] I *have* suggested elsewhere that in the broadest sense "God is hidden" is equivalent to a fairly large *disjunction* of claims, referring to *various* experiences and evidences and beliefs that might be said to be absent (see "What the Hiddenness of God Reveals: A Collaborative Discussion," in *Divine Hiddenness: New Essays,* ed. Daniel Howard-Snyder and Paul Moser [Cambridge: Cambridge University Press, 2002], pp. 34–35), and in some contexts it may be appropriate to read it this broadly; but our present context is not one of them.

the more general claim that there are nonresistant nonbelievers. So I will not spend much time citing examples. Those who need examples might consult certain recent popular books.[2] Better yet (for at any rate the first three categories) would be a resolution to widen the circle of one's acquaintances!

1. *Former Believers*

Imagine yourself in the following situation. You're a child playing hide-and-seek with your mother in the woods back of your house. You've been crouching for some time now behind a large oak tree, quite a fine hiding place but not undiscoverable—certainly not for someone as clever as your mother. However, she does not appear. The sun is setting and it will soon be bedtime, but still no mother. Not only isn't she finding you, but, more disconcerting, you can't *hear* her anywhere: she's not beating the nearby bushes, making those exaggerated "looking for you" noises and talking to you meanwhile as mothers playing this game usually do.

Now imagine that you start *calling* for your mother. Coming out from behind the tree, you yell out her name, over and over again. But no answer. Oh, there *is* a moment when suddenly you hear sounds you are sure must signal your mother looking for you, but they turn out to come from nothing more than leaves rolling in the wind. So you go back to calling and looking everywhere: through the woods, in the house, down to the road. Several hours pass and you are growing hoarse from calling. Is she anywhere around? Would your mother—loving and responsible parent that she is—fail to answer if she were around?

This exercise of the imagination illustrates the problematic qualities of a certain type of nonresistant nonbelief. Some persons start out assured of the power and presence of God in their lives and of their participation in a meaningful conscious relationship with God, and then they *lose* all this—often by being exposed to reasons for doubt about the reliability of the support they have for theistic belief. And though they grieve what they have lost and seek to regain it, looking for God in all the old familiar places as well as in new, unfamiliar, locales, they fail to do so: God seems simply absent, and their belief is gone. Oh, there may be times when they think

[2] Many sources might be cited. I will cite four interesting books—two each—by the journalists John Horgan and Winifred Gallagher. See Gallagher, *Working on God* (New York: Random House, 2000) and *Spiritual Genius* (New York: Random House, 2002), and Horgan, *The End of Science* (New York: Broadway Books, 1996) and *Rational Mysticism* (New York: Houghton Mifflin, 2003).

they have detected traces of God in some public event or argument or experience. But it is only for a moment: the event's theological significance is soon undermined by convincing reinterpretation or the argument is proven unsound or the experience is rendered doubtful by reflection on their psychological state or on *conflicting* experiences—whether their own or others'.

This most poignant type of nonresistant nonbelief of those who regret the loss of belief and wish to regain it but fail to do so, all within a broader psychological and intellectual context involving a search for God fueled by a desire and willingness to love and serve God, I call the nonresistant nonbelief of *former believers*. I touched on this phenomenon in the last chapter when introducing the general concept of nonresistant nonbelief. Here I want to examine it more closely. In particular, I want to ask whether, given such experiences, we can really suppose that *God* is "anywhere around." Would there fail to be a response to the calls of former believers if God *were* around?

In developing the argument suggested here, we must take care to emphasize that the individuals in question were, from the perspective of theism, *on the right path* when they lost belief. (If there is a God, it is certainly appropriate to believe that such is the case and to respond accordingly, in prayer and worship and service, etc., as did these former believers.) If theism is true, indeed, then these individuals *already were* in relationship with God and the loss of belief has *terminated* that relationship. And it is the fact that such a thing—such a termination of a genuine and meaningful relationship with God and the absence of a response from God to requests for its resumption—apparently could not occur that I am saying should instead suggest to us that theism is false. Really, what is suggested is that the theist is here committed to a contradiction, which follows from the conjunction of the claim that God exists with the claim that our former believers exist. The relevant moves can be clarified as follows.

(1) God exists, and there are former believers (assume for reductio).

(2) Necessarily, God would not permit the loss of relationship that is experienced by former believers.

(3) Necessarily, if God exists, there are no former believers (from 2).

(4) There are no former believers (from 1 and 3).

(5) There are former believers and there are no former believers (from 1 and 4).

So the problematic fact in this case is something more specific than what we were discussing in the last chapter, where we focused on how the presence of nonresistant nonbelief of whatever kind indicates that meaningful relationship with God is not accessible to everyone capable of it and open to it. It is one thing for God not to make relationship available to everyone; it is another for God to take it away from those who have already had it and prevent its resumption.[3] How could a perfectly good and loving God countenance one-time believers trying to make their way home without being able to do so? This would be like disowning one's own child—not just shutting him out of the house but shutting him out of your life—without any infraction to give this behavior so much as a patina of legitimacy. (Indeed, where there are apparent signs of God's presence that turn out to be misleading, we have something comparable to shutting your child out, then tantalizingly suggesting that he may be welcome after all, only to slam the door in his face again.)

What all this means is that we have a powerful new argument, an argument whose success does not presuppose that of the other, more general hiddenness argument, though also making use of a claim—a narrower one—about relational love to support its critical premise, (2). And, furthermore, here we may, as suggested, appeal to additional facts about the Divine moral character, such as the *responsive* love and caring and *noncapriciousness,* and also *justice* (why should some believers be bereft of relationship with God and others not?) and *faithfulness* (would not a God remain true to those who have committed themselves to God?), that must necessarily characterize Divine dispositions and behavior.

Let us now consider some objections. Perhaps the most straightforward objection would question the critical claim that a theist must hold these individuals to have already been in a relationship with God and thus to have had that relationship terminated by the loss of belief. Perhaps these persons never were in a relationship with God in the first place—even if God exists. Perhaps they only *thought* they were and really were not, due to spiritual immaturity or misunderstanding of some kind.

But then God would have had to *permit* them inculpably to think that they were in a relationship with God (for example, to have permitted illusory versions of a loving, comforting, guiding presence to successfully

---

[3] A central point is that here we can be sure that the persons involved *would* be in a meaningful relationship with God if it were available to them. The importance of knowing this is emphasized by Chris Tucker in connection with the general hiddenness argument in his unpublished paper "The Value of Divine-Human Relationships and the Atheistic Argument from Non-belief"; and although I do not think it necessary, as he supposes, for *that* argument, knowing this facilitates, as we see here, an additional, more specific, hiddenness argument.

pass themselves off as the real thing), and also—given the "searching and calling" element of this case—to have done nothing to manifest the *right* way of relating to God in response to a willingness to be made aware of such things. And this simply suggests *another* argument against the existence of God (one emphasizing the truthfulness and nondeceptiveness of the Divine moral character, as well as the caring already mentioned), an argument at least as strong as the one presently being considered. In any case, given the nature of God there must *always* be some measure of immaturity and misunderstanding on the part of creatures in relation to Divine things, and this fact, we might expect, would simply be woven into any authentic relationship with God—become part of its very texture, as it were—instead of being an insurmountable impediment to it.

An objector might also claim that former believers who search for God are not very much like the children of my story—the vulnerability we attach to the latter and need to be able to transfer to the former in the argument I have used is in fact not transferable in this way. But this objection appears to assume that all former believers are adult humans, and that is not at all obvious: actual children may (and do) lose belief in God too, without in every case having their ensuing search rewarded with positive results. More important, because of the evil we face and the evident frailty of our natures, even human grownups are not appropriately construed, theologically speaking, as mature and resilient adults. Theology has traditionally pictured us this way (while also referring to us as "God's children"), but a close look at the world suggests that a better picture would portray us as young and unformed, still needing a home—in particular, still in need of Parental support and encouragement in the development of a character and self-esteem that can withstand the pressures toward fragmentation and despair life represents, and make the achievement of our full potential possible.

A third objection to the argument suggests that there is something presumptuous about *expecting* a response from God. God is not obligated to respond to our every whim; and if God responds, it will be in God's own way, not necessarily as we expect. But the argument I have developed is not suggesting that God should satisfy our every *whim*, our every sudden and unreflective and unreasonable desire; only that a God would respond to serious attempts to be reunited with God in loving relationship. Observe how much more plausible the latter claim is than the former. The objection is here dealing with a caricature of our argument, not the real thing. As for presumption: the expectation of a former believer does not come in the form of a *demand*, but as anticipation or reasoned inference. Are we really to imagine people walking around demanding that God "show himself"? Some *philosophers* may do this, but they are usually individuals who have long since concluded that God does not exist and think the world is better off that way; it would be a mistake to confuse them with the earnest and hopeful former believers of our argument, or with those who after careful reflection on all the available information conclude that it would be in the nature of a God to be in some way revealed to former believers.

Finally, we have an objection pointing to the value of a search for God on the part of individuals who may have always quite unreflectively believed and taken God for granted. In response to this it seems necessary to distinguish between (i) *doubts and questions* arising *within* a relationship and motivating a search that leads to deeper understanding and stronger character and more mature modes of relating to God and (ii) doubts and questions motivating a search that leads (conscientiously) to *nonbelief* and the *end* of the relationship. Why should it be (ii) instead of (i)? Why should a *search* only *confirm* the former believer in her nonbelief?

One way of seeing the problem here is to notice the deviation from that "secondary" sort of hiddenness introduced at the end of the previous chapter. We saw there how God might conceivably withdraw from individuals who are already in a relationship with God to facilitate certain hiddenness-related goods, though without removing the conditions of relationship—and in particular, without removing evidence sufficient for belief. This sort of move on God's part, an event within relationship, is sometimes extolled by theologians. Here, for example, is John Macquarrie: "As happens also in some of our deepest human relationships, the lover reveals himself enough to awaken the love of the beloved, yet veils himself enough to draw the beloved into an even deeper exploration of that love. In the love affair with God . . . there is an alternation of consolation and desolation and it is in this way that the finite being is constantly drawn beyond self into the depths of the divine."[4] Well, one is inclined to say, that's the way it would be if there really were a God wishing to facilitate hiddenness-related goods for believers in relationship with God. But that is not the way it is—instead we see persons losing their belief and losing what they took to be meaningful relationship with God and unable to get it back though they have tried to do so through every legitimate avenue known to them, rather finding only stronger evidence for atheism, for a picture of the world in which God is not just hidden but absent. And this is a very serious *problem* for theistic belief, as our discussion makes clear.

---

[4] John Macquarrie, *In Search of Deity* (London: SCM Press, 1984), p. 198.

2. *Lifelong Seekers*

Another type of nonresistant nonbelief is represented by what I call *lifelong seekers,* individuals who don't start out in what they consider to be a relationship with God and may not even be explicitly searching for *God,* but who are trying to find out where they belong and, in their wanderings, are open to finding and being found by a Divine Parent—all without ever achieving their goal. These are individuals who seek but do not find.

To illustrate their situation, we might make a few changes to our imagined events above. So picture yourself as a child with amnesia. Apparently because of a blow to the head (which of course you don't remember) your memory goes back only a few days, and you don't even know whether you *have* a mother or a home of any kind. You see other children going home at the end of the day and think it would be nice to be able to do the same. So you ask everyone you meet where your home might be and look everywhere you can, but without forwarding your goal in the slightest. You take up the search anew each day, looking diligently, even though the strangers who took you in assure you that your parents must be dead. But to no avail. Would this be the case if you really have a home and a loving mother, and if she is around and aware of your search? When in the middle of the night you tentatively call out, would she not answer, if she were really within earshot?

Similarly, if there really were a God who is the true home of every seeker, a being perfectly good and loving and the source and goal of our own being, would the existence of this God not represent a sufficient condition of *there being no lifelong seekers?* If there were such a God, would we really have individuals sensitive to the truth who—perhaps because of that very sensitivity (in conjunction with the weakness of the evidence that becomes available to them)—remain always in a condition of nonbelief and, thus, in a condition inimical to finding God? Wouldn't the twists and turns of their investigation somewhere, somehow, bring them into contact with God—a God whose search for them is as earnest as their own?

The answers yes, no, and yes, respectively, seem undeniable. When we look with unblinkered eyes at not just the love and caring of God but also the justice and generosity of God, how could we say otherwise? In particular, consider justice. A *lack* of Divine justice would seem to be evidenced in the lives of lifelong seekers both by virtue of their own, often prodigious, efforts and genuine sensitivity to the truth—here we are talking about retributive injustice—and in their condition as compared with that of others, who are, if God exists, able to enjoy relationship with God, often without anything like the efforts of the seeker or her sensitivity—here we notice *distributive* injustice. But God is, if God exists, neither unjust nor (to reintroduce the other relevant attributes) ungenerous, uncaring, or unloving. Thus the existence of lifelong seekers suggests the nonexistence of God.[5]

Perhaps it will be said that the reason these individuals never find God is the sin that stands in between and clouds their vision. Those who apparently are seeking aright in fact are (or may well be) *prevented* from doing so by some hidden flaw, maybe a well-disguised self-seeking agenda. But this reference to sin seems quite unsubstantiated—many lifelong seekers appear in fact to be quite blameless in the relevant respects. And, of course, we have to remember that we are talking about *nonresistant* nonbelievers. Where given such circumstances critics continue to claim that an inhibiting culpability may well be present, the influence of a previously acquired theistic belief and associated allegiance is generally unmistakable. It is important to notice here that beyond looking thoroughly and carefully at the evidence and removing all observed impediments to success in the search, there is nothing the seeker *can do* to bring about theistic belief or any other sort of belief. Belief as such is involuntary—it is something that happens to you when evidence adds up to a certain point, not something you can "do" directly. Thus if a search of the sort in question has been undertaken, the seeker and nonbeliever cannot be to blame for not believing.

But the objector may persist, as does Paul K. Moser, saying that it is in God's "appointed time" that the evidence for theism will appear, not necessarily when we demand to have it. This point, however, neglects to notice that many who seek God do so *humbly*, and that when we have established a theologically sensitive criterion for determining when and how God's presence will be felt—"a morally transforming sign [will be available to] seekers actively open to moral transformation toward God's moral character"—we are not in a position to say to those who *satisfy* it that it may not yet be God's appointed time.[6]

---

[5] Is *this* a conclusion to which we are driven by the apparent *logical impossibility* of God doing otherwise? When we see the role that the various concepts associated with the Divine moral character are again playing, we may well wish to answer in the affirmative (remembering that all such a priori conclusions are still defeasible and must be able to withstand objection). But I do not find myself saying this with as much confidence as in the earlier case of former believers, where the *termination* of relationship was involved. Perhaps many will be led by some such consideration to construe the conditional claim of the argument—"If God exists, there are no lifelong seekers"—as true but not necessarily true, and the evidence we have adduced as capable of strongly supporting its truth though not its necessary truth. That too would be sufficient for my purposes. (Similar points apply to the next two arguments developed in this chapter.)

[6] See Paul K. Moser, "Divine Hiddenness Does Not Justify Atheism," in *Contemporary Debates in Philosophy of Religion*, ed. Michael Peterson and Raymond VanArragon (Oxford: Blackwell, 2004), esp. pp. 51–52.

Another objection that may be tempting here claims that the crumbs we all—including former believers—receive from the Divine table are enough. We shouldn't complain about the silence of God; we should be grateful instead for all the good things God provides. But as well as begging the question—simply assuming the existence of God—the point of this objection may be compared to saying that the falsehoods God tells are small and unimportant and that we should be grateful for all the truths. In other words, it simply ignores the logic of Divine perfection. Indeed, the standard to which it is willing to hold the Divine is not even as high as that to which most of us hold *ourselves* in personal relations. Perhaps there is an echo in the objection of that older way of thinking that sometimes characterized (and sometimes still does characterize) the parent/child relationship: "Don't bother the great, good God, so busy as He must be with matters more important than relating to his puny and error-prone human creations!" But it is *this way of thinking* that is subject to error and needs to be outgrown, as suggested at the beginning of the previous chapter.

What about the possibility that God does respond and seekers simply miss the response, expecting something else—something other than what God has in mind? Well, what else might God have in mind? If what is needed for the search to reach a theistic conclusion and resolution is belief that there is Someone to relate to, what *could* count both as *loving* and as a *response* apart from some noticeable indication of God's presence? Certainly in the imaginary case of the unencumbered mother and her child, nothing apart from the mother actually coming to her child in a manner recognized by the child would qualify as a loving (or just or generous or caring) response. What makes us think that something else would do in the case of God's immeasurably greater goodness and love? Perhaps it will be said that God, unlike the mother, is able to be present to us all the time without our noticing it. That is indeed true, if God exists. But it still doesn't qualify as a response to the cry of the lifelong seeker. And we need to recognize that the absence of love in one respect is not compensated for by *other* forms of love when what we're dealing with is not the love of a finite being but the perfect love of an unlimited God. Indeed, it is starting to look as though the relevant differences between God and ourselves make it harder to mount an "other response" objection, not easier.

The obvious replies to the objections we have considered, and to others that might be formed on the model of objections considered in the previous section (especially such as emphasize the value to be gained in a search for God—something one need not even deny to decry permission of a *lifelong* search), show that here too we have a powerful new argument for atheism.

3. *Converts to Nontheistic Religion*

Those who emphasize the importance of searching for God sometimes suggest that the searcher needs to continue in this for some considerable period of time, at *various* levels of life (emotional, moral, spiritual, intellectual), without succumbing to the belief that God does not exist. Here it is again ignored that belief is not a voluntary affair—indeed, such investigation as this view recommends may itself at some stage produce the belief in question, without the investigator being able to do anything (short of self-deception) to change it. Further, given the impartial interest in the truth that ought to be the motive for any such investigation, it is hard to see how investigators may avoid the obligation of equally scrupulous investigation into *other* serious conceptions of the Ultimate. Such investigation may of course turn up evidence that produces religious belief of another kind—perhaps in the context of nontheistic religious communities and/or on account of nontheistic religious experiences—and the truth of atheistic claims may be seen to follow by implication. (That atheism can be produced in this manner is often neglected by contemporary philosophers of religion, whose own main interests and investigations are often restricted to Western perspectives.) Call such nonresistant nonbelievers as are here described *converts to nontheistic religion*.

The situation of converts to nontheistic religion, and the problem it represents for theism, can be illustrated by means of a continuation of the imaginary exercise begun in sections 1 and 2. Suppose that after looking for your mother for many days and nights without success, or else sometime after your memory-erasing accident, you are taken in by strangers and eventually adopted by them. And suppose that they bring you up in a manner that leaves you predisposed to deny that you *have* a (living) mother and to rewrite your whole life story in those terms, or produces experiences causing you to deny the importance of personal relationship with a mother in the development of a child. Can we imagine that you really have a good and loving mother and she is just standing by, allowing all this to take place without lifting a finger? Surely not.

Likewise, it can hardly be supposed that God would permit a nonresistant nonbeliever—perhaps a former believer, perhaps a seeker who has never yet held theistic belief—to arrive as a result of honest inquiry at *nontheistic* experiences and beliefs. For such individuals would honestly take themselves to have found a truth that in fact only enmeshed them in a meaning system *distortive* of (what must, if God exists, be) the truth—a system according to which (for example) there is no loving personal God and no substantial self either, or according to which all distinctions between the world and the Ultimate must finally be erased. How could a truthful, nondeceptive God countenance such a state of affairs?

Descartes asked a similar question, concluding that God would allow us to fall into significant error only through the inappropriate exercise of our own wills (i.e., culpably). But, as I have indicated, in the individuals we are talking about it is an *honest and conscientious search* that has brought them to nontheistic belief. So we cannot avail ourselves of Descartes's way out here. And then consider also certain other moral labels that must necessarily apply to God (some already mentioned in previous sections)— for example, "caring" (could a caring God allow a life-changing sense of significant insight following on careful inquiry that is in fact delusory?), "supportive" (how do one's life choices reflect Divine support if they are grounded in error?), "faithful" (how is God faithful to a former believer if that individual not only is excluded from continuing relationship with God but allowed to form false beliefs that lead her further away from God and the source of her true well-being?), "providential guide" (would a providential guide lead us into such significant error?). Clearly, each of these also provides a reason to deny that there would ever be nonresistant nonbelievers who are converts to nontheistic religion, if there were a God. And so again we have powerful grounds for denying that there is a God.

Are there any objections to this argument that cannot, mutatis mutandis, be met by replies to objections already considered in previous sections? Perhaps it could be argued that I have made too much of the importance of correct belief. Without falling back on the argument of the last chapter (something I don't want to do, so as not to compromise the independence of this chapter's arguments), how can I maintain that emphasis? For it seems that what *really* matters are certain *dispositions,* such as the ones I have been using in my descriptions of God. It is good for us to have opportunities to become more caring, just, faithful, and so on, and it is good of God to provide us with such opportunities. And now the central point: such opportunities are afforded us as much by participation in nontheistic religion as by participation in theistic religion. For, as is well known, *all* religious traditions emphasize the need to become less self-centered and more caring, just, and so on.

But here again we seem to meet the "you already have enough—silence yourself and be grateful" sort of move, which, as we saw earlier, ignores the logic of Divine perfection. Certainly it is fine to be afforded opportunities to deepen the development of one's moral character, and perhaps any form of religious practice can provide this. However, the God we are considering—the personal being than which a greater cannot be thought— would do much more. Even if dispositions are what *really* matters, correct beliefs matter too, and none but a deity given to slipshod behavior and inclined to underestimate the intrinsic value of understanding the world could fail to be influenced by this. Not only that, but correct beliefs are intimately *connected* to certain more specific dispositions God would surely wish us to have the opportunity to display, such as dispositions to be grateful to *God,* love *God,* and serve *God.* Beyond this, if reality is indeed to be understood theistically, why would any deity other than the inordinately self-effacing deity of the critic's objection wish humans to waste their time and energy on other understandings, which not only prop up moral dispositions of various desirable sorts but become completely intertwined with a person's sense of identity and place in the world in such a way as to make their uprooting a traumatic and psychologically far-reaching event (and presumably uprooted they would be at some future point in the careers of these individuals, unless we are to suppose that God would *never* deliver them from error)? By considerations such as these, then, I suggest that the present objection can be answered. Since no other, halfway plausible objection suggests itself, I move on.

4. *Isolated Nontheists*

Consider now the nonresistant nonbelief of those who have never been in a *position* to resist God because they have never so much as had the idea of an all-knowing and all-powerful spiritual being who is separate from a created universe but related to it in love squarely before their minds—individuals who are entirely formed by, and unavoidably live their whole lives within, what must, if God exists, be a fundamentally misleading meaning system. Perhaps they think and live and feel as though there are many limited gods interacting with worldly beings, or take their natural surroundings to be infused with a (nonpersonal) spiritual energy, or are not conceptually equipped to make a distinction of any kind between the world and a Divine reality. I call such individuals *isolated nontheists* because they are intellectually (and often also geographically) isolated from such as possess theistic concepts and who orient themselves in the world by means of them. Of course, if we go far enough back in time, we will find a world in which virtually *everyone* falls into the former category (it is really only in the present and the fairly recent past that the "isolated" part of my label has any work to do), and that matters here: such arguments as we are developing are nurtured as much by nonresistant nonbelief of the past as by such as is presently occurring.

Why should we suppose that *this* sort of nonresistant nonbelief is problematic for theism? Well, for much the same reasons as were mentioned in the previous section in connection with *converts* to nontheistic religion—the reasons arising from the notions of a truthful and nondeceptive, but also caring and supportive, Providence concerned to help us form dispositions appropriate to the nature of the world in which we live. We all know about isolated nontheists and have got used to finding a place for them in our worldview, perhaps in some corner segregated from the rest of what concerns us. But if we seriously consider the idea that there is a God and what all this means (among other things, the presence of a passion for truth and providential care unsurpassably great), shouldn't we find their presence rather troubling, at least insofar as we are theists? Would a God of integrity who was concerned for the well-being of all creatures permit such pervasive and all-embracing and unavoidable error to take hold—let alone flourish and persist—in any part of the Divine creation? It certainly seems not.

Here we might again benefit from the aid to faltering or recalcitrant intuition supplied by imagination. I suggest we try a role reversal, imagining ourselves in the position of a parent instead of that of a child. Suppose you are a parent with several children who has the primary responsibility for their care. And suppose you notice that they have picked up from their friends or from movies or video games some totally false picture of how things are, and are starting to think and act in terms of it, since they really believe that it represents the truth. Suppose also that although on the surface this picture may—apart from being completely false—seem relatively harmless, you are aware that there are subtle ways in which a preoccupation with it could lead your children to fail to notice responsibilities toward yourself that they would be able to see were they to take a more accurate measure of things, and that it could, over time, so penetrate their sense of themselves and of the world as to make its eventual removal in the face of adult realities frightening and painful. If all this were the case, and if the means for doing so successfully were available to you, wouldn't you immediately recognize a responsibility to try to ease your children back into the real world before the erroneous picture in question puts them completely under its spell? Wouldn't you be seriously neglectful if you did not do so? The application to the religious situation should be obvious.

Perhaps the critic will object that there are, if God exists, great goods that require erroneous religious beliefs on the part of some—in particular, the opportunity for others to set them straight! There is, inter alia, a deep and very meaningful *responsibility* here that a God might well wish (some of) us to have. God is not neglectful in relation to such individuals as have been mentioned if, in general, the misfortunes of some human beings are required to produce great goods (including important responsibilities) for others—and also for the some, insofar as in experiencing those misfortunes they are able to be of use.[7]

---

[7] For argument along these lines, see Richard Swinburne, *Providence and the Problem of Evil* (Oxford: Clarendon Press, 1998), chap. 11.

The general claims involved here I have addressed elsewhere[8] and will touch on again in the next chapter. They have also been trenchantly criticized by Draper.[9] But it should be evident on its face that a principle justifying the misfortune of certain individuals on the grounds of their usefulness when those individuals are *unaware* of their usefulness and might not choose to be thus useful if the matter were put to them, and when perfectly fine goods—including important responsibilities (see Chapter 11, section 3)—may be secured in other ways, is at the very least problematic.

There is also the factual problem that for long periods of human history perhaps no one was in a position to *have* or (thus) to fulfill the responsibility at issue here, since all the world was in the same boat in respect of ignorance of theism. Hence this objection does not explain why in those generations ignorance was needed. If it is said that ignorance *then* is needed to have it now, since the present intellectual state of a culture is thus dependent on its past, we may point out that *universal* ignorance is never needed—past *pockets* of ignorance are all that would be needed to generate similar pockets today even on the critic's view—and that the dependence cited by the critic is in any case not a logical one: recent generations or cultures of today could be completely ignorant of God even if long-past ones weren't, provided that the knowledge possessed by those in the distant past was, as we neared the present, somehow removed, not a very difficult task for omnipotence.

Finally, as has just been suggested, all that is needed for the responsibility in question is *ignorance,* and though erroneous religious belief represents a *sufficient* condition of such ignorance, it is not a necessary condition. For persons could be completely ignorant of God even if their view of things (correct as far as it went) were only *incomplete,* lacking any spiritual dimension, and including no beliefs at all as to the presence or absence of a realm beyond the mundane. Hence, the notion that there should be completely *erroneous* beliefs about religious matters, which a truth-loving and nondeceiving God might certainly be thought to abjure, has not been justified.

But another objection may immediately spring up to replace the first. And this (as it might seem) obvious but overlooked objection may be presented as being of quite general relevance, affecting much of the earlier discussion in this chapter and, indeed, discussion in the previous chapter

---

[8] See *Divine Hiddenness and Human Reason,* chap. 7, and also my "Stalemate and Strategy: Rethinking the Evidential Argument from Evil," *American Philosophical Quarterly* 37 (2000), 405–419.

[9] See his critical study of Swinburne's *Providence and the Problem of Evil* in *Nous* 35 (2001), 456–474.

as well.[10] What does it say? Well, that the *evolutionary structure of the universe* is required to preserve the *freedom* of God's creatures, and that given evolutionary processes, long periods of ignorance and error on matters from the mundane to the sublime must be expected to precede the dawning of knowledge and understanding. God cannot step in and ensure that correct beliefs are held without undermining the splendid architectonic of this movement of free creatures toward an ever-fuller intellectual and spiritual engagement with the Divine. Stories like this are often told these days, especially by a certain brand of scientist-cum-theologian seeking to reconcile the latest results of biology and physics with a fairly traditional theism, enamored of the picture of science and religion marching arm in arm into the sunset (though, if that sounds deprecatory, it must be said that their program is much more respectable than that of those—whom they oppose—who would like to have the direction of scientific research determined by a literal reading of the biblical book of Genesis). Here, for example, is Kenneth R. Miller, a molecular biologist at Brown University: "In biological terms, evolution is the only way a Creator could have made us the creatures we are—free beings in a world of authentic and meaningful moral and spiritual choices."[11] What should we say about this basis for a defense of aeons of religious error?

I would suggest that it is itself an example of error. To cut to the chase, we again have a sufficient condition confused with a necessary one. It is indeed *sufficient* for what Miller calls authentic and meaningful creaturely freedom that there be interposed between God and creatures a screen of the sort that the evolutionary processes of the actual world provide, but it is hardly necessary. There could be very different evolutionary processes or none at all without creaturely freedom being compromised. The screen could be thinner or of a very different kind. As an example perhaps too obvious to be noticed in this connection, we might cite the sort of scenario of which biblical literalists are fond (of course we need not incorporate all their details, and we certainly need not concede that the scenario obtains): one in which the universe is created ready-made as a theater for Divine-creature interaction, but with gross physical features and a preoccupation on the part of creatures with their physical environment and with short-range desires sponsored by it that serve as a screen, making an engagement with the spiritual dimension something that requires work

---

[10] *Each* of the objections taken up in this chapter is potentially relevant to the last chapter inasmuch as any successful justification of a *type* of nonresistant nonbelief will also refute the more general claim defended there.

[11] Kenneth R. Miller, *Finding Darwin's God: A Scientist's Search for Common Ground between God and Evolution* (New York: HarperCollins, 2002), p. 291.

and discipline, an openness to "hearing the word of the Lord." Clearly the possibilities here are limited only by the imagination and by one's willingness to exercise it.

This brings us to what really generates confusions of the sort Miller's quote represents: here again we see the theologian's task being undertaken instead of the philosopher's. The religious thinker sees a world in which evolutionary processes prevail and tries to figure out how to fit God into that picture. There is no incentive in such a situation to exercise one's imagination in an attempt to get some sense of the *range* of options from which God might select; no, we are stuck with what we've got. And the temptation then to take something that *is afforded* by the actual world and treat it as afforded *only* by the actual world—thus to justify God's creation of the latter—is nearly irresistible. But it should hardly need to be said that a philosopher must resist such temptation and cannot rest content with such maneuvering, and so it should hardly need to be said that the present objection furnishes no better basis for accepting aeons of religious ignorance than did the previous one, with its emphasis on responsibility.[12]

5. *Conclusion*

We have seen that by looking inside certain *types* of nonresistant nonbelief and getting a closer view of the problems for theism lurking there, we are able to notice some additional, and powerful, means of arguing to atheism from facts about Divine hiddenness. Each of these types generates convincing grounds for atheism (though perhaps the first argument is strongest—see note 5), grounds that can function quite independently of the more general hiddenness argument developed and defended in the previous chapter.[13] Thus with this chapter's results, atheism is further ahead.

---

[12] Another problem with the evolutionary approach we have considered is that it simply assumes that creaturely freedom of the sort we take ourselves to possess is a great good, and one embodying a value greater than the disvalue obviously to be associated with our evolutionary world—which, though it may be beautiful in its larger features, gets extremely messy and mean in its details. Since there is more discussion of this issue in the next two chapters, I simply mention it here as a matter that would leave the approach in question incomplete even if the other problems for it that I have raised could somehow be circumvented.

[13] No doubt yet other hiddenness arguments can be developed. For example, see Stephen Maitzen, "Divine Hiddenness and the Demographics of Theism," *Religious Studies* 42 (2006): 177–191.

CHAPTER 11

The Argument from Horrors

In this chapter I turn from the much-neglected and little-explored territory I have labeled the problem of Divine hiddenness to the much-traveled (one might say trampled) neighboring territory of the problem of evil. Superhighways crisscross this philosophical province. Sophisticated infrastructure supports the many cosmopolitan centers that dot its terrain. But though the problem of evil is well known and much discussed, it is a larger and more complex problem, more multifaceted, than is commonly recognized: there remain sizable tracts of this territory that are underinvestigated and pathways of discussion that no one has developed. I want us to work on some of these. And what we will see if we do, I suggest, is that Epicurus and Hume and Mackie were right in supposing that a very formidable disproof of the existence of God may be lurking here (even if the pathways they followed in pursuit of it turned out to be dead ends or were successfully co-opted by theistic highway builders).

1. Developing the Argument

There are several important signposts along the way—several neglected considerations to which I shall appeal in developing my version of the argument from evil—and I want to begin by briefly identifying them. The first neglected consideration is that a God both perfect and personal, being necessarily omniscient, would necessarily have *maximally full knowledge by acquaintance of each possible occasion of horrific suffering.* (And let us follow Marilyn Adams and think of horrific suffering—or horrendous suffering, as it is sometimes called—as that most awe-full form of suffering that

243

gives the victim and/or the perpetrator a prima facie reason to think that his life is not worth living.)[1] Every aspect of *what it is like* to experience horrific suffering in every moment of its occurrence in every possible world in which it occurs must be present in complete detail to the awareness of God. This knowledge, taken together with the infinite compassion we are independently required to ascribe to the Divine, yields what I call the unsurpassable *empathy* of God.

The second neglected consideration to which I want to draw attention concerns the relation between the following: (i) *outweighing* goods and (ii) the *deepest* good of personal creatures. These seem conceptually distinct. In particular, it seems that someone's horrific suffering might serve what is by some reliable calculation an outweighing good without being required for her deepest good (or for that matter, for anyone else's). Thus is permitted to arise the question whether God would allow horrific suffering for just any outweighing good, or only for an outweighing good that was also the deepest good of creatures.

The third neglected consideration I want to bring into focus—and here we borrow from Chapter 9—is that the deepest good of finite personal beings in any world created by God is *known* to us: it is quite evidently an ever-increasing knowledge by acquaintance of God. If indeed God is to be construed as perfection personified, then what could be better for finite creatures than to enter ever more fully into the maximally great richness and beauty and glory of God? Of course, theists are already committed to this. But even nontheists should be able to agree that *such would be* the nature of the good for finite personal creatures, if there were a God.

The fourth neglected consideration to which I will be helping myself is that there appears to be nothing to prevent finite created persons who do not experience horrific suffering from realizing a relationship with God of the sort just mentioned. Take persons in the actual world, for example. Clearly not *all* of us experience horrific suffering. Are we to suppose that those who don't are for that reason debarred from experiencing relationship with God? Surely not. Again, this follows from what most theists believe. But there is plenty of other support too. We may point out, for example, that if God is unsurpassably deep and rich, then even where no horrors are experienced there must be an *infinite number* of ways of developing a relationship with God—an infinite number of possible journeys into self, the world, and God that realize the ultimate in meaning and goodness for finite created persons.

---

[1] See Marilyn McCord Adams, *Horrendous Evils and the Goodness of God* (Ithaca: Cornell University Press, 1999), pp. 26–29.

The fifth and last neglected consideration is like the fourth, except that it focuses more single-mindedly on the notion of a finite created person. There would seem to be a very large number of *subtypes* hidden within that notion: perhaps an infinite number of *ways* in which that notion can be realized. We tend, because of the peculiar nature of our own finitude, to focus obsessively on the finite persons we know to exist, with their peculiar problems and possibilities. But a God would not be similarly limited, and so when thinking of what might be, if there were a God, and even when operating on the assumption that God would wish there to be finite persons, we need to open ourselves to a more expansive understanding of the relevant set of possibilities.

Having thus identified some of the major signposts in the terrain we are exploring, let us now take a closer look at some of the details of the topography to which they draw our attention. We may start by sharpening the point about knowledge by acquaintance. Analytic philosophers are quite comfortable with the idea that an omniscient being would have perfect *propositional* knowledge—knowledge of every *truth* that it is possible for such a being to cognize—and in fact they usually define "omniscience" precisely and exclusively in such propositional terms. But here it is overlooked that a perfect creator must have, to a maximally great degree, *every* sort of knowledge it is good to possess, and that knowledge by acquaintance of horrific suffering belongs in that category. Without such knowledge, God might still be able to make correct comparative judgments of experiential value through knowing the relevant propositions but, as degree of value often depends on the nature of experienced qualities, would be denied direct apprehension of the *basis* of truth in such value judgments. More specifically, a God unable to experience with possible creatures their suffering would be unacquainted with their inner lives, could never know what it feels like from the inside to be one of those creatures. Such a God might know *that* there was suffering in a possible world inspected by the Divine mind and know *that* this was very bad. Perhaps she would be able to project herself, through imagination, into some faint likeness of the mental state of sufferers, which is of course what human empathizers do. But she would not possess the maximally rich and penetrating and meaningful understanding of suffering that we must surely associate with divine perfection. If a deeper acquaintance is possible—if, let us say, it is possible for God to have experiences qualitatively indistinguishable from experiences undergone by sufferers, whether actual or possible, which reveal to God what it is like to *be* those sufferers—it therefore follows that such knowledge must be possessed by a personal God. It seems evident that the deeper acquaintance *is* possible. Thus I derive the mentioned conclusion.

So what can be done with this conclusion? Well, we need to think about the enormity of its implications for the inner life and creative dispositions of any God there may be. Think, in particular, of what would result from an infinitely compassionate being experiencing so fully all the horrific suffering of *our* world, held before the Divine mind as a candidate for creation. This might seem a mind-boggling task. But perhaps we can make a beginning in it if we think a little about the effects of somewhat similar states in human beings. Think first of humans who are in some measure compassionate but not in any sense very "close" to any horrific suffering at all. This might describe most of us, who make do with journalists' reports or with imaginative extrapolation from our own—not very high—peaks of pain, and occasionally make some effort in the direction of relieving suffering through a donation to Oxfam or some such thing. We have "normalized" suffering to a considerable extent. (Familiarity breeds tolerance.) Even while calling it horrific, we really can hardly help not knowing—and underestimating—how bad horrific suffering truly is and having our own motivation to do something about it diluted by other concerns.[2]

But imagine next being given a shot of compassion and immediately transported from that comfortable spot in front of your television into the heart of the human devastation left behind by a tsunami or a terrorist bombing, or think of those who actually are day by day brought close to horrific suffering in this way: journalists, doctors, and (for the most intensified version of compassion plus proximity to horrific suffering) the Mother Teresas and Gandhis of our world. It would appear that with greater compassion and with greater proximity to much horrific suffering— more of a sense of what it is like to suffer thus—comes also a *stronger opposition to such suffering*, a fuller investment of time and energy devoted to its elimination and prevention.

And now let's intensify compassion and proximity to horrific suffering one more time. In particular, let's think of those whose "proximity" to it is as great as it can be for us humans, because they have experienced such suffering for themselves. Of course it is in the nature of the case that the number of such sufferers who survive and return to active life is relatively small, but some do, and from their experience and subsequent dispositions we might hope to glean the fullest glimpse of the effects of such empathy

---

[2] It is disconcerting to think of how, though we know horrific suffering is going on around us and hear of it every day, *precisely because* we ourselves are alive and well and able to take in the news at our leisure, we are disqualified from really knowing what the suffering we read about is like. *Everyone* who is talking about it is, for that reason, unable really to comprehend it, and so what is going on around us every day may be far more awful than we tend to imagine. (The responses of those who *do* experience it and survive provide support for the latter assessment—see immediately below.)

as I have ascribed to God—involving maximal compassion and maximal knowledge of what it is like *from the inside* to experience horrific suffering. Now it certainly appears from the examples that could be cited (take Elie Wiesel, the author of the well-known and disturbing little book *Night,* for one) that those who have experienced such suffering and are compassionate become strongly and indeed unalterably opposed to its occurrence in other cases: few who suffer thus can subsequently think of anything other than the eradication and prevention of such suffering.

Therefore, taking stock of our human cases, it appears we can say that the *greater* someone's empathy (i.e., the greater their compassion and the deeper and fuller their acquaintance with horrific suffering), the *stronger* is their opposition to horrific suffering—their disposition to seek to eliminate and prevent it wherever they can. But God would, if existent, be *maximally* empathetic (maximally compassionate and maximally well acquainted from every vantage point, and in particular from the inside, with *every* instance of the horrific suffering going on somewhere in our world at virtually every moment). So what should prevent us from drawing the conclusion that God would, if existent, be *maximally opposed* to the existence of all this suffering, and thus maximally opposed to actualizing our world? And if maximally opposed to the latter action—well, shouldn't that be enough to prevent God from performing it? At the very least, it seems we should say that God would be *more* opposed to horrific suffering than any of us are, and that too should suffice to prevent God from performing the action in question, given what many of us with our limited awareness of such suffering would already be quite willing to do with it, if we had the power.

Someone will no doubt say, however, that we should be deterred from the conclusion to which I am here drawn by the fact that God, unlike ourselves, is incapable of being *overwhelmed* by contact with horrific suffering, and thus is able to *also* see and respond positively to *outweighing goods* for which the permission of horrific suffering is necessary.

Now to this introduction of the notion of "outweighing goods" one might certainly be inclined to respond by saying that God, so far from being an exception to the rule of empathy, would exemplify it most fully, and (relatedly) that horrific suffering has the effects it does have in those who are empathetic not because of their limited psychological capacities to bear its awfulness but because of its *recognized importance.* However, instead of dwelling on these points, I will be content if I am allowed at this stage to reintroduce the *second* neglected consideration earlier adumbrated, and if the reader will grant me at least this much on the basis of serious reflection on empathy considerations: that it is a necessary condition of God's permission of horrific suffering that the outweighing good in question be the realization, by created persons, of their *deepest* good (notice that I make no concession as to the sufficiency of this condition). Put otherwise: if there can, in the absence of horrific suffering, be finite personal beings who realize their deepest good, then no merely greater or outweighing good *distinct* from the deepest would ever move a maximally empathetic God to permit such suffering.

Writers in the philosophy of religion have generally assumed that the horrific suffering of creatures might well be countenanced by God for the sake of some good so long as *permitting* that suffering did not stand in the way of their deepest good. What I am suggesting here is that, in the place of this common but far too lax assumption, we should nail the thesis that the horrific suffering of creatures would *not* be countenanced by God, *even* for the sake of a "greater good," so long as *preventing* that suffering did not stand in the way of their deepest good. The permission of horrific suffering might well be required for some possible good whose total goodness, on some utilitarian scale, outweighs the evil, or even for some good representing *one way* of experiencing the good most appropriate to creaturely life. But if there can be persons capable of experiencing the deepest good available to them even where there is no horrific suffering, who could be justified in permitting such suffering? Who, while perfectly empathetic, *would* permit it?

To test the claim I am making,[3] we need to try to bring together in our minds the idea of a God so exquisitely empathetic being able to make available to every creature not just some good but his deepest good—the richest, most all-embracing, and meaningful good possible for him—even if horrific suffering is altogether *prevented,* and the idea of God permitting some of those creatures to experience horrific suffering in all its awfulness anyway. Can we do it without the sense of jarring that signals inconsistency? The whole idea behind the notion of "outweighing goods" is that there may be heights of goodness that a creature cannot reach without suffering being permitted. But if we now see that the *greatest possible* heights of goodness are realizable without horrific suffering, what then? If the deepest good of creatures did not in any way require it, would the idea of permitting them to suffer horrifically so much as come to mind for an unsurpassably loving and empathetic God?

We need to think hard about this, considering it in light of what we know about the sort of empathy at issue here and about outweighing goods, and also recognizing that we are likely to underestimate the awfulness of

---

[3] A claim, I might add, that is considerably weaker than other claims that might be made here with considerable plausibility, such as the claim that God would not permit horrific suffering so long as a *good* life could be facilitated without it. The true principle, in other words, might seem to an inquirer to be quite a bit stronger than the one I am defending here—which fact should add to the latter's credibility.

horrific suffering. (Perhaps religious believers need to take special care here: despite much empathy, it is possible for a believer to "normalize" the hideous things their God is said to permit—much as any human being might, through loyalty or familiarity, normalize the offensive behavior of, say, a spouse.) If we do, I suggest, we will sense the inconsistency. Just *try* to conceive of a God whose empathy is unimaginably greater than that of your mother or of Mother Teresa permitting children to slowly burn to death, experiencing with them each moment of their horror, when everyone including those children can achieve not only very great goods but even their deepest good without the permission of such suffering.

Some critics of our argument may try to do just that.[4] What they may say is that if there really *were* a good that was (in some way unimaginable by us) great enough to outweigh the awfulness of horrific suffering and could not otherwise be obtained, a reasonable person might very well be willing to undergo horrific suffering for the sake of that good, *even* if he saw that his deepest good given the existence of God was obtainable either way; and so God would only be respecting what we would on reflection and full awareness of the facts want for ourselves by permitting horrific suffering to occur.

What my reply to this point would emphasize is, first, that we are talking here about the very *worst* sort of suffering, suffering that engulfs its victims and all they hold dear. Think of being brutally raped and repeatedly tortured, having your limbs chopped off with an ax, and being driven into a tormented and permanent insanity as a result. Such things happen. We need to look this suffering in the face and recognize how awful it is.

Then, second, we need to consider how great our deepest good would be, given the existence of God. But how, it may be asked, are we to do this? After all, might not our deepest good be quite unknown to us? Even if we can say what it is for other creatures, won't we find ourselves hesitating when it comes to complex personal creatures like ourselves? Well, we don't have to know what this good would be to recognize that, by virtue of being the deepest, it would be *more* desirable than any merely greater good of the sort to which horrific suffering might be linked. Why would a rational person be willing to undergo—or to permit—horrific suffering for the sake of an outweighing good that is itself outweighed by a good she is quite capable of realizing—or bringing about—without such awful suffering? But more to the point, drawing on our *third* neglected consideration from before, we may say that we are *not* in the dark even about what is the greatest and deepest good any personal being can experience given the

---

[4] I am indebted to Paul Draper for helping me see how these objections might be fleshed out.

existence of God: it is a positive, ongoing (indeed unending), and constantly growing relationship with God. Whatever difficulty might attend an
attempt to imagine the range of possible outweighing goods and all the
members of the corresponding set (a difficulty made much of in contemporary discussions of the problem of evil),[5] we *can* imagine something of
what our *deepest* good given the existence of God would be like.

And having done so, we will find it hard to imagine anyone on reflection and with full awareness of the relevant facts preferring to undergo
truly horrific suffering for the sake of a merely outweighing good, however great it might be, or regretting the loss of that good. (After all,
we are talking about endless intimate relationship with unsurpassable
greatness!) Why would someone who recognized what was waiting for
her in relationship with God wish to do anything other than move into
it ever more deeply? Why take time off to suffer horrifically in service of
a good that, no matter how great, will inevitably be transcended as she
continues her journey into God? And it *would* be time off, for horrific
suffering is absolutely inimical to the development of relationship with
God: it blows the fragile, developing person all to smithereens, causing unspeakable damage to physical, psychological, and (because of the
interrelatedness of the various aspects of personal life) also spiritual aspects of her being.

We can look at this another way. To gain the wonderful outweighing
good in question, the individual we are imagining would have to countenance the *ruin* of his earthly life (and perhaps much of any life that may
follow—who knows how long the destructive effects of horrific suffering might last?), and all this while recognizing that what is *most* desirable
(a good immeasurably more wonderful still) does not depend on his doing
so, and that his entering into it is in fact being put off by undergoing horrific suffering. Now a rational individual wants both to experience good
and avoid suffering. Obviously, these urges sometimes conflict, and up to a
point, the latter will give way to the former. But when the suffering linked
to an outweighing good is as immense as the suffering we are talking about,
and when, moreover, there is a recognition that to pursue one's deepest
good is to pursue a good whose greatness can increase forever, and is compatible with the avoidance of horrific suffering, and that entering into it
fully will indeed only be *delayed* by such suffering, then the former urge
must give way to the latter. Only this way can *both* urges be accommodated

[5] See, for example, Daniel Howard-Snyder, *The Evidential Argument from Evil* (Bloomington: Indiana University Press, 1996), most of whose essays either defend or oppose an
objection to arguments from evil based on this alleged difficulty. (There will be more on
these matters in Chapter 14.)

in a manner that is tolerable for a rational individual (not to mention a loving mother or an unsurpassably empathetic God).

Consider this further point as well, which fills out some earlier allusions. We have to remember here all the goods that are *lost* through horrific suffering and the profound, and often morally significant, attachments we may have to them. Horrific suffering, in other words, is awful not just intrinsically but also instrumentally. Most obviously, of course, it removes basic well-being and the sense of a meaningful existence. But it may also stand in the way of the development of one's personal gifts or of virtue, and prevent the fulfillment of important projects. It can interrupt and unravel or simply stamp out important moments of spiritual development. Furthermore, it often involves losing connections of various sorts with people who are deeply important to the sufferer and to whom he feels very strong loyalty.[6] The idea that a sufferer might prefer to give *all this* up because of other goods in the wings seems morally and rationally bizarre.

But perhaps a deeper point to be made here—drawing on the discussion at the outset of Chapter 9—is that the goodness of God's nature embraces *all* goodness in such a way as to make the distinction between our deepest good and another, competing good that we have been working with somewhat artificial, at least from an ultimate (all-things-considered) perspective. Earlier we talked about the urge to pursue the lesser good "giving way" to the urge to avoid suffering. But at a more fundamental level we can see that there is no giving way, for if every good apart from God is a dim reflection of good *in* God, then it is, ironically, through a deeper acquaintance with God that the value of the apparently competing good in question can best be known and experienced.

But the critic may persist, raising the following question. What if that good "in the wings" referred to above were not (at least not in the first instance) a good for *creatures,* as all my responses assume? What if it were some non-creaturely good somehow making the world as a whole much better (metaphysically, aesthetically . . .) than it could otherwise be?

---

[6] It is all too easy for a theistic critic to say here that all this can be made up for in a happy afterlife. Why would a rational individual *be* happy if the fabric of his life is suddenly torn away and the basic form of his existence is completely altered? The predictable answer is that God can wipe away all tears, but with this answer we also wipe away the value that is naturally and rightly attributed to the fabric of an undisturbed earthly life—the *intrinsic* value that in a proper assessment will stubbornly refuse to yield to the forward-looking orientation of the critic. (Theists, in other words, often underestimate not only the intrinsic badness of horrific suffering but also the intrinsic *goodness* of ordinary and undisturbed human life on earth, a proper estimate of which would bring with it, as I say in the text, an enlarged sense of the *instrumental* badness of horrific suffering.)

In response we might point out that, were God to permit horrific suffering for some such reason disconnected from any creaturely good, God would be simply using us and horribly—in a manner incompatible not only with the deepest empathy (which could hardly calculate from a distance as to what might be done with us and indeed *against* us to enhance the universe) but also with other obvious facets of Divine goodness, such as justice and love and respect.

But what if God could somehow turn the horrific suffering involved to *our* greater good as well, in some unfathomable fashion linking a significant improvement in our own overall condition to the good involved and thus indirectly to the permission of horrific suffering? Here, I suggest, we encounter the problem of giving sense to the idea of a significant improvement in our overall condition—a significant enough improvement to match the dreadful deficit represented by horrific suffering—being possible when the deepest good of creatures in continual relationship with God is *unsurpassably great* and can *otherwise* be achieved. How can a life graced by the continuing experience of such a good be significantly improved? Thus on the assumption (which I shall defend in a moment) that our deepest good *can* otherwise be achieved, the present objection too must be unsuccessful. I therefore conclude that the claim I have been defending—namely, that it is a necessary condition of God's permission of horrific suffering that such be required for there to be created persons who realize their deepest good—survives scrutiny.

So what can be done with *this* conclusion? Given awareness of the *fourth* neglected consideration mentioned earlier, it may not be too hard to see just what. Reflection on the traditional conception of a personal and perfect creator shows that the necessary condition our claim specifies is not satisfied: personal creatures can realize their deepest good even where there is no horrific suffering. Although, as many writers have undertaken to show, horrific suffering need not prevent the realization of this deepest good, its absence need not prevent it either. By appealing to Divine resourcefulness many have sought to establish that lives horribly marred by suffering may nonetheless participate in the good of relationship with God, but the very same point surely justifies the claim that the permission of horrific suffering is not *required* for persons to experience this greatest of all goods. (Notice that this is quite compatible with the claim that the permission of various other sorts of suffering *is* required.) Indeed, as we noted earlier, if God is infinitely deep and unsurpassably rich, then even if horrors are by some metaphysical mechanism or by the nature of the world God chooses to create excluded from personal life from the beginning, there must remain an *infinite number* of ways of growing into wholeness and fulfillment in God. (Here the *objector* fails to ruminate long enough on the differences between God and ourselves.) The idea that the permission of horrific suffering is required for anyone's deepest good in a world including God is therefore implausible in the extreme. But if so, then, given the apparent obviousness of the claim which says that if it is *not* thus required, God would not be prevented from preventing it, we may conclude that the latter proposition is indeed true: there is nothing to stop God from acting on the Divine empathy and barring horrific suffering from the universe.[7]

The argument we have arrived at can be stated more formally. Since the points for which I have argued all seem necessarily true if true at all, I offer a necessitarian formulation (and here it is assumed that the horrific suffering referred to is the horrific suffering of finite persons).

(1) Necessarily, if God exists, finite persons who ever more fully experience the reality of God realize their deepest good.

(2) Necessarily, if God exists, the prevention of horrific suffering does not prevent there being finite persons who ever more fully experience the reality of God.

(3) Necessarily, if God exists, the prevention of horrific suffering does not prevent there being finite persons who realize their deepest good (from 1 and 2).

---

[7] To some of the points I have been making Marilyn Adams can be seen as suggesting a reply with her idea of horrific suffering as a "vision into the inner life of God." (See Adams, *Horrendous Evils*, pp. 161–162.) This idea faces grave difficulties, however. For even if horrific suffering, by being "disproportioned to the human psyche and, as such, 'mind-blowing,' anxiety-producing, incapacitating, and humiliating," were to have something like numinous features, what it would communicate concerning the Divine could only be how far *distant* we remain from God's "inner life": to say of such experience that, even objectively, it can represent "moments of intimacy with God" is just unconvincing. If now it is suggested, rather differently, that the sufferer is making contact with that part of the inner life of God that, as I myself have argued, must be acquainted with horrific suffering, we should respond by pointing out that two quite distinct possibilities are being conflated: (i) becoming aware of God's experience and (ii) having one's *own* experience that in some way is *like* God's. While it is—at best—(ii) that we might link with horrific suffering, only (i) could fairly be thought to represent a moment of intimacy with God. (Here compare my experience of a vivid awareness that $2 + 2 = 4$ with somehow consciously experiencing *God's* mental interaction with that mathematical fact. Though I might regard the latter experience as valuable because of the connection to God, any connection to God in the former case must be too thin to generate anything of special religious interest.) But, regardless of the interpretation of her view that we select, the main problem faced by Adams's idea, given the contours of our present discussion, is expressed by Adams herself when a few pages farther on (p. 167) she admits that "a horror-free life that ended in beatific intimacy with God would also be one in which the individual enjoyed incommensurate good."

(4) Necessarily, if God exists, there is horrific suffering only if its prevention *would* prevent there being finite persons who realize their deepest good.

(5) Necessarily, if God exists, there is no horrific suffering (from 3 and 4).

(6) There is horrific suffering.

(7) God does not exist (from 5 and 6).

It seems to me that there is something strangely moving in this argument's idea that worlds in which God permits the worst and most awe-full tragedies to occur are not so much as possible—something strangely moving in the idea of a God who is *that utterly and implacably opposed* to the existence of such unspeakable horrors. But if so, then there is something strangely moving about the idea of God that only an atheist can appreciate.[8]

2. *An Objection to the Argument*

A variety of objections to the argument from horrors, as stated above, have already been dealt with in the course of its development. But I also want to examine a number of points not yet explicitly introduced. I particularly want to consider the free-will theodicy and the free-will defense. But before doing so, let me take up a specific point that will be easier to formulate now that we have the completed argument before us.[9]

This point says that (4) is not true as it stands, but true only if we add to it the following words: "or would prevent them from realizing such goods as are needed to experience it in the deepest possible way." That is, even if everyone could achieve relationship with God without horrific suffering, we cannot rule out God permitting horrific suffering if it were needed to make that relationship *as deep as possible*, and so to get the clearly necessary condition I want here, I need to make the suggested alteration. But then

---

[8] There may appear to be something odd in affirming that our world would be viewed thus by a perfect being while also affirming—as most of us would (if only because we value our own existence!)—that we love our world and wouldn't trade it for any other. But these two things are no more incapable of being harmonized than the similar pair of assertions that I wouldn't trade my present life for any other even though I should have—and had I been wiser at the time, would have—avoided certain mistakes when I was young, mistakes whose non-occurrence would have made for a very different present life.

[9] For the details of the objection taken up here I am indebted to several helpful e-mail discussions (undertaken separately) with Paul Draper and Michael Bergmann.

(3) is no longer strong enough—in conjunction with (the now revised) (4)—to facilitate the deduction of (5). To make it so, I would have to somehow justify adding to it the same alteration. And how could I do so? How could I rule out there being a good distinct from the deepest and necessary for the deepest to be as deep as possible *that requires the permission of horrific suffering?* Put otherwise, whereas what I have said we ought to be concerned with is

R: having a growing relationship with God in some way or other,

perhaps instead it is

RF: having a growing relationship with God that has feature F.

And perhaps RF requires experience of some good that cannot be had unless God permits horrific suffering.

But to make her case here, the critic needs to be able to show how one form of everlasting and ever-developing relationship with God might be a deeper or greater good for finite creatures than another (that RF1 might be better than RF2 or RF3, etc.), and it seems evident that, given the greatness of God, no such distinction can be made. Here we need to remember that "growing relationship with God" is short for something like "an everlasting journey into the heart of God in which ever fuller and richer experience and knowledge is obtained." How could one way of doing *this* be better than another? Given what God would have to show them (and here we can speak of an infinite good—that is, *God* is infinitely good—as well as of infinite richness), any number of finite persons could begin from the place determined by their makeup and move off in any direction, never exhausting the wonders of God, finding themselves stretched to the limits of their capacities for whole-making experience at every point along the way. This seems to just follow from what God is (an infinite and inexhaustible good) and from what such persons would be (finite and limited in all their capacities).

But now it may be suggested that the critic's point is not that some ways of knowing God ever more fully are better than others but that precisely because the notion of relationship with God is a developmental notion and because creatures may *not* find the development of relationship endlessly progressive (may *not* be knowing God ever more fully but stuck instead), horrific suffering might in some cases be needed to facilitate *further* spiritual development. (The relevant comparison is between a relationship that goes only so far and one that proceeds *beyond* that point and thus moves deeper into the deepest good.) We might on account of our own limitations—not God's—hit a wall at some point and be unable to progress. Perhaps horrific suffering is necessary for some good that enables some of us to scale that wall and progress further.

I would reply as follows. In the world in question God is the source of whatever limitations of constitution finite persons experience and has designed them with continuing relationship in mind; God is moreover infinitely wise and resourceful; so it is inconceivable that any creatures would remain at "the wall" for any significant length of time. If nothing else, God can always release whatever measure of infinite *attractiveness* is required in order to get someone moving. Something quite *contrary* to horrific suffering is thus available to God for the purpose in question and (unlike horrific suffering, which is extremely likely simply to embitter the individual or to destroy the very qualities and capacities needed here, and thus to fortify the wall) can immediately be seen by us to be the sort of thing capable of doing the job.

I suggest, therefore, that even if we accept the emendation to our argument suggested by the present objection (perhaps stipulating that "realize their deepest good" be interpreted throughout as "realize their deepest good in the deepest possible way"), the objection itself cannot be made successful.

3. *More Objections: The Free-Will Theodicy*

So is the argument from horrors sound? I think it is. But to confirm that this is so, I want to consider an additional roadblock that some may seek to throw up here, whose basic contours readers will no doubt find familiar. What I am referring to is an argument (or set of arguments) appealing to the value of free will.[10] How might this sort of move be developed and applied here? I will consider it first as a *theodicy* (which claims that, for some reason it specifies, God would, or probably would, permit evil) and then also as a *defense* (which, in line with current discussion, I shall understand as more modestly phrased in terms of epistemic or logical possibility). As a theodicy (and indeed also as a defense, as we will see later), this move will seek to absorb the point about our deepest good, making the well-known

---

[10] I shall assume, with the rest of philosophy of religion, that the free will in question is free will that permits choices having a significant impact, either good or evil, on how the world goes. For more on such arguments as belong to the background of my discussion here, see Alvin Plantinga, *The Nature of Necessity* (Oxford: Clarendon Press, 1974); John Hick, *Evil and the God of Love* (New York: Harper & Row, 1978); Richard Swinburne, *Providence and the Problem of Evil* (Oxford: Clarendon Press, 1998); and Peter van Inwagen, *The Problem of Evil* (Oxford: Clarendon Press, 2006).

claim that for personal creatures to achieve what is *truly* their deepest good in relation to God, they must be given deeply significant freedom and responsibility. In particular (and now I continue specifically with the theodicy for horrors), it must be up to us whether we develop our lives for good or ill and how we affect the lives and the similar development of others. But then God might be expected to permit individuals to cause or to remove suffering, including what we are calling *horrific* suffering: permitting such a thing is indeed a requirement of a sufficiently serious world in which what we do or don't do really *matters,* and in which genuine soul-making and deeply significant choices of destiny are possible.

This argument, while perennially interesting, is flawed. That is because creatures can have plenty of moral and spiritual freedom and responsibility even in a world in which choices leading to or resulting from horrific suffering are not open to them. Notice first certain features of the actual world, in which (the critic will allow) we *have* such freedom and responsibility. In the case of many (most?) of those whose actions do in fact lead to horrific suffering—rapists, mass murderers, and the like—it is at least dubious that the actions taken are free in the relevant sense (even theists and others who say we sometimes act freely will allow that often we do not, and it seems that actions of the sort at issue here may quite *commonly* be determined by prior states of the world—for example, by a horrifying upbringing, itself fully explicable in sociological and psychological terms—and so fall into the category of unfreedom). As for the rest of us, who reject the idea of perpetrating horrific suffering: it is not at all obvious that we are capable of doing anything else! (At any rate, this is the case if we mean by "capable" what is normally meant by it in these contexts: that although I may at a certain time have rejected the idea of perpetrating horrors, I could *at that very same time* have chosen to do otherwise.) Indeed, whatever might be the result of processes—for example, of brainwashing or attempted psychic reorganization—set in motion in the future, it seems clear that many of us are now and always have been by virtue of genetics and socialization quite *incapable* of performing actions that we know lead to horrific suffering: no matter how hard we tried, we could not bring ourselves, right now, to rape or torture or viciously murder another human being or drop nuclear bombs over inhabited areas. There seems no relevant sense, then, in which we may be said to be *free* in respect of such actions.[11]

---

[11] It is surely of relevance to questions about the value of free will in this connection when one notices that if someone *were* able to do such horrific things as are here listed, she should arguably consider that not a generous gift but a curse! In distancing ourselves from such things as we do, we indicate that we do not even want to be *able* to do them.

It follows from all this that our freedom in the actual world is not bound up with the capacity to cause horrific suffering. And if it is not, then perhaps God could ensure that *all* creatures are, throughout their developmental careers, incapable of actions leading to horrific suffering without rendering them less free than creatures are in fact. (Of course the result of this action might be a set of creatures other than the one that is actual, but, again, why suppose that God should, in advance of creation, be biased in favor of *us*?)

But perhaps we are wrong about this, and many in the actual world do have the capacity to deliberately produce horrific suffering, and do sometimes exercise that capacity freely. And of course we must also remember that there is much horrific suffering in the actual world that is not in *any* way the work of human hands, which we have the (no doubt significant) responsibility to seek to *remove*. Are things any better for the free-will theodicy when the former concession is made and the latter reminder heeded? It seems not. For now we need only think about a world in which these things are *not* present, and notice the freedom and responsibility that remain in it. I can be given a nontrivial share in the molding of the world even if the choice to cause horrific suffering is never open to me, for there are many *non*horrific evils I can cause or influence others to cause, remove or influence others to remove. It should also be noted that there are many varieties and levels of possible goodness in human life (especially a life lived in conscious relationship with God, which, given the richness of God, is capable of ever more development and deepening). And so I might, for example, influence you to stay at some *lower* level of goodness with narrow preoccupations—concerned only about a minimal attention to obligations and focused on sensual pleasure, say—instead of helping you grow and mature and ascend through the moral and spiritual ranks.

Let's look a bit more closely at what would be left to us in a world like ours from which horrific suffering had been excluded. As attention to experience reveals, there would still be rather a lot to work on in a world like this. There would, for example, still be innumerable conflicts of interest and sources of emotional pain, as well as illness, fear of death, self-centeredness and ego attachment of various kinds—all generating choices of great significance both morally and spiritually. Much of the work that would remain is of a sort that is only gradually revealed as we progress through the stages of life (if we do), and depends on earlier developments, which we may or may not have chosen to pursue. The human sciences, themselves relatively undeveloped, suggest that matters here are much more complex and messy than we may realize. Marilyn Adams has a nice summarizing passage:

> We human beings start life ignorant, weak, and helpless, psychologically so lacking in a self-concept as to be incapable of choice. We

learn to "construct" a picture of the world, ourselves, and other people only with difficulty over a long period of time and under the extensive influence of other nonideal choosers. Human development is the interactive product of human nature and its environment, and from early on we humans are confronted with problems that we cannot adequately grasp or cope with and in response to which we mount (without fully conscious calculation) inefficient adaptational strategies. Yet, the human psyche is habit forming in such a way that these reactive patterns, based as they are on a child's inaccurate view of the world and its strategic options, become entrenched in the individual's personality. Typically, they are unconsciously acted out for years, causing much suffering to self and others before (if ever) they are recognized and undone through a difficult and painful process of therapy and/or spiritual formation. Having thus begun immature, we arrive at adulthood in a state of impaired freedom, as our childhood adaptational strategies continue to distort our perceptions and behavior.[12]

Our freedom is indeed quite limited—"impaired," as Adams puts it. But by its own exercise it can be extended; and through considerable effort our damaged state can be made to evolve into something better, clearer, purer, and more open to others and to any God there may be. And of course, open to others, we are able to assist them in the navigation of their own developmental careers, and can choose whether to do so or not. *This* is where our moral and spiritual responsibility lies, and while as Adams shows, it may involve pain and suffering, it is quite detachable from *horrific* suffering, and indeed, in a sense inimical to it, given the disastrous physical, psychological, and spiritual effects of the latter. Nontheists, therefore, have an attractive option to advance as an alternative to the theist's view on freedom and responsibility, which must accommodate horrific suffering.

Perhaps it will be replied to this that it is precisely people as messy, psychologically, as those described in the Adams passage who are *capable* of atrocities. And it may be added that any kind of personal development through time of the sort I am emphasizing must occur against the backdrop of a law-abiding universe, which as we know can kill and maim as well as heal. As Keith Ward has recently put it: "Some of the findings of modern cosmology suggest that the fundamental constraints and principles of the natural order need to be just what they are if organic life is to exist.

---

[12] Adams, *Horrendous Evils*, p. 37.

One may not say that God could have produced a better universe with beings like us in it. Perhaps the sorts of harms this universe produces are the price of personal lives like ours."[13]

Let's take these points in turn. The first, I would suggest, betrays a certain naïveté about human nature—the idea that only a few pathological killers and their victims (or victims of the earth when *it* becomes a pathological killer) have serious work to do, psychologically, and that the rest of us are "normal" and have no "problems." As careful reflection on Adams's passage and insights from the human sciences on which it is based will show, the truth is rather different; and it is only conventionality and complacency that prevent us from recognizing this fact. Most of us are sleepwalking through life, unaware of the extent to which what we say and do is not the product of conscious reflection, but rather the present manifestation of imperfect "adaptational strategies" from the past or the work of hands other than our own; and even when we wake up to these facts, we are often unwilling to meet the difficult challenge with which they present us—of taking charge of our lives and working to form patterns of thought and feeling and behavior that reflect values and goals that we have consciously and carefully considered and made our own. Now, as already indicated, many serious choices face us here, and this is true just as much for those of us who are quite incapable of atrocities as it is for those who are capable. (Indeed, as already suggested, it is unclear to what extent the doings of those causally responsible for atrocities are a matter of *free choice* at all; and even if their doings *are* free, the range of morally and spiritually significant actions that are realistic options for such individuals, given their narrow preoccupations, is rather small.) God can therefore bring about the existence of individuals facing a variety of highly significant developmental tasks without making them capable of atrocities.

As for the second, "natural order," suggestion: this seems to result from a fixation with what is actually the case. The mistake is a common one in these discussions, so common that it deserves a name. Call it the *Familiarity Fallacy.* We are so familiar with the way personal life is realized in the actual world that we can hardly imagine things being otherwise and are inclined to infer that they cannot be otherwise. Yet the state of affairs that consists in *our* possessing personal life is but a single instance or token of the type *personal life.* Drawing on our fifth and last neglected consideration from the beginning of this chapter, which alerts us to the breadth of God's creative options, we may point out that there are many ways other than the actual of realizing personal life (other tokens of the type), and that some of these

[13] Keith Ward, *Religion and Community* (Oxford: Clarendon Press, 2000), p. 350.

are instantiated in worlds in which horrific suffering is absent. Beginning with possible worlds close to ours, in which the "goal" is developmental organic life and the general parameters are such as actually obtain, it would still be within the power of an omnipotent God to prevent the subset of events constituting horrific suffering by making adjustments *within those parameters,* either case by case or by simply willing "from the foundation of the world" that there shall be no such suffering and that the direction of orderly development within the universe shall be one consistent with this constraint. (A prohibition on horrific suffering might thus constitute a higher-level "fundamental constraint and principle of the natural order.")

It should also be noted that even if Ward is right to suggest that organic life requires a universe more precisely like ours, he goes too far when he suggests that *personal life is necessarily organic.* Imagination—or reflection on the claims of spiritual traditions of the sort to which Ward belongs—will reveal that a God would not be restricted to organic or physical options when contemplating the creation of personal lives with developmental potential. (Presumably anyone who thinks a *God* is possible will not have reason to shrink from the idea of *other* personal but non-embodied entities.) No doubt our existence as limited embodied creatures within an orderly physical universe affords us opportunities to learn and develop and grow or not to do so, but why should we suppose that this is the *only* sort of environment conducive to such things? Finite non-embodied persons within any number of orderly environments that can be conceived would also be able to learn and grow and make critical choices in relation to their own lives and those of others. (If it is suggested that we need a physical world of trial and temptation as a precursor to a spiritual world in which such things are done away with, we may reply that different *orders* or *levels* of spiritual existence, with appropriately different conditions, can be conceived.) Now within such nonphysical or spiritual environments the horror-causing regularities of the actual world would obviously not operate. Hence the claim that personal, developmental life is necessarily bound up with horror-generating physical conditions of the sort that actually obtain is false.

4. *More Objections: The Free-Will Defense*

The free-will theodicy therefore appears to be without any force in this context. But what about the free-will *defense*? This comes in two flavors: an *epistemic possibility* defense (or epistemic defense), which in response to our issue will argue that it is epistemically possible, even if not probable, that for some reason connected to free will God would permit horrors, and a *logical possibility* defense (or logical defense), which claims, more modestly still, that there is at any rate a possible world in which God has a reason deriving from the value of free will to permit horrors. I begin with the epistemic defense.

This defense has recently been developed in concrete and colorful detail by van Inwagen in his book on the problem of evil, based on his Gifford Lectures on the subject, and I will focus on his discussion. Here we find fleshed out a certain *story* about God, free will, and horrors that, according to van Inwagen, there is clearly no good reason to regard as false, even if there is also no good reason to regard it as true. (The broad outlines of the story will not be unfamiliar to anyone acquainted with the orthodox Christian picture of the world and its history.) Applying his argument to our own, what we can say is that *if the epistemic possibility of the story is clear,* then we must infer that it is epistemically possible that God permits horrors, and that my argument, which denies this, is unsound.

So what is van Inwagen's story, and *should* we regard it as epistemically possible? It is a story, developed at some length, of primates being miraculously raised to a human status involving rationality and free will by God; being given the gift of the beatific vision and living in peace and power and pleasure with each other and other creatures; then inexplicably rebelling and separating themselves from union with God, over time becoming corrupted through the influence of inherited self-centered genes, and needing to be freely reconciled to God—after which reconciliation (still somewhere in our future), in part to be effected by permitting *random horrors* in order to bring humanity to an appropriately motivating realization of the consequences of separation from God, humans will experience an eternity of spiritual bliss in relationship with God. Here are some central passages:

> Any plan with the object of restoring separated humanity to union with God would have to have this feature: its object is to bring it about that human beings once more love God. And, since love essentially involves free will, love is not something that can be imposed from the outside, by an act of sheer power. Human beings must choose freely to be reunited with God and to love him, and this is something they are unable to do by their own efforts. They must therefore cooperate with God.

> For human beings to cooperate with God in this rescue operation, they must know that they need to be rescued. They must know what it means to be separated from him. And what it means to be separated from God is to live in a world of horrors. If God simply "canceled" all the horrors of this world by an endless series of miracles, he would thereby frustrate his own plan of reconciliation. If he did

that, we should be content with our lot and should see no reason to cooperate with him.

However much evil God shields us from, he must leave in place a vast amount of evil if he is not to deceive us about what separation from him means.

According to the story I have told, there is generally no explanation of why *this* evil happened to *that* person. What there is, is an explanation of why evils happen to people without any reason. If a much-loved child dies of leukemia, there may well be no explanation of why that happened—although there is an explanation of why events of that *sort* happen. And the explanation is: that is part of what being separated from God means; it means being the playthings of chance. It means living in a world in which innocent children die horribly, and it means something worse than that: it means living in a world in which innocent children die horribly *for no reason at all*. It means living in a world in which the wicked, through sheer luck, often prosper. Anyone who does not want to live in such a world, a world in which we are the playthings of chance, had better accept God's offer of a way out of that world.[14]

Of his story, van Inwagen says this: "I contend that, given that the central character of the story, God, exists, the rest of the story might well be true. I contend that, in the present state of human knowledge, we could have no reason for thinking that the story was false unless we had some reason—a reason other than the existence of evil—for thinking that there was no God."[15] And it is this contention that I will now assess.

I suggest that it is implausible. This is because certain assumptions that it demands be true are instead false. Here are the assumptions (I shall use "might" to express the element of alleged epistemic possibility):

(1) That love might essentially involve free will.

(2) That creatures gifted with the beatific vision might nonetheless rebel against God and "leave paradise."

(3) That what it means to be separated from God might be to live in a world of horrors.

(4) That seeing the horror of life without God might for such creatures as van Inwagen describes provide the most effective motive of cooperation and return.

[14] Van Inwagen, *Problem of Evil*, pp. 87–89.
[15] Ibid., p. 90.

(5) That if a reconciliation plan involving horrors was implemented when the rebellion first occurred, many millennia ago, that plan might nonetheless not yet have proved successful.

(6) That those who experience horrors might all know of the existence and nature of God and of God's call to return.

(7) That if God's plan is as van Inwagen imagines, the number (and distribution) of horrors today might be great (and wide) *enough*.

Perhaps just looking at these assumptions, presented in this way, will raise some worries about their joint believability. But now let us consider the details that lead to justified denial. First, it seems odd that van Inwagen should wish to make (1)'s strong assumption (the "might" does not do much to make it less strong given the "essentially"). There will be more on this in the next chapter, but already we can see that if determinism turned out to be true and it were shown that humans lack free will, we would not be barred from loving each other or other things, including God, or required to conclude that what we had always thought was love really was not. For we would still be able to form emotional attachments and grow in propositional knowledge and knowledge by acquaintance of other persons, thus deepening our appreciation for them; and we would still be able to decide on the basis of reasons to become committed to them and act on our commitments. And what is all this if not love? (We might in such a situation realize that our decisions were unfreely made and that we therefore could not do other than what we did. But that would not make it inappropriate to decide and act as we did—the reasons on which we acted would retain their force—or make it false that we had thus decided or acted. Indeed, all the while we might be thanking our lucky stars—or God—that we were *able* to love in this way, instead of being otherwise constructed!) Now in this connection van Inwagen reminds his readers that "love is not love that alters when it alteration finds."[16] But why suppose that determined love would be transient and fickle? It seems that finite beings could be determined (in both senses) also to *stick with* their commitments, having been made to learn about and act on the good reasons for doing *that*.

But perhaps all van Inwagen needs (and really wants?) to say is that the *best* love *between humans and God* essentially involves free will. Such a claim might seem more plausible. Unfortunately it is still false (here again the Familiarity Fallacy looms). Since this is shown by the detailed discussion of

---

[16] Ibid., p. 167.

the next chapter, I simply issue the reader a promissory note to that effect and move on.

The next worry that can be turned into justified denial concerns the idea of creatures gifted with the beatific vision perhaps rebelling against God and separating themselves from union with God. I suggest that if we seek an appropriately enlarged understanding of what intimate knowledge by acquaintance of *God* would involve, we will find ourselves unable to conceive of such a thing. Here our understanding can, indeed, never be large *enough*, for God would by definition have to be the *ultimate* reality, unsurpassably and unimaginably beautiful and wonderful and rich. The trouble is that most of us tend to think of even a full and deep relationship with God of the sort to which van Inwagen refers in somewhat arid and abstract (or else mundane and shallow) terms, instead of imaginatively projecting ourselves into blissful union with the most wonderful reality we can bring to mind. Recognizing that even the latter would fall unimaginably far short of a real beatific vision, we must surely deny that creatures who truly *realize* the beatific vision would ever be moved to rebel against God, to seek to separate themselves from a good they would necessarily experience as most completely satisfying and entrancing.

Now perhaps the reply will be that the beings in question must be imagined as *human* beings, still earth-bound and therefore still influenced, to some extent, by self-centered desires and urges inherited from distant and much more primitive ancestors. But precisely this point can be used to make the problem here seem even more acute. For if the individuals in question are indeed to be pictured as influenced by self-centered tendencies, whatever could possess them to leave the paradisal situation van Inwagen describes, in which their powers and pleasures are complete? Perhaps another reply would be that we can *weaken* the emphasis, in the story, on the depth of acquaintance with God. But that would only serve to threaten the story as a whole, whose central theme, after all, is on facilitating a *return* to the completely paradisal and beatific state that is God's original and permanent wish for us. The assumption we are considering therefore seems at once an assumption that is false and an assumption van Inwagen's story cannot do without.

Assumption (3) also seems false. What it means to be separated from God, one wants to say, has nothing to do with living in a state of horrors but is rather to *lack* the special state of *loving communion* just described (and of course if *that* is horror-inducing, then we only see in another way the implausibility of the previous assumption). Any number of conditions—such as mediocrity in one's existence—would be sufficient for such a lack, so what need for horrors? And if God wished to bring home to us that we need to be rescued from such a condition, would not unremitting and intense tedium and boredom (for one example) do quite nicely? Is there any chance that we—beings like *us*—really would be *content* with such a lot, as van Inwagen's case implies?

This brings us to assumption (4), with its suggestion that experiencing horrors might provide the most effective motive of cooperation and return. The point just made seems to refute this suggestion. And we could add to it by pointing, more positively, to the likely efficacy of fresh infusions of the appropriate experience of God or, in a less exciting but all too realistic vein, of the appropriate operation of a system of rewards. Again, if humans really are self-centered, will not seeing "what's in it for them" clearly get them moving, however immaturely, along a path that, smoothed by the Divine resourcefulness, eventuates in a mature relationship of love with God? When we look at what in the actual world gets humans moving Godward, is it horrors or other things of the sort I have mentioned? I suggest that even van Inwagen's modest-seeming emphasis on the epistemic possibility of the need for horrors will seem gratuitous and strained when considered in the light of such reflections.

What about assumption (5)? Here one is inclined to ask why, if horrors are just the ticket, they have not produced serious results by now. Surely God would have sought to stem the rebellion immediately, before it grew into the advanced disease van Inwagen describes, and to do so by whatever was the most effective method available, if as the first part of the story implies, the beatific vision really was the Divine wish for human beings. And if horrors represent the most effective method, surely a massive infusion of horrors into human life early on would have been the most effective implementation of that method. And surely the latter would have produced the desired result very swiftly indeed. (Free will or no, we are not exactly distinguished for our bravery.) Thus the present assumption too seems implausible.

Assumption (6) allows to be epistemically possible the idea, common in some forms of orthodox theology, that in our heart of hearts all of us, including those who experience horrors, know that there is a God who is calling to us to return. But (as suggested in Chapters 9 and 10) this idea is quickly falsified by a bit of empirical inquiry—and if the apparently honest doubt of Western seekers is insufficient to satisfy here, then a glance at what in the previous chapter I called isolated nontheists (of other times as well as our own) should do. The idea of a personal God who is calling human persons to return to relationship is quite evidently not an idea that everyone has had or now has. Thus, contrary to assumption (6), there are many who experience or have experienced horrors but without being in a position to be motivated by them in the manner that van Inwagen's story demands.

Finally, we come to assumption (7). Van Inwagen clearly holds that the number (and distribution) of horrors today might be great (and wide) enough to motivate a return to God—indeed, that it might be just what is needed for the purposes of an omniscient God seeking reconciliation to be satisfied. But *do* we have an epistemic possibility here? If we require horrors to recognize our separation from God and be moved to cooperate with God's rescue plan, and God exists, why do so many of us not ever experience them? Why do those who really are proud and self-centered (not all are—here is another mistaken assumption) so often sail through life with the greatest of ease, while horrors fall on the poor and helpless, on those who are already committed to God, or on those who—as earlier noted—are lacking the conceptual resources to be motivated in the manner in question? "Just the luck of the draw," van Inwagen may say, emphasizing the *randomness* of horrors in a world without God. But if horrors are part of God's plan for that world, designed to motivate cooperation and return, and if God's love is impartial, then shouldn't God see to it that all of us experience horrors *sometime,* even if this means supplementing what chance produces? (Van Inwagen makes a similar point about God *limiting* horrors in many cases, so clearly it's not a completely "hands off" God that his story envisages.) In sum, if God has the plan van Inwagen imagines, then there should be *more* horrors than there are. That there are not shows that there is no such plan and that even van Inwagen's modest epistemic possibility claim to the contrary is false.

I conclude, therefore, that there are strong and straightforward arguments against each of the seven assumptions critical to van Inwagen's case that I have identified. There is good reason to believe that all are false. Of course, if even *one* of them is false, van Inwagen's epistemic defense fails. Not surprisingly, I therefore conclude that his epistemic defense fails.

Are there other stories that might be successful even if van Inwagen's is not? Critics are welcome to produce them, but I suspect that when the net of reflection is spread widely enough to include serious and nonpartisan consideration of the reasoning that got the argument from horrors going in the first place, as well as the reasoning I have used against van Inwagen's case (which shows, among other things, just how unwarranted is the hold on us of intuitions about freedom, love, and the behavior of God sponsored by orthodox theologies), such stories as are produced will be seen to lack the power to persuade.

What about the second version of the free-will defense? Let us turn our attention now to this rather different move. (Since a version of it was already discussed in some detail in Chapter 9, we can be relatively brief here.) Applied to our issue, what it suggests is that despite what I have said, there is a way of showing that it is logically possible that God permits horrific suffering for the sake of our deepest good since, again, that good entails the possession of free will. (As this logical defense will be quick to point out, because my argument is stated in necessitarian terms, only a logical possibility is required to defeat it.) Notice that this claim is not simply a weakened, more modest version of the free-will theodicy or of the epistemic defense, saying that even if it is not probable, it is at least logically *possible* that horrific suffering is needed to make life in the world challenging enough for free creatures, or that even if it is not *epistemically* possible, it is at least *logically* possible that horrific suffering is needed to motivate our return to God. No, instead it relies on the logic of incompatibilist free will. What it tells us is that it is logically possible that what God saw when contemplating creative options is this: that the distribution of truth-values on the set of counterfactuals of creaturely freedom is such that, for each world without horrific suffering in which free creatures (with whatever measure of freedom) achieve their deepest good in freely chosen relationship with God, the attempt to actualize it would be stymied by uncooperative behavior on the part of its free denizens. But if it *is* possible that God cannot achieve that worthy goal of freely chosen relationship with God without permitting horrific suffering, then, on my own terms, the suggestion that God would *necessarily prevent* horrific suffering turns out to be unjustified.

In line with our similar discussion in Chapter 9, let us assume that the point about a possible impossibility is, if not clearly true, at least true for all we know. Even so, our proper conclusion in light of this is somewhat different from what the free-will defender suggests. On my own terms, the suggestion that God would necessarily prevent horrific suffering turns out to be unjustified only if *freely chosen relationship with God* is entailed by possession of the deepest good for creatures. And it seems clear that it is not. In the above presentation of the free-will defense, a subtle shift occurred from the assumption (which I have accepted through much of the previous discussion for the sake of argument) that free will is entailed by our deepest good to this more specific claim. But considering again that neglected point about the breadth of God's creative options (in particular, the infinite number of *modes* of relationship with God), we can see that there are many ways in which our deepest good can be achieved in the absence of a freely chosen relationship with God. Along the lines of Chapter 9, we might again tell our own story about the beauty and glory of God being made so clear to creatures (one might even imagine an incarnation event whose occurrence and ramifications are more evident to all than is the Christian story in the actual world) that the contrary desires or false beliefs supporting their previous resistance fade away and a positive response to God inevitably follows. This scenario is but one of an infinite number that God would see in blazing detail were one of those Plantinga situations to arise in which the only way freely chosen relationship with God can be achieved is by permitting horrific suffering. Since God would always have to consider not just the great good of such freely chosen relationship but also the *other* modes of relationship—*alternatives* to permitting horrific suffering that are still compatible with the deepest good of creatures being realized—and since the latter *are equally splendid,* one of those alternatives is always going to seem preferable to a world with horrific suffering, when viewed from the perspective of unsurpassable empathy, even if the latter world includes freely chosen relationship with God. After all, if a perfectly good and loving and empathetic and wise God is able to choose between a scenario whose goodness is very great but requires the permission of horrific suffering and a scenario with goodness *equally* great and *no* need for the permission of horrific suffering, how might we suppose the Divine choice will be made?

What one notices if one accepts these arguments is that although there may be a possible world in which God sees what the free-will defense says God might see and in which certain freedom-related states cannot be achieved without horrific suffering, there is no possible world in which these things are so *and God goes ahead and permits horrific suffering.* To see the difference between these two things is to see the Achilles' heel of the logical defense, to which the argument appealing to empathy considerations (and the unconsidered alternative scenarios) directs its arrows. Since the free-will theodicy and epistemic free-will defense are, as we have seen, equally vulnerable, it may therefore be concluded that the potential roadblock to the success of that argument which we have been considering can be dismantled. Considerations of free will represent no significant barrier to the conclusion that the argument from horrors is sound.

The Free-Will Offense

In the last two sections of the previous chapter I (at most points) went along with the common assumption that for finite personal creatures to achieve their deepest good in relation to God, they must be given incompatibilist free will. Here I challenge that assumption. Indeed, I argue that, correctly construed, free will is a *problem* for theism—the basis, if it exists and is distributed and exercised in the ways it appears to be, for a distinctive argument (or set of arguments) against the existence of God. And thus we are taken from the free-will *defense* to the free-will *offense.*[1]

This sort of move is of course going to seem initially controversial: few of those who have views on such things would be prepared to deny that the deepest good of personal beings in some way depends on free will. The drama regularly rehearsed in the literature, involving the progress toward deeper perfection (or recovery from deep imperfection) of creatures who are the ultimate source of their own actions, has caught the imagination of pretty much everyone, and philosophers have little inclination to consider alternatives to this picture when thinking about what sort of world a perfectly good creator would actualize. But here again we must beware of the Familiarity Fallacy. While there is no doubt that these familiar commodities, and a relationship with God mediated by them, would be great goods for personal beings, why suppose that a relationship with God mediated

---

[1] Now, of course, perhaps it will turn out that none of us actually possesses free will. But most of us believe and consider it to be a justified belief that we do possess it, and so I shall take it as appropriate to use this assumption in the arguments against theism developed in this chapter. In any case, if free will does not exist, then free-will theodicies and defenses cannot get off the ground for *that* reason, and a problem quite similar to one of the problems developed here is faced by theism anyway.

in any number of other ways would be inferior? The fact that this question has to date hardly been so much as raised in philosophy suggests that the aforementioned consensus is cause for suspicion. Complacency or acquiescence in cultural or religious prejudice may as well be the source of it as genuine and indisputable insight. After our discussion here, such suspicion should appear the more justified.

In this chapter's first section I examine some possibilities of personal development compatible with an absence of free will. My conclusion is that God can do quite as much to forward the good of persons in a world in which free will is absent as in one in which it is present. Then, in the second section, I argue that certain strides the famous free-will defense against the argument from evil may have appeared to make in the absence of awareness of this fact are to be viewed as ill-gotten gains. What careful reflection actually shows is that the consensus view (that God would decide in favor of free will) is false, and that belief in free will serves the atheist's purposes rather better than the theist's. Finally, in section 3, I reveal another side to the free-will offense, to wit the argument that if an all-wise God were *going* to grant us free will, the pattern of opportunities for its exercise would be rather different than in fact it is.

1. *A World without Free Will*

I propose to begin by going directly to what many would consider the heart of the issue: the question how anyone without free will can enjoy authentic personal relationship with the Divine of a sort that, as I myself have emphasized, would be greatly valued by a creator whose relational-personal love was the *most perfect* possible. A common argument here, associated with the work of John Hick,[2] is that if finite persons lacked free will, their responses to God would be "fixed" in advance and thus mechanical and lacking in spontaneity. Indeed, the relationship between themselves and God would be like that between a hypnotized patient and the hypnotist, or between a puppet and the puppeteer, or between a robot and its designer—which is to say grounded in one-sided manipulation and control and so not authentic or truly personal at all. Hick produced this argument in response to an earlier (and in my view somewhat misguided)

---

[2] See his *Evil and the God of Love* (London: Macmillan, 1985), pp. 271–275. Hick (p. 266) goes so far as to suggest that individuals without free will cannot really be persons at all, but (in part, no doubt, on the basis of such considerations as I advance immediately below) few have followed him in this, and I ignore this suggestion in my characterization of the argument.

attempt to support the thesis that God would create persons without free will associated with the names of Antony Flew and J. L. Mackie,[3] and most philosophical writers these days proceed as though he settled the issue.[4] The Hickian sort of argument is also very popular in writing emerging from the current science/religion debates. As an example, here again is Kenneth R. Miller, the molecular biologist whom we first encountered at the end of Chapter 10: "A world without meaning would be one in which a Deity pulled the string of every human puppet, and every material particle as well. . . . All things would move towards the Creator's clear, distinct, established goals. . . . By always being in control, the Creator would deny His creatures any real opportunity to know and worship Him. Authentic love requires freedom, not manipulation. Such freedom is best supplied by the open contingency of evolution."[5]

The Hickian argument—and in particular its connection to the notion of evolution—bears examination, however. It claims, as we have seen, that created persons who lacked free will would be like God's puppets. But there are puppets and then there are puppets! Take ourselves, for example, the human beings who actually exist. We are persons, and surely this is the case even if we lack free will. The image of a sea of wooden Pinocchios can make us forget that, even if it turned out that we lack free will, we would not suddenly be required to look on ourselves as less than the psychologically and intellectually complex and ever changing and (potentially) developing social creatures that we are. The mysteries of our nature would, given such a scenario, still be considerable, yielding only to much patient investigation, as would the mysteries of the larger reality of which we are a part. There would still be moments of sudden insight and discovery. We would still be making a living intellectual contact with truths and falsehoods, still struggling with how to be true to what we know and fashion it into a life, still navigating the intricate and subtle highways and byways of interpersonal relationship, still growing or failing to grow toward deeper maturity in various respects. In a world without free will, for

[3] See Antony Flew, "Divine Omnipotence and Human Freedom," in *New Essays in Philosophical Theology*, ed. Antony Flew and Alasdair MacIntyre (London: S.C.M. Press, 1955), and J. L. Mackie, "Evil and Omnipotence," *Mind* 64 (1955). A defect of the Flew and Mackie approach, as I see it, is that it seeks to meet the theist on her own playing field—where an emphasis on *some* sort of freedom and on moral character is a prerequisite of participation—instead of inviting the theist into another ball park altogether, from which a variety of goods that take us beyond moral character and do not require free will may become visible.

[4] See, for example, Robert M. Adams, "Plantinga on the Problem of Evil," in *Alvin Plantinga*, ed. James E. Tomberlin and Peter van Inwagen (Dordrecht: D. Reidel, 1985), p. 228.

[5] Kenneth R. Miller, *Finding Darwin's God: A Scientist's Search for Common Ground between God and Evolution* (New York: HarperCollins, 2002), p. 289.

example, I might still *decide* to take on certain commitments, *feel* the tension between these and competing concerns, *think* of ways to strengthen the psychological power and efficacy of the former and diminish that of the latter, and so on.[6] Of course perhaps none of us wants it to be the case that nothing we think and feel and decide is in the incompatibilist sense up to us—though why we should see more than a tendency toward ego-centeredness here I'm not sure. But there can be no doubt that we are still amazing creatures with a potentially amazing future even if we lack free will.

This, however (or so it will be claimed), does not yet address the critic's central concern: that in a *Divinely produced* scenario including persons but no free will, God must *manipulatively control* everything that happens to persons and in persons in a manner incompatible with any kind of authentic personal relationship between them and God. But I would suggest that a fuller development of points already advanced will suffice to deal with this. If we consider the possibilities of an evolutionary picture of the sort suggested by the actual world (but not, of course, restricted to it)—a picture in which, instead of existing complete and whole from the beginning of their careers, created persons are given the opportunity to ever more fully develop the finite psychological, social, spiritual, and perhaps physical capacities they are given in an environment that develops and changes with them as they grow[7]—and use our imaginations when thinking about God and determination, we will find a way of alleviating the critic's concern and gain a better appreciation for what is possible without free will. As we have just seen, such an evolutionary picture does not require free

---

[6] It may be said that although these things could occur without free will, they could not occur without the *belief* that we have free will—how, for example, can I think of myself as deciding between two actions A and B unless I think of myself as *able to choose either A or B?* But then, if despite thinking thus we are made to *lack* free will by God, God would be guilty of deceit. I suggest, however, that the sense in which one sees oneself as deciding between two actions can vary with the nature of one's belief about matters metaphysical. If (to take an example discussed more fully later on) I see it as determined by God that I shall progressively learn more of the truth, forming beliefs and desires and purposes appropriate thereto, I will think of my decision between A and B in this way: I do not know which of the two I will do, but whichever it is, it will be done only at the end of a process involving my thinking of the reasons for doing A and the reasons for doing B and selecting the action best supported by reasons. One who thinks thus and goes through the mentioned process is clearly making a decision, and all without—in the usual sense—thinking that she is able to do either A or B. (Perhaps in going through this process it will *seem* as though she is able to do either A or B; but this "seeming" is as innocuous, in the presence of the belief that such is not in fact the case, as its "seeming" to us as though the sun goes around the earth.)

[7] I say "perhaps physical" to underline the fact that an omnipotent and nonphysical God would presumably not be *restricted* to physical options when thinking about what sort of world finite persons should inhabit.

will, and as I will now argue, it can be attractively filled in without depicting God as controlling and manipulating or even as determining every creaturely thought and feeling and choice.

There are several points here. (1) Though it is tempting to assume, as does the Hickian argument, that if in a Divinely created world persons have no free will, everything about them (including any development they undergo) must be determined by God, "fixed" in advance, this assumption is false: determination by God does not follow from being created without free will. God may choose to make it the case that not all events—or even all creaturely choices—are determined in advance while not giving anyone free will, for free will notoriously requires more than choices not determined by antecedent conditions outside the agent's control: it entails as well *the agent's control over those choices*—something that, as everyone knows, has proven difficult to provide with an intelligible description, and might well be absent even if determinism is false. It is not hard to see how in such a world, in which genuine surprises may occur at various levels (perhaps within parameters that *are* predetermined), God would not be in the position of controlling or manipulating everything that happens in and to persons as the evolutionary process unfolds.

(2) But let us assume that such a scenario is for some reason unacceptable. I want to attempt the harder task of showing that a world without free will poses no religious problems even on this assumption. Consider first that even if everything about persons in a world created by God is fully caused by prior states outside their control, it does not follow that God is tinkering with their psyches every moment of every day, as the Hickian argument's use of words like "manipulate" might lead us to think. In a deterministic scenario, provided with an evolutionary frame, the responses of persons can be seen as part of a process whose laws God has ordained, and as occurring in accordance with those laws, not in accordance with special Divine decrees.

(3) To find further reason to resist the apparent force of the Hickian argument even while accepting the deterministic assumption, notice that at least in the hypnotist example the subject is caused to do what she might otherwise choose to avoid, and may easily be led down delusional pathways that serve purposes other than her own—this is at least part of what gives content to "manipulation" and "control" here. But in a deterministic scenario involving God, persons do what it is in their nature to do; there is nothing *they* would rather do if only they had the freedom to do it, and so there is no manipulation of the sort one might associate with the hypnotist example. They are also continually being led into a deeper acquaintance with the truth, and so are progressively, in every way compatible with finitude, *overcoming* delusion and approaching enlightenment

on various fronts. This is significant because it alerts us to the fact that in a deterministic evolutionary scenario, interestingly designed, God does not build into persons a certain limited store of knowledge and then wind them up and watch them do the Divine bidding on the basis of the knowledge given. Rather God builds into persons capacities that can grow and yield ever richer results, including a capacity to discover ever more of what there is. Persons, in this picture, are constantly learning more of what *God* knows—they are, if aimed at anything, aimed at the truth. Surely it would be a privilege to be "manipulated" in this way![8]

(4) The previous point also allows us to see what is wrong with the idea that free will is required for an authentic love and trust in response to God, an oft-repeated refrain in the hymnbook of theistic metaphysics. If we lacked free will and all our responses were determined by God, so we are told, we would be "preprogrammed," and thus any response of love and trust toward God would be triggered by the program, not by real awareness of how things are—specifically, not by awareness of God's own personal qualities and merits. Implanted desires would be activated instead of ones naturally acquired in response to the facts. But this does not follow, as in effect we have already seen. For if I am programmed to learn the truth, and to form beliefs and desires and purposes appropriate thereto, then I *cannot* respond to the program without responding to the facts. Coming to learn truths about God, individuals in the scenario I have in mind naturally and appropriately respond with an ever deeper love and trust, just as in meaningful personal relationships with each other in the actual world we may respond positively and appropriately to our awareness of facts about the other—for example, to our recognition of a

---

[8] It may be objected that while the agent may not be caused to do what she might otherwise choose to avoid, it is still the case that she is caused by factors over which she has no control to have the nature she has and to want to do the things she does, and that this point—perhaps the central point Hick and others are trying to make—may have force even if the hypnotist example isn't quite right. I reply as follows. The hypnotist example is commonly used and commonly taken as forceful and so needs to be exposed as inadequate by anyone with my argumentative aims. That is what this paragraph was about. And the more general "control" issue that remains when this is done is directly addressed in points 6 through 9 below. Here I would add that if persons being caused by factors over which they have no control to have the nature they have and to want to do the things they do is a problem, *then even a scenario including human free will must be problematic*, since agents whose nature it is to be free, if created by God, are also "caused by factors over which they have no control to have the nature they have," and they no more choose their wants than do those who are unfree. Nor, we might add, is the *range* of their freedom chosen by them. Notice that free creatures might well wish to rid themselves of their freedom (or of the sort of freedom they possess) but without being able to do so, if it is written into their natures. Freedom, too, in a certain sense, constrains. Indeed, as the points below bring out more fully, a lopsided, asymmetrical relation between Creator and created in which the former has much "control" over the latter is quite unavoidable.

parent's biological relationship to ourselves, his gentle, caring nature, his helpfulness in difficult situations already experienced, and so on.[9]

(5) It may now be objected that despite the refinements I have added, in a deterministic scenario of the sort we are considering, God still must *know* everything that will happen to finite persons in a manner quite incompatible with authentic relationship and the uncertainties and vulnerabilities it entails (this will of course not trouble the Molinist encountered at the end of each of the previous two chapters, but, as we have seen, Molinism may well be false). Later we will see another reason for supposing that this is not a problem, but for now we may simply point out that, having ordained the laws of the developmental process and thus knowing what will happen, God may also *suspend* knowledge of some or all of these laws or of some or all of their consequences. There does not seem to be anything incoherent about this notion. (Indeed, it is not unlike a notion of Divine self-limitation already accepted by some philosophers of religion who reject a full-blown Molinism—who accept that God is *capable* of knowing counterfactuals of creaturely freedom but graciously chooses not to *exercise* this capacity.) Thus it seems that we lack any grounds for speaking of control or manipulation here.

(6) Perhaps it will be claimed that in my deterministic scenario there remains a lamentable sort of one-sided control, since even if God only ordains the laws of the process and sees to it that they lead us ever further into truth, and even if God suspends knowledge of exactly how the process will unfold, the whole thing has objectively been *set up* to run the way it does, and will inevitably proceed according to Divine decree. The only relationship this makes possible between God and created persons is significantly unlike that existing between individuals in a genuine, personal relationship of mutuality, respect, and "letting be." But this suggestion only permits us to make a deeper point about any relationship between God and created persons—a point that shows how inapt the analogies we have been considering really are. The force of the hypnotist analogy, for example, depends on the contrast brought to mind there, a contrast between the relationship the hypnotist has to the patient when he determines her responses and the more equal and mutual relationship in which she might participate if he did not do so. However, in the religious case the contrast between control given determinism and equality or mutuality given free will must inevitably be severely diminished or disappear altogether.

To see this, consider that in any world created by God, even one that includes their free will, the persons we are talking about are *creatures,* and

---

[9] This point seems to be missed by, among others, Richard Swinburne in his *Providence and the Problem of Evil* (Oxford: Clarendon Press, 1998), p. 195.

so the relationship between them and God necessarily lacks symmetry in deep and important ways: God creates finite persons, but finite persons do not create God; the potential of finite persons and the number of ways in which they may pursue it are determined by God, but finite persons do not determine anything like this for God; unless Divine knowledge is suspended, God knows, even if not precisely what finite persons will do, the exact disjunction of possibilities, but finite creatures cannot ever have a similarly comprehensive understanding of what God might do; God (consequently) has or can have "contingency plans" likely to be successful for anything that finite persons do, but finite persons have no such unlimited resources for managing the relationship with God; the appropriate response of persons to God is one that includes worship and adoration, but God owes creatures nothing of the sort; and so on. And the ways in which the relationship lacks symmetry, as should be evident, show that something very like the "control" lamented by the objector is *ineliminable* from a relationship with God and must simply be accepted by finite persons—and indeed become part of the very texture of that relationship insofar as it is properly understood. In a relationship with an infinite being who is the very source of your existence and nature, things will always be "set up" to a large extent and there must always be a rather significant power differential. Even for creatures who have free will, such a relationship can in no possible circumstances be anything like the "equal" and "mutually influencing" and "mutually vulnerable" relationship the hypnotist could choose to have with his patient if he gave up the idea of hypnotizing her.

(7) It may now seem that my points, if correct, prove too much—that *no* authentic personal relationship between finite persons and God is *ever* possible if what I have said is true. But this is not the case. We must simply look for better analogies. Instead of thinking about what is true of meaningful relationships between ourselves and other adult humans when considering what an "authentic" personal relationship with God might involve, we can, for example, look at how as adults we are related to our children and how they are related to us. (This can hardly be seen as a novel suggestion, given well-known and typical patterns of religious discourse about our relation to God.) We are, most obviously, responsible for bringing our children into the world in the first place. And when relating to our small children with a modicum of child psychology in mind, we often know very well what they will do and how they will respond to us and to others in various circumstances, or at least we often know the relevant disjunction of possibilities: when they meet someone new they will be wary or prefer staying close to us, when afraid they will look to us for comfort or run and hide, when hungry they will cry or ask us for food, and so on. None

of this prevents us from having an authentic personal relationship with our children appropriate to our different roles and places in the world. This relationship is ideally and indeed typically expressed in the natural disposition of a parent to feed and shelter and clothe and protect and play with and teach the child, and in the natural disposition of the child to receive and participate in all these things, and to share with the parent in a life that is structured by them (notice that for the parent of a small child, there is therefore little of the "vulnerability" to being rejected that a Hickian will consider essential to personal relationship).

When we think in terms of *this* analogy, we are much less likely to find significant the changes that would go along with a more thoroughgoing parental responsibility for the existence and nature of the child. Suppose, for example, that the child is the result of sophisticated genetic engineering initiated by the parent, and indeed that the depth of the parent's knowledge of the child's constitution is such that the parent is potentially aware of everything the child will do (including all its responses to the parent) in future life. Is it not evident that an authentic, personal, loving relationship between the parent and child remains possible? (We could, if we wished, suppose that the parent decides not to access much of what she is able to be aware of, but, interestingly, this does not seem to affect significantly the reasonableness of answering in the affirmative here.) And is it not evident that this is because the relationship is structured by—and indeed requires—a very different role and place in the world for parent and child? Think of the delight of those times when we experience with our children the usual passages of life (for example, learning how to walk) or help them to see something we ourselves have known for a long time (why the sky is blue, where babies come from, how large is the known universe)—something that, given their curiosity, we realize will interest them and stimulate certain additional questions, often easily predictable in advance. Surely there are some very deeply meaningful moments of personal relationship here.

(8) All this suggests a model for understanding authentic personal relationship between Creator and created quite different from the conventional one—call it the *sharing* model. (It might not, of course, be a model applicable in the actual world, but that is neither here nor there: we are not trying to make God conform to the world as we know it—or would like it to be—but to conform our understanding to the truth about what a Divine creator would do.) Imagine that morally bad actions and the rejection of God are not options for finite persons, that persons are created good and well-disposed toward their creator within a deterministic but evolving physical or spiritual universe without evil, which is designed to extend everlastingly the richness of their experience and opportunities

for creative endeavor.[10] Imagine further that God is related to each finite person or to communities of such persons somewhat as a parent is related to his children, or—to use a notion functionally similar—in a manner analogous to the relationship existing between a supremely wise teacher and her disciples, and that finite persons are in this way given the privilege of coming to see and understand and experience ever more fully, through unending time, the amazing wonders of the universe and of its infinitely transcending creator, and to participate in the positive evolution of the universe toward a state that ever more fully reflected the Divinity of its creator. (Thus we might expect work and challenge to be involved, though not such work and challenge as degenerate into suffering. Notice that an "unfinished" universe is not the same as a bad one, just as an unfinished house is not the same as a house poorly built.)

What, among many other things, is interesting about persons—for themselves and, we may surmise, for any Divine creator—is their deep capacity for understanding and self-awareness and self-regulation, as well as for creative activity (however determined such capacities and the circumstances of their exercise may be by prior states). This permits growth and insightful, reflective change in response to experience in ways not possible for other creatures, and it does so no matter whether free will is exercised in the process or not, and even if there is no evil. Because of these facts there could be deeply interesting and meaningful interaction between God and finite persons in a scenario of the sort I have described without free will and without evil. In that scenario, God expresses a loving desire to share by creating and nurturing finite persons and facilitating their development in alignment with the truth. Respecting the precious nature of personal life, God permits it to unfold as it will, governed, perhaps, only by a disposition to become and remain conformed to the truth—a disposition that, in the nondevelopmental sense appropriate to an infinite and unsurpassably great creator, governs God's life too. Why should we suppose this scenario to be inferior to one including creaturely free will?

(9) "An interesting scenario," my critic will say, "and one that sounds a great deal like Heaven! But a relationship involving the creature's free will, exercised in a hostile world that through heroic effort and, yes, suffering she has the opportunity to tame, and that is ultimately *followed* by Heaven,

---

[10] Many have argued that, if there were a God, there would be free will *of a different kind* (perhaps restricted to choices between goods or between goods and minor evils) and *less* evil. But it is hard to be clear when discussing such scenarios—where should we draw the line? So it will be interesting instead to reconsider the merits of a world without free will of any kind and without any evil at all, and apply the results of *this* discussion to the problem of evil.

is better than what you have in mind. In particular, it is better for the creature. Even if an authentic personal relationship with God does not necessitate such a prelude, it is still true that finite creatures receive a much more generous privilege and can potentially attain to a much higher degree of dignity if they are given such freedom and responsibility than otherwise. And surely these are good reasons to suppose that a loving creator would give to at least some creatures free will in a world like ours before giving them access to a world of the sort you have described."[11]

How should we respond to this argument? The most generous interpretation of what the critic has to say about generosity and dignity would have us consider that perhaps God can create beings more dignified, and can exercise more generosity, by creating persons who at first possess free will than otherwise (it is clear that if God creates creatures who never possess free will, *they* would not have been benefited had God chosen otherwise, for otherwise *they* would not exist). But results we have already arrived at, carefully considered, together with a simple point about the knowledge of God, suggest that this claim is false. As we have already observed, the beings God can create who never possess free will include truly wondrous creatures who are afforded the marvelous privilege of experiencing a more unfettered conscious awareness and a more constantly unfolding knowledge of the truth about themselves, their environment, and their creator from the beginning (and there is therefore a way in which they are privileged and afforded dignity that is denied most humans in the actual world). Just imagine, for example, the opportunity to acquire ever deeper and more detailed knowledge, both propositional and by acquaintance, of the intricacies of nature and of conceptual space

---

[11] See, for example, Swinburne, *Providence*, passim. Another development of the "dignity" point might say, as does Peter van Inwagen (*The Problem of Evil* [Oxford: Clarendon Press, 2006], p. 166), that since God loves each thing essentially, finite love best imitates Divine love (and thus is the better) if it too comes *from within*, which for us means being the product of free will. But when thinking about the best love and how to imitate it, should we be thinking about where it *comes from* or about its *content*? Even when talking about God's perfect love van Inwagen says only that it involves having essentially the property of loving each thing—what God *does* if God loves is not addressed. Presumably the answer would mention such things as valuing finite personal life and relating to finite beings in the most appropriate manner and being fully committed to their good. But then one might think that to best imitate Divine love, we should seek with all our might to approximate such attitudes and dispositions, something one could do even if all one's attitudes and dispositions were—in the incompatibilist sense—unfree. Indeed, if the property of so loving were to fall among our essential properties—or among the essential properties of whatever finite beings God caused to exist—it appears that we would also have the clearest imitation of Divine love in *van Inwagen's* sense. And couldn't God create beings for whom such love *was* an essential property? (Van Inwagen appears to claim otherwise, but in doing so he seems to be misled by a focus specifically on human beings, and to be rather more confident about what is possible or impossible than he famously is elsewhere.)

as well. Imagine being created with more of a *taste* for such things (a taste anyone can see as appropriate when gripped by the sublime as revealed in the humblest shadings of a leaf or surfaces of a twig or an elegant scientific theory or mathematical proof). Imagine being given gifts of consciousness and awareness sufficiently enlarged to *progressively take this all in,* moving far beyond the levels of understanding any of us on earth actually ever achieve. When, in the grip of this fantasy, one remembers the emphasis on "free will" as something of surpassing great value, one feels *perplexed.* "Free will"—it is only a dim echo of something once deemed valuable in another world.

Here we can also think again about the conclusion we would draw about *ourselves* should it be discovered that we lack free will. Would we think of ourselves—would we be *right* to think of ourselves—as lacking in the relevant respects in that case? Would we no longer be able to say, if we are religious, that God has made us but a "little lower than the angels" and has crowned us with "glory and honor" (Psalm 8:5)? Surely not. Surely the birth of a human child and our recognition of its amazing complexity and the potential it must realize as it grows would rightly continue to fill us with awe. (Here someone may interject that, in a scenario of the sort I have sketched, no one would grow *past* the level of childhood—that in such a scenario finite persons would be prevented from ever growing into anything like adulthood in relation to God. But the notion of a "child" that I have been using is of course metaphorical, and insofar as we are humble, we will perhaps recognize the metaphorical status of a child as appropriate to the vast differences between ourselves and any Divine Maker. We should also recognize that it is quite compatible with all the sorts of development and maturation normally associated with the literal use of the term "adult"—and, indeed, with more than these, for we are thinking of *everlasting* growth in knowledge and in the sophistication of one's responses thereto.)

Now no doubt free will plus Heaven would be a great good for anyone who possessed it. But great value is also realized by those who are naturally and spontaneously good and diligent from the start, and whose lives are continually enriched by new and diverse experience and knowledge. It's just a different kind of goodness. Notice that any assessment of comparative value here must refer to more than just the way in which *choices* are made: in particular, the scenario I have developed must be considered as a total state of affairs in which free will may be absent but many other goods are present. The tendency of writers in the past to focus exclusively on the value of different kinds of choices and actions has, I think, contributed to their arriving at a false sense of the importance of free will.

Add to this now the aforementioned point about knowing God, which should be becoming familiar. If creatures are growing in experience of *God* unendingly, they are ever more fully experiencing and knowing not just finite nature but a reality unsurpassably deep and rich. And the privilege involved in *any* way of experiencing an everlasting and ever-growing intimacy with a reality unsurpassably deep and rich is *so* great, one wants to say, as to render ridiculously irrelevant whether those experiencing it do so freely or not. Anyone afforded such a privilege will rightly see what most deeply benefits them and dignifies them as bound up *with this privilege*, not with this or that fact of their own nature (except insofar as it moves them more decisively toward God). Indeed, it seems that, while a relationship marked by human free will is one *style* of relationship God might be free to choose, so long as intimacy with God is not excluded by different styles of relationship, the latter could not reasonably be regarded as inferior. (Remember that we're talking about *ever*lasting, *ever*-growing intimacy with *unsurpassable* greatness.) But then we have an even more forceful reason to infer that the value realizable by creatures without free will would not be surpassed by the value to be associated with free will—a reason that, together with the other points previously adduced, puts that claim altogether beyond doubt.

2. A World without the Free-Will Defense

If what I have been arguing is along the right lines, then we must accept certain additional repercussions for the free-will defenses and theodicy discussed in the previous chapter (for simplicity, these arguments are here grouped under the label "defense"). While there is no doubt that various familiar commodities associated with free will, and a relationship with God mediated by them, might facilitate great things for personal beings, it is also evident that an everlasting and ever-growing relationship with God mediated in any number of other ways—including the way I have sketched above—could hardly be thought inferior. Thus we have another good reason for denying that free-will arguments can defeat the argument from horrors.

But there is, as it turns out, also a wider and deeper consequence for the free-will defense which must affect even the views of those who do not accept my argument from horrors. For especially given the obvious risk of serious suffering bound up with permitting free will of the sort we are talking about, it seems a necessary truth that a benevolent creator would not do so unless there were at least some chance that the contribution to value of free will would be greater than the contribution to value of alternative states of affairs God would be capable of producing.[12] Only thus could the additional risk of evil given free will be justified. And as the arguments of the previous section help us to see, this condition necessarily cannot be satisfied: even the option involving no free will and no evil at all can clearly be instantiated in such a way as to contribute to value fully as much as a state of affairs involving free will (I shall call its tendency to do so a tendency to *counter* the value of free will). It follows that God would *not* countenance free will and that free-will arguments cannot even get started as defenses against the atheistic force of serious suffering.

A more formal presentation of this argument may seem desirable. Let "F" stand for the state of affairs that consists in finite persons possessing and exercising free will. Let "p" stand for "God exists"; "q" for "F obtains"; "r" for "F poses a serious risk of evil"; and "s" for "There is no option available to God that counters F." With this in place, the argument may be formalized as follows:

(1) $[(p \,\&\, q) \,\&\, r] \rightarrow s$		Premise
(2) $\sim s$		Premise
(3) $\sim[(p \,\&\, q) \,\&\, r]$		1, 2 MT
(4) $\sim(p \,\&\, q) \lor \sim r$		3 DM
(5) r		Premise
(6) $\sim(p \,\&\, q)$		4, 5 DS
(7) $\sim p \lor \sim q$		6 DM

Conclusion (3) follows from the conjunction of (1) and (2) by modus tollens; De Morgan's law applied to (3) yields (4); (4) and (5) together lead to (6) by disjunctive syllogism; and another application of De Morgan's law takes us from (6) to the final conclusion, according to which either God exists or there is free will (but not both).

So the argument has a valid form. But what about the premises? Can we say anything more in their support? Well, premise (1) receives support from the very plausible and commonly accepted claim that any good for the sake of which God permits evil must be, if not a greater good, at least an *equally great* good—one such that the world is as good with the evil and this good as it would be given any alternative state of affairs God can actualize. To see that it does, notice that if there is a countering option, then God can obtain a world as good as is potentially realized through F

---

[12] My term "serious" in this sentence should be taken as indicating a category of sufferings broader than that named by "horrific" and compatible with its absence—the category of sufferings, let us say, that in some way significantly interfere with the proper functioning of the sufferer in everyday life.

without as much of a risk of evil, and perhaps with none at all. But then if there is such an option, the world in which F obtains along with the attendant risks is *less* good than an alternative world God can actualize, and so F is *not* at least an equally great good. But if F is not at least an equally great good, then, according to the claim we are calling in our support, God will have nothing to do with F and the evil it may involve. Hence (by hypothetical syllogism) if there is a countering option, God will have nothing to do with F and the evil it may involve. But then (by contraposition) if God countenances F and the evil it may involve, there is *no* countering option—which is what premise (1) says.

So premise (1) seems plausible enough. What about premises (2) and (5)? As we have seen, the truth of (2) follows from the various considerations advanced in the previous section of this chapter: if what we said there is correct, then there is indeed an option that counters F—namely, one in which God adopts the sharing model of personal relationship with finite persons. As we noted, if God does so, a degree of value no less great than that obtainable through any form of free will would be realized in the lives of finite persons created by God, and without evil of any sort. But why focus on finite persons in this way? Am I illegitimately assuming that the only value-related difference made by free will is one involving such persons? To answer this we may observe that free-will defenders have always claimed that the value of the free will they emphasize resides in its contribution to the value of finite persons' lives and to the possibility of a valuable sort of relationship between themselves and any God there may be,[13] and observe also the plausibility of their claim. Notice that it can be interpreted as a large (and inclusive) disjunctive claim: the value in question need not be viewed as restricted to those who suffer on account of free will or to persons who have free will or even to persons on our planet! What the claim says is that free will has value if and only if *someone or other* is made better or benefited by it. And in this form it does seem to be an unexceptionable claim.

All that remains, then, is to defend the truth of premise (5)—and this is not a difficult task. For giving finite persons free will must *always* carry with it a serious risk. Indeed, philosophers who defend the free-will defense will admit that the risk in question has obviously been turned into a

---

[13] And here we must of course assume that such relationship does not make *God's* life better than it would otherwise be. But this seems to follow from God being by God's very nature unsurpassably great, and from the generally accepted idea that if God creates, it is through an *overflowing* of goodness and not in order to get any Divine *needs* met. (Even if this were not accepted, we would, in order to meet the needs of our argument, only have to say that God's life is as improved by a sharing sort of relationship with finite persons as by one involving their free will; and it is not hard to see how such a claim might be defended.)

most disturbing reality in the actual world. Premise (5) is therefore true, in which case our argument is apparently not just valid but sound.

Now this yields some rather interesting results. First, the consensus view mentioned at the beginning of this chapter, namely, that a God who created persons would give them free will, ought to lose that status, for it appears to be false. But we can go further. Most of us—and certainly theists—would regard the belief that free will exists as justified. But if that belief is justified, then we are vulnerable to a simple disjunctive syllogism involving the proposition it affirms and the conclusion, (7), of our argument above, which generates the further conclusion that God does not exist. And thus we see how open-minded reflection on free will, far from leading to an impressive defense of theism, simply suggests another reason for denying that it is true.

3. *The Problems of Free Will*

Given the circumstances described in the previous section, someone might want to say that free will *itself* counts as a kind of evil, and that the problem of free will detailed there is thus a species of the problem of evil. But that is not quite right. Free will is a *cause* of evil but does not count as evil itself, much as hurricanes and tornadoes and other natural phenomena may be causes of evil without counting as evil themselves. However, it is clear that free will is itself a *problem* for theism—in particular, for belief in a God whose moral character includes benevolence—inasmuch as it *gratuitously* causes evil, as we have just seen.

But there is (at least) one more aspect to the problem of free will, and in this section I want to introduce it and examine it more closely. I call it a problem of *opportunity*. This issue is about how things *would* be *if* a God—a God not just benevolent but also wise—were going to grant us free will. To develop this issue we do not have to assume that God would permit free will of some kind, and that is a good thing, given that in the previous section we saw reason to suppose that this is not the case. All we need is the hypothetical "if." For should it be the case that *if* God permits free will, a certain condition obtains, and that condition does *not* obtain, then we can conclude not only that God would not permit free will but, given the presence of free will, that God does not exist. The basic argument, more precisely and somewhat more formally expressed, is as follows:

(1) If human free will were caused by God, then there would obtain a certain set *O* of opportunities for its exercise.

(2) *O* does not obtain.

(3) Human free will is not caused by God (from 1 and 2).

(4) If God exists, then human free will is caused by God.

(5) God does not exist (from 3 and 4).[14]

So what is this "set of opportunities *O*" to which I have referred? The basic idea is that there are many instances of serious suffering in the actual world that might have been prevented if free agents (other than the victims) had been made aware of them and brought into close enough proximity to the suffering to do something about it. If there is any suffering at all, God must surely wish it to be kept to a minimum, and if there is free will at all, presumably something like the rationale utilized by theistic free-will arguments applies and God wishes us to use our free will (at least in part) in the prevention and elimination or amelioration of suffering. Any opportunity to do so, theodicists tell us, is an opportunity for soul-making, character development, a responsible choice of destiny, and the like. So surely if God exists and there is suffering and there are free agents about who could under suitable circumstances respond to the suffering if they chose, God will see to it that those agents are brought into those circumstances. But there are an *awful lot* of cases (and "awful lot" can be taken in both senses) where this does not occur. Opportunities that might have existed for the meritorious exercise of freedom in the prevention or elimination or amelioration of suffering are not just missed but *do not come to exist* because the agents who *might* have been made aware of the suffering and *might* have been brought close enough to it to do something about it are not. The set of *such opportunities* is the set to which the argument above refers.

As an example, consider the true story of three boys, ages 5, 8, and 11, who were found suffocated in the trunk of a car on June 25, 2005, in Camden, New Jersey. They climbed in and were trapped when the heavy trunk (which would not stay up on its own) slammed down on top of them. A huge search of the town and area was undertaken, but no one thought to check the trunk of that car. Camden is (at the time of writing) economically

---

[14] On the basis of reasoning developed below and my refutation of objections, I would say that the first premise of this argument is strongly supported, but as in the case of several of the arguments of Chapter 10, I would not go so far as to claim that it appears necessarily true. Premise (2), as we will see, seems clearly true as well. And the truth of premise (4) follows directly from the evident truths that if God exists, God is the cause of all human powers and that free will is a human power.

depressed and faces many social problems, but its people rallied in these circumstances—here was something to bring them together. However, when the three bodies were finally found, people were grief-stricken and felt disheartened and let down, and the spirit of the town sank to a new low.

Now imagine that the boys had suffered but had also been discovered before it was too late, when someone thought to check that trunk. People might well have asked, "Why would God allow those poor boys to suffer so?" And the answer would certainly have come: "Look at the town rallying, needing a boost and getting it, and look at the free will and responsibility exercised by the individual who thought to check the trunk and did so—which events brought all those good things about. . . . *That's* why God allowed it." My point here is this: it *could* have been that way if one of the searchers had thought of the importance of examining that trunk—if God had brought that thought to someone's mind. They would then have had the opportunity to exercise their free will (instead of negligently dismissing the thought and going for coffee, or whatever) and to exercise it in a very important way, where much hung in the balance. But that is not how things actually occurred. And so we have to say that here an opportunity for the exercise of free will was prevented by God, if God exists—an opportunity of just the sort that free-will defenders will say God *wishes* us to have, and use to *justify* suffering. If we have free will and God exists, the atheist should agree, God *would* wish us to have these opportunities. But here (as so often) the critical opportunities are not made available when so easily they might have been. (So many suffer alone when there are individuals about who might have helped if only they had known of the suffering.) And that is reason to believe that God does not exist, as the argument above shows.

Now it may be objected to this reasoning that God cannot ensure the prevention or elimination or amelioration of the relevant suffering by bringing free agents within range, for, after all, they are *free* agents and may choose not to help. But it is an *opportunity* for free and responsible choice to which I have referred, and this can exist regardless of how it is used or misused. As theodicies correctly insist, it is the *opportunity* that is most fundamentally important if we have free will—the *chance* to do something helpful or brave or noble or whatever, to which we must then choose how to respond. Besides, there are many circumstances where if any average, decent person had been brought within range, there is excellent inductive reason to expect that something would have been done. Moreover, God can also choose to move into place individuals whose wills are already firmly set on the good because of *previous* free choices, and who are therefore very likely to respond appropriately.

But would not the sort of action I have in mind—with God bringing thoughts to mind or "moving individuals into place"—be unacceptably intrusive and perhaps itself freedom-removing? I don't see why. The individual finds herself in a certain situation, physically and mentally, because of Divine activity, but she still has a choice to make, which God does not make for her. And indeed, had she not been thus affected, this serious choice would not exist. So the Divine activity I envisage is freedom-enhancing rather than inhibiting. At a deeper level, what we should notice is that if God is the source of our existence, then *any* situation we find ourselves in is one we are in because of God's activity. Further, theists already accept that many of the specific thoughts and inclinations they experience (for example, an inclination to telephone a sister who just happens to be depressed) are gifts from God, and is this not just how we should expect things to be if God enters into *loving relationship* with finite creatures who are suitably disposed?

But perhaps it will be said that most of the situations we *in fact* find ourselves in owe something to our previous free choices. So if God were to pull us out of such a situation and move us into another, where someone was suffering, God would in effect be overriding our (previously exercised) free will. This can be dealt with by noticing that we do not *always* act freely, and often find ourselves where we are for no particular reason, or because of the operation on us of external (inanimate) forces. In any case, by pulling us out of a situation, God (obviously) does not prevent us from having acted on our choice to get into it but simply prevents us from staying in it. And often no choice to stay in it for any particular or long period of time will have been made. And often the new free choice with which we would be presented were we to be thus acted on by God is far more serious and valuable than any free choice that may have brought us to or led us to remain in—say—that armchair in the living room, and so would be · preferred by God even if a conflict of the sort in question were to occur.

It appears, therefore, that the argument we have been considering is forceful. But if so, then once again we must conclude that free will of the sort we find in the actual world ought to be viewed as an insurmountable *impediment* to theistic belief rather than a help.

4. *This Chapter and Previous Arguments*

We have seen that free will is as much of a problem for theism as the evil whose effects it is often thought to assuage—indeed, there even appears to be a strong argument for supposing that there would be no free will of the sort the actual world contains at all, if there were a God. Considering these results, the reader may be left wondering whether they are such as to require us to modify earlier arguments, in which, after all, free will was often mentioned in a more positive tone of voice. To what extent is this the case, and is it a problem for those arguments?

Our results here do at least allow for a more precise and focused and sharply limited position on free will than I have taken elsewhere in discussions of evil and hiddenness or in the previous chapters of this part of the book. In those chapters I said little to suggest that, on my view, there would be no free will if there were a God. Indeed, there was occasional talk of free choices *against* God and their potential value, and allusions to responsibilities we might have in connection with the removal of suffering and other forms of evil even if hiddenness and *horrific* suffering were removed. But it will also be noticed that I questioned such talk a time or two (e.g., Chapter 9, note 8), and often what I had to say about the value of free will was couched in conditional form: *if* God gives creatures free will, then this or that exercise of it (e.g., in rejection of God) has value. And that is quite compatible with equal or greater value being realizable without free will. At a number of points I also suggested ways in which goods commonly associated with free will could be achieved without it, or with free will of some modified sort (e.g., in connection with the Swinburne/ Murray prudence argument in chapter 9 and the discussion of responsibility in relation to a free-will theodicy in Chapter 11). So our earlier discussion should really be seen as leading up to and pointing in the direction of the results of our fuller discussion in this chapter concerning what can be done without free will.

Moreover it ought to be noted that suffering need not always be the result of creaturely choices: even if we lacked the capacity to freely produce suffering and other evils, such things might still exist as a result of inanimate causes in nature (in other words, there can be natural evil). And it is also important to recognize that even if such serious bad choices *as are possible in the actual world* were to be impossible, it would not follow that *all* bad choices, of whatever degree of badness, were impossible (here one should not be misled by my "countering scenario" above involving determinism and no free will—it is only an *example,* the most radical one, of how even without free will of the sort our world contains, creatures could achieve their deepest good). For the sake of our discussions, I have sometimes understood free will as involving the possibility of serious bad choices, but it can be otherwise understood, and without moving from an incompatibilist to a compatibilist conception.

All in all, then, no real modification of earlier arguments and results is called for by this chapter's investigations. That being said, one can still see in Part 3's buildup to the fuller recognition of how free will should be understood in relation to theism an example of what I earlier said would be found in it: an illustration of contentions earlier still as to the limitations of our understanding, and the likelihood of new views arising to fill out or overturn old ones (my present views on free will *have* overturned views I once defended—e.g., in my 1993 book *Divine Hiddenness and Human Reason*—even if not the views developed in earlier chapters of this book). Thus from another perspective one may say that the aspect of this part's results at issue here not only poses no problem in relation to other of its results, but is quite capable of being integrated into the *overall* results pursued in this book and of furthering the latter's most general goals.

CHAPTER 13

Consolidating Forces
The Arguments Combined

The four ways of arguing for atheism represented by the last four chapters—including the two kinds of hiddenness argumentation, the argument from horrors, and the free-will offense—can be represented schematically (Figure 5).

9. H.I	11. H
10. H.II	12. F

Figure 5

Each of these patterns of reasoning embodies powerful support for atheism on its own. But having seen this, we may now see as well that these arguments (more exactly, certain elements therefrom) may be combined to create additional forms of argument, each distinct from the others and even more powerful than the others. There are various ways of doing this. Here we will start by thinking about combining 9 and 10, noticing the emergence of the *Consolidated Hiddenness Argument* (CH), which is a form of argument more powerful than either H.I or H.II alone. Then we will combine elements from 11 and 12 to realize the *Consolidated Argument from Horrors and Free Will* (CHF), which surpasses in force both H and F. Finally, we will bring *these* two—9.10 and 11.12, or CH and CHF—together, thus achieving the most powerful argument of all, which we may call the *Consolidated Argument from Hiddenness, Horrors, and Free Will* (CHHF). All told, then, a slightly more complicated representation of our forms of argument is called for (Figure 6).

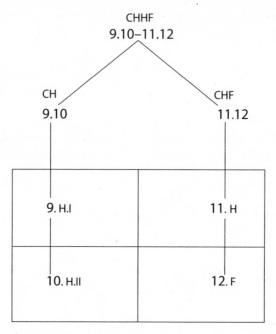

Figure 6

The remainder of this chapter is devoted to explicating these additional forms of argument, following the blueprint of Chapter 5, thus completing the construction of our edifice of *atheism.*

1. *The Consolidated Hiddenness Argument*

As suggested above (and also in Chapter 5), in thinking about patterns of consolidation, we are really dealing with argument *types* that can have various tokens or instances instead of individual arguments. I shall develop two consolidated arguments here. The first becomes visible when we see how it is possible to develop an argument that expands on what was said concerning any *one* of Chapter 10's types of nonresistant nonbelief (here I will focus on the first of the four, former believers) by adding to it the general results of Chapter 9. Clearly, if *all* types of nonresistant nonbelief will be prevented, then *this or that particular type* will, and so any support for the former claim must strengthen any support one has for a claim of the latter sort. Filling this out, if we have support for the claim that all nonresistant nonbelief would be prevented by God, then (by entailment) we also have support for the claim that the nonresistant nonbelief of *former believers* would be prevented. But then we can *add* this form of support to the independent support from Chapter 10 for the claim about former believers. The result? The claim that there would be no former believers if there were a God is now upheld from two sides, and in each case by deductive considerations supporting its necessary truth. This is powerful support indeed.

Another way that reasoning might proceed here moves in the opposite direction. Remember that the argument of Chapter 9 focused on nonresistant nonbelief quite *generally,* without dividing it into types: my argument there was that perfect relational-personal love would lead a Divine creator to prevent nonresistant nonbelief of *any* kind because of how such nonbelief precludes access to personal relationship with God. But clearly whatever independent considerations we have for supposing that various *types* of nonresistant nonbelief will not be instantiated if there is a God must *add* force to that claim. If, over and above the general point about how a loving God would never leave anyone without access to relationship with God, we can locate, more specifically, reasons why a loving or just or generous or faithful or nondeceiving God would never countenance one-time believers trying to make their way home without being able to do so, or dedicated seekers failing to find, or taking themselves to have found a truth that only enmeshes them in a meaning system distortive of (what must, if God exists, be) the truth, or individuals being entirely formed by, and living their whole lives within, a fundamentally misleading meaning system, then we can *reinforce* the case for supposing that a God of the sort represented by traditional theism would prevent nonresistant nonbelief.[1]

---

[1] Notice that in the case of hiddenness we were able to advance *both* the general argument *and* the more specific one(s), whereas in the case of the problem of evil, the more general argument is commonly viewed as discredited (very few these days are trying to make the case that there would be *no evil of any kind* if there were a God), and philosophers wishing to develop the problem of evil have turned to making more specific arguments focused on this or that type of evil—for example, some type of suffering—instead. In the case of nonresistant nonbelief, I suggest, there clearly need be no turning; it is rather a matter of adding. (Thus there is a way in which the hiddenness arguments have an advantage over arguments from evil.) And, of course, here we are seeing how there are other sorts of adding as well: for example, the consolidating of the general and specific arguments to make the *general* one stronger.

Now it will be noted that even between them, the four types of nonre-sistant nonbelief discussed in Chapter 10 may not cover the *whole* range of nonresistant nonbelief, and so it may be wondered how we are to com-bine the arguments concerning them into an argument for the conclu-sion that *all* nonresistant nonbelief will be prevented if there is a God, which can then be added to the argument of Chapter 9. The answer is "inductively and probabilistically." Consider an analogy. Suppose I am aware that my new friend's mother is very wealthy, and—somewhat envi-ously and resentfully—I form the hypothesis that he and all his siblings have recently received some sort of monetary benefit from her. Suppose also that on investigating I learn that this is indeed the case for my friend and *three* of his five siblings: one has received from his mother money to put a down payment on a car, another the sum required to pay rent, and so on. Surely I now have evidence in support of my hypothesis, for the re-sults of my investigation are just what one would expect if the hypothesis is true. Similarly, the results of our inquiries in Chapter 10, though per-haps focused only on *most* types of nonresistant nonbelief, are just as one might expect if the hypothesis that God would prevent *all* nonresistant nonbelief were true. Thus they provide support for the truth of that hy-pothesis. And therefore someone who has both the argument of Chapter 9 and the results of Chapter 10 to go on has more support for Chapter 9's claim about nonresistant nonbelief than someone who has only one or the other—that is, both deductive and inductive support.

In either of these ways, then, we may produce a powerful *consolidated* hiddenness argument from the results of Chapters 9 and 10—an argu-ment stronger than any of the arguments involved in the combination taken on its own.

2. *The Consolidated Argument from Horrors and Free Will*

In Chapter 12 we developed an argument to the effect that free will of the sort we actually find would not be let loose in the world by a morally perfect God, because doing so might lead to serious suffering uncompen-sated by any countervailing benefit greater than what could otherwise be achieved. Now, clearly, the *more* serious the suffering to which free will can lead, the more forceful the claim of this argument must be. Hence, given the fact of *horrific* suffering freely caused (and most of us—and certainly theists—would allow that at any rate *some* of the actions by which hor-rific suffering is brought about in the actual world *are* free in the relevant sense), we can see that the argument is capable of being made very force-ful indeed. And thus the problem of free will is intensified by introducing this fact from the argument of Chapter 11. (Free will *might not* generate horrific suffering even if it is associated with *serious* suffering, so given the argument of Chapter 12 alone, we cannot make the more specific claim required for the intensification; but if we add Chapter 11 into the mix, we can.) In this way the claim that free will would not be permitted by God is made even more plausible than it could otherwise be, and so is the conclusion shared by these two arguments—that God does not exist—which obviously may be inferred from that claim conjoined with the claim that free will exists.

Moving in the opposite direction now: horrific suffering might have never had non-natural causes, so when we say God would prevent horrific suffering, we commit ourselves to this being the case whether it is ever freely caused or not. We are not arguing from *freely caused* horrific suffering. But in Chapter 11 we noticed that horrific suffering can be horrific because of victim *and/or* perpetrator. And in the worst cases of freely caused horrific suffering, clearly, both the victim and the perpetrator are given a prima facie reason to think that their life is not worth living. Thus when we look closely at free will and notice that it *is* sometimes the cause of horrific suffering, we see how that suffering is made worse—for now *both* the victim *and* the perpetrator may have their lives ruined. And looking at it through the lens of Chapter 12, we also see that there is no unique value in free will sufficient to prevent us, all things considered, from making use of this intensification in an argument from freely caused horrific suffering. This point could not have been arrived at on the strength of Chapter 11 alone, but if we introduce the relevant facts about free will, we can reach it, and in so doing we generate a stronger premise from which to argue than the one that refers to horrific suffering simpliciter.

In both these ways, then, the consolidation of what was discussed in Chapters 11 and 12 into *freely caused horrific suffering* produces arguments more powerful than what we had from either of those chapters to begin with.

3. *The Consolidated Argument from Hiddenness, Horrors, and Free Will*

But the strongest argument of all has not yet been considered, as we will realize if we consider the possibility of making the higher-level move of combining elements from the previous two *consolidated* arguments.

We can summarize the basic sort of fact made use of here in terms of *horrific suffering freely caused that is experienced by individuals lacking conscious access to any personal God there may be.* Here, for the first time, horrific suffering and hiddenness are brought together—and the results are interesting and significant. For suppose one notices that some victims of horrific suffering of the freedom-involving sort discussed in the previous section are *also* nonresistant nonbelievers of a certain kind. One might in that case say that we have reason from both the previous (consolidated) arguments to say that such a thing would not be found if there were a God. But one can also go further. For now a new argument is suggested, which has a premise stating that even were God to permit one or other of these phenomena (for simplicity, hiddenness or horrors), their *conjunction* in any individual case would be avoided. Perhaps we have good reason to say, separately, that horrors would be prevented and that hiddenness would be prevented, and even *more* reason (drawn from the grounds supporting those previous arguments but others as well) to say that the *conjunction* of these things would not be found in any individual life if there were a God.

For what the hiddenness discussion reveals to us is that through experience of the presence of God horrific suffering could in a sense be *relieved* by God even if it could not be *removed*. And so the possibility arises of becoming doubly troubled where *neither* of these is found. Would not an omnibenevolent God seek to provide at least *one* of these—if not removal, then relief? And yet in many cases *both* are absent. Thus we have the basis for a new consolidated argument for atheism. (This argument can draw, of course, on such things as former believers who endure much freely caused horrific suffering without the Divine reassurance they have sought. But it might also be developed in terms of those easy-to-forget nontheists from times long past who suffered horrors at the hands of others without so much as the concepts that an experience of the theist's God would require.) Notice that this is not just the conjunction of the two previous arguments, which points out that in a certain case we have both freedom-involving horrific suffering and hiddenness of a certain kind.[2] No, it is a new argument that, while drawing on the others, also points out an independent reason for denying that considerations of the sorts one finds in the other two would be realized in any single individual, if there were a God. This argument therefore takes us to an entirely new level in atheistic reasoning.

[2] Neither is it reducible to a similar suggestion recently discussed by Daniel Howard-Snyder and William Rowe in connection with the latter's inductive argument from evil, where the conclusion drawn is not atheism but that we are likely to know of reasons for our suffering if there is a God. See, for example, Daniel Howard-Snyder, "The Argument from Inscrutable Evil," in Howard-Snyder's collection *The Evidential Argument from Evil* (Bloomington: Indiana University Press, 1996), pp. 305–307; and, in the same collection, William Rowe, "The Evidential Argument from Evil: A Second Look," pp. 274–276. (However, I note that in his most recent discussion of these issues—"Friendly Atheism, Skeptical Theism, and the Problem of Evil," *International Journal for Philosophy of Religion* 59 [2006]: 79–92—Rowe appears to be moving in the direction of a more straightforward atheistic argument from the conjunction of horrors and hiddenness.)

CHAPTER 14

Closing the Case
Seven Proofs and a Skeptical Conclusion

1. *The Force of the Proofs: An Opening Worry*

In the previous five chapters I developed seven new arguments (or forms of argument) for atheism. My main aim in this final chapter of Part 3 is to show the role that can be played by my seven arguments in justifying at least *skepticism* about theism given various assumptions theists might make—and thus in justifying, for all theists, a position on this most popular form of religious belief that is in accord with my earlier findings concerning ultimism. But let us begin by seeing whether more than this might credibly be claimed for them, and, if so, how much more. After all, the job of those arguments, ostensibly, was to *prove theism false* and so to justify *disbelief* of theism. How do they fare when cast in that role?

Not very well, many will say. Indeed, quite a tempting response at this stage will be that, given the larger argumentative context of this book, and particularly my capacity skepticism, according to which we may not yet be in a position to discern "basic truths concerning the existence or nature of the Ultimate," any claim as to the provability of atheism I might make would be self-defeating: because of the nature of my arguments in Part 1 and Part 2, I am in no position to think of my arguments in Part 3 as successful proofs. Let us consider this worry more closely.[1]

---

[1] A related worry can be dealt with more quickly. If the arguments I have offered are indeed successful as proofs, have I shown too much? That is, does the falsity of not just theism but also of ultimism follow? The answer is no. For the religious idea we are working with in the latter case is much more general and does not involve the specific personal notions and axiological concepts from familiar personal contexts of behavior and interaction that seem capable of generating disproofs in the narrower context. Now it might be thought that claims about evil in particular would be transferable to the more general context,

Notice first that the availability of a proof of the sort in question would not entail that we had discovered a "basic truth about the existence and nature of the Ultimate." This point was already made in my *Prolegomena* (p. 101), where I observed that to discern the absence of a being (here, a personal God) that, were it to exist, would instantiate an ultimate reality is not to discern the absence of such a reality, and thus to discover a basic truth about it, unless there is no *other* way for such a reality to be instantiated. For the critic to maintain her criticism in light of this point would require rather parochial thinking—the assumption that the class of candidates for ultimacy has but one member, namely, traditional theism.

A related point is that in discussing traditional theism we are "closer to home," dealing with notions that are far from incomprehensible. For the basic idea of a personal God, as traditionally understood, is derived from what we know of ourselves—and from human qualities that we *do* understand even at the present stage of our development. All my claims about how *such* a God could be revealed to us or would be empathetically disposed toward us are unaffected by the awareness that many *other* conceptions of the Divine remain to be explored. Further, some of my arguments make use of insights that draw on recent developments, for example in psychology and feminist thought, and so their claims need to be considered as contenders for the status of propositions quite "clear" in themselves but only now becoming clear to us.

Let me develop the central issue here a little more deeply. My earlier arguments never claimed that in just *any* instance of reasoning, problems resulting from (say) the possibility of unrecognized counterarguments should be expected to intrude. It was acknowledged in Chapter 1 that there are commonly available grounds sufficient to justify belief, and that grounds supporting the necessity of a proposition and certain powerful kinds of inductive grounds are among them. (It was simply denied that grounds supporting the affirmation or the denial of *ultimism* are among them.) And in Part 2 we saw how the deliverances of certain belief-forming practices, including the rational/intuitive belief-forming practice, must be taken as innocent until proven guilty. Hence, insofar as there appear

---

given that a truly ultimate reality, even if nonpersonal, would have to be absolutely perfect. But although evil *is troubling* even in the more general context (and may contribute to doubt about ultimism), *arguments* from evil do not so immediately and naturally suggest themselves there since, if we do not assume a personalist interpretation, we cannot assume that familiar axiological concepts tell the complete and final truth about value, but must rather acknowledge that the latter might be quite beyond us (to do otherwise would be something like taking facts about planet Earth as representative of the full truth about the universe).

to be grounds of these kinds for atheism, belief of atheism may become justified. Then also it is appropriate to *put forward* such grounds as justifying atheism.

And precisely such grounds do seem to be available. Indeed, it was the main burden of the previous five chapters to show just how powerful are these new arguments for atheism. Of course, the reasoning is always defeasible. But such arguments as I have developed would pass muster even given heightened sensitivity to defeasibility if (for example) the connection between Divine love and the availability of meaningful conscious relationship with God I have emphasized seemed, as we considered it, more and more a necessary one and undeniable, and if my discussion of objections seemed more and more to be simply the removal of obstacles obscuring a necessary truth (therefore) not previously apprehended but now (given their removal) capable of being clearly recognized. If this *were* our situation (and I am proposing that it is), the discussion of these objections would be not so much a constant reminder of how much we may not know in this area as an ever more clearly discernible signal of an *advance* in our understanding.[2]

2. *The Force of the Proofs: Skeptical Theism*

Another sort of objection that should be considered, however (one that is of a type rather common in the literature these days), does not try, futilely, to catch me in inconsistency but will be said to follow from claims we should accept even if my claims in Part 1 are *false and wrongheaded*. It can also be said to be grounded precisely in the personalist notion of the Ultimate whose familiarity, I am claiming, is a *buffer* against the general skepticism I earlier defended. The type of argument involved here is developed by theists, which is why Draper dubbed the position it represents "skeptical theism."[3] What it says is that we have no way of ruling out that the *omnipotent and omniscient* personal being who is God has great and

---

[2] Of course, it is not as though I am expecting my arguments about this to be accepted without discussion. I am making (and defending) *proposals* here, one of which is that there are good arguments for atheism, and these are indeed subject to discussion. As stated in the Introduction, my task, as I see it, is to express as clearly and strongly as I can the arguments that seem to me to point in one direction as opposed to another, as part of a community attempt to reach consensus on where the truth about the worthiness of various responses to religious claims lies. Thus I certainly am not against discussion of my arguments, and want indeed to inspire it.

[3] See his "The Skeptical Theist," in *The Evidential Problem of Evil*, ed. Daniel Howard-Snyder (Bloomington: Indiana University Press, 1996).

good plans for the universe quite at odds with what our puny intelligences tell us would be good. Applied to our arguments, what it says is that although we may not be able to discern any good reasons for God to permit horrors or hiddenness, and so on, we cannot infer that there *are* no such reasons. (Another way of putting this is to say that the reasons for doing this or that which are available to us may not be *representative* of *God's* reasons.) Hence we have no justification for my claims to the effect that God would not permit these things.[4]

It might seem, given my own skeptical tendencies, that this more specific skeptical ploy of a somewhat similar sort would be hard for me to resist. However, I feel no temptation to accept it. Why? Well, notice once again that in my case for atheism I have utilized deductive arguments with premises that seem clearly true or (in many cases) *necessarily* true. I have not reasoned, as do the arguments (in particular the evidential arguments of William Rowe)[5] which the skeptical theist move was designed to answer that it is probable that God would not permit horrific suffering *because we cannot think of any good reason for God to permit it,* or that we have a reason to think theism improbable because such suffering is *less likely on the hypothesis of theism than on competing hypotheses.*[6] Such arguments get embroiled in the relevant sort of reasons talk, and invite comparisons between human and Divine cognitive abilities and information. But my arguments are different. In particular, they depend on no inference from facts about our reasons to facts about God's. Instead we have the claim that certain propositions entailing—sometimes in conjunction with other highly plausible propositions—that God would not permit the phenomena in question are clearly true or necessarily true.

It seems clearly necessarily true, for example, that the permission of horrific suffering is not required for a finite personal creature to achieve its deepest good. Just thinking about the splendid and commodious notion of relationship with an unsurpassably great reality (and about certain connections among relevant propositions) is sufficient to generate a sense

---

[4] Many Christian philosophers have defended this sort of move recently. (For a sample of their work, see the essays by Alston, Howard-Snyder, Plantinga, van Inwagen, and Wykstra in *Evidential Problem of Evil,* ed. Howard-Snyder.) It comes in two varieties: one more concrete (developed in terms of some specific and perhaps elaborate "story" that it is alleged we have no reason to rule out as false) and the other more abstract (developed in terms of the general point that our reasoning cannot be taken as representative of God's). The more concrete variety we have already met and dealt with in responding to van Inwagen in Chapter 11. Here it is the more abstract move that will be the focus of attention.

[5] See his contributions to *Evidential Problem of Evil,* ed. Howard-Snyder.

[6] The latter is Draper's style of reasoning against theism. See his contributions to *Evidential Problem of Evil,* ed. Howard-Snyder.

of necessity here. And just thinking about the notions of perfect love and perfect empathy generates a similar sense of necessity for the proposition that if a perfectly loving and empathetic God can achieve even our *deepest* good without permitting horrific suffering, such a God would not permit horrific suffering. In this way we can arrive at the conclusion that God would not permit horrific suffering without ever making an inference about God's reasons. (It is not because I cannot see any reason for God to permit horrific suffering that I end up in this position or—interestingly— even because of some reason I *can* see which I think would lead God *not* to do so. The relevant reason is not the sort of reason God might consult in figuring out what to do at all, but rather a reason *I* have, generated by apparent necessity, for taking certain claims as conceptual truths.)

Now if we take as necessarily true a claim to the effect that God would not permit *x*, we do have a way of showing that God has no good enough reason to permit *x*, for that just *follows*. But this will normally be no more than an afterthought, and is not at all a move essential to the argument. Of course if skeptical theists seek to reapply their skepticism, arguing that I have not yet shown that God lacks reason to permit the item in question, it can become a strategy of response instead of an afterthought. For then I will argue that, given the implication just mentioned, their move is question-begging: if my arguments are right, then that God lacks such reason simply follows, and so to suggest that I have not yet shown that such is the case *assumes that my arguments are unsuccessful*—which is never a good way to try to make one's case in a philosophical context.[7]

All in all, then, the skeptical strategy discussed here seems simply inapplicable to my arguments, and thus unsuccessful. Theists need to think carefully not just about what we don't know concerning the details of the Divine plan but about what we *do* know concerning love and empathy. But some additional arguments against skeptical theism can be given. First, consider that—as Rowe has pointed out more than once—the skeptical theistic strategy can be *abused:* surely there must be states of affairs such that it would be unreasonable to say that a perfectly good and loving God might have—unknown to us—some reason to permit them to obtain. But then we require some indication of *how to avoid* such abuse: we should ask what the criterion is by which we may determine where to draw the line

[7] For further reasoning along these lines—though in defense of an argument more modestly construed as evidential and probabilistic, developed in an attempt to extricate us from conventional ways of construing evidential arguments before I saw how naturally the move back in the direction of a "logical" argument could be made—see my "Stalemate and Strategy: Rethinking the Evidential Argument from Evil," *American Philosophical Quarterly* 37 (2000): 405–419.

and (thus) whether the strategy is being abused or not by the skeptical theist who applies it in response to such arguments as I have given. If no persuasive answer is forthcoming (and it is hard to imagine what such an answer might look like), then we must remain at the very least skeptical as to whether the general skeptical theistic strategy, as applied to my arguments, should be deemed acceptable or not, for we lack any way of *discriminating* between acceptable and unacceptable uses of it.

Second, we should recognize that, as Draper has suggested, skeptical theism is a double-edged sword, since theists themselves typically rely on claims to the effect that God would create such-and-such a world or be revealed through prophets and miracles or permit suffering of certain moderately intense sorts to realize purposes of such-and-such a kind. And how can we be even halfway sure about such things if the relevant parts of the design plan and reasoning of an omniscient being might well be beyond our grasp? Isn't the skeptical theist required to say that there might be great goods we cannot understand on account of which God does *none* of these things? If he does *not* wish to say this, isn't he required to admit that sometimes there can be clear reasons for supposing that some claim about what a God would do is *correct*, which renders pointless investigation into reasons God might have to do some contrary action?[8]

Perhaps the most effective rebuttal of this kind is one focusing on propositions about what a God would do that just anyone can see are clearly true or necessarily true. Consider the following proposition, for example:

(A) If a perfectly loving God exists and creates finite personal beings in a world like ours, then for at any rate some such beings physical death is not the end.

Many thinkers—and not just theists—would on reflection judge this proposition to be clearly true and perhaps even necessarily true. For if God exists, disembodied personal existence is not impossible (since God, by definition, is personal and lacks a body), and one might expect as well that a perfectly loving God would seek to keep in existence those who have entered into a loving relationship with God but not traveled very far in it, so that the relationship might be more fully consummated. (Within the bounds of earthly existence, the sort of unrestricted communion perfect

---

[8] See Draper, "Skeptical Theist," p. 188. My development of this point, immediately below, in terms of the afterlife first appeared in my "Stalemate and Strategy." The afterlife example was subsequently taken up and developed in a similar fashion (though with a specific application to Christians) by Rowe. See his "Friendly Atheism, Skeptical Theism, and the Problem of Evil," *International Journal for Philosophy of Religion* 59 (2006): 90–91.

love would seek is just not possible, and of course for many in a world like ours even *restricted* communion will be unavailable.)

Such considerations are available to theist and nontheist alike, and may (and do) lead to the belief that (A) is true in reasonable individuals who reflect on them. Notice how easily such a belief is reached. No talk *here* of reasons a God might have for *not* seeing to it that at any rate some of us survive death. Yet surely there are as many areas of human ignorance relevant to the exclusion on independent grounds of *such* reasons as there are in the case of the propositions I have defended. How could we show, on independent grounds, that there is no great good God might seek to realize that is essential to the execution of God's design plan and requires that death be the end for us all? But such problems do not exercise us. No skeptical tradition has arisen seeking to undermine (A). Why? One may hope it is not because (A), unlike the propositions about hiddenness or horrors, does not threaten theism. Is it, perhaps, because our reasons *for* believing that (A) is true are sufficiently powerful to render unnecessary such probing into God's reasons? Notice that even theists who say they believe (A) partly on the basis of revelation would rule out the idea of overriding reasons for God to make death the end on the basis of their positive case *for* (A) (it's just a different case). And surely this is, in principle, an acceptable approach. But then what is to prevent us from applying it in the case of premises about horrific suffering or hiddenness? Surely not skeptical theism.

What we can see here is that the skeptical theistic maneuver is quite *selectively* skeptical. If it were to be applied consistently, we would have a claim that is not (as suggested at the beginning of this discussion) *less* skeptical than my arguments in Part 1 but rather much *more* skeptical. For then we would have to say that even when certain propositions persistently strike us as *necessarily* true, we have no reason to do other than suspend judgment. And, as we have seen, a view so skeptical as this cannot be upheld.[9]

Even if it should be shown that the arguments of the skeptical theist do not lead to a stance more skeptical than mine, it would still be clear that they lead to a stance *as* skeptical as mine. My earlier case for a more general religious skepticism rests on (among other things) what is essentially an expansion of the skeptical theist's own point, one that with reflection on such matters as are raised in the text will be seen to be more plausible than the latter—namely, that our finite limitations (at least at the present stage of our development) should leave us unsure as to whether what we

---

[9] Here I might introduce once again the emphasis on seeking understanding and the assumptions made in connection with that: if apparent *necessity* won't do to generate something contributing to understanding, whatever would?

have to go on in judging the truth of ultimism is representative of the total evidence relevant to this matter. Thus skeptical theists really have good reason, *given the content of their own stance,* to accept the modes I have developed and their conclusion—which is to say that they have good reason to become skeptical *non*theists.

Finally, even if some way around the previous arguments can be found, it seems quite clear that the skeptical theist will, on his own terms, be required to concede that the various claims of my arguments about what God would do—prevent nonresistant nonbelief, prevent horrors, and so on—are *epistemically possible.* If God's ways really are beyond our grasp, then how could we rule out that those ways might include the prevention of such things as nonresistant nonbelief and horrors? (It might be replied that the skeptical theist can fall back on religious experience to defend a view about what God would do, claiming only that *reason* is unreliable here, but that sort of move was discredited in Chapter 8.) Thus even if the skeptical theist is not required to hold that *disbelief* with respect to theism has been justified by my arguments, he will be required to reconcile himself to doubt.

3. *The Force of the Proofs: Other Theists*

We have seen how those who accept the popular position of skeptical theism are here required either to give up their stance or to accept a broader skepticism embracing theism. But how about other theists? All theists are either skeptical theists or not. Having dealt with the former category, let us now turn our attention to the latter.

In thinking about these other theists (really, the positions they represent), we can again proceed by division of cases. Theists in the nonskeptical category (that is, those who are not skeptical theists) will either find my proofs convincing or they will not. (When I say "find my proofs convincing," I mean "find *at least one* of my proofs convincing.") If they do find my proofs convincing, either they will *also* find at least one *theistic* proof convincing or they will not. Suppose they do *not* find at least one theistic proof convincing. Then it immediately follows (given, again, that there is no falling back on religious experience) that *disbelief* of theism has been justified for them. However, suppose that they *do* find at least one theistic proof convincing. Still, they will be rationally required to give up theistic belief since they will now be required to view theism and atheism as equally well supported. (Applying the principle of justification utilized at the outset of Chapter 6, we must here too concede that available information does not permit a judgment of sufficient and overall good evidence for theism *over* atheism and that theistic *skepticism* is justified instead of belief.)[10]

So, as might be expected, if theists find my proofs convincing (and regardless of what else may belong to their situation), theistic belief is unjustified for them. (That is, insofar as they are aware of all that bears on their case, they should not instantiate that type of belief.) But now let's consider the category remaining: those who are *not* convinced by my proofs. Several strategies apply here. First, I would be inclined to argue that, whatever the force of my proofs, there is nothing *better* on the side of theism, and so at least suspense of judgment is called for.

Let us consider this initial strategy more closely. All of us are familiar with the various versions of ontological, cosmological, teleological (etc.) arguments for theism, and also with the various shortcomings that remain in them after a thousand years or more of meticulous attempts to make them successful—especially when they are cast as deductive proofs. It is indeed because of such shortcomings that the foremost natural theologian of our time, Richard Swinburne, sought to reconceive the theistic proofs and turn them into a powerful inductive cumulative case in his famous book *The Existence of God*.[11] That case is very interesting and at many points persuasive, but we need only point out that it *is* inductive and probabilistic, and also that it crucially depends, in the end, on an appeal to religious experience, undermined in our Chapter 8, to show that it can hardly be deemed *more* forceful than the proofs of atheism I have defended, even by one who is left unconvinced by the latter.

Here is an additional point that only adds force to this result: there are possible arguments for atheism *suggested by* those unsuccessful theistic arguments—arguments for atheism we have not discussed. In light of this fact we must say that theistic arguments might in the end only generate arguments *supporting* my case for atheism, and in such circumstances we would surely be required to conclude that "there is nothing better [than our arguments] on the side of theism"! Among the arguments in question are ontological disproofs,[12] cosmological arguments *against* God,[13]

---

[10] Subject, of course, to the absence of relevant non-truth-oriented considerations, a matter addressed in n. 16.

[11] See Richard Swinburne, *The Existence of God*, 2nd ed. (Oxford: Clarendon Press, 2004).

[12] For the classical attempt at an ontological disproof, see J. N. Findlay, "Can God's Existence Be Disproved?" *Mind* 57 (1948): 176–183. As is well known, Plantinga's famous ontological argument seems to breed counterparts (see Chapter 1, section 7).

[13] A cosmological argument against God is developed by Quentin Smith in Quentin Smith and William Lane Craig, *Theism, Atheism, and Big Bang Cosmology* (New York: Oxford University Press, 1993), pp. 200–201.

dysteleological arguments,[14] and so on. These "counterparts" to theistic arguments have not often been touched on by atheists except in passing, and thus they represent a neglected area of possible discussion concerning the existence of God. By introducing this "gap" we muddy the waters still further for theists not convinced by my proofs, for not nearly as much attention has been given to seeing how such arguments might be developed as to their theistic counterparts, and it is quite possible—and it seems that theists not convinced by my proofs should regard it as (epistemically) possible—that such further discussion would be a fertile source of new and powerful objections to the truth of theism. Thus it appears that even theists in the category we are presently considering—who are not convinced by my proofs—have reason to give up their theistic belief.

4. *God and the Gaps*

The last point made here brings me to some more particular observations about possibilities of the future, which connect our discussion to that other interesting feature of our proofs which must be taken account of even by those who do not think they *succeed* as proofs—namely, their novelty. (I take no special pride in their novelty. Indeed, I think the ideas they embody are quite commonsensical, even elementary. It's just that at our stage of development we are still overlooking and neglecting elementary ideas.) And in seeing what is involved in properly taking account of this feature, we hit on another strategy or two for converting individuals in that last remaining category of nonskeptical theists unconvinced by my proofs to at least skepticism about theism.

Here we are returned to what I said, in introducing Part 3, about how, whatever one might think of the force of these arguments, their *very existence,* in the argumentative context I have outlined, suffices to provide strong extra support for religious skepticism—and, in particular, at least skepticism as to whether present theistic discussion is on the right track. Our reasoning has exposed many "gaps" in human thinking about God and suggested the possibility of many future changes in it. And this *itself* provides justification for at least skepticism about theism, even for one who is unconvinced by that reasoning.

---

[14] Hume's *Dialogues Concerning Natural Religion* is the classical source of dysteleological ideas. A modern exponent of such ideas is Paul Draper. See his "Natural Selection and the Problem of Evil," a contribution to the forthcoming Internet debate moderated by Draper: *God or Blind Nature? Philosophers Debate the Evidence.*

In a moment we will look more closely at just how it does so, but first let's bring fully before our minds the gaps that have been exposed (and sometimes filled) and the future changes that have been suggested. It will have been noticed, for example, that my seven proofs, with their particular ways of dealing with hiddenness, horrors, and free will and the unifying emphasis on relationship with God and the diverse aspects of the Divine moral character, represent a new phase of discussion in support of atheism—very little from earlier defenses of atheism will be found here. So (the one unconvinced by my proofs should be led to ask) what else might be waiting for us in the future? Here we find the contentions of Chapter 4 illustrated and confirmed with specific reference to theism.

More specific examples can be found by considering particular arguments. Take the general hiddenness argument of Chapter 9, for example. Until recently there was no developed hiddenness *argument* in the literature at all. Of course a certain philosophical *notion* of Divine hiddenness and of its problematic nature has been with us for a long time, hovering like a wraith over discussions of the existence of God. Long before any of us ever came on the scene, hints of it could be found in Hume and Nietzsche and other writers, and there must have been many reflective women and men in times past who have wondered why God's existence is not more evident than it is. But only in the last few years has the problem been fully developed and its atheistic potential thoroughly explored. So we have—as Chapters 1 and 4 of Part 1 in particular would lead us to expect—a new development that may suffice to cast into question much that was formerly taken for granted. As for the arguments in Chapter 10 from *types* of hiddenness (i.e., from types of nonresistant nonbelief), they appear for the first time in this book.

So why have these things not been explored before? An obvious answer is that we really have not been at this philosophy thing all that long—a few thousand years might give us no more than a start where ultimate investigations are concerned. But, as I have suggested a time or two, the correct answer may also have something to do with patriarchal elements in our culture that have obscured important necessary truths about the nature of a perfect personal God. And it seems further (and relatedly) to have to do with the powerful influence that theology of many centuries ago still exerts on our imaginations. Here we see confirmation of points made in developing the Retrospective Mode of Chapter 3 and also of points in Chapter 2 about the unworthiness of many past and present conceptions of the Ultimate.

Similar observations can be made about the argument from horrors of Chapter 11. That piece of reasoning seems to show, by utilizing only necessary truths as premises, that the existence of God and the existence of horrific suffering are *logically incompatible*. What this means is that we are here revisiting what has been called the "logical" problem of evil, discovering that in the apparently dead and cold ashes left by Plantinga's well-known and sophisticated solution,[15] there remains a spark that can be fanned into a flame. Better put, there has all the while, in the same general neighborhood, been raging a fire to which no one has been giving due attention. To notice it, one needs to recognize, in particular, the work that can be done in such a proof by the notion of relationship with God, given a proper distinction between outweighing goods and our deepest good and a proper appreciation of Divine empathy. Noticing the many unexplored alternatives to the idea of *freely chosen* relationship with God helps too. Now why have these things not been explored before? It is tempting to point once again to the grip of theology and also to our own love of independence and autonomy, which make free will attractive but reflect intellectual and emotional immaturity of just the sorts discussed in Chapter 3 of Part 1. Of course it might also be mentioned that notions of love, relationship, and empathy have not often been high on male philosophers' lists of things to think about, and that philosophers have always been predominantly male. If things are changing in this respect, it is for the good, and no doubt with many possible results yet uncatalogued.

Finally, let me mention the full-blown discussion undertaken in Chapter 12 questioning our understanding of the role of free will in all these debates. Here we only see intensified the point—central to much in the skeptical modes of Part 1—that alternatives to comfortable conventional views on matters religious often go unexplored. That there might be a serious *problem* of free will in addition to the problem of evil rather than a powerful free-will *defense against* the argument from evil seems hardly to have crossed most philosophers' minds. And yet in Chapter 12 we see how persuasive this claim can be made to be. This sort of result illustrates and strongly confirms the idea that our species may well have traveled only a relatively short distance along the path of religious investigation and spiritual development.

All this the theist left unconvinced by my proofs must still take into account. And taking account of it properly will lead to skepticism about theism. Two strategies suggest themselves here. First, we may emphasize, on the basis of all the points just made, that unpredictable changes are to be expected in future discussions specifically of theism. Even if the theist is not convinced by my arguments, what she has learned in considering them should lead her to *this* awareness and thence to skepticism.

[15] See his *The Nature of Necessity* (Oxford: Clarendon Press, 1974), chap. 9.

But another approach is possible too. We may reason, using all the references just made to chapters from Part 1, that my arguments and our discussion thereof provide a *clear illustration* of how the more general claims of Part 1 are indeed true. Those arguments must therefore be taken, even by someone who is left unconvinced by them, as reflecting and confirming the main contentions of our earlier modes of religious skepticism—as providing *more support* for taking those modes as sound and for in *this* way inferring that theistic belief (like all other religious belief) is unjustified. Thus here again we find that individuals who are in the category of non-skeptical theists unconvinced by my arguments must still be led by those arguments to see the doubtfulness of theism.

With connections of the sort I have just mentioned between my arguments for atheism and the arguments of Part 1, we are, as it were, brought full circle. And the circle is unbroken. There is no special dispensation for theism; no special refutation of earlier arguments that theists, by virtue of the intellectual security of their belief, are in a position to offer. Rather, at the finish line (or is it the starting line?), theists of every description should stand with all other inquirers, ready and willing to exchange their belief for skepticism.[16]

---

[16] Someone might say that, as in Chapter 6, and for the same reasons as were discussed there, we must add the following qualification: *provided that there are no non-truth-oriented, pragmatic considerations with sufficient countervailing force.* But it will not take long to see that the additional condition suggested here is well satisfied. If the arguments made in Chapter 6 against the force of non-truth-oriented considerations can be successfully applied in that context, then they apply a fortiori in this one. Specifically, all the points made there about self-deception, nonreligious motivational beliefs, and the alternative of faith apply here with equal strength. Furthermore, in this context one of the potentially counterbalancing pragmatist arguments we considered in the earlier discussion—the argument alleging special investigative benefits of a form of religious belief focused on generic ultimism—is not so much as relevant and can indeed be co-opted (this because specifically theistic belief, for reasons suggested in Chapter 3, not only does not open one up to the exploration of new conceptions of the Divine but tends to militate against it). It follows that *both* the conditions cited by our principle as jointly sufficient for the positive justification of a skeptical response apply to theism with at least as much force as to ultimism.

Epilogue

It seems abundantly clear that the truth about religion is unclear. Responses to religion involving belief—whether that be religious (perhaps theistic) or irreligious belief—are too neat and tidy, too smooth and definite for our world. The religious landscape is in many ways rough and snarled and forbidding. And the rough places have not yet been made plain. No highway has been made straight in the wilderness of our ignorance, and the glory of the Lord has not been revealed.

Such is the conclusion to which we have been led in this book. My proposal, the central outcome of the inquiry it represents, is that complete religious skepticism is positively justified. Connecting this result to the order of discussion in my *Prolegomena*, it may be said that in determining the proper response to religion, lovers of wisdom will rise above—transcend— the avenues involving belief, discussed in its second and third chapters, to embrace the most thoroughly skeptical of the skeptical positions outlined in *Prolegomena*, Chapter 4.

Now skepticism is not often "embraced" by philosophers, in philosophy of religion or elsewhere. Whatever the proposition involved, a skeptical position is not, at first sight, a very attractive position to be in: it is not especially comfortable to be poised between one form of belief and the other, awkwardly seeking to maintain one's balance, straining to see in the half-light generated by our best arguments and most illuminating experiences. Thus it might seem odd to speak in this connection of *rising above* or of *transcending* religious and irreligious belief (except in the minimal and purely descriptive sense of finding ourselves in a position on religion *other than* a believing or a disbelieving one), and one might also wonder whether there is not a sense in which, for the religious skeptic, the pursuit of wisdom must be given up. Maybe the positive evaluative meaning of "transcendence" would be applicable where simple belief of one kind or another is replaced by knowledge—but *skepticism*? And how is wisdom in matters of religion to be achieved if the rationality of *believing* things about it is impugned?

In bringing this book to a close, however, I want to return to a contrary point suggested in the Preface: that skepticism about religion of the sort I have defended may very well represent a positive step forward instead of a step backward, intellectually speaking, and that it may in a deep sense be wise to acquiesce in doubt about ultimate things. Consider an analogy. If in some artistic or construction project we have been complacently thinking of ourselves as making serious progress and then are brought up short, reminded of its many defects, forced to look at it with fresh eyes and perhaps led to notice entirely new and more interesting ways of proceeding, are we really in a worse place than we would be in if we were still regarding the project as virtually complete? Is it not possible to make a significant advance by noticing how far behind we really are?

So it is, I suggest, with the investigation of matters religious. Instead of uncritically accepting the conventional associations of "skepticism," we must ask ourselves whether religious skepticism really is a dead end, or whether the awareness that it is the only stance appropriate to our present situation might in some sense be the condition of imagining a new and more illuminating beginning. We have indeed been led into the dark valley of religious skepticism, but perhaps there are important intellectual vistas we can see only from there. If so, then there may come a time when all who inquire into religion will sincerely seek, and be exceedingly glad to have found, the wisdom to doubt.

Definitions

S is religious (or exhibits religion):

(1) *S* takes there to be a reality that is ultimate, in relation to which an ultimate good can be attained.

(2) *S*'s ultimate commitment is to the cultivation of dispositions appropriate to this state of affairs.[1]

S believes that *p:*

S is disposed to apprehend the state of affairs reported by *p*, when that state of affairs comes to mind, under the concept *reality.*[2]

S believes in *x:*

(1) *S* believes that *x* has value or is in some way a good thing.

These definitions are taken from my *Prolegomena to a Philosophy of Religion* (Ithaca: Cornell University Press, 2005), chaps. 1–6, to which source the reader is referred for fuller discussion.

[1] For the meanings of "ultimate" and associated terms, see the Introduction.

[2] Earlier in the chapter from which this definition is taken, I give this alternative definition of "*S* believes that *p*": "*S* has a disposition such that (normally) it is only in the thick sense that the state of affairs reported by *p* comes to mind for *S*." By "the thick sense" should be understood the sense we are using when, in saying that someone has thought of a state of affairs, we mean that he has had a thought of the relevant arrangement of things being actual. This is to be distinguished from the "thin" sense, which we are using when in uttering the same sentence we mean only that the person has had a thought of *what it would be like* if the relevant arrangement of things were actual.

(2) S is disposed, when x comes to mind, to experience a feeling state that, when conjoined with the fact represented by (1), produces a blended experience of approving, trusting, and loyal emotions toward x.

S possesses (propositional) religious belief:

(1) S is disposed to apprehend the state of affairs reported by a certain proposition p, when that state of affairs comes to mind, under the concept *reality*.

(2) p entails the existence of an ultimate and salvific reality.

(3) p is independently capable of informing a religious practice.

(4) S recognizes the religious character of her belief.

S possesses (affective) religious belief:

(1) S believes that a certain item x has value or is in some way a good thing.

(2) At least a part of S's reason for valuing x is that S values the existence of an ultimate and salvific reality or, more directly, the good obtainable in relation to such a reality, if it exists.

(3) S is disposed, when x comes to mind, to experience a feeling state that, when conjoined with the facts represented by (1) and (2), produces a blended experience of approving, trusting, and loyal emotions toward x.

S possesses (propositional) religious disbelief:

(1) S is disposed to apprehend the state of affairs reported by a certain proposition p, when that state of affairs comes to mind, under the concept *reality*.

(2) p entails the nonexistence of an ultimate and salvific reality.

(3) S recognizes the nonreligious character of her belief.

S possesses (affective) religious disbelief:

(1) S believes that a certain item x has disvalue or is in some way a bad thing.

(2) At least a part of *S*'s reason for disvaluing *x* is that *S* disvalues the valuing of the existence of an ultimate and salvific reality or, more directly, disvalues the valuing of a good obtainable in relation to it, if it exists.

(3) *S* is disposed, when *x* comes to mind, to experience a feeling state that, when conjoined with the facts represented by (1) and (2), produces a blended experience of disapproving and distrusting emotions toward *x*.

S is a religious skeptic:

S is in doubt and/or withholds judgment, because of the apparent inconclusiveness of the relevant evidence, with respect to (i) this or that particular religious proposition or limited set of religious propositions (common skepticism), or (ii) the proposition that there is an ultimate and salvific reality (categorical skepticism), or (iii) the proposition—qualified or unqualified—that human beings are capable of discovering at least some basic truths concerning such a reality (capacity skepticism), or (iv) both (ii) and (iii) together (complete skepticism).[3]

S has faith in *x* (a putative ultimate and salvific reality):

(1) *S* believes or has faith that *p* (where *p* is the religious proposition that *x*—a putative ultimate and salvific reality—will be or do for *S* what *S* needs or wants).

(2) *S* lacks evidence rendering *p* certain.

(3) If *S* is disposed to act on her belief or faith that *p*, and *p* is false, *S* will suffer bad consequences.

(4) *S* *is* disposed to act on this belief or faith: that is, to do what seems appropriate to the truth of *p*, given *S*'s other purposes and the rest of *S*'s worldview.[4]

S has faith that *p* (where *p* is a religious proposition), and *S*'s faith is religious faith:

(1) *S* lacks evidence causally sufficient for *S* to believe that *p*.

[3] For an explanation of the distinction between "qualified" and "unqualified" capacity skepticism, see the Introduction.

[4] This "faith-in" was in *Prolegomena* called *operational* faith.

(2) *S* considers the state of affairs reported by *p* to be good or desirable.

(3) *S* tenaciously and persistently represents the world to herself as including that state of affairs.

(4) *S* voluntarily and committedly adopts a policy of assent toward that representation—or, more broadly, toward *p*.

(5) *S* recognizes the religious character of her attitude.[5]

---

[5] This "faith-that" was in *Prolegomena* called *propositional* faith.

Principles

P1. A response to religious claims is justified at a time t if and only if there is at t no better alternative response that can be made.[1]

P2. A response to religious claims is justified if and only if it is either negatively or positively justified.[2]

P3. If a response to religious claims is unjustified, then some alternative response is justified.

P4. If a believing or disbelieving response is epistemically justified, then all alternative responses are epistemically unjustified.

P5. If neither a believing nor a disbelieving response is justified, then some form of skepticism is justified.

P6. If a faith response is positively justified, then a purely skeptical response is unjustified.

These principles of response justification are taken from my *Prolegomena to a Philosophy of Religion* (Ithaca: Cornell University Press, 2005), chap. 8, to which source the reader is referred for fuller discussion.

[1] Hereafter I omit the temporal reference and commonly also the qualification "that can be made" when speaking of responses to religious claims, on the assumption that they will be understood to apply in every case (and the reader will recall that it is not token responses and the particular times at which they are justifiedly made that are at issue here, but response *types* and the times at which they are examined or recommended).

[2] For an explanation of the distinction between positive and negative justification, see the Introduction.

P7. If a purely skeptical response is positively justified, then a faith response is unjustified.

P8. If a faith response is justified, then some form of skepticism is justified.

P9. If, in certain circumstances C in which one might have faith, some other disposition or action is more appropriate to the aim apparently sanctioning faith, then faith is in C unjustified.

P10. If, in certain circumstances C in which one might have faith, it would not be good for the proposition involved to be true, then faith is in C unjustified.

P11. If, in certain circumstances C in which one might have faith, belief in the falsity of the proposition involved is epistemically justified, then faith is in C unjustified.

P12. If, in certain circumstances C in which one might have faith, some aim (independent of the aim apparently calling for faith) that should all things considered be pursued by anyone in C can only or best be pursued by not having faith, then faith is in C unjustified.

P13. If one of principles 9–12 applies to it, then a faith response is unjustified.

P14. If a faith response is unjustified, then one of principles 9–12 applies to it.

P15. If none of principles 9–12 applies to it, then a faith response is negatively justified.

P16. A faith response is positively justified if (1) it is negatively justified and (2) some aim that should all things considered be pursued by us can only or best be pursued by making such a response.

P17. For any response r, other than the faith response, if r is negatively justified, then r is at least as good as the faith response.

P18. A believing or disbelieving response is *negatively* justified if (1) there is sufficient and overall good evidence for the truth of the proposition involved and (2) there are no non-truth-oriented considerations with sufficient force to show some alternative response to be better and thus preferable in the circumstances.

P19. A believing or disbelieving response is *positively* justified if (1) it is negatively justified and (2) there are no non-truth-oriented considerations with sufficient force to show some alternative response to be as good and thus equally worthy of being made in the circumstances.

P20. A skeptical response is *negatively* justified if (1) available information does not permit a judgment of sufficient and overall good evidence for either the proposition that would be believed in a believing response or the proposition that would be believed in a disbelieving response and (2) there are no non-truth-oriented considerations with sufficient force to show some alternative response to be better and thus preferable in the circumstances.

P21. A skeptical response is *positively* justified if (1) it is negatively justified and (2) there are no non-truth-oriented considerations with sufficient force to show some alternative response to be as good and thus equally worthy of being made in the circumstances.

P22. A purely skeptical response is *negatively* justified if (1) available information does not permit a judgment of sufficient and overall good evidence for either the proposition that would be believed in a believing response or the proposition that would be believed in a disbelieving response, (2) a faith response is no more than negatively justified, and (3) there are no non-truth-oriented considerations with sufficient force to show some nonskeptical alternative response to be better and thus preferable in the circumstances.

P23. A purely skeptical response is *positively* justified if (1) it is negatively justified, (2) a faith response is unjustified, and (3) there are no non-truth-oriented considerations with sufficient force to show some alternative response to be as good and thus equally worthy of being made in the circumstances.

Index